The Last Great Subsistence Crisis in the Western World

The Last
Great Subsistence Crisis
in the Western World

John D. Post

The Johns Hopkins University Press
Baltimore and London

Copyright © 1977 by The Johns Hopkins University Press

Manufactured in the United States of America

The Johns Hopkins University Press, Baltimore, Maryland 21218
The Johns Hopkins Press Ltd., London

Library of Congress Catalog Card Number 76–41239
ISBN 0–8018–1850–8

Library of Congress Cataloging in Publication Data

Post, John Dexter, 1925–
    The last great subsistence crisis in the Western World.

    Bibliography: pp. 215–35
    Includes index.
    1. Food supply—Europe—History.   2.   Climatic
changes—Economic aspects—Europe—History.
3.   Crops and climate—Europe—History.
4.   Epidemics—Europe—History.   I.   Title.
HD9015.A3P67   338.1′9   76–41239
ISBN 0–8018–1850–8

To
Herbert Moller
Professor of History, Boston University
friend and mentor

Contents

Acknowledgments

This work owes much to the inspiration and critical judgment of Professor Herbert Moller, who has always been unstinting with his time and his wisdom. I am indebted to my wife, Ruth, who, through her continuing confidence and forbearance, has in more ways than I can recount lightened the task. I also owe a debt of gratitude to Ivy R. DeRosier of Northeastern University, who typed the manuscript flawlessly and in the process suggested stylistic improvements.

Introduction

The years 1816–19 were marked by a crisis of hemispheric and, to some extent, world-wide proportions. The Western economy was shaken by violent price fluctuations, large numbers of people were exposed to basic food shortages, and governments were required to cope with distressed populations and the danger of public disturbances. Yet historians have looked for explanations on the various national levels, pointing to postwar dislocations of trade, manufacture, and agriculture as the cause of the malaise, and for each national economy excessive weight has been given to changes in the money supply The downswing and contraction of 1816–19 and its portentous social consequences cannot, however, be adequately interpreted by the fragmented approach of national history, or even within the framework of a North Atlantic economy.

Furthermore, it will be argued that the crisis owed its supranational scope only to a minor extent to the newer economic forces, i.e., industrialization and the improved commercial and monetary communications. To a greater degree the sudden downswing must be accounted for by fluctuations in agricultural productivity, especially grain yields.

Finally, if harvest failures were of pivotal importance, it follows that the dislocations of the Western economy cannot be reduced exclusively to market relationships, but that ultimately extraeconomic "shocks" to the system must be introduced as independent variables. It will be argued that these factors were meteorological in nature and that it was the interaction between economic and climatic fluctuations rather than political decisions that led to the disruption of commodity market relationships and the attendant social upheavals. While the impact of weather patterns on preindustrial and nineteenth-century crises has been noted by economic historians, climatic irregularities have usually been perceived as swings of good or bad luck. Some authors have unsuccessfully attempted to establish a connection between solar cycles and trade cycles. The present study, by contrast, is not predicated upon elusive extraterrestrial forces, but will venture on a systematic geophysical explanation, dealing with observed and documented meteorological phenomena.

Though this study focuses primarily on the second decade of the nineteenth century, it will be apparent that its findings apply to other economic crises of the past—and possibly to future events. Recent investigations have deepened our understanding of the history of climate. This research has been directed toward the influence of secular climatic change on human ecology and economic discontinuity as well as toward shorter-range consequences of weather patterns. On a secular time scale, the three centuries *circa* 1550–1850, referred to as the "Little Ice Age," registered measurably lower atmospheric temperatures compared either to medieval or contemporary times. These changes were not limited to Europe; similar patterns have been found in North America and East Asia. Then, a century of warmer climate more accommodating to agriculture began about the middle of the nineteenth century.[1] The last half of the century also witnessed lower food prices and a rise in the real wages of the working population. To what extent were the political and social troubles which peaked during the period 1800–50 prompted by the economic consequences of harsher climate, as well as by the discontinuities associated with early industrialization?

The weather patterns of the second decade of the nineteenth century were even more anomalous than the secular trend of the Little Ice Age and present an independent problem in climate history. Multiple variables determine the large-scale wind circulation and hence also the weather generated on the surface of the earth. The evidence here, however, indicates that extraordinary volcanic activity during the years 1811 to 1818 proved mainly responsible for the calamitous weather. Volcanic dust veils in the stratosphere will decrease the absorption of incoming radiation by reducing the transparency of the atmosphere, which in turn produces lower surface temperatures. The correlation of dense volcanic dust veils and intercontinental economic disturbances marked by high agricultural commodity prices can be documented also for other historical periods. A partial list of the years when the two phenomena were present together (1597– 1601, 1638–41, 1693–98, 1709–12, 1766–71, 1783–86, 1811–18, 1835–41, 1845–50) resembles a catalog of the preindustrial crisis years, not only in Europe but often in North America and East Asia.[2]

The postwar trade cycle, nonetheless, was not determined solely by weather patterns. Economic destabilization also ensued from the influence of self-generating cyclical variables. It has been convincingly established that the financial panic and subsequent depression of 1818–19 derived chiefly from monetary deflation and from changes in inventory investment. Yet these events remain unclear without reference to the agricultural calamity of 1816–17. The postwar economic distress originated in a subsistence crisis which affected the entire Western world and probably touched the whole northern hemisphere. While the influence of industrial and monetary variables on the trade cycle varied considerably from economy to economy, it will be shown that only the fluctuations of agricultural production and prices registered a critical impact on every economy from 1816 to 1819.

The term "subsistence crisis" refers primarily to the demographic and economic consequences of doubled or tripled cereal prices and, while the effects are due more to the high cost than to the absolute shortage of food, the conditions may range from dearth and scarcity to actual famine, with deaths from starvation. The subsistence crisis ushered in by the harvest failures of 1816 was not the last occasion when regions of Europe suffered from dearth and famine. The Irish famine and the food scarcities in Belgium, Germany, and France during 1845–47, which resulted largely from widespread potato blight, are well known. The famine of 1816–17, however, extended for the last time over extensive regions of the Western world, not just parts of Europe. Even though in Ireland the famine proved more extreme in 1845–47 than was the case in 1816–17, during the earlier crisis genuine famine conditions also prevailed in large areas of Switzerland, Italy, the Habsburg Monarchy, and the Ottoman empire, as was likewise true in smaller regions of eastern France and southwestern Germany. Dearth, moreover, was common throughout Europe west of the Russian empire, and food shortages occurred in North Africa and also in some districts of North America.

The subsistence crisis registered an immediate impact on vital events. The postwar changes in birth, death, and marriage rates point to a telling degree of social disruption. The decline in marriage and birth rates represented mostly a voluntary adjustment to a worsening economic outlook; the rising death rate, however, derived from a deteriorating level of public health and physical well-being. Fluctuating mortality rates reflected not merely economic conditions, but the interaction of nutrition and infection. This correspondence between famine and contagion touches several long-standing problems of demographic history which need clarification.

To begin, a fundamental change occurred in the demographic experience of Europe after the 1740s: subsistence crises no longer produced major mortality peaks. Up to the years 1740–42, famine and coincident surges in mortality had periodically reduced the population surplus that had been generated by the excess of births over deaths during years of ample agricultural production. After the middle decades of the eighteenth century, death from natural causes has never again taken such a heavy toll. Pierre Goubert has posed the problem of causation by his summary statement: "Something had changed, whether in the nature, level, yield, or cost of production, the speed or cost of transportation, the resources of the consumer, or perhaps in government policy."[3]

The continuous improvement of economic and social conditions, and especially the abatement of famines, has generally been accepted as the explanation for the decline of epidemics. Even if few historians today assume that medical advance was a major factor in the leveling of mortality peaks, a few authors, nevertheless, have remained skeptical of the thesis that the conquest of epidemic disease flowed from improved economic productivity. Since European famines were in fact not invariably followed by serious epidemics, it is possible that bubonic plague and similar crises of public health were essentially autonomous in origin and not directly related to problems of subsistence and nutrition. Additional hypotheses suggest that the declining mortality rate ensued from an increase in the natural immunity of human populations long exposed to contagion and from changes in the ecology of disease-carrying animal vectors.

Consideration of these issues is a major concern of this study. The last European preindustrial subsistence crisis, the famine of 1816–17, constitutes an appropriate case-study for several reasons. Since the dearth directly affected the United Kingdom, France, Belgium, the Netherlands, Germany, Switzerland, Italy, the Habsburg empire, and the Balkan peninsula, a comparative examination of the variables responsible for the taming of famines becomes possible. Moreover, the wide regional variation in European development and modernization in the first quarter of the nineteenth century lends a longitudinal dimension to the work. The concomitant appearance of a major typhus epidemic in the Italian peninsula, the Alpine region, and the British Isles, together with an outbreak of epidemic bubonic plague in southeastern and Mediterranean Europe, offers an opportunity to examine the question of autonomous or dependent epidemic disease in historical detail. For the resolution of the fundamental issue—whether the famine was primarily responsible for the typhus and plague epidemics—it proves necessary to reconcile the historical evidence with the current findings and hypotheses in the fields of public health and human ecology.

The degree of interrelationship between economic events and political policies is the last concern of this work. European governments labored under an unrelieved sequence of popular disturbances that began with the postwar dislocations of 1815 and persisted until the social commotion and demonstrations of 1819. Interaction between socioeconomic factors and political action flowed from such phenomena as the increase in the number of beggars and vagabonds spawned by unemployment and hunger. Vagrancy, on occasion, led to looting and rioting on a scale serious enough to require military force for pacification. Subsistence rather than rebellion remained the chief goal; but hypersensitive governments were not always capable of drawing fine distinctions, especially when hostile political sentiment was rife. Social stability was compromised in the greater Rhine region (western Germany, Alsace, Switzerland) by massive emigration westward to America and eastward to the Russian empire. Anti-Semitism was aroused in southwestern Germany, where the Hep-Hep riots erupted in 1819, paralleled by less virulent forms of abuse and discrimination in neighboring lands. While Restoration governments exhibited mixed responses to emigration and anti-Semitism, the net outcome was to produce elevated social and political tension. It is not difficult to believe that economic crisis and social unrest fused with political conservatism to foreclose the emerging liberal ideas of 1815, which by 1820 were in retreat almost everywhere in Europe, both in the constitutional and economic spheres.

chapter
one

Weather Patterns and
Agricultural Consequences

WEATHER PATTERNS

The spring and summer months of 1816 registered mean seasonal temperatures which were among the lowest in the recorded meteorological history of
the Western world. Reportedly, snow and ice remained somewhere in New
England twelve months of the year. Abnormally low temperatures in western
and central Europe were accompanied by excessive precipitation during the
growing season. Even though the weather was apparently less severe in northeastern Europe and along the Mediterranean littoral, observers reported deficient harvests and elevated agricultural commodity prices. Needless to say,
the weather of 1816 was of international interest, and numerous impressionistic references to the events of that year are available. Since this study intends
to illustrate a connection between meteorological and economic fluctuations,
however, the investigation will focus on systematic and instrumental evidence, and should begin with a few observations concerning the history of
climate and the variables that regulate climate changes.

The systematic application of meteorology to economic history became a
possibility a quarter century ago with the appearance of a seminal work by C.
E. P. Brooks.[1] Brooks elaborated an approximate but comprehensive outline
of the "climates of the historical past" stretching back to the retreat of the last
ice sheets; and he also identified a period of climatic "decline," *circa* 1550–
1850, termed the Little Ice Age. Gustaf Utterström was probably the first
historian to attempt to correlate climatic fluctuations with economic and demographic fluctuations in early modern Europe, in effect the centuries of the
Little Ice Age.[2] Although his investigations have been invaluable and his

1

suggestive conclusions insightful, critics have found the work to be excessively speculative, perhaps with some justification. Emmanuel Le Roy Ladurie has been the most severe critic of Utterström's findings and also has remained skeptical of the ecological or economic significance of climatic fluctuation—or at least skeptical concerning changes of sufficient magnitude to affect economic conditions. While Le Roy Ladurie admits that agricultural history was vulnerable to the caprices of the weather in the short term, he continues to question the possibility of a systematic application of meteorology to economic history.[3]

Two studies which appeared in the latter half of the 1960s, however, have demonstrated that the concept of the Little Ice Age can no longer be questioned, even if its precise significance for economic history remains to be investigated. The climatologist H. H. Lamb has not only traced the climatic changes of the present millennium but has also displayed evidence of the consequences for human ecology and economics.[4] And the meteorologist Hans von Rudloff has published a remarkably comprehensive record of surviving instrumental weather observations dating back to 1670, together with season-by-season weather summaries by half centuries.[5] In addition to the accumulation of geological, botanical, and documentary evidence by Le Roy Ladurie and Lamb, thermometric and barometric readings indicate the advent of a century of warmer climate more beneficial to agriculture beginning about the middle of the nineteenth century. What, if any, significance have these climatic fluctuations had for economic history; and, more immediately, what variables that elicit such changes might constitute an appropriate concern for historians?

To begin, the large-scale atmospheric circulation determines the weather of the earth, and changes in the large-scale wind circulation are determined by fluctuations of the earth's radiation balance. The character of one season, or of a group of years, or of an entire climatic epoch, "may be defined by some long-lasting anomaly in the position and alignment of the mainstream of the upper westerlies. This steers the sequence of surface depressions and anticyclones and even controls the places where they develop." The flow of the surface winds transports heat, drives the warm and cold ocean currents, and determines areas of radiation heating and cooling in such a way as to maintain the particular hemispheric thermal pattern which continually regenerates the same circulation regime. But the basic conditions of a stationary pattern tend to fade with a change in radiation input.[6] Although there are many elements that determine the wind circulation and the climatic patterns generated, probably only three represent causes that fall potentially within the historian's field of research: the extent of ice on the polar seas; solar disturbance or its absence; and volcanic dust veils in the stratosphere. All three may exert a simultaneous influence, but the meteorological effects of volcanic dust veils are particularly relevant in the case of anomalous intradecennial weather patterns because they last no more than several years after a sudden onset. Since preindustrial intercontinental economic crises followed a similar pattern, the association between the two is examined here, focusing on the period after the Napoleonic wars.

Some apparent connection between volcanic activity and social crisis has been noted since the eighteenth century. Until the development of the pyrheliometer, and hence the ability to measure incoming solar radiation, however, it remained impossible to determine the precise relationship between volcanic eruptions and weather patterns. The intensity of the solar beam at the earth's distance from the sun has been measured since 1883—the calculated value termed the solar constant; it represents the amount of radiation available to heat the surface of the earth, assuming a perfectly transparent atmosphere. According to meteorological theory, volcanic dust and debris thrust up to heights of 20 to 40 kilometers and more in the stratosphere will deplete normal-incidence solar radiation. The solid particles, dust, and haze suspended in the atmosphere will intercept, absorb, scatter, and reflect back to space incoming radiation. Persistent volcanic dust veils made up of the smallest particles may remain in the lower stratosphere up to twelve years before falling into the troposphere, where they become washed out by precipitation. The majority of the particles, however, probably do not remain in the stratosphere beyond two years. But the particles that do remain as long as a year or two are the most significant. Because of their dimensions, these smaller particles (especially those of about one micron cross-measurement) are able to absorb and therefore deplete the incoming short-wave solar radiation. More than three-quarters of incoming radiation is at wave lengths equal to or smaller than these particles. At the same time, most of the outgoing radiation reflected from the surface of the earth is long-wave radiation (mostly at wave lengths of 5 to 50 microns), which the smaller particles cannot absorb or intercept. This is known as the reverse greenhouse effect, and its consequence is to lower the temperature of the air.[7]

Some idea of the magnitude and duration of the atmospheric effect of great volcanic explosions can be gained from the monthly averages of measured incoming solar radiation. After the eruptions of the years 1883, 1888, 1902, and 1912, the monthly average of direct solar radiation as measured by pyrheliometric observations fell in some months as far as 20–22 percent below the mean value 1883–1938, with a substantial effect still noticeable two to three years after the eruptions. The effect on the net total radiation reaching the surface was not so great as these measurements of the direct solar beam would suggest, however. The depletion of the solar beam is mostly compensated for by an increase in the scattered light and heat (diffuse radiation) reaching the surface. The net effect (direct radiation minus diffuse radiation) appears to be a reduction of the total radiation equal to a ratio of 0.16 (i.e., of the depletion of radiation received at the surface to depletion of the direct solar beam) at 30 degrees of latitude, with a higher ratio of 0.24 in the polar regions and a lower ratio of 0.13 in the equatorial zone. A fluctuation of only one percent of the solar energy absorbed by the earth, nevertheless, can change the surface temperature by about 1.5° C.[8]

Temperature fluctuations are inevitably associated with changes in the strength of the general zonal circulation, involving shifts in the location of the principal semi-permanent meteorological "centers of action," which in the North Atlantic are the Iceland "low" and the Azores "high." Other things remaining equal, a decrease in the radiation absorbed by the earth should weaken the zonal circulation and transfer the mainstream of the upper wester-lies to lower latitudes, and in addition shift equatorward the latitude of the North Atlantic subpolar cyclonic activity or the so-called depression tracks (the Iceland low). As a concrete example, volcanic dust veils would decrease energy transmission and should initially produce a lowering of temperature everywhere; they should produce lessened temperature gradients between equator and pole, and weaken the zonal circulation. The end result in the northern temperate zone of the Western world would be spring-summer weather that is cooler and duller and probably stormier than normal. Shifts in the forty-year running mean latitudes of the depression tracks (subpolar lows) and of the subtropical anticyclone belts (Azores high) have been found in the North Atlantic. These shifts are of the order of 1° to 4° of latitude, varying approximately between 60° and 64°N for the semipermanent Iceland low, and between 32° and 36°N for the semipermanent Azores high during the summer months, the critical season for agricultural production in the temperate zone.

These shifts in the semipermanent centers of action seem to be correlated with the fluctuations in the intensity of solar radiation absorbed by the surface of the earth. For example, during the decade of cold summers, from 1811 through 1820, the average latitude of the subpolar low in July was 60.7°N; whereas during the warm decade from 1925 to 1934, the average latitude was a much more northerly 66.9°N. Lamb is inclined to believe that the latitude of the Iceland low represents the prime indicator of climatic fluctuation.[9]

H. H. Lamb's study of volcanic dust in the atmosphere spans the years from 1500 to 1968. Within the Little Ice Age (1550 to 1850) the chronological association of dense volcanic dust veils in the stratosphere and intercontinen-tal economic disturbances marked by high commodity prices is striking. Lamb has devised an atmospheric "dust veil index" based on a series of formulas that include a numerical factor designed to bring the index to 1,000 for the Krakatoa eruption in 1883, which was chosen as the basis of comparison. Historical eruptions are rated on a scale beginning with 10, index numbers below 100 being considered meteorologically insignificant. The eruption of Coseguina (Nicaragua) in 1835 secured the largest value, with an index of 4,000; while the explosion of Tomboro (Indonesia) in 1815 received the second highest index number of 3,000. No volcanic eruption in the twentieth century secured a value as large as 1,000.[10]

Measured by the total volume of debris, not merely the finest particles, volcanologists tend to consider the explosion of Tomboro on the island of Sumbawa in 1815 as the greatest eruption since 1500. Although estimates have varied greatly regarding the volume of ash discharged into the atmosphere during this eruption, ranging from a low of 150 to a high of 1,000 cubic kilometers, the smaller figure is more generally accepted.[11] Volcanic activity, moreover, has tended to occur in waves, successive eruptions reinforcing the density of the stratospheric dust veils. When the eruptions of the years 1811 to 1818 are grouped together, they amount to a value of 4,400 on Lamb's scale of index numbers, while the eruptions occurring during the years 1835 to 1841 correspond to an index number of 4,200. These two periods, coming at the end of the Little Ice Age, could be expected to have experienced unusually adverse weather.

Restating the meteorological theory at this point, volcanic dust veils in the stratosphere decrease the absorption of radiation by reducing the transparency of the atmosphere, which has the further effect of lowering surface temperatures. Since the atmospheric circulation patterns have been reconstructed to a certain extent back to 1750, and since temperature, rainfall, and other weather observations are available as far in the past as the seventeenth century, the theory should be capable of verification. Lamb has correlated the index of the dust veil with temperature, the long-term atmospheric circulation, and year-to-year variations of the atmospheric circulation, but the results are on the whole inconclusive. The weakening of the zonal westerlies in the year of a great volcanic eruption in the low latitudes proved the one statistically significant result. In the first July after a great eruption, the subpolar low-pressure zone in the longitude of Greenwich exhibited a southward displacement of 3° to 6° of latitude on the average. After a high-latitude eruption, this southward anomaly tendency appears to continue for three or four years. Six degrees of latitude will, of course, cover the entire British Isles. These findings are in line with the observation that many of the coldest, wettest summers in Britain, eastern North America, and Japan occur in years of volcanic dust veils. There is also a tendency for cold winters in Europe after volcanic eruptions in low latitudes that produce world-wide dust veils.[12]

At the same time, the two most celebrated severe winters in Europe during the eighteenth century, the winters of 1708–09 and 1739–40, did not derive from great volcanic eruptions in low latitudes, so far as the available evidence indicates. Of course, the more remote in time and the more isolated the location of the volcanic explosion, the less precise the values represented by these index numbers become. Even so, the explosive eruptions of three middle latitude volcanoes during 1707—Vesuvius (41°N), Santorin (36 ½°N), and Fujiyama (35°N), assigned a combined dust-veil index of 1,300—were almost certainly responsible for the cold spell during 1708–09.[13] This season, as was the case in 1816 and 1740, ushered in a period of famine, high food prices, and elevated mortality levels.[14]

The severe winter of 1739–40 cannot be attributed to volcanic dust veils with the same degree of assurance. Although it is well established that the Kamchatka peninsula was the scene of recurrent volcanic eruptions during the years immediately prior to 1740, its remote location has precluded precise knowledge of their magnitude.[15] Meteorological theory suggests, nevertheless, that the cold winter of 1740 probably resulted from volcanic dust in the atmosphere. In brief, large volcanic eruptions produce a reservoir of dust in the lower stratosphere at the latitude of injection, and then dust veils spread slowly over the earth in the direction of the zonal circulation. Of most importance here is the fact that equatorial reservoirs have a stratospheric residence time of about two years (Tomboro is located at 8°S), while middle- and high-latitude injections have a shorter residence time of three to nine months (the Kamchatka volcanoes are located near 55°N). Also, poleward dispersion of volcanic dust is more readily accomplished than transport toward the equator. Finally, dust injected at high latitudes tends to spread over all latitudes between the pole and 30° in the hemisphere of eruption, but apparently no farther south.[16] These theoretical considerations, fortified by the known weather patterns of the eighteenth century, indicate that middle- and high-latitude eruptions are more likely to produce one severe winter in the northern temperate zone, such as in 1709 and 1740, than an extended period of below-normal temperatures, as was the case following the low-latitude eruption of Tomboro in 1815. Even though an explanation for the cold winter of 1739–40 must remain problematical, the famine and mortality crisis that followed this severe season prove valuable reference points which help to illuminate this study.[17]

Lamb has cautioned, however, that these meteorological findings represent mainly statistical tendencies, "since the initial thermal state of the atmosphere, the oceans, and the land surface at the time of a volcanic eruption must affect the weather patterns developing."[18] In an attempt to subject the theory to additional empirical tests, this investigation examines the climate of the second decade of the nineteenth century, in particular the anomalous year 1816, by surveying both the instrumental observations and the documentary evidence. Two specific issues are considered. First, what was the effect of volcanic activity on the weather patterns of this decade? Second, what was the effect of the weather on agricultural productivity?

AGRICULTURAL CONSEQUENCES

W. Köppen's computations of average surface air temperature over the Western world for each year from 1750 to 1871 remain the only available series of annual thermometric values incorporating a large area of the earth. Since the year 1816 should have registered the most noticeable meteorological effects produced by volcanic dust veils during the second decade of the nineteenth century, only the deviations from mean temperature for the years surrounding 1816 are displayed in Table 1.[19] The predominance of minus values before 1818 is unmistakable, particularly during 1816, when the negative deviations were greatest. Although these deviations suggest similar weather changes throughout much of the northern hemisphere, it is necessary to trace temperature curves more comprehensively to establish economic effects. Annual means represent the net value of monthly plus or minus deviations and thus may be distorted by even one extreme monthly anomaly. In the case of agricultural production, moreover, the weather of the growing season primarily determines differential yields.

Table 2 displays the monthly deviations from normal means during the years 1815–16 for eleven locations in eleven countries and on three continents. The occurrence of lower readings during the last half of 1815 and the sharp negative departures in the summer months seem apparent. In addition to this seasonal pattern, the data suggest the relative escape of the Baltic region. Central Europe, on the other hand, sustained the full brunt of the calamitous weather. A convincing argument for the economic consequences of the post-war meteorological conditions, however, requires a microscopic investigation of multiple regions.

To begin with, the spring and summer months of 1816 were unseasonably cold in the eastern half of North America. The surviving weather observations indicate that the principal cause of the subnormal cold proved to be a succession of cold fronts which brought freezing temperatures to the entire northeastern region of the continent.[20] If annual temperature means frequently conceal critically large seasonal or monthly variations, the latter in turn may mask destructive weekly or even daily deviations. A relatively brief period of temperature extremes, or of untimely precipitation, can become crucial for the survival of vegetation. Micrometeorological data are indispensable in ascertaining the extent of injury to growing crops. Reliable observations made at Williamstown, Massachusetts, from 1816 to 1838 provide daily weather information and also serve as a general point of reference for northeastern North America. Measured by annual mean temperature, the year 1816 was by no means the coldest, even though its average of 44.3°F fell 1.3°F below normal for the period 1816–38. The two coldest years, each averaging 42.6°F or 3.0°F below normal, were 1836 and 1837—the years following the epochal eruption of Coseguina. At first glance, then, 1816 was not a year of record-breaking cold, a point which underscores the indispensability of monthly and even daily temperature values. The damagingly cold months from May through September were partially offset by above-average temperatures during February, October, November, and December—which was essentially the

Table 1. Temperature Deviations from the Mean 1768–1819 (Degrees of Fahrenheit Scale)

Year	Near East	Italy	Austria	West Central Europe	New England	British Isles	Northern Germany, Holland	Northwest Russia	Northern Europe
1814	-0.4	-1.2	-1.8	-1.6	-0.4	-2.5	-2.4	-2.1	-1.3
1815	-0.4	-0.1	-0.3	-0.9	-1.5	-0.4	-0.9	-1.5	+0.4
1816	-0.7	-1.5	-1.3	-2.5	-2.2	-2.4	-2.1	-1.4	-0.1
1817	-0.6	-0.1	-0.7	-0.5	-1.8	-0.2	-0.2	-0.7	-1.2
1818	-0.9	-0.7	-0.8	-0.4	-1.3	+1.8	+0.1	+0.6	+0.6
1819	-0.7	-0.9	-1.4	-0.7	+0.9	+0.4	+1.2	+0.6	+0.8

Source: W. Köppen, "Ueber mehrjährige Perioden der Witterung," *Zeitschrift der Österreichischen Gesellschaft für Meteorologie,* 8 (September 1873): 260. Temperature deviations form Centigrade scale.

Table 2. Temperature Deviations 1815–1816 from the Mean 1807–24 (Degrees of Fahrenheit Scale)

Months 1815	Madras	Salem U.S.A.	London	Dumfries Scotland	Paris	Haarlem Holland	Stockholm	Berlin	Vienna	Geneva	Milan
Jan	-2.2	-1.9	-2.4	-1.7	-4.6	-5.4	+1.7	-5.5	-2.5	-5.5	-4.1
Feb	+0.5	-3.5	+5.3	+2.9	+4.6	+2.2	+2.2	+2.5	+3.9	+3.1	-1.1
Mar	-1.3	+2.6	+5.5	+2.5	+5.5	+5.6	+2.6	+3.3	+4.0	+4.9	+4.5
Apr	+3.7	-2.6	+1.5	+1.4	+0.9	+2.2	+4.4	+0.2	+0.4	+1.4	+2.2
May	+2.1	-2.2	+4.0	+1.3	+0.4	+1.5	-1.6	+0.4	+0.2	+2.8	+2.1
Jun	-3.5	+0.5	+0.9	+0.4	-0.9	+0.8	-4.3	+2.4	+0.7	+0.6	-0.3
Jul	-2.9	+3.1	-1.3	+0.1	-1.4	-1.7	-4.3	-5.3	-3.3	+1.1	-1.7
Aug	+0.2	-3.2	+0.2	+0.2	-0.8	-0.9	+0.1	-2.8	-3.3	-0.4	-2.4
Sep	+0.7	-0.9	-1.5	-1.3	-0.1	-0.2	-2.0	-3.3	-2.7	+1.7	+0.5
Oct	-1.5	-2.0	0.0	+0.1	+1.8	+1.2	+1.5	+1.0	-0.5	+3.6	+1.5
Nov	-2.3	+1.8	-4.2	-3.3	-6.0	-2.9	+1.2	-2.2	-3.1	-1.3	-3.1
Dec	-2.1	-1.6	-1.4	-2.5	-2.7	-2.4	+0.1	-3.1	-6.4	-0.7	-3.8

Months 1816	Madras	Salem U.S.A.	London	Dumfries Scotland	Paris	Haarlem Holland	Stockholm	Berlin	Vienna	Geneva	Milan
Jan	-2.4	+0.6	+0.9	-0.4	+1.1	+1.9	+1.9	+2.9	+4.0	+3.1	-0.7
Feb	-3.4	+1.1	-5.8	-2.4	-4.7	-3.5	-8.0	-5.2	-3.3	-2.8	-7.0
Mar	-3.3	-2.8	-2.5	-2.4	-1.2	-1.4	-3.2	-1.7	-1.0	-0.7	-2.5
Apr	-2.8	-0.2	-1.8	-3.7	+0.3	+0.2	+0.1	+0.8	+0.4	+0.2	-1.7
May	-0.4	-1.9	-3.4	-0.5	-3.2	-3.6	-5.2	-5.3	-3.0	-1.4	-1.9
Jun	+0.4	-4.4	-1.6	-1.4	-3.0	-4.1	+2.7	-2.4	-1.5	-3.0	-2.6
Jul	-1.7	-4.9	-2.7	-2.9	-5.0	-2.8	+2.1	-1.6	-3.4	-4.9	-4.0
Aug	-2.0	-2.1	-2.7	-2.6	-4.9	-3.5	-6.6	-5.1	-3.5	-3.8	-7.6
Sep	-1.5	-3.8	-2.6	-1.5	-2.6	-2.5	-0.6	-2.6	-2.1	-0.9	-1.3
Oct	-0.3	-0.1	+0.2	-0.1	+0.7	+0.2	-2.4	-2.7	-2.3	+1.7	+0.6
Nov	+0.5	+3.4	-5.3	-2.2	-4.9	-4.4	-2.4	-5.1	-1.6	-1.6	-3.5
Dec	-1.4	+1.0	-1.8	-1.4	+0.5	+0.7	+3.1	-0.9	-3.2	+0.1	-4.0

Source: H. W. Dove, "Uber die nicht periodischen Anderungen der Temperaturvertheilung auf der Oberfläsche der Erde," *Abhandlungen der Königlichen Akademie der Wissenschaften zu Berlin,* part 1 (1838): 360–65; and part 3 (1842): 143–44. Temperature deviations converted from Réaumur scale.

case throughout western Europe, as Table 2 indicates. At the same time, the lowest temperatures recorded at the regular 7 A.M. observation (they would be some 4°F lower at 5 A.M.) during June, July, and August 1816 (respectively 35.0°F, 43.0°F, and 37.5°F) were the lowest readings for these three months in the course of the 23-year observation period.[21]

Accordingly, an examination of daily temperature means is essential for a comprehensive understanding of the American weather patterns in 1816, but the survey can be limited to the critical agricultural months of May through September; these readings are displayed in Table 3. The descriptive comments

Table 3. Daily Mean Temperature Williamstown, Mass., May–September 1816 (Degrees of Fahrenheit Scale)

Day	May	June	July	August	September
1	63	70	63	65	54
2	44	69	69	67	64
3	56	56	67	70	67
4	61	56	61	66	62
5	60	68	64	65	62
6	56	43	59	63	61
7	48	43	55	64	61
8	41	44	58	67	67
9	44	48	54	65	57
10	50	44	62	65	51
11	49	54	68	71	50
12	54	65	65	69	52
13	55	62	65	67	51
14	39	69	67	66	56
15	46	64	71	74	60
16	45	62	79	73	56
17	40	62	59	68	51
18	45	60	58	71	56
19	56	73	69	73	57
20	58	56	71	63	62
21	65	64	66	51	47
22	67	74	71	59	51
23	50	76	73	61	56
24	52	77	66	66	58
25	44	56	60	61	51
26	53	61	62	63	40
27	58	62	63	57	40
28	59	56	60	50	42
29	47	57	59	54	46
30	58	58	62	64	50
31	65	—	66	62	—
Monthly Mean	52	60	64	64	55
High Reading	78	90	90	87	85
Low Reading	33	35	43	37	25

Source: Chester Dewey, "Results of Meteorological Observations Made At Williamstown, Massachusetts," *Memoirs of the American Academy of Arts and Sciences* 4(1818–21): 387. Tenths of degrees are given but not reproduced.

found with the weather log leave no doubt that the anomalous conditions of 1816 reduced agricultural yields to a significant degree:

Frosts are extremely rare here in either of the summer months; but this year there was frost in each of them. . . . June 6th the temperature about 44° through the day—snowed several times. . . . June 7th no frost, but the ground frozen, and water frozen in many places. . . . Moist earth was frozen half an inch thick, and could be raised from round Indian corn, the corn slipping through and standing unhurt. June 8th, some ice was seen in the morning—earth very little frozen—no frost—wind still strong and piercing from the N.W. Cucumbers and other vegetables nearly destroyed. June 9th, less wind and some warmer. June 10th, severe frost in the morning. . . . Ten days after the frost, the trees on the sides of the hills presented for miles the appearance of having been scorched. June 29th and 30th some frost. July 9th, frost, which killed parts of cucumbers. August 22nd, cucumbers killed by the frost. August 29th, severe frost. Some fields of Indian corn were killed on the low grounds, while that on the higher was unhurt. Very little Indian corn became ripe in the region.[22]

Williamstown is located near the border of Massachusetts and New York and, though in southern New England, the town is more than one hundred miles from the sea. If New England and New York are considered a geographical unit, Williamstown is a representative central location.

Although damage caused by low temperature is usually referred to as frost injury, implying that the temperature fell below freezing and ice formed in the plant tissues, above-freezing temperatures can also be injurious. Moreover, the rate of temperature drop is often more significant than the temperature extremes in causing plant damage. Also, young plants are normally far more sensitive to frost than older tissues, a circumstance that maximizes the damage caused by low temperature in late spring. Finally, many strains of corn are killed by a succession of cold nights in which temperatures range from 33°F to 45°F, while other strains can withstand 30°F and a few as low as 28°F.[23]

Agreement among six New England weather stations corroborates the cold summer of 1816, the departure from normal mean temperature being substantially identical for Williamstown, Salem, Cambridge, New Bedford, New Haven, and Brunswick, Maine.[24] June and July at Salem registered the lowest temperatures for these two months during the 33-year period 1786–1818, each falling 5.2°F below the mean. The average temperature for the summer season declined to 4.4°F below normal, while the minus deviation for the year 1816 only amounted to 1.5°F. The surviving literary evidence, moreover, leaves little doubt concerning either the severity of the season or the economic outcome in New England.

In fact, the interaction between temperature changes and crop yields must be validated by surveying the agricultural season month-by-month from contemporary accounts. Reports complaining of severe cold, late snow storms, and retarded vegetation appeared in April, and by the middle of May it was observed that spring was "nearly six weeks less forward than common."[25] Frosts were recorded in southern New England throughout the month of May; the damage was minimized by the retardation of the growing season, however, until the end of the month when frost then became a threat to growing crops.[26] But temperatures turned more seasonable in early June, permitting farmers to repair the injury with some hope for a successful harvest. These hopes were shattered during the period from June 5 to June 11, which witnessed the remarkable cold wave recorded at Williamstown. While the effects of snow, frost, and subfreezing temperature were harsh enough in southern New England, the agricultural consequences proved disastrous for the northern districts of New England and New York, where snow accumulated to a depth of five or six inches. Most vegetables and Indian corn in New England were destroyed.[27]

Replanting was still possible, nevertheless, and four weeks of good growing weather following June 11 (one of the two periods during the summer of 1816 that was frost free for more than three weeks) restored hopes for a good harvest. July 1816, however, brought the lowest mean temperature for that month in American meteorological history, averaging more than 5.0°F below normal. The hay crop began to suffer, which meant a reduction in the number of animals that could be maintained through the winter. Wheat and rye, hardier grains, survived better than corn. The new cold front recorded on July 6 produced fear of a general famine in New England, New York, and Canada. Then the weather moderated at the end of July and concern for the grain harvest diminished.[28] Before the crops were completely harvested, however, a new frost occurred on August 13, which proved especially severe in the interior of New York and in northern New England. Once again corn represented the principal agricultural loss. Southern New England was reprieved until August 28, when another cold wave overspread the region. A succession of frosts terminated the growing season before the end of September. The harvest assessments from every section of New England were in basic agreement: the corn crop almost a total loss, the hay crop small, wheat and rye harvests fair to normal.[29]

Despite the inordinately cold summer in New England some meteorologists have insisted that reliable evidence of low temperatures elsewhere is lacking. While it is true that virtually no systematic records of atmospheric temperature for 1816 are available outside of New England, the presence of similar weather patterns can nevertheless be documented for almost the entire eastern North America. The weather attracted considerable press comment, which has compensated for the absence of thermometric readings.[30] New York, New Jersey, Delaware, and Pennsylvania hardly fared better than New England. For example, the Philadelphia Society for Promoting Agriculture resolved on October 30, 1816, "to collect facts relating to agriculture and Horticulture, and of all circumstances connected therewith, which have occurred through the extraordinary season of 1816; and particularly the effects of frost on the vegetation." Respondents from Pennsylvania and elsewhere in the northeastern states agreed that the frosts had damaged corn most, buckwheat to some extent, but wheat, rye, barley, and oats only to a limited degree.[31] Complaints of frost and drought during the spring, summer, and autumn, with ensuing harvest deficiencies and fears of dearth were widely expressed.[32]

The United States midwest seems to have escaped the worst agricultural consequences of the bad weather, but the entire western region experienced the same late spring frosts which were so damaging to the northeast. Moreover, the region was not exempt from the late summer-early autumn frosts.[33] In all probability topographical conditions led to varied magnitudes of crop damage from district to district; but it is clear that the western region suffered less than did the northeast. Indeed, the former was to profit from the agricultural calamity at the expense of western Europe.

The weather was just as bad in the south, the American heartland for the production of agricultural staples. As elsewhere in the United States, the majority of southern observers cited drought as the cause of deficient harvest yields in 1816, but the evidence that the cold waves also penetrated this region is overwhelming. An editorial in the *Richmond Compiler* at the end of August depicted a season not unlike the northeast experience: "The corn is very backward—and it is generally supposed will be an uncommonly short crop. The same case perhaps with tobacco."[34] North Carolina appears to have shared the same weather as Virginia, as well as similar harvest outcomes. The journals maintained by the Moravian settlements in North Carolina provide a comprehensive account of the progress of the seasons in 1816. Heavy frosts were recorded during April. Both the severe cold front of June 6 and the cold waves of late August penetrated as far south as North Carolina.[35] The final outcome of the harvest of 1816 was summed up in the Bethania Memorabilia on September 1: "The very cool and dry weather in spring and summer hurt our grain fields badly, and it was with sorrowful and troubled hearts that we gathered our second crop of hay and our corn crop, which were so scanty that we reaped only a third of what we usually get, and wondered how we could subsist until next year's harvest."[36] Similar agricultural conditions existed almost everywhere in North Carolina, with more telling damage in the western districts.[37]

In the lower south, the subtropical region of the United States, one would not expect to encounter low summer temperatures. Nonetheless, South Carolina experienced frost as late as mid-May, and the familiar late August cold waves were also noticed there. Crop deficiencies occurred in at least some districts of South Carolina in 1816; in addition to the heavy damage to corn, tobacco and cotton yields also suffered.[38] Georgia appears to have escaped the season of 1816 without significant agricultural injury. The same was not true of the Territory of Alabama to the west, where crop failures produced a genuine dearth during 1816, and forced numerous settlers to evacuate owing to the lack of provisions. The cold weather of 1816 also caused some damage to the sugar crop in Louisiana.[39]

The anomalous weather patterns, in fact, penetrated as far south as the Caribbean region, where they reduced the yields of ''colonial'' products and contributed to the dearth conditions that prevailed in Havana and Vera Cruz.[40] The scarcity of provisions was also a problem in the British West Indies, where a partial failure of the sugar harvest occurred.[41] The merchants and planters on St. Kitt's petitioned the governor to open the ports for food imports to ''secure them against the horrors of famine.''[42] Nonetheless, the agricultural consequences of the weather were less destructive in the Caribbean.

In Canada, by contrast, the weather was as severe as in any region of the Western world. Snowfall accumulation was still interfering with normal husbandry as late as the middle of April. In early June, the same cold wave noticed in the United States swept from west to east preceded by snow. The death toll among nestlings, lambs, and other young animals was higher in Quebec province than in New York and New England. To make matters worse, the backward spring and cold summer of 1816 followed a year in which the weather had been almost equally bad.[43] Canada also had the abnormally low July and August temperatures recorded in the United States and, as a consequence, harvest outcomes remained uncertain. The government of Lower Canada established an embargo on the export of all bread grains from July 9 to September 10, 1816.[44] But despite some distress among the poorer classes, Canada passed through the threatening dearth without serious social problems—an outcome not unexpected in a land with such a favorable population–resource ratio.[45]

Of further economic and social significance, as well as of meteorological importance, the years 1812–18 were colder than normal as a group. For example, the average temperature at New Haven 1778–1935 was exactly 50.0°F, while each year from 1812–18 proved considerably colder than this mean: 46.4°F, 48.5°F, 48.1°F, 46.8°F, 46.1°F, 46.0°F, and 46.3°F in chronological segquence.[46] The historical significance of this sequence of cold years was magnified by its parallel occurrence in Europe and elsewhere in the northern hemisphere.

The abnormally low temperatures in western and central Europe were accompanied by excessive precipitation during the growing season. Also the agricultural dislocations occasioned by the recent wars reinforced the calamity. Turning first to the United Kingdom, monthly mean temperatures representative of the English Midlands for the period 1698–1952 indicate that the summer months of 1816 were all considerably colder than the mean, ranging from a −2.3°F deviation for May to a −4.6°F deviation for July. July 1816

registered the lowest mean temperature for that month during the entire observation period.[47] On the Lancashire plain, the decade 1811–20 registered the
lowest decennial mean temperature during the period 1754–1940.[48] Compared over the observation period 1659–1973, however, 1816's mean of
46.0°F was considerably higher than the record low temperature of 44.2°F
measured in 1740. Nonetheless, it is significant from the standpoing of agricultural productivity that the largest minus temperature deviations in 1740
occurred during the months January–May and October–December, whereas in
1816 they fell during the months July–September.[49] English phenological
records support a conclusion that summer temperature values are more critical
for grain harvests. Observations made at Farningham, Kent, from 1808 to
1861 record the latest "harvest finishing" date on October 13, 1816, compared to an average date of September 3, and also record the latest "wheat in
ear" date on July 15, 1816, compared to an average date of June 25.[50] At
Edinburgh, to the north, the same abnormally low mean temperature was
recorded during the crop season of 1816, with readings slightly below those in
England.[51]

Although systematic observations are not available for Ireland, a medical
historian has documented both the low atmospheric temperatures and the
injury to vegetation:

In 1816 the spring was unusually late; the summer and autumn excessively wet, cold,
and cloudy: the quantity of rain which fell in this year measured in the gauge nearly 31
inches, a circumstance perhaps unprecedented in this country; there were 142 wet
days, and these principally in the summer and autumnal months. The mean temperature of the spring, summer, and autumn, was 3 ½ degrees below that of the preceding
year. ... the winter of 1816 was remarkably mild. The year 1817 was almost as
remarkable as 1816 for being wet and cold.[52]

As a consequence of these meteorological conditions, the wheat, oat, and
potato crops failed in Ireland, unleashing a famine that struck hardest in the
north and southwest.

The years 1740–41, like the years 1816–17, produced severe famine in
Ireland, but the weather played a somewhat different role. As elsewhere in
western and central Europe, the agricultural losses in 1740 resulted primarily
from the "great frost" that began the last week in December and continued
almost uninterruptedly into late February. Famine conditions were even further extended in Ireland because of widespread reliance on potatoes as a
substitute for grain. Apparently, it was customary at this time either to leave
the potato crop in the ground or in shallow pits until Christmas or so. The soil
covering the potatoes proved scant protection from the severe frost and reportedly most of the crop was destroyed in a single night. Wheat prices in Dublin
advanced until they doubled between January 1740 and January 1741, and

then reached a peak in the summer months of 1741.[53] Weather patterns across the Irish Sea in Lancashire were just as bad, and grain prices rose nearly as sharply, but famine was avoided.[54]

In 1816 the Irish harvest deficiencies and dearth conditions were again paralleled to varying lesser degrees in England, Scotland, and Wales. The British press was tardy in reporting the approaching crisis; as elsewhere in Europe, this policy ensued from a reluctance to promote speculation in grain. *The Times* finally noted the precariousness of the harvest outlook in late July: "Should the present wet weather continue, the corn will inevitably be laid, and the effects of such a calamity and at such a time cannot be otherwise than ruinous to the farmers, and even to the people at large."[55] The inclement weather continued with night frosts in August, and even snowfall was reported from several locations in England before the harvests were complete.[56] Districts in Britain related varying harvest fortunes, with the most pessimistic accounts emanating from Wales, the northern counties, and Scotland.[57]

Despite repeated comments by European observers concerning the damaging precipitation in 1816, the records of measured rainfall fail to disclose extraordinary levels. At Edinburgh, rainfall totaled 25.24 inches during 1816, while the annual average for 1770–1896 amounted to a similar 25.85 inches. The abnormal circumstance in 1816 was rainfall of 5.22 inches during July, and a combined total of 10.44 inches for the months of July, August, and September.[58] Precipitation patterns were similar in the London area, where measured rainfall amounted to 29.74 inches in 1816, and where 16.34 inches fell between June 17 and September 13.[59] Despite complaints of drought in New England, on the other hand, measured precipitation at Williamstown from May through August amounted to 11.04 inches, even though the annual total of 25.98 inches in 1816 was considerably below normal.[60] Both rainfall patterns occurred elsewhere in Europe. Whether maximum crop damage ensued from low temperature or from untimely precipitation remains unclear. Widespread and severe hailstorms throughout the Western world during the summer of 1816 also added to the agricultural losses.

The cold and wet summer of 1816 spared neither half of the new kingdom of the United Netherlands. Although no systematic data are available for the Belgian provinces, a weather log kept at Ghent in Flanders has preserved detailed observations beginning in 1791. According to the observer, the weather continued cold and wet with snow and sleet until the middle of May. Even June was cold and rainy, the maximum temperature reaching no higher than 64°F. July turned out excessively wet, with violent hailstorms; and in August, when the rye harvest began, the weather continued alternately fair and stormy. September proved mainly wet. The first apricots did not ripen until September 16; the grape harvest was virtually a complete failure; the potatoes rotted in several cantons; and a general dearth ensued.[61]

Weather conditions were equally bad in the Dutch half of the kingdom. The seasonal and annual means for the Zwanenburg-Utrecht district of Holland during the second decade of the nineteenth century disclose the unusually low summer temperatures of 1816, as well as the abrupt drop in temperature during 1812 and the recovery to normal means by 1818. The deviation from the long-range mean for the summer of 1816 measured −4.0°F and thus approximated the departure elsewhere in the Western world, as was the case in the series of cool summers in the Netherlands from 1812 to 1817.[62] The Netherlands witnessed a destructive conjunction of low temperature, excessive or untimely precipitation, and violent summer storms, causing harvest deficiencies and famine conditions, which were maximized in the northern provinces.[63]

In northern France, summer temperatures were consistently below normal in 1816; the Paris Observatory recorded a −5.4°F seasonal deviation from the mean for 1740–1870, while the annual mean amounted to a departure of −2.9°F.[64] Despite the record of below-normal temperature in France, observers believed that the agricultural losses were caused primarily by excessive precipitation. Regional and local studies have confirmed contemporary testimony of persistent rain, flooding, and destructive hail, especially in the eastern half of France.[65] But once again the records of measured precipitation fail to indicate that 1816 was a year of strikingly high rainfall. Even the precipitation that fell during the critical growing season from May to September measured less than the rainfall recorded in 1817 and about the same quantity as in 1819.[66]

While it may not be possible to determine which of the three elements—cold, rain, or hail—was principally responsible for the crop deficiencies, the case for low temperature is supported by the records of *vendange* (grape-harvesting) dates in France. The *vendange,* or vintage season, was the official date when the grape harvest could begin in a given locality, indicating the date when the grapes ripened. For example, at Argenteuil (Seine et Oise), the average *vendange* date in a 215-year series occurred on September 28, with a deviation of 51 days separating the extreme dates. The latest recorded date fell on October 23, 1816; moreover, from 1601 to 1926 there were only six dates in the Paris region later than October 15.[67] In addition, all the French and Swiss wine-growing stations whose harvest dates are known (i.e., from 1782 to 1879) disclose that the latest *vendange* occurred in the year 1816; the sixty-three locations included in the series indicate a mean harvest date of October 29, 1816.[68] The significance of small temperature variations, as well as the severity of the growing season in 1816, may be deduced from the fact that in Verdun the grapes failed to ripen that year.[69]

Public or official notice of the unprecedented agricultural season was as rare in France as in Britain. Once again this stance was dictated by the pressing need to dampen grain speculation and to avoid social unrest. Nevertheless, with the exception of a few individuals, most persons in positions of authority seemed unaware of the precariousness of the agricultural outlook. Public prayers were offered in hopes of improving the weather, but many participants had shared this experience in earlier years. Neither the *Moniteur* nor the Parisian dailies commented on the weather in 1816, except to notice late snowfalls, severe storms, and the superabundant rain in a casual way. By contrast, the Ministry of Interior's circulars, addressed to the prefects, warned as early as August 13, 1816, that the excessive precipitation would reduce the supply of fodder and thus constitute a health hazard for the livestock population. The next major communication concerned with the weather failed to appear until February 17, 1817.[70]

Table 4 indicates that weather conditions were more harsh in central than in western Europe. The decline to minus temperature deviations in 1812 and the continued absence of positive departures until 1819 are apparent for these twelve central European stations. Literary accounts of the year 1816 substantiate the instrumental data as far eastward as the borders of the Russian empire; also, they document the harvest failures resulting from the inclement weather.

Every region of Germany experienced cold and wet weather during the crop cycle of 1816. A privy councillor in Bavaria compared 1816 to the dearth years 1770 and 1570, because of the unending rain and frequent hail in each of the summer seasons. Not only was the harvest delayed and deficient in Bavaria; the grain that reached full maturity turned out excessively wet. Grain prices rose sharply in the markets, prompting a public outcry against profiteers and *Kornjuden*.[71] In the kingdom of Württemberg, the new yearbook focused on the weather patterns of 1816 and the ensuing harvest failures; the editors believed that the agricultural tragedy overshadowed the recent European political events. The poor harvest was the culmination of a consecutive series of deficient yields throughout central Europe. Summer cold waves reminiscent of the American experience penetrated southwestern Germany. "Every storm of the past summer moreover was followed by the most severe cold, so that it regularly felt like November, and no month went by in which many houses were not heated."[72] The harvest was delayed by more than a month, and then rain hindered reaping in some districts so that crops were still standing in the fields as late as the middle of October. Finally, a severe frost supervened on October 17, followed by snow a few days later; as a result, fields in the highland districts could not be harvested at all, and more than two-thirds of the oat fields rotted under snow and ice.[73] Neighboring Baden witnessed the worst harvest disaster in four centuries.[74]

Upper Franconia and the area around Frankfurt am Main were inundated by violent summer storms and unending precipitation, which dimmed the agricultural outlook as early as July. The losses in grain, hay, tobacco, and pulses were termed "incalculable."[75] Neither Franconia nor Swabia was reprieved by an Indian summer. Rather the fall season set in prematurely and by

Table 4. Temperature Deviations from the Mean 1851–1950 (Degrees of Fahrenheit Scale)

Year	Basel	Strass-burg	Karls-ruhe	Stutt-gart	Geneva	Berlin	Prague	Vienna	Trieste	Milan	Turin	Hohen-peissen-berg
1811	+1.6	+2.9	+0.9	+1.3	+1.4	+0.9	+3.6	+3.2	+2.0	+1.4	+0.2	+3.6
1812	−2.7	−2.1	−2.9	−2.7	−2.3	−4.3	−1.1	−0.9	−1.3	−2.7	−3.8	−1.1
1813	−2.0	−1.3	−1.6	−2.3	−1.4	−1.4	+0.5	−0.4	+0.5	−0.7	−2.7	−1.1
1814	−2.0	−1.6	−2.2	−2.3	−2.0	−3.6	−1.3	−0.9	−0.7	−2.3	−2.5	−1.3
1815	−0.9	−0.4	−1.4	−1.3	−0.2	−2.2	+0.5	−0.2	−0.9	−0.9	−0.5	−0.7
1816	−3.2	−2.5	−3.4	−3.4	−2.2	−3.6	−0.4	−1.6	−2.2	−3.8	−1.1	−2.9
1817	−1.1	0.0	−1.3	−1.1	0.0	−0.7	+1.3	+1.4	−0.4	−1.6	+1.4	−0.4
1818	−0.2	+0.5	+0.5	0.0	−0.4	−0.2	+1.6	+2.0	+0.2	+0.4	+1.6	+1.6
1819	+0.7	+1.1	0.0	+1.1	+0.4	+0.9	+2.2	+1.8	+1.1	+0.4	+1.6	+1.4

Source: M. Bider, M. Schüepp, and Hans von Rudloff, "Die Reduktion der 200-jährigen Basler Temperaturreihe," *Archiv für Meteorologie, Geophysik und Bioklimatologie*, serie B, 9 (1959). Temperature deviations converted from Centigrade scale.

November winter conditions prevailed, with snow a foot deep in some locations.[76] Saxony and the Hessian states likewise experienced a sequence of spectacular storms, cold waves, superabundant rainfall, and threatened harvests during 1816.[77]

The Prussian provinces (the Rhineland and Westphalia) located in northwestern Germany witnessed weather patterns similar to those in southwestern and central Germany. The flooding in Lower Rhine, which persisted for five months, was extended by the closing of a Dutch sluice on May 11.[78] Düsseldorf counted 166 days of precipitation in 1816; total rainfall amounted to 32 inches for the year, but almost 13 inches fell during June, July, and August. Potatoes were still in the earth and grain uncut under a foot of snow at the end of 1816 in the higher elevations around Cologne.[79] The eastern provinces of Prussia escaped the full brunt of the destructive weather; but, like the northeastern United States, a spring drought threatened crops in the East-Elbian districts, and then overabundant rain in mid-summer reduced harvest yields. Despite a steep advance in grain prices in eastern Prussia, agricultural output seems to have fallen only slightly below normal levels.[80]

Northern Germany was even less touched by the adverse weather, though this statement was less true for the hinterlands than for the coastal districts.[81] For example, the grand duchy of Mecklenburg-Schwerin encountered an unusual number of cold and wet days in both May and July, which led to the death of numerous cattle as well as to deficient grain yields. Dearth prices finally prevailed for all provisions, but famine never became a threat.[82] Holstein fared better; and Lower Saxony escaped with nothing more than a shortage of rye.[83]

Scandinavia and the northern Baltic region, where temperatures remained nearer normal values, reaped average grain volumes; but prices rose to dearth levels nonetheless, and the united kingdom of Sweden and Norway found it expedient to subsidize bakers and to place an embargo on grain exports in 1816. Moreover, as elsewhere in Europe, the elevated food prices spawned bread riots and the looting of grain supplies, especially in Norway.[84] Russia also seems to have harvested average crop volumes in 1816, a conclusion which is consistent with the contemporary observation that the more easterly or northerly the location the more the weather improved.[85]

Compared to the grim experience of northern Europe in 1740, moreover, this region virtually escaped the severe weather of 1816. While the major rivers of Europe and the Zyder Zee were frozen during the winter months of 1740, temperatures in northern Europe fell low enough for an extended period to freeze the Sound between Denmark and Sweden and the Baltic Sea between Stockholm and Abo. This deep frost occurred in all Baltic ports; reportedly, it was possible to build a palace from blocks of ice at St. Petersburg. Scandinavian harvest yields were compromised further when the cold winter of 1740 was followed by a cool, wet summer.[86] Under normal meteorological conditions it would, of course, be expected that northern Europe would experience more severe winters and lower temperatures than western Europe. This was not the case, however, in the winter of 1708–09, when western Europe encountered more extreme weather than the Baltic region. Moreover, the spring and summer months of 1816, contrary to normal patterns, brought lower temperatures to northwestern than to northeastern Europe. Apparently, the latitude of eruption is a major factor in determining subsequent European weather patterns in years when they are influenced by volcanic dust veils, or at least the empirical circumstances suggest this. Northern Europe likewise escaped a mortality crisis in 1816–17, again in contrast to the appalling death rates recorded in Norway, Sweden, Finland, and Denmark in the years 1740–43.[87]

Switzerland was not so fortunate; no land suffered more during the years 1816 and 1817. Many of the Swiss cantons had become dependent upon foreign grain supplies for basic subsistence. The extreme cold of 1816 worsened this problem by interfering with the cattle-breeding and dairying industry. In the words of the pastor of the St. Gall parish, these were years of hunger, want, sickness, death, manufacturing unemployment, trade stagnation, and calamitous weather.[88] The famine of 1816–17 followed a series of deficient harvests, as elsewhere in central Europe. Swiss grain harvests during the first half of the nineteenth century have been systematically classified according to yields. Each year has been assigned a numerical value on a scale from one to six, the higher number representing more abundant harvests; the values for the years relevant to this study are reproduced:[89]

1812 2
1813 3
1814 3
1815 2
1816 1
1817 2
1818 6
1819 6

Although a glance at Table 4 will reveal that fluctuations of agricultural yields followed the temperature curve, the 130 days of rain counted in Switzerland from April to September 1816 also must have reduced harvest volumes. Grain and potato harvests were delayed too long, a significant part of the hay crop was destroyed, and the grape harvest failed. Contrary to the widespread hope that potato culture had eliminated famine, hunger became generalized in eastern Switzerland during 1817, engendering hordes of beggars and vagrants.[90]

Despite its enormous expanse, no province of the Habsburg Monarchy avoided the economic and social distress traceable to the weather, though some districts fared better than others. One high government official claimed that 1816 had been a worse year for the Monarchy than any of the twenty previous war years, the territorial losses and the huge indemnities associated with a succession of lost battles notwithstanding. Of course, the calamitous harvests of 1816 were preceded by several deficient crop years and accompanied by chronic monetary inflation.[91] The more underdeveloped provinces of the empire seem to have suffered almost as severely in 1815, another year of excessive precipitation. The continuing bad weather was also blamed for the epidemic of bubonic plague that raged in the Balkans and threatened to spread into the traditional Habsburg lands.[92]

The year 1816 began inauspiciously in Hungary when a devastating two-day blizzard struck at the end of January. Houses virtually disappeared from view; and hundreds of thousands of cattle, sheep, and horses perished, for livestock were still pastured out-of-doors in the winter. ''The snow was not white, but brown or flesh colored.''[93] This statement was no doubt a reference to volcanic dust in the atmosphere, a phenomenon reported at several Western locations in the winter of 1815–16. Deficient temperature and excessive precipitation during the growing season reduced harvest volumes throughout the Hungarian realm—Hungary, Slavonia, Croatia, Transylvania. Poor communications and transportation, made worse by storms and flooding, hampered attempts to provide relief to the more isolated districts. While the grain deficiencies produced dearth in Hungary proper, famine conditions developed in Transylvania and in several Slavic districts.[94]

Harvest outcomes were uneven in the Czech lands, with highland districts reporting the lowest yields. While dearth prices became the rule as elsewhere, there was no famine in Moravia because of proximity to the grain lands of eastern Europe.[95] Many families in the highlands of Bohemia would have died from starvation without public assistance; the Budweiser and Bunzlauer districts both reported low grain yields.[96] Not even the Polish province of Galicia escaped deficient grain yields, in spite of its easterly location. Although famine never became a realistic concern in this rich grain land, neighboring provinces were unable to count on customary rye imports from Galicia during 1816–17. The potato crop, the principal nourishment for the highland population, also turned out badly in Galicia.[97]

In Austria proper, grain harvests also proved deficient, but not alarmingly so. Although yields suffered from the late spring frosts and the damp weather, the wheat, barley, and oats harvests were better than expected. The combination of lower crop yields and a Bavarian grain embargo, however, pushed grain, flour, and bread prices to dearth levels in Upper Austria. Rye and grapes failed to a substantial degree, especially in Lower Austria.[98] The harvest failures in Styria, Carinthia, and Carniola represented the culmination of a series of poor years. The winter grains had failed for three consecutive years in Carinthia, creating a desperate situation for the peasants in the mountainous areas. Because of time lost to the weather in 1816, two-thirds of the rye fields could not be plowed and planted for the coming winter. Harvests also turned out badly in the Tyrol and Vorarlberg, with no possibility of assistance from neighboring Switzerland, Bavaria, Carinthia, or Venetia, where subsistence conditions were likewise unfavorable.[99]

The Balkan provinces in a similar pattern witnessed damaging weather and concomitant harvest failures that necessitated extensive public assistance, particularly in the Austrian Military Frontier.[100] The Ottoman Balkan provinces encountered the same hardships. "This calamity appears almost general: all travelers assert that it is experienced in Turkey, Hungary, Italy, and Germany, and throughout all the East of Europe."[101] Not only did European journals report dearth conditions at Constantinople; they maintained a closer watch on the plague epidemic in the Ottoman domains that threatened to invade the Habsburg lands and Italy.[102]

In Habsburg Italy, harvests were grievously deficient in the highland districts, and grain prices climbed steeply in Milan and other markets during 1816. The weather in Italy that year was cold and wet, with snow still on the ground in Lombardy–Venetia as late as April and May. The snowfalls were succeeded by cold rain and floods during the late spring and early summer. Observers attributed the cold winter in Italy to the refrigerating influence of the glaciers in Switzerland and the Tyrol, which in fact had advanced considerably in the previous year. Both northern and southern Italy experienced below-normal temperature readings during the growing season; Sicily, however, appears to have substantially escaped. Throughout much of Italy, as in all of central Europe, partial and in some instances complete crop failures had occurred for several years prior to 1816. Instead of fulfilling anxious hopes, the weather of 1816 brought near disaster.[103] The grain had to be cut at the beginning of September in many districts of Italy. Because of the early autumn frosts, much of the crop proved suitable only for fodder, provided it had not been destroyed while still standing in the fields. In the higher elevations of Lombardy and Venetia the grains either were ruined by floods or failed to mature because of the low temperatures.[104] Harvest outcomes were scarcely better in the Papal States or on the mainland of the kingdom of Naples; only Sicily reported a good harvest.[105] Most of Italy faced misery and dearth in the spring of 1816; by the spring of 1817 outright famine appeared.[106]

The Iberian peninsula fared better than the Italian peninsula, but unfavorable weather produced a sharp advance in food prices, which was accompanied by social unrest in northeastern Spain. The only complete Spanish price series for the nineteenth century pertains to Barcelona from 1812 to 1914; these data indicate that food prices paralleled the rise throughout the Western world during 1816–17. Spain also witnessed the damaging late summer rains of 1816, and a definite shortage of provisions prevailed by spring

1817.[107] In Portugal, the late summer and early fall rains of 1816 ruined the indispensable grape harvest and created distress in the wine districts. Olive oil, the other principal agricultural commodity, exhibited an unbroken series of price increases from September 1816 to August 1817, the average annual price at Lisbon in 1817 reaching the highest figure between 1750 and 1854.[108] "The oil and wine crops had also failed" in Italy owing to the absence of "the usual heat of the summer," according to the United States consul at Leghorn.[109] Wheat prices at Lisbon rose approximately 50 percent from 1815 to 1817.[110]

The postwar years initiated a period of noticeable political and social decline in the Barbary states across the Mediterranean. It remains unclear whether climatic change played a primary role; however, beginning with the crop year 1814/1815, a series of poor harvests ensued in Tunis and in Algiers. Dearth conditions prevailed during 1816–17, followed by the first epidemic of bubonic plague since 1784–85. Morocco avoided famine conditions, but the emperor placed an embargo on the export of grain at the end of 1816.[111]

Although systematic meteorological evidence is not available for Asia, anamalous weather patterns were apparently not absent. In Japan, rice yields fell in the years 1813–17, while prices rose in 1814 and again in 1816–17, even though climatic conditions did not approximate the severe decades of the 1780s and 1830s.[112] If peasant uprisings in Japan constitute an index of harvest deficiencies, during the second decade of the nineteenth century the number reached the largest figure recorded between the 1780s and the 1830s.[113]

The evidence is less equivocal for India. James Jameson, assistant surgeon of the East India Company and secretary to the Medical Board of Bengal, introduced his full study of the first modern pandemic of Asiatic cholera with a detailed essay that described the unusual weather patterns experienced in India from the end of 1815 to 1817. Abnormally low temperatures and excessive precipitation during the temperate season, as in the Western world, and then untimely drought during the rainy season reduced grain yields throughout the eastern half of India. Cold and damp weather during the winters and springs of 1815/1816 and 1816/1817 "greatly injured the spring grain crop, and the new sown Indigo lands." Drought during the rainy season of 1816, succeeded by heavy rains in September, blighted the rice crop. These conditions possibly facilitated the cholera pandemic, which originated in Bengal during the years 1816–17.[114]

METEOROLOGICAL EXPLANATIONS

The majority of observers attributed the anomalous weather to the sunspot maximum that occurred in 1816. Popular opinion, especially, exaggerated the significance of the solar phenomena; and the combination of bizarre weather and sunspots visible to the naked eye gave rise to predictions of the approaching "end of the world."[115] Informed opinion both in Europe and America tended, however, to question the connection between sunspots and low temperature.[116] While it is probable that solar cycles affect weather patterns on the earth, agreement concerning the precise correlation has not been reached.[117] Observers were likewise impressed by the accumulation of ice and snow in the temperate zone, both as sea ice in the Atlantic shipping lanes and as advancing glaciers in the mountainous regions.[118] Again, while it is certain that the volume and latitude of sea ice affects weather and climate by inducing anomalous patterns of the atmospheric circulation, the precise relationships remain incompletely understood.[119]

The principal cause of the thermal deficit, volcanic dust in the atmosphere, was disclosed in a medical account of the "atmospheric constitution" concerned with the suspended radiance of the sun:

What rendered it more astonishing in its diurnal variation, was its coexistence with mist or vapour equally dense and diaphanous all over the horizon. It had nothing of the nature of a humid fog. It was like that smoking vapour which overspread Europe about thirty years ago. The learned, who made experiments to ascertain its nature, could only state its remarkable dryness, by which no polished surface or mirror could be obscured. . . . While the human eye could thus, during the long days, gaze on the great luminary of nature, . . . deprived of its dazzling splendour and radiance; then the numerous dark spots were discovered on its face, without the help of telescopic or obscured glasses; these among the multitude became the theme of popular apprehension of a calamitous sign in heaven, and others thought to have found a visible cause of the long refrigeration of our atmosphere.[120]

Benjamin Franklin noticed in 1784 that "this fog was of a permanent nature; it was dry, and the rays of the sun seemed to have little effect toward dissipating it, as they easily do a moist fog, arising from water." Franklin already suspected the volcanic origin of the vapor.[121]

Other atmospheric phenomena widely reported during the postwar years confirm the presence of volcanic dust veils. Anomalous sky effects are trustworthy indications of volcanic explosions that discharge dust into the stratosphere—such as reddish sun and moon, blue or green sun or moon, richly colored twilights, dust veils dimming the horizon sun, and "colored" precipitation.[122] The great Hungarian blizzard of 1816 that produced snow described as brown or flesh-colored was not an isolated incident. A red and yellow snowfall terrorized the inhabitants of Taranto in southern Italy, where snow itself was a rare occurrence.[123] The snowfalls of April and May 1816 in Maryland were reported to be tinted brown, bluish, or red.[124] But the most persuasive evidence is the atmospheric dust or vapor or dry fog observed in the Western world. "During the entire season the sun arose each morning as though in a cloud of smoke, red and rayless, shedding little light or warmth and setting at night behind a thick cloud of vapor, leaving hardly a trace of its having passed over the face of the earth."[125] The French Academy of Science and the British Museum also reported extraordinary dust loads; and the sky effects of the Tomboro eruption were noted throughout the balance of the year 1815 in the form of streaky skies, haziness, long twilights, and red sunsets.[126]

The conclusion that the dust in the stratosphere was indeed the debris produced by the explosion of Tomboro is corroborated by contemporary evidence. Despite the isolation of Sumbawa in 1815, detailed accounts of the explosion have survived as the result of British military occupation of the East Indies. The reports claim that the explosions were audible hundreds of miles from the volcano, and also that ash accumulated at this distance.[127] Sir Thomas Raffles, British military governor of Java, drew up the most comprehensive account, which leaves little doubt that Tomboro corresponded to an epochal volcanic explosion. "This eruption extended perceptible evidences of its existence over the whole of the Molucca islands, over Java, a considerable portion of Celebes, Sumatra, and Borneo, to a circumference of a thousand statute miles from its centre, by tremulous motions, and the report of explosions." Java, three hundred miles distant, was showered with ash to a depth of several inches.[128] About 12,000 inhabitants of Sumbawa perished as a direct result of the explosions, while another 44,000 persons died on the neighboring island of Lombok, in large part from famine produced by the destruction of the field crops by falling ash. According to the Dutch naturalist Franz Junghuhn, the explosions were audible at a location in Sumatra some 1,950 kilometers to the west of Tomboro, and as far as New Guinea to the east.[129] If the distance between these extreme points is plotted on a map of the Western world, the lines will extend from Madrid to Moscow or from Leningrad to Suez.

For the economic historian, the inability to explain anomalous weather patterns with quantitative exactness is less critical than it is to remember that the elements can become an uncontrolled independent variable affecting the intensity, duration, and perhaps the occurrence of trade cycles.

chapter
two

The Subsistence Crisis
of 1816–1817

POSTWAR ECONOMIC BACKGROUND

The subsistence crisis of 1816–17 was the worst European famine since 1709–10 and probably amounted to the most severe scarcity since the seventeenth century. The Western world has never again witnessed a dearth of such extensive range. Factors other than the weather were responsible for the acute distress, however. Postwar dislocation and readjustments in trade and industry in particular added to the disequilibrium as falling price levels and declining production increased unemployment rates. Even though the history of the postwar industrial and international trade sectors is well known, and though this work concentrates on the dominating economic effects produced by weather patterns, it is necessary to examine the continuing influence of wartime arrangements and the behavior of self-generating cyclical variables. The fluctuations of agricultural output serve as the connecting link between the weather and each national economy; but not all economies confronted the same postwar economic legacy, and thus national experiences differed.

The *Annual Register* in Britain summed up the year 1816 by calling attention to the pan-European nature of the economic distress and pointed to twenty-five years of war as its origin. The prevailing commercial stagnation in Britain was traced to the failure to recapture European markets after the British trade monopolies created by the sea blockades were terminated by the peace. Not only were Britain's former customers on the Continent impoverished by wartime expenditures and losses, now they were eager to supply their own industrial wants. "British manufactures, therefore, which by the improvements of mechanical ingenuity, had been accumulated to a vast amount in the merchants' warehouses found no regular demand, but were forced by speculation into foreign markets, where they could obtain a sale only at a price much below the prime cost." Manufacturers consequently found it necessary either to suspend or to reduce production, thereby raising unemployment levels in almost every branch of industry.[1] While this account represented a reasonably accurate description of commercial and industrial conditions in Britain, the European postwar economic conjuncture was much more complex.

To begin with, the drastic sea blockade had ruined French, Dutch, and Spanish colonial commerce and also had seriously dislocated most continental industries from 1807 onward. The economic life of such great ports as Amsterdam, Bordeaux, and Marseilles was badly crippled; harbors were deserted, population declined, and industrial production collapsed both in the ports and in their hinterlands. The linen industry proved to be the most important European casualty, though it was doomed in any event from the competition of the rising cotton industry. Linen in France had been principally an export industry of the western provinces with overseas markets in the West Indies and Spanish America.[2] Beyond its contribution to foreign exchange earnings, the linen industry on the Continent was counted on to furnish supplementary employment in regions where small landholdings were the rule, which was especially the case in the southwestern German states and in Bohemia but was an economic factor nearly everywhere.[3] At the same time, linen exports determined the income and wage levels of workers in the industrial locations of Prussia, Bohemia, Moravia, Upper Austria, and the United Netherlands.[4] Linen remained the principal German textile industry in the postwar years and also represented the only large-scale export, even though British cottons and Irish linens had preempted overseas markets. Although nearly all German manufactures slumped in the first years of peace, the depressed linen industry was chiefly responsible for declining industrial wages and income. Flax spinning and linen weaving achieved preeminent economic importance in Prussian Silesia, Westphalia, and the southwestern states. The inability to sell German linens abroad became a factor in the massive postwar emigration from Württemberg.[5]

A thriving continental beet-sugar industry proved another industrial casualty, in this case as a result of the ending of the blockade. Although of much less economic importance than linen, some one hundred sugar refineries had flourished in Amsterdam at the peak of the industry. At the end of the war only three factories remained in the entire Netherlands.[6] The isolation of the Continent from colonial products created the new sugar industry in the Habsburg Monarchy. By 1810 a substantial refining industry had been established in Bohemia, but it remained economically viable only in the absence of cane sugar. Despite temporary disaster after the reappearance of West Indian sugar, this industry was destined to secure a significant role in the economy of central Europe. The final blow was delivered in 1816 by the crop failure, which drove up the price of sugar beets and compelled the Austrian factories to close.[7]

The blockade and Continental System also gave added momentum to the cotton textile industry, for British competition had previously been almost an insuperable barrier. Peace, correspondingly, brought temporary disaster to the continental cotton industry. Bonaparte's Continental System had given French trade and industry a decided competitive advantage, but the termination of this artificial economic condition made postwar competition all the more difficult for merchants and manufacturers; the fall of the Empire in 1814 coincided with the end of the growth of the cotton industry.[8] The southern provinces of the Netherlands had become the birthplace of the industrial revolution on the Continent during the two decades in which Belgium had been incorporated within France. Belgian manufactures and coal had commanded the French imperial market, which was effectively protected against competing British products. With the introduction of textile machines, Ghent became the continental center of the cotton industry. But with the return of British cottons in 1814, the future of the Belgian industry depended on expansion and a reduction in production costs, neither of which materialized in time. Then, the textile industry was depressed further when new tariff barriers severely restricted the previous flow of Belgian manufactured goods into France.[9]

Whereas the German linen export trade suffered from the loss of overseas and European markets during the years of the Continental System, the German cotton industry prospered from the artificial conditions. With the return of peace, however, British cottons captured a significant share of both the German cotton and linen markets. Although the German cotton industry remained less important in the postwar period than either linen or wool, geographical concentration and mechanized production made its difficulties highly visible. For example, an impressive cotton textile industry had evolved in and around Plauen in Saxony, providing some 30,000 jobs; but these workers suffered severely from high unemployment during the immediate postwar years.[10] The Swiss cotton industry had likewise benefited from the barriers erected by the Continental System. Centered in the eastern cantons, cotton textiles had become the major industry, employing some 150,000 workers as early as 1780 and more than 200,000 by 1815. But the return of British textile competition and the proliferation of customs barriers in neighboring states in 1816 translated into rising unemployment and falling prices in the Swiss cotton industry.[11] Austrian cotton production also increased considerably during the years 1800–15, benefiting from rapid monetary inflation that led to investment in new businesses, as well as the absence of British competition. The introduction of spinning machines was accelerated not only by the wartime manpower shortage but also by the currency revaluation and financial crisis of 1811, which disrupted normal credit relationships.

At least twelve mechanized spinning mills were operating in the Monarchy by 1814; but few new installations appeared thereafter, and with the return of British cottons even the strongest firms tottered.[12] The entire European textile industry, moreover, slumped badly in 1816.

Needless to say, continental merchants and producers became convinced that the textile industry, and indeed the entire economy, was being ruined by an avalanche of cheap British goods. Most historians also have adopted the contemporary view. But then as now complaints about the destructive competition of imports should not be taken merely at face value. The commercial stagnation of 1816 flowed both from the supply side and the demand side. Gayer, Rostow, and Schwartz found the source of the British slump to be located in the contracting phase of an inventory investment cycle. "As in 1792–3, 1799–1800, and 1810–11, we have a crisis the basis of which was prior investment in consumption goods for export and re-export," moreover, "even more than in other cases thus far examined, the sources of this cycle lay strictly in foreign trade."[13] In fact, the declared value of British exports and reexports declined from £68.4 million in 1815 to £54.3 million in 1816, while the value of imports fell even more steeply from £71.3 million in 1815 to £50.2 in 1816. These figures also represented substantial declines from the postwar peaks of 1814, when imports reached £80.8 million and exports totaled £70.3 million, of which £24.8 were reexports—the highest figure found in the trade statistics until 1859.[14]

While it is true that foreign-trade levels had become a critical indicator of the state of the trade cycle in the British economy, the level of internal trade was still more significant for the economic well-being of the majority of the European population. The entire Western economy, moreover, remained preeminently agricultural in the early decades of the nineteenth century. Even in Britain, the least agrarian economy, agriculture made up the largest component in the national income and was still the largest industry both in terms of capital and labor force.[15] Economic well-being still varied decisively with the outcome of the harvests and with the price of cereals. Correspondingly, the level of real national income must have moved directly with agricultural productivity and inversely to the price of grain.

Even so, the trade cycle was markedly influenced by fluctuations of international trade, and it is necessary to attempt to assess the economic signifiance of British exports for the continental postwar crisis. The strongest protests against British goods issued from Belgian manufacturers, who demanded not only high tariffs but the prohibition of all textile imports. Textile producers attributed all industrial difficulties to the foreign competition to which the new unpopular political settlement exposed them, "telling dismissed workers to blame the government."[16] The Belgian viewpoint was ceremonialized by the public burning of British cottons at Ghent in August 1816, an event that prompted a violent press polemic on both sides. It was widely believed that British goods were priced below cost to ruin Belgian industry.[17]

Yet as far as the cotton industry at Ghent was concerned 1816 was a year of partial recovery. ''Both in terms of numbers of factories and size of labour force, the position in 1816 was healthier than in 1811 or 1812. The number of cotton workers at Ghent fell to 6,150 in 1813, after having reached 10,600 in 1812; in 1816 the number stood at 11,928.''[18] It is difficult to reconcile these figures with the complaints against destructive British competition. Foreign trade values are not available for Belgium, but the British trade statistics lend perspective to the issue, even if they do not furnish all the data wanted. The British figures, displayed in Table 5, provide aggregate trade totals with the Netherlands in 1814; manufactures are distinguished from colonial goods in 1815; and trade values are separated between Belgium and Holland in 1816. Exports and imports are expressed in official rather than current market values, and therefore measure volume fluctuations more accurately than changes in aggregate values. Since British export prices declined from 1816 to 1820, the figures are not an accurate record of changes in the balance of trade.[19]

The most striking fact is the share of British exports to the Netherlands represented by colonial or foreign goods. Although these figures are not available for either 1814 or 1815, the large value of total British reexports for

Table 5. Official Values of International Trade between Great Britain and the Netherlands 1814–20 (in millions of pounds sterling)

	A. British imports from and exports to the Netherlands			B. British manufactured exports to the Netherlands			
Year	Imports	Exports	Exports foreign products	Total	Cottons	Woolens	Others
1814	2.2	8.9	—	—	—	—	—
1815	1.2	8.2	—	2.7	1.7	0.3	0.6
1816	0.7	6.6	4.2	2.3	1.3	0.3	0.6
1817	0.9	4.4	2.6	1.8	0.9	0.2	0.7
1818	1.7	4.0	2.2	1.8	1.0	0.3	0.4
1819	0.8	4.0	2.2	1.9	1.2	0.2	0.3
1820	0.7	3.6	1.7	1.9	1.3	0.3	0.4

C. British exports to the provinces of the Netherlands

	Dutch Provinces			Belgian Provinces		
Year	Manufactured Products	Foreign Products	Total	Manufactured Products	Foreign Products	Total
1816	1.5	2.3	3.8	0.9	1.9	2.8
1817	1.2	1.4	3.6	0.6	1.2	1.8
1818	1.0	1.0	2.0	0.7	1.2	1.9
1819	1.2	1.1	2.3	0.7	1.1	1.8
1820	1.2	0.8	2.0	0.7	0.8	1.5

Source: Robert Demoulin, Guillaume I er et la transformation économique des provinces belges, 1815–1830 (Liège, 1938), pp. 423–25.

1814 and independent evidence for 1815 suggest that the percentage of colonial goods shipped to the Netherlands was at least as large as in 1816.[20]
Cottons made up the major manufactured export to the Netherlands; however,
as Table 5 indicates, the aggregate volume remained modest. Moreover, the
larger share both of manufactured products and colonial goods was imported
by the Dutch rather than the Belgian provinces. In 1816, the peak year for
which separate Belgian figures are available, total manufactured imports
amounted to £0.9 million or approximately 10.5 million florins. Although no
benchmarks such as national income are at hand to assess the economic
significance of the imports, measured against the Belgian population of 3.4
million in 1816, manufactured imports from Britain averaged slightly more
than three florins per capita. If two-thirds of these imports were cotton textiles, the corresponding value is reduced to two florins. Additional perspective
may be gained from the fact that Britain contributed 12 million florins to the
expense of erecting fortifications along the Franco-Belgian frontier, a project
that ultimately cost more than 80 million florins.[21] Apparently the sums
expended for British cottons were not a staggering amount, but even modest
quantities of British goods must have applied more downward price pressure
on the already depressed Belgian textiles. Of more importance was that effective demand for all industrial goods began to decline as the price of foodstuffs
advanced in Belgium and elsewhere in Europe in the spring months of 1816.

The same complaints against the flood of British exports were echoed
virtually everywhere on the Continent. In the absence of comprehensive foreign trade values, it is not possible to determine the true magnitude of foreign
imports. The French trade statistics are available, however, and they boast a
rough degree of accuracy.[22] These values, shown in Table 6, tend to reinforce
the patterns disclosed by the figures for the Netherlands. The volume of
imports from Britain equaled about one-third of all French imports during the
peak year of 1814. These values then declined sharply in 1815, to approximately one-sixth of total French imports. In 1816 British imports amounted to
less than the value of Dutch imports, but the aggregate volume of British
products still remained significant and it is necessary to examine their compo-
sition. As Table 6 indicates, the steep decline of British imports in 1815 was
paralleled by an equally precipitous fall in the value of colonial products,
whereas manufactured textiles exhibited no more than a slight decline. Colonial wares included such staple commodities as sugar, tobacco, coffee—and
in 1814, as the result of wartime control of the sea lanes, only Britain disposed
of a large quantity of these products. The figures displayed in Tables 5 and 6
do not suggest the conclusion that the postwar continental economic crisis
derived chiefly from an avalanche of British exports produced by the new
textile machines. Nonetheless, the Western textile markets were oversupplied
by British industry in light of the decline in demand that ensued both from the
European dearth and the postwar disruption in commerce and markets.

Table 6. Value of International Trade—France, 1814–20 (in millions of francs)

Year	Exports total	Imports total	Imports from the Netherlands	Imports from Britain	Imports industrial products	Imports manufactured textiles	Imports textile fibers	Colonial products
1814	346	239	36	77	10	16	50	65
1815	433	296	46	51	14	15	82	42
1816	444	334	72	46	22	20	78	52
1817	380	427	69	47	38	19	91	65
1818	428	444	58	43	19	16	130	63
1819	383	387	42	36	23	15	110	77
1820	373	360	53	38	22	17	116	95

Source: Alexandre Chabert, *Essai sur les movements des revenus et de l'activité économique en France de 1789 à 1820* (Paris, 1949), pp. 321–24.

The wars also had produced a degree of generalized impoverishment on the Continent as the outcome of twenty-five years of taxation, requisitions, plunder, conscription, and marching armies. Some economies of belligerent Europe, nevertheless, faced a more burdensome economic legacy than others, which in turn influenced the differential severity of the postwar crisis. Northern Italy, for example, had been especially unfortunate; for the economy of Bonaparte's kingdom of Italy had been regulated in accordance with French commercial and international self-interest with scant concern for Italian needs. French military requisitions and taxation levied a heavy burden on Italian property owners. The measures adopted by the Austrian administration that replaced the French in 1814 contributed to rather than alleviated unemployment and commercial stagnation. Austria disbanded the former French–Italian army that had sustained 60,000 Italians, the majority of the employees of the French regime were dismissed, and public works projects discontinued. These steps were taken in the face of deficient cereal harvests from 1813 onward.[23]

France, the major continental economy, also encountered trying postwar economic disabilities, most of the burdens flowing from the consequences of military defeat. Not only was France saddled with an army of occupation and the economic costs incident to the lost war, the two foreign invasions had destroyed or consumed agricultural, industrial, and residential property valued at 1,400 million francs.[24] The occupation army of 800,000 was supported chiefly by forced requisitions and cost the French government 1.75 million francs per day. By the terms of the Second Treaty of Paris, signed on November 20, 1815, France agreed to pay an indemnity of 700 million francs and the expenses associated with foreign occupation for five years. The frontier departments in the north and east were to be occupied by 150,000 troops for at least three but not more than five years; the estimated occupation costs of 150 million francs were to be added to the indemnity. The restored Bourbon government also promised to settle all debts incurred by preceding French governments, including those contracted in Allied countries during the imperial period.[25] The total expenses of the second invasion, the occupation, and the indemnity ultimately amounted to 1,290 million francs, or to 1,833 million if the foreign civilian debts are included.[26] Even apportioned over three years, sums of this magnitude obviously influenced the postwar trade cycle; but the economic effect would not approach impoverishment in a wealthy and populous country like France.

Nonetheless, the French government was confronted by a fiscal crisis in 1816. It proved impossible to secure approval of the ministerial budget by the legislative assembly, the ultra-royalist *Chambre introuvable*. The administration had planned to sell 400,000 hectares of national forest land in order to balance income and expenditures. But the fact that most of the forests had belonged to the church and the intention to apply the proceeds to the debts contracted by the Empire was too much for the royalist assembly to accept. The king dismissed the assembly on September 5, 1816, with the agreement of the Allied control commission in Paris.[27] It was necessary to secure 380 million francs to balance the budget; receipts had fallen 153 million francs below anticipations, while expenses had exceeded expectations by 248 million francs.[28] Since no apparent funds were available to meet the indemnity installment falling due in November, a loan proved the only realistic solution. Also, since public credit had fallen so low, a foreign rather than a domestic loan was agreed upon.[29] By September, moreover, the impending subsistence crisis had become undeniable, and meeting the budget deficit by levying increased taxes became unthinkable; now, government expenditures would be forced upward to meet the higher occupation costs.

Not all regions of Europe had experienced deficient harvest yields in 1815, and this fact again created different postwar economic conditions. British agriculture was in fact seriously depressed by low grain prices at the beginning of 1816. Five million acres had been added to British wheat-producing capacity by 1815, encouraged by high wartime prices and the absence of foreign competition. Ample yields in 1813 and 1814 and the return of competing grain supplies from Baltic ports forced wheat prices below 65 shillings per quarter (they averaged 125 shillings in 1815) early in 1816, the lowest average since 1804. Agricultural distress led to the new Corn Law of 1815 to alleviate the rural depression.[30] In addition to the one-third of the English population still working at agricultural pursuits, the tradesmen, innkeepers, and shopkeepers of country towns also suffered from the agrarian depression, and blacksmiths, wheelwrights, collar-makers, harness-makers, and carpenters found no work.[31]

East-Elbian Prussia was similarly burdened with grain surpluses at the beginning of 1816. Although the decline of linen exports contributed to commercial stagnation in the eastern provinces, cereal culture made up the principal economic activity of the region and trade interests centered on the export of grain.[32] All of Prussia of course remained an agrarian economy, but urban textile and metals industries flourished in Berlin and the large Rhenish towns of Coblenz, Cologne, Aachen, Elberfeld, Barmen, Düsseldorf, Krefeld, and Trier.[33] The sale of Prussian cereals depended heavily on markets in the more industrialized states, particularly in Britain and the Netherlands. Large production units were still the rule in an agricultural system that was both manorial and capitalistic, and therefore economic prosperity in eastern Prussia was contingent on high grain prices and a brisk demand from western Europe.[34] Trade with Britain had been interrupted during the Continental System, but with the return of peace the eastern landowners and the Prussian state hoped to recover some of the wartime losses by the export of cereals. This expectation was not realized, however, owing to the tariff protection granted to British wheat producers by the Corn Law of 1815. In fact, Prussian grain exports to

Britain fell from 186,200 quarters in 1814 to 19,400 quarters in 1815. The deficient European grain yields reversed this trend during 1816, however, and Prussian exports to Britain rose to 94,800 quarters.[35] The harvest failures of 1816 were to convert stagnation into prosperity not only in East-Elbian Prussia but throughout the eastern European grain lands and in the agrarian economy of the United States as well. At the same time, the harvest failures of 1816 produced dearth and famine throughout the balance of the Western economy.

THE SUBSISTENCE CRISIS

The harvest failures of 1816 came at an inopportune time, superimposing a subsistence crisis not only on a stagnating economy but also on a Western society still unsettled as a residue of the war years. A measure of industrial unemployment and the appearance in the labor market of several million men released from the armed forces had already created subsistence problems for numerous working-class families. The shortfall of cereal production, however, drove bread prices beyond the reach even of the majority who were employed at customary wage levels. While fluctuations in per capita food supplies are the ideal measure of changes in subsistence conditions, reliable figures for preindustrial agricultural output are not available. Cereal prices, therefore, must be used as an approximate index of harvest outcomes.

Table 7 presents indexes of wholesale grain prices computed for the years 1815–20; these values are based on either national, regional, or market averages derived from fifteen locations in the Western world, and they represent prices of the principal domestic breadstuff, wheat or rye. The numbers indicate that wholesale cereal prices virtually doubled between 1815 and 1817 and then declined to one-third of the peak and to three-fourths of the 1815 average by the end of the decade. Differential harvest yields and transportation costs from the main centers of grain export were responsible for the postwar price curve. Grain prices were still a regional rather than a national phenomenon, and national averages in locations like France conceal even more extreme fluctuation in areas large enough to be of economic significance. Some synchronization of price trends had begun to appear with improving commercial and monetary communications, but the massive flows of grain from North America and southern Russia still lay in the future. Nonetheless, sufficient information and ocean transportation had become available to arbitrage grain prices in the outports of the North and Baltic Seas, a fact which is noticeable in Table 7 from the less fluctuating indexes for Britain, Prussia, Hamburg, and Mecklenburg. At the other extreme, Switzerland, Bavaria, Württemberg, and Baden remained exposed to the vicissitudes of the weather—which was likewise true for eastern France and

Table 7. Indexes of Wholesale Grain[a] Prices Western World, 1815–20 (1815=100)

Location	1815	1816	1817	1818	1819	1820
United States[b]	100	124	154	127	86	59
Britain	100	117	146	131	114	102
France	100	145	185	126	94	98
Holland (Utrecht)	100	133	221	156	111	90
Belgium (Antwerp)	100	138	200	155	105	91
Switzerland	100	162	235	121	81	75
Austria (Vienna)	100	188	183	52	30	40
Prussia (Berlin + Danzig)	100	108	160	141	97	79
Bavaria (Munich)	100	190	301	131	n.a.	46
Württemberg	100	169	239	108	62	44
Baden	100	171	268	119	84	81
Saxony (Leipzig)	100	157	198	138	87	n.a.
Hamburg	100	111	167	139	94	78
Mecklenburg (Rostock)	100	96	186	170	136	83
Poland (Cracow)	100	98	124	66	44	47
Unweighted averages	100	140	198	125	88	72

[a]The index numbers represent wheat prices for the United States, Britain, France, Holland, Belgium, Switzerland, Prussia, Baden, Hamburg, and Mecklenburg-Schwerin; rye prices for Austria, Bavaria, Württemberg, Saxony, and Poland.

[b]Unless a particular market is stated, such as Utrecht, the index numbers are computed from national averages, with the exception of Switzerland where the indexes are based on the combined averages of the markets at Zürich, Lucerne, Bern, and Lausanne.

Sources: United States, Bureau of the Census, Historical Statistics of the United States: Colonial Times to 1957 (Washington, D.C.: Government Printing Office, 1960), p. 124; Thomas Tooke, Thoughts and Details on the High and Low Prices of the Last Thirty Years (London: John Murray, 1823), part III, p. 177; France, Statistique générale, Archives statistiques du ministère des travaux publics, de l'agriculture et du commerce (Paris: Imprimerie royale, 1837), pp. 8–13; Nicholaas W. Posthumus, Inquiry into the History of Prices in Holland (2 vols., Leiden: E. J. Brill, 1946–64), 2: 422; Robert Demoulin, Guillaume Ier et la transformation économique des provinces belges 1815–1830 (Liège: Faculté de Philosophe et Lettres, 1938), p. 401; Hans Brugger, Die schweizerische Landwirtschaft in der ersten Hälfte des 19, Jahrhunderts (Frauenfeld: Huber & Co., 1956), p. 110; Alfred Francis Pribram, Materialen zur Geschichte der Preise und Löhne in Österreich (Vienna: Carl Ueberreuters Verlag, 1938), p. 393; Wilhelm Abel, Agrarkrisen und Agrarkonjunktur (2d ed., Hamburg and Berlin: Paul Parey, 1966), p. 290; Moritz J. Elsas, Umriss einer Geschichte der Preise und Löhne in Deutschland vom ausgehenden Mittelalter bis zum Beginn des 19, Jahrhunderts (2 vols., Leiden: A. W. Sijthoff, 1936–49), 2, B: 127; Mack Walker, Germany and the Emigration 1816–1885 (Cambridge: Harvard University Press, 1964), p. 249; A. J. V. Heunisch, Das Grossherzogtum Baden (Heidelberg: Julius Groos, 1857), p. 454; William Jacob, Report of the Trade in Foreign Corn and on the Agriculture of the North of Europe (3d ed., London: James Ridgway, 1826), pp. 180–89, 242–43.

highland districts of the Habsburg empire. A situation of lower peaks is evident in states like Poland and the United States, which normally produced grain surpluses for export.

For a more focused view of the subsistence crisis, index numbers have also been computed for monthly grain prices during 1817, the year in which price levels peaked. These indexes are displayed in Table 8 and illustrate the drastic effect of high cereal prices on the cost of living of the "harvest-sensitive"

Table 8. Indexes of Monthly Wholesale Grain^a Prices Western World, 1817 (1815=100)

Location	Jan	Feb	Mar	Apr	May	Jun	Jul	Aug	Sep	Oct	Nov	Dec
United States[b]	192	192	192	186	199	147	147	147	109	108	108	122
Britain	162	158	159	161	164	175	159	134	122	120	125	131
France	179	187	190	203	230	233	185	165	159	162	162	166
Holland (Utrecht)	210	226	221	214	240	251	243	228	220	214	204	195
Switzerland (St. Gall)	243	211	242	358	437	448	435	333	190	210	204	196
Austria (Vienna)	255	242	219	232	240	244	163	134	130	125	113	101
Prussia (Düsseldorf)	131	132	134	134	163	195	128	101	101	101	102	n.a.
Bavaria (Munich)	295	284	253	299	342	371	301	327	214	322	332	267
Saxony (Leipzig)	233	232	204	189	202	233	188	177	172	187	184	182
Hamburg	185	180	167	163	163	196	178	178	156	141	148	141
Poland (Cracow)	146	150	143	125	122	146	154	118	104	86	90	90
Unweighted Averages	186	183	177	189	209	222	190	170	139	148	148	145

^aThe idnex numbers represent wheat prices for the United States, Britain, France, Holland, and Hamburg; rye for Switzerland, Austria, Prussia, Bavaria, Saxony, and Poland.

^bUnless a particular market is stated, such as Utrecht, the index numbers are computed from national averages.

Sources: Arthur H. Cole. *Wholesale Commodity Prices in the United States, 1700–1861* (Cambridge: Harvard University Press, 1938), supplement, pp. 171, 174, 178, 182, 186, 191; Thomas Tooke and William Newmarch, *A History of Prices and of the State of Circulation from 1792 to 1856* (6 vols., New York: Adelphi, 1857), 2:390; France, Statistique générale, *Archives statistiques du ministère des travaux publics, de l'agriculture et du commerce* (Paris: Imprimerie royale, 1837), pp. 20–21; Nicholaas W. Posthumus, *Inquiry into the History of Prices in Holland* (2 vols., Leiden: E. J. Brill, 1946–64), 2: 422; Ruprecht Zollikofer, *Der Osten meinen Vaterlandes, oder die Kantone St. Gallen und Appenzell im Hungerjahre 1817* (2 vols., St. Gall: Zollikofer and Züblin, 1818–19), 1: 282; Alfred Francis Pribram, *Materialen zur Geschichte der Preise und Löhne in Österreich* (Vienna: Carl Ueberreuters Verlag, 1938), p. 393; Wilhelm Sandkaulen, *Das Notjahr 1816/17 mit besonderer Berücksichtigung der Verhältnisse am Niederrhein* (Munster: n.p., 1927), pp. 12–13; Moritz J. Elsas, *Umriss einer Geschichte der Preise und Löhne in Deutschland vom ausgehenden Mittelalter bis zum Beginn des 19. Jahrhunderts* (2 vols., Leiden: A. W. Sijthoff, 1936–49), 1: 677; 2, B: 127; William Jacob. *Report of the Trade in Foreign Corn and on the Agriculture of the North of Europe* (3d ed., London: James Ridgway, 1826), pp. 180–89, 242–43.

fraction of the population. National monthly averages, moreover, conceal higher regional prices. For example, wheat prices in France reached their highest average in June 1817 at 45.46 francs per hectoliter. In the northeastern departments, however, wheat prices averaged 64.29 francs in this month, and in the Alsatian department of Haut-Rhin alone, this figure averaged 81.69 francs. Even within Alsace, wheat sold for 108 francs the hectoliter at Strasbourg on June 17, 1817, and wheat prices climbed higher still in the markets of Colmar and Belfort.[36]

Cereal prices represent the best index of subsistence levels because bread continued to occupy first place by far in popular budgets, claiming at least half of a laboring family's income, even when normal grain prices prevailed. It has been estimated that two-thirds of an English laboring family's budget was spent on food and drink.[37] The real income of all strata of the European working population must have declined markedly in light of the rise in cereal prices during 1816–17. Some rough but systematic indication of the increase in the cost of living can be gained from the index numbers reproduced in Table 9. Even though the components used to construct the indexes vary, and although the values are approximate, the numbers still convey the impact of the dearth on popular budgets and real income. It is not in dispute, moreover, that the majority of the European population was made up of wage-earners and agricultural laborers compelled in whole or in part to procure bread, flour, or cereals at market prices.

Sir William Beveridge's index of wheat prices in western and central Europe corroborates the severity of the harvest deficiencies in 1816. Beveridge utilized price lists derived from forty-eight market locations, but the index omits Switzerland and the less-developed provinces of the Habsburg

Table 9. Indexes of Urban Cost of Living, 1815–20

Year	France (1820=100)	Antwerp, Belgium (1815=100)	Bath, England (1838=100)	Germany (1820=100)
1815	142	100	116	120
1816	142	119	129	134
1817	164	149	157	172
1818	137	127	132	144
1819	112	114	120	119
1820	100	98	119	100

Sources: Alexandre Chabert, *Essai sur les mouvements des revenus et de l'activité économique en France de 1789 à 1820* (Paris, 1949), pp. 234, 264; Robert Demoulin, *Guillaume I ᵉʳ et la transformation économique des provinces belges, 1815–1830* (Liège, 1938), p. 408; R. S. Neal, "The Standard of Living, 1770–1844: a Regional and Class Study," *Economic History Review*, 2d ser., 19 (December 1966): 606; Jürgen Kuczynski, *Germany, 1800 to the Present Day*, vol. 3, part 1, *A Short History of Labour Conditions under Industrial Capitalism* (4 vols.; London, 1942–46), p. 63.

Monarchy, where genuine famine conditions appeared. In addition, Beveridge included only eight markets in southern Germany, Alsace, Bohemia, and Austria—locations where domestic cereal prices advanced more steeply than in northwestern Europe. Nonetheless, the index number of 381 for the agricultural year 1816 is by far the largest value in the entire series, which includes the period from 1500 to 1869.[38] The wartime year 1811 yielded the second highest value, 302. Prices are converted into index numbers on a base of 100 for the mean 1700–45. To take account of the secular upward price movement, and to eliminate the trend so far as possible, Beveridge also computed an "index of fluctuation," which shows the number for each year "as a percentage of the mean for the period of 31 years of which it is the centre." Once again the largest value in the entire series, 178, is found in the year 1816. A comparison of both indexes for the famine periods centering on the agricultural years 1709, 1740, and 1816 indicate that subsistence conditions became most acute during the last of these three great European dearths (the index of fluctuation is found within the parentheses):

YEAR	INDEX	YEAR	INDEX	YEAR	INDEX
1708	134(125)	1739	125(122)	1815	280(130)
1709	183(175)	1740	162(159)	1816	381(178)
1710	113(108)	1741	113(110)	1817	266(126)
1711	108(103)	1742	94(90)	1818	197(94)
1712	121(115)	1743	85(81)	1819	177(86)

The last regional European dearth, which occurred during the agricultural years 1845–46, saw the wheat price index rise only to 278, and the index of fluctuation to 139 in 1846, far lower than the values reached in 1816, 1709, and 1740.

Contemporary sources, whether systematic or impressionistic, remove any doubt that per capita food supplies dropped markedly during 1816–17. While it is true that inelasticity of demand drove grain prices to disproportionately high levels in comparison to the volume deficits, nonetheless, cereal yields departed significantly from normal averages, some regions experiencing more calamitious shortfalls than others. English wheat yields in 1816 were the lowest recorded from 1815 to 1857. The mean yield fell to 25.3 bushels per acre in 1816, contrasted to a yield of 37.0 bushels in 1815. Wheat yields then recovered to 33.4 and 32.6 bushels in 1817 and 1818, respectively.[39] The evidence indicates, in fact, that the low yield recorded in 1816 represents an overestimation. A parliamentary committee investigating the state of agriculture in 1821 heard testimony from a Liverpool firm dealing in the international grain trade that the harvest failures were more severe than originally believed. As a matter of strategy the firm conducted an annual 1,000-mile survey of the wheat crop on the eve of the harvest in order to determine the average yield and to predict both the price and the import needs of the following year. The witness, a partner in the firm, stated that they had seriously overestimated the yield in 1816 by disregarding the flour content of the wheat. "We were so thoroughly satisfied of the deficiency, that we were rather inattentive, and did not weigh nearly the same number; we had gained our point in respect of information and did not pursue it further; but it was very much worse than the survey; it was nearly rotten."[40] The survey had produced the yield of 25.3 bushels quoted above. Thomas Tooke's observations suggest a similar conclusion: "a lamentable deficiency in quantity, and a miserable inferiority of quality." Tooke added that "nearly all that had been saved of the crop was in so damp a condition, as to be unfit for immediate use."[41] The large surplus of wheat from previous seasons, unlike the supply situation prevailing in central Europe, prevented cereal prices from rising to famine levels in England during 1816.

In France the deficient flour content of the wheat crop in 1816 was noticed almost immediately. A circular from the Ministry of Interior to the prefects, dated February 17, 1817, disclosed the extent of the qualitative deficiency. Whereas the best wheat in both 1815 and 1816 weighed 75 kilograms per hectoliter, the weight of even slightly damaged wheat in 1816 scarcely reached 61, and the weight fell to 56 kilograms if deterioration was advanced.[42] At the more impressionistic level, a Briard peasant noticed that "You could not eat the bread. It stuck to the knife."[43] Estimates of deficient grain yields which boasted varying degrees of precision, appeared in almost every region of the Continent. In Württemberg it was reported that the wheat yield of 1816 amounted to 85 percent of the volume of 1815, and only to 75 percent of the yield in 1812, which had been the last satisfactory harvest. But inasmuch as the wheat proved deficient in flour, even this reduced output was deemed illusory. Considering both quantity and quality, the effective wheat yield was estimated at one-half of a normal year.[44] Both the west-central and east-central regions of Europe witnessed similar harvest outcomes. A *Scheffel* of rye harvested in Bavaria weighed only 240 to 250 pounds, instead of the more normal 290 pounds;[45] grain yields in the Budweiser district of Bohemia reportedly amounted to one-half the normal number of sheaves in the lowlands and only to one-quarter in the highlands.[46] If the estimates can be trusted, the rye crop in Galicia turned out in 1816 only one-third the volume of the previous year, while the wheat-yield equaled one-half.[47] The wheat crop yielded an average volume in the plains of Lombardy–Venetia; but all grains were virtually ruined in the highlands, and the combined harvests corresponded to about one-half a normal yield.[48] Assuming that impressionistic observations probably exaggerated the volume deficiencies, it is still clear that European grain shortages were acute and widespread.

Even though yield deficiencies of the several bread grains varied, the price of wheat, rye, barley, and oats advanced by similar magnitudes. Because all cereal yields fell, and because the four grains were substitutes for one another, short-term price movements tended to duplicate one another and therefore to limit the ability to shift demand from higher- to lower-priced grains. The demand for wheat, rye, barley, and oats was expressed primarily by the need for bread and fodder, and these were needs for which no real alternatives existed. While it is true that potatoes were becoming a supplement to the grain supply in some European locations, the importance of this plant as a major field crop still lay in the future. The price movements and the price relationships that prevailed to a like degree throughout the Western economy can be seen in Table 10, which shows the course of wholesale grain prices for the years 1814–20 at the Rotterdam and Antwerp markets in the Netherlands.[49] The apparent inability to shift demand significantly from cereals to meat and dairy products can be seen in Table 11, which displays indexes of Swiss agricultural commodity prices during the same years. Despite the severe famine in Switzerland, a land that had developed a major cattle-raising industry, the prices of milk, cheese, and butter rose only slightly during the subsistence crisis, while beef prices advanced 25 percent. Grain prices by contrast almost tripled, while potato

Table 10. Wholesale Grain Prices the Kingdom of the Netherlands, 1814–20 (in florins and cents)

A. Prices at the Rotterdam market per *Last*.[a]

Year	Flour	Wheat	Rye	Barley	Oats	Potatoes[b]
1814	—	216	144	92	86	—
1815	—	208	143	91	84	—
1816	—	288	195	135	91	—
1817	—	459	250	185	129	—
1818	—	312	193	159	124	—
1819	—	214	156	127	98	—
1820	—	193	121	85	74	—

B. Prices at the Antwerp market per hectoliter.

Year	Flour	Wheat	Rye	Barley	Oats	Potatoes
1814	—	—	—	—	—	—
1815	10.48	8.98	6.09	4.53	2.82	1.95
1816	20.37	12.42	9.14	6.32	3.60	3.07
1817	24.96	17.99	11.30	8.38	5.30	4.48
1818	14.60	13.95	8.59	7.73	5.12	2.40
1819	10.33	9.46	6.85	6.63	4.53	1.77
1820	9.11	8.22	4.78	4.21	3.25	1.64

[a]A large grain measure used in sea-borne shipping which varied in volume from port to port; generally, but not in all ports, a Dutch *Last* at this time measured slightly more than 3,000 liters.

[b]Price per *Rasière*.

Sources: Kamer van Koophandel en Fabrieken Rotterdam (Rotterdam, 1928), p. 140; Robert Demoulin, *Guillaume 1er et la transformation économique des provinces belges, 1815–1830* (Liège, 1938), p. 401.

Table 11. Indexes of Agricultural Products Prices Switzerland, 1814–20 (1850=100)

Year	Grain	Potatoes	Wine	Beef	Milk	Butter	Cheese
1814	129	70	212	110	91	103	106
1815	131	52	282	110	91	101	102
1816	212	121	279	114	91	103	106
1817	307	172	328	138	100	113	113
1818	158	60	311	124	100	107	106
1819	106	61	194	107	91	93	84
1820	98	63	147	93	91	87	75

Source: Hans Brugger, *Die schweizerische Landwirtschaft in der ersten Hälfte des 19. Jahrhunderts* (Frauenfeld, 1956), p. 126.

prices more than tripled. These price relationships were not merely a local or even a European phenomenon; wholesale grain and beef prices at the Philadelphia market, in fact, followed an inverse relationship during 1816—17.[50] Meat prices might have been dampened in part by the increased number of animals slaughtered as a result of the fodder shortage, and also by the persistence of traditional cereal consumption patterns. More likely, however, a major shift in demand in Europe was foreclosed by the fact that meat prices remained higher than grain prices on a per calorie basis despite the disproportionate changes in price levels.[51]

Under these circumstances, the single best index of the severity of a European subsistence crisis in the early decades of the nineteenth century is the movement of bread prices. Bread prices followed the course of wholesale grain prices, as might be expected; but some significant variations appeared. As a general European pattern, bread prices failed to rise as steeply in cities and coastal districts as in rural towns and interior districts. Bread prices in France, similar to cereal prices, approximately doubled between 1814 and 1817, and then declined to 1814 levels in 1819–20. The course of bread prices in Paris proved a noticeable exception to this pattern, since political wisdom dictated keeping these prices as low as possible. The two patterns can be seen by comparing average bread prices at Paris and at Strasbourg (prices are expressed in fractions of a franc for a four-pound loaf):[52]

YEAR	PARIS	STRASBOURG
1814	0.312	0.38
1815	0.298	0.40
1816	0.410	0.64
1817	0.482	0.85
1818	0.390	0.52
1819	0.306	0.42
1820	0.363	0.36

The price of bread rose more sharply during the dearth than these annual figures indicate, however. At Paris, for example, despite an average price of 0.48 francs during 1817, the four-pound loaf actually sold for one franc on 234 days of that year.[53] On balance, the price of bread in France increased two to three times between the spring of 1816 and the summer of 1817. In an isolated department like Meurthe in Lorraine, bread prices increased 3.6 times between July 1816 and June 1817; at Lyons, by contrast, bread prices advanced only from 0.18 francs per pound in 1815 to 0.35 francs in spring 1817, but climbed much higher in the surrounding countryside.[54] The consumer was, of course, compelled to make purchases weekly or possibly daily and thus had to pay the prices demanded, which reached famine levels in the northeastern region of France, where the price of wheat exceeded 100 francs per hectoliter in June 1817.[55]

Assessing the extent of the subsistence crisis in France as a whole, it is best described as a severe dearth not a famine, and the same generalization is valid for the Netherlands. The price of grain, flour, and bread in spring 1817 reached levels two to three times higher than those prevailing in 1815. Index numbers based chiefly on the prices of cereals, bread, and meat in Antwerp indicate that these commodities rose from 100.0 in 1815 to a peak of 178.7 in the month of May 1817.[56] Even though food prices advanced in 1817 to levels never before experienced in the Netherlands,[57] true famine conditions remained absent. A similar conclusion can be applied to the subsistence crisis in England. The price of bread began to climb during the second quarter of 1816, reached maximum levels in the second quarter of 1817, and then exhibited a more or less uninterrupted decline. Prices paid by the Charterhouse (London) advanced from 2.58 s. in the first quarter of 1816 to 4.58 s. in the second quarter of 1817, or some 80 percent.[58] At the retail level, bakers raised the price of the quartern loaf of best bread from 11 pence in May 1816 to a top price of 20 pence in June 1817.[59]

The subsistence crisis tended toward a deeper level of distress in the German lands, especially in the rural and southwestern locations, where food prices climbed higher than in urban and northern locations. When Carl von Clausewitz toured the Prussian Rhineland in the spring of 1817, he concluded that as a result of "a complete harvest failure in all of southern and western Germany," the Rhineland faced "a true famine." Even though he qualified the statement with the observation, "so far as this is still possible in the state of civilization in which we find ourselves," his description of the social scene is bleak enough: "The author, who traveled on horseback through the Eifel region in spring 1817, where he passed the night in villages and little towns, often had a heartrending view of this misery, because these areas belong to the poorest classes in the land. He saw ruined figures, scarcely resembling men, prowling around the fields searching for food among the unharvested and already half rotten potatoes that never grew to maturity."[60] Yet, measured by cereal and grain prices, the subsistence crisis was worse still in Württemberg and Baden. The six-pound rye loaf in Württemberg quadrupled in price from a customary figure of 3 to 4 kreutzer per pound to highs of 12 to 17 in late spring 1817, depending on the location. Prices fell abruptly after the 1817 harvests, as elsewhere, and in spring 1818 the rye loaf declined to a more normal price of 20 kreutzer.[61] Cereal and bread prices in Baden likewise rose nearly fourfold; the price of rye in 1817 reached the highest recorded figure in the history of Baden between the years 1484 and 1849.[62] The subsistence crisis was almost as severe in Bavaria, where cereal prices also advanced fourfold between January 1815 and June 1817.[63]

No other German state experienced famine conditions, even though some rural districts like the Eifel in the Rhineland and the Odenwald in Hesse-Darmstadt suffered badly.[64] Although wheat and rye prices doubled in the Prussian Rhenish towns, and the price of bread more than doubled in Cologne and more than tripled in Barmen, the institution of municipal bread subsidies minimized distress.[65] Subsistence problems became serious but less severe still in the northern cities of Hamburg, Rostock, Danzig, Bremen, and Göttingen, where cereal prices tended to increase less than 100 percent in the dearth period.[66] But in the rural districts, as elsewhere in Europe, the price of cereals climbed higher and the level of distress plunged deeper.[67] Leipzig, Berlin, and Breslau also experienced moderate increases in the price of cereals, and in these cities the subsistence crisis did not progress beyond a moderate dearth.[68]

The Habsburg Monarchy, owing to its vast expanse, witnessed varying degrees of distress; but unlike northwestern Europe, famine conditions became widespread and no province escaped lightly. Although the index numbers found in Tables 7 and 8 indicate that average grain prices in Austria increased 2.5 times between 1815 and 1817, these indexes tend to understate the movement of cereal and bread prices. A combination of deficient harvests and currency inflation had already doubled grain prices from 1814 to 1815; and, in fact, wholesale wheat and rye prices increased fivefold in the Vienna market between January 1814 and January 1817.[69] This price rise was in part a function of the depreciation of the currency, which lost approximately half its value between these two dates, with the exchange rate rising from 185 to 378 paper florins per 100 specie florins, and thus responsible for about 40 percent of the price increases.[70]

It is necessary to glance at the postwar monetary history in order to assess the severity of the crisis in the Habsburg empire. To begin with, the finance minister's patent of February 20, 1811, had depreciated the paper currency in circulation to one-fifth of its nominal value. The government then issued new paper currency and proclaimed these notes to be equal in value to silver equivalents and thus legal tender. The government promised not to issue notes beyond the new circulation of 212 million florins (the figure at which the old currency had last been quoted at par), in order to maintain the value of the new paper currency. Additional notes were issued starting in 1812, however, and the value of the paper currency fell to less than one-third of its silver equivalent by 1816. A complex exchange mechanism was then enacted on June 1, 1816, to stabilize the value of the currency; in brief, holders of paper currency interested in redemption could exchange 140 florins for 100 florins in bonds and 40 florins in banknotes, the latter redeemable in silver. A sinking fund was created to redeem the banknotes and a national bank was authorized to facilitate the fiscal operations of the state. The discount quoted for paper currency fell slightly below 300 during the summer of 1816, but rose to a peak of 383 in March 1817, and then the currency gradually appreciated in value until 1819 when the exchange rate was stabilized at 250.[71]

After price movements are adjusted for currency depreciation, the advance of cereal prices in Austria approximated the increases encountered in southwestern Germany and northeastern France, with the notable exception that sharper price increases occurred earlier in the Habsburg domains. Dearth prices had in fact already appeared in 1815. The price of rye bread in Vienna more than doubled from 4.20 kreutzer per pound in July 1814 to 10.38 kreutzer in July 1815. The highest price was reached in both January and July 1817, when rye bread sold for 23.27 kreutzer per pound; after that the price declined steeply to 3.62 kreutzer at the end of 1817. White breads exhibited similar price fluctuations, as did flour, both wheat and rye.[72] The prices of all cereal grains moved in virtually the same patterns in Bohemia, Moravia, and Hungary. Wheat prices in the spring of 1817 advanced to 2,052 kreutzer per *Metzen* in Vienna, 1,853 kreutzer in Prague, 1,680 kreutzer in Brüun, and 1,840 kreutzer in Hungarian markets.[73] Barley prices in Vienna paralleled those of wheat, advancing fivefold from 1814 to 1817; while oats exhibited a less pronounced threefold increase.[74]

The subsistence crisis in the Habsburg domain reached its most forbidding level in Transylvania and the eastern counties of Hungary. Reportedly, some 18,000 persons starved to death in the county of Arad, and 26,000 died from famine in Szatmar, Krasso Bihar, and Bereg.[75] The Balkan provinces, Styria, Carinthia, Carniola, and the Tyrol experienced both food shortages and high cereal prices, but apparently escaped elevated death rates from widespread famine.[76]

Habsburg Italy, by contrast, witnessed smaller increases in the price of cereals (primarily because the debased Austrian paper currency was not made legal tender),[77] but higher famine mortality. A portion of the highland population in Lombardy was compelled to subsist largely on roots and herbs. Virtually everywhere on the Italian peninsula the subsistence crisis approached famine conditions.[78] A true famine with deaths from starvation prevailed in the cantons of eastern Switzerland, while dearth prices were the rule in the remaining Swiss lands. Not only were prices in Switzerland during

1817 the highest recorded in the first half of the nineteenth century, even the lower 1816 averages exceeded the prices reached in the crisis year of 1847.[79] The price of bread in the cantons of St. Gall and Appenzell rose from a level of six kreutzer per pound in 1814–15 to 28 kreutzer in June 1817.[80] On balance, Swiss grain and bread prices increased four to five times, measured from lows to highs during the postwar years.[81] Only in Ireland was the subsistence crisis to produce more appalling results. Because of the large yield deficiencies, the Irish peasants' harvest was substantially consumed by the end of 1816. Small-holders were forced to abandon their homes in the spring of 1817 in order to subsist by begging. The shortage of food became so pressing that seed potatoes, nettles, and wild vegetables were sought after to satisfy hunger.[82]

The postwar subsistence crisis was so extensive that not even the agrarian American economy escaped traces of dearth and famine. American cereal prices followed the same movement as those in northern Europe, and for the same reasons: prices reflected both deficient domestic grain yields and the increased European demand. Average wheat prices at the Philadelphia market rose from $1.50 per bushel in April 1816 to a peak of $3.11 in May 1817. The price of Indian corn, a better indicator of domestic subsistence conditions, increased from $0.85 per bushel in April 1816 to a maximum price of $1.73 in May 1817.[83] Comparable to the experience in European markets, cereal prices advanced sharply in the summer of 1816, reached their highest figures in the spring of 1817, and fell off steeply in the autumn of 1817. Since transatlantic communications were still slow and uncertain, the rise in grain prices during the early summer months of 1816 was more a response to American weather conditions than to the impending European harvest deficiencies. Corn, unlike wheat and flour, represented neither an important American export commodity nor a significant European import. In fact, corn yields proved so deficient in some parts of the eastern United States that not enough grain matured to meet seed requirements.[84]

As a consequence, dearth conditions appeared in the United States as in Europe during the years 1816–17. The distress was concentrated mainly in the northeastern region, especially in New England, but also in scattered districts of the Atlantic states. The poor in the hardest-hit areas resorted to make-shift diets reminiscent of famine districts in Europe. The interior towns and settlements of northern New England experienced the worst food shortages. The scarcity of cereals in the Maine districts of Massachusetts produced "fears of a famine before the close of another winter."[85] In the interior of New Hampshire, "the cattle died for want of fodder, and many of the inhabitants came near perishing from starvation" in the spring of 1817.[86] In Vermont, "the scarcity and high provisions occasioned extreme privation and suffering."[87] Most of the corn consumed in Vermont during the crop year 1816–17 had to be imported from outside the state; some families even subsisted on hedgehogs, boiled nettles, and clover heads.[88] State legislatures in New Jersey, Delaware, and Maryland proposed a national embargo on the export of flour and grain, a proposal that gained wide currency by the end of 1816.[89] A subsistence crisis also materialized in some districts of Virginia and North Carolina during the spring of 1817.[90] An influx of new settlers and the poor corn harvests of 1816 combined to produce serious food shortages in the territory of Alabama early in 1817. The majority of the new settlers were forced to abandon their improvements and to return to older settlements to avoid starvation.[91]

If Indian corn proved in most short supply in the winter of 1816–17, the Indian population was of course confronted with the most serious subsistence crisis. Timely public assistance prevented famine in some locations, particularly in Alabama, where the federal government preserved the local Indians from starvation.[92] The remnants of the Indian tribes located in Maine, 500 to 600 persons mostly women and children in 1816, survived the winter of 1816–17 because the Massachusetts General Court voted to furnish them with 300 bushels of corn.[93] The more numerous Indian population of New York, collectively called the Six Nations, suffered severely during the winter as a result of the nearly total failure of the corn crop. Reportedly, a tribe that usually raised more than 7,000 bushels of Indian corn harvested only 50 bushels in 1816. Even though the several tribes received annuities from New York or the federal government, the sums amounted to no more than $3 per man and thus were inadequate for subsistence. Apparently, the charity dispensed by a few missionaries and other private groups successfully carried them through the famine period.[94] The most destitute inhabitants of virtually every region of the Western world required some degree of welfare assistance to survive the postwar subsistence crisis.

One of the reasons was that incomes and wage-levels did not follow prices, unlike the general rule prevailing in the Western world in the second half of the twentieth century. Even though comprehensive income series are lacking, the evidence clearly indicates that the income levels of the majority of the population were insufficient to meet the increased outlays required for subsistence. At the same time, early nineteenth-century wage data still present unresolved problems; it is difficult to reconcile famine food prices with weekly wage rates. Weekly wage rates were not, of course, the same as actual family earnings, which is the more revealing figure, since the household was the basic economic unit and shared expenses for food, fuel, clothing, and rent. On the other hand, wage rates must be discounted for periods of unemployment. Here, however, the concern is with the sources of income or food that kept famine, disease, and malnutrition at the observed levels rather than at the higher levels which the disproportion between wage rates and subsistence costs would have induced. Sources of income or food that existed then probably have since become concealed. Vegetable gardens and poultry could have been universally available to the working population. That wages were paid in food products to a greater extent than commonly recognized is a probability. Agricultural day laborers invariably received extra wages for occasional piecework; and almost all laborers received added compensation in the form of rent-free cottages, food, drink, coal, and small items.[95] Annual earnings were not necessarily the weekly wage multiplied by fifty-two; unemployment and overtime, the income of wives and children, and compensation in kind are not reflected in wage series. Nevertheless, the way in which laboring persons bridged the gap between income and outlay in times of dearth still awaits a systematic exploration.

Indeed, the evidence suggests a decline in money wages for the majority of industrial workers during the postwar years; while the residue that maintained wartime wage levels did not always maintain employment. The investigations of Arthur L. Bowley indicate a fall in wages for British agricultural laborers, as well as for the majority of workers in the building trades. Bowley's index of English agricultural wages (1891 = 100) declined from 103 in 1814 to 98 in 1818; the index for cotton factory workers declined only from 62 to 61 for the same period; whereas the index for all cotton textile workers declined from 92 in 1814 to 53 in 1818.[96] In money wages, English agricultural laborers secured from 12 s. to 15 s. a week in 1814.[97] But it is difficult to generalize about rural wages. For example, the offenders brought to trial in East Anglia in connection with the riots at Ely and Littleport earned from 4 s. to 20 s. weekly, the majority receiving between 6 s. and 15 s.; but some laborers were unemployed, while others were underemployed.[98] Cotton spinners in Manchester and other centers of cotton manufacture maintained a money wage of 32 s. per week for the entire postwar period 1814–20. Hand weavers, by contrast, saw weekly wages decline from 15 s. 7 d. in 1814 to 9 s. 6 d. in 1817. Carpenters and bricklayers seem to have maintained weekly wages at 25 s. and 22 s. 6 d. respectively.[99] It is clear that hand weavers, like agricultural laborers, experienced much more distress than spinners and artisans who remained in employment. Ironworkers as an occupational group probably suffered the greatest decline in manufacturing wages. Not only did the iron industry exhibit the usual sharp cyclical downturn; the cessation of hostilities and the decline in military orders further depressed the metals industry. Wage rates for ironworkers fell from 18–42 s. in 1810 to 10–18 s. in 1817.[100] Even so, inasmuch as the four-pound loaf of bread sold for a shilling or so and did not rise above 20 pence, widespread starvation did not become a serious threat in Britain, even for lower-paid workers, so long as employment continued.

On the Continent as in Ireland, however, where food supplies became scarcer and bread prices climbed higher, and where wage levels were lower and full-time employment became less available, a significant fraction of the work force was reduced to vagrancy or begging, and starvation became a pressing anxiety. While the available regional wage quotations varied by trade, location, sex, age, and skill and thus defy systematic presentation, the data nevertheless suggest wage levels far too low to absorb a two- or threefold increase in the price of bread. In France, for example, the average daily wage in the building trades amounted to 3.50 francs in Paris and ranged between 2.00 and 2.15 francs elsewhere. Male cotton spinners in Paris secured a daily wage that varied from 2.25 to 3.00 francs; female spinners earned between 0.60 and 1.30 francs; while children's wages ranged from 0.30 to 0.75 francs daily. Day wages for male workers in the various trades and crafts varied between 1.00 and 2.00 francs, female workers received between 0.60 and 1.50 francs, while children could scarcely hope to earn more than 0.80 francs. Some industrial wage levels were higher in the East, ranging from 1.90 francs for journeymen to a maximum of 3.00 francs. In the textile industries of the southeast, daily wages ranged from 1.50 to 3.00 francs, and some skilled workers were able to earn as much as 5.00 francs.[101] In light of contemporary estimates of a daily bread consumption of one pound per capita, even the smallest price increase of 0.15 francs per pound, recorded at Paris, multiplied by four or five family members will result in a budget increase of at least 0.60 francs daily; and bread prices in some eastern departments rose more than 0.25 francs per pound.[102] Measured against the prevailing wage rates, a variation of 0.10 francs in the price of bread was important in a family's living costs; increases several times this figure must have created severe hardship, while the enormous price increases experienced in the northeastern departments can only have proved calamitous.

Urban wage earners in western Germany faced a similar subsistence crisis. For example, the eight-pound rye loaf that sold for 15 Stüber (one-quarter of a reichstaler) in 1815 cost between 30 and 40 Stüber in Barmen during the dearth period. Male industrial workers earned from 2.0 to 3.5 taler weekly in 1815, while female workers received 1.5–2.0 taler and children 1.0–1.5 taler. Assuming that a family could subsist on one loaf of bread per day, only family income based on the higher wage rates quoted would have been sufficient when dearth prices prevailed. Moreover, wage levels declined and unemployment mounted in Barmen as bread prices advanced.[103] The reduction in wages flowed from the commercial depression. The Rhenish provinces, like the Belgian provinces, had been part of the French empire and incorporation within the imperial economy had stimulated the manufacturing sector; but now the closing of French markets and the end of military orders resulted in deep stagnation, especially in the metals industry.[104] Industrial wage rates in Baden also were insufficient to meet rising bread prices. The price of a loaf of bread rose from the customary 8 or 9 kreutzer to as high as 35 kreutzer. Although highly skilled weavers earned 60 kreutzer per work day, in one large industrial weaving enterprise the average wage amounted to 20 kreutzer.[105]

Cotton and wool textile workers in Austria seem to have been the only European artisans who secured wage increases during the subsistence crisis. Higher wages apparently became mandatory in light of the sevenfold increase in bread prices that ensued from the grain shortage and the currency inflation. Linen workers, nonetheless, experienced a decline in income; and flax spinners were the lowest paid as well as the most numerous industrial workers in the Monarchy.[106] Swiss industrial workers, however, were confronted with the most desperate subsistence problems. Bread prices approached and in some towns exceeded one-half franc per pound, while a skilled cotton spinner in 1817 earned a daily wage of one-tenth of a franc and a weaver netted two francs per week after expenses. Cotton-spinning-machine operators and silk workers were better paid, but the majority netted one franc per day. The weekly earnings of a hand-spinner in 1817, moreover, were less than the price of a pound of bread.[107] At the same time, income levels and employment declined not only for industrial workers and artisans but also for day-laborers.[108]

The majority of Europe's working population was, of course, made up of subsistence peasants and agricultural laborers, and the cereal deficiencies and ensuing dearth naturally produced mixed economic results in the agricultural districts. Large and middling grain producers on balance saw income rise, not only because of the extreme inelasticity of demand for cereals but from the ability to withhold produce from the market as prices were advancing. Agricultural day-laborers and small peasant proprietors suffered as much as urban workers. Opportunities for agricultural wage-work diminished; farmers attempted to offset low grain yields by curbing expenses to a minimum, either by dismissing servants or simply by not hiring day-laborers. The competition of small peasant proprietors searching for supplemental income reduced employment opportunities still further. Indeed, the majority of peasant proprietors in western Europe could not support their families from landholdings alone; it was necessary to find additional income either by earning wages as artisans or by competing with day-laborers. In France, moreover, the majority of the 3.8 million proprietors counted in 1815 lacked sufficient land to earn a livelihood; the majority of all French land cultivators were in fact tenants, share-croppers, or day-laborers and not proprietors. As a consequence, the rural population also found itself in a precarious subsistence position. The same loaf of bread that sold as low as 1.25 francs in Paris, Lyons, and Rouen because of public subsidies often cost rural inhabitants 3, 4, and even 5 francs.[109]

Rural wage earners everywhere in western Europe found themselves unable to cope with high cereal prices. Agricultural laborers in Ireland who were fortunate enough to find employment received four- to sixpence a day without food, while weavers scarcely earned more than three pence a day.[110] Swiss agricultural day-laborers received 0.55–0.60 francs with board, and 0.85–

1.30 without board.[111] With bread at one-half franc per pound, married day-laborers with small children faced an impossible situation. Earnings of a day-laborer in the district of Cologne averaged about 20 Stüber, while the price of an eight-pound loaf of rye bread reached 30 Stüber as early as October 1816. Because of the growing supply of labor in the Prussian Rhineland, moreover, wages tended to decline during 1817, when bread prices rose even higher.[112] The prevailing day-labor wage in Cleves was reduced from 10 to 6 groschen during 1816–17.[113] The large-scale emigration from the small-peasant region of southwestern Germany in 1816–17 suggests that the rural subsistence crisis was even more severe there.

The agricultural day-laborer was still the most numerous class of wage earner in the Habsburg lands. Although specific wage data for the postwar period are lacking, wage levels on balance proved insufficient to meet increased living costs.[114] The extensive survival of the manorial system and feudal relationships, however, insulated many peasants against the extreme distress witnessed in France and Germany. Manorial tenure systems existed in Bohemia, Moravia-Silesia, Upper Austria, Lower Austria, Styria, Carinthia, Hungary, Transylvania, and Galicia. These lands made up 80 percent of the Monarchy and contained some 77 percent of the population. Peasant freeholds also existed in these provinces, but were comparatively few in number.[115] One of the attributes of the system continued to be the expectation that landowners would provide for tenants in time of distress. A clear example of this obligation, together with its consequences in a year like 1816, is found in the account of a Moravian landowner:

The late year met with misfortune, all winter grains are still green. Nobody in my manor has any seed grain. The price is so high that it hurts! Nobody is able to buy, and also my private means is not in proportion to the enormity of the need for assistance: so several thousand persons become impoverished as the year progresses. Calamitous enough, that every farmer dismisses farmhands and maid-servants, and because of dearth and lack of fodder sells half of his cattle. . . . Now I am left with introducing a Rumford soup plan in order to save the majority of my dependents from starvation.[116]

Even allowing for some exaggeration, the conditions were somber enough. The relative absence of manorial tenure in the Italian provinces was one of the reasons why distress reached greater depths in Lombardy–Venetia, and elsewhere in the Italian countryside from Piedmont to Apulia.[117]

Even if documented yield deficiencies and cereal price series were not available, the severity of the subsistence crisis can be deduced from the social upheaval engendered by fears of starvation. A rebellious upsurge of pillage, rioting, vagrancy, and criminal violence attested to the level of distress. Food riots erupted in the towns of France, Belgium, and Britain in 1816 and then climaxed in the spring of 1817, by which time the disorders were also present in the towns of Germany, Holland, Ireland, Switzerland, Italy, and even

Norway. Agrarian disturbances marked by arson and the destruction of grain stores, livestock, and farm buildings swept through the French, British, Irish, and Belgian countrysides. Theft and crimes against property multiplied to the point where offenders were no longer pursued or prosecuted. Vagrants became a threat to the security and stability of rural districts, especially in France, where bands were large enough to risk armed clashes with the military. In central Europe 1817 was called the year of the beggars; and while all states saw a striking increase in the number of mendicants, the Swiss cantons, southwestern Germany, Bohemia, eastern France, Italy, and Ireland were inundated by destitute men, women, and children. The most visible social phenomenon was a massive wave of migrants traveling down the Rhine from Baden, Württemberg, Alsace, and the Swiss cantons to the ports of the Netherlands. Other emigrant groups moved overland in an attempt to reach the Russian empire. These events reflected the deteriorating European social scene.

POLITICAL RESPONSES AND ADMINISTRATIVE REMEDIES

The primary task of European governments was to compensate for the grain deficit and thus to keep food prices within reach of the poorest segment of the population. Various measures were adopted, timid at first, such as the French government's edict of August 10, 1816, which exempted grains, flour, bread, and biscuit from the new import duties that had been enacted as recently as April 28. The mounting subsistence crisis dictated a more positive attempt to encourage food imports, however, and on November 26 import premiums were instituted for wheat, rye, barley, and flour.[118] At the same time the Paris ministry remained convinced that a domestic policy of free trade in cereals would both depress prices and channel supplies into dearth areas. But the French population opposed the principle of free trade in grain, remembering the recent Napoleonic policy of controlled prices, and local officials on occasion were compelled to requisition grain supplies or to control prices in the face of popular disturbances.[119] The same conflict of views took place in the Netherlands, where the Dutch commercial interests clung to the advantages their ports had acquired as the granaries of Europe, whereas the Belgian provinces opposed the free-trade policy of the government and demanded an embargo on grain exports. As the pressure of the dearth intensified, the king compromised by prohibiting the export of food products by land but continuing the freedom of the grain trade by sea. Since the principal exports were shipped by sea, however, the restrictions failed to dampen domestic grain prices.[120] The Habsburg empire likewise followed a policy of free trade in grain, in spite of the increasing criticism of this policy during 1817.[121]

The majority of the west-central European states, by contrast, adopted a series of measures to restrict the export of cereals. Outright prohibitions against the export of cereals were widely enacted in the German states; but this step of course only worsened the subsistence crisis within the dearth-stricken area of Europe. The proliferation of grain embargoes and export restrictions gave rise to an early attempt to form a German Zollverein; the movement foundered, however, when the Austrian emperor vetoed Metternich's approval of the free exchange of essential foodstuffs.[122] The measures adopted by the Bavarian government were representative of the most extensive attempts to control the trade in grain; the administration commandeered granaries, closely supervised grain markets, taxed and then prohibited the export of cereal products.[123] Other west German states instituted similar internal grain policies, which included embargoes, export taxes, distilling restrictions, market regulations, and price controls.[124] The embargoes deprived the Swiss cantons of essential grain supplies that were customarily procured in Bavaria, Württemberg, and Baden. The subsistence crisis in Switzerland was further aggravated by its federal political structure, which resulted not only in badly coordinated government regulations but prompted each canton to act independently even to the point of closing markets, granaries, and frontiers to less fortunate neighbors and rendering it almost impossible to transport grain shipments.[125] Grain export embargoes also became the rule on the Italian peninsula; even after the harvests of 1817 the export of cereals from the Papal states remained strictly prohibited.[126]

The only effective relief measure for the dearth-ridden regions, however, was to secure grain supplies from areas of surplus production. Government grain purchases abroad became unavoidable when cereal prices continued to rise instead of falling in the usual pattern after the harvests of 1816 were completed. If nothing else, political wisdom had long since included the injunction to supply wheat to millers and flour to bakers, and to watch bread prices in large cities like Paris and London. Despite the growing predisposition in western Europe not to interfere in economic life, administrations found themselves compelled to make public grain purchases.

Securing large supplies of grain in the international market of 1817 presented obstacles, however, not the least of which were transportation problems. Since the extensive harvest failures of 1816 affected all of western and central Europe, cereal imports perforce had to originate either in the distant markets of eastern Europe, the Ottoman empire, or in North America. Moreover, the world grain supply had been compromised by the absence of customary reserves owing both to below-average harvest yields in 1815 and to wartime dislocations. Also, the Baltic seaports, which represented the logical source of grain for northwestern Europe, were unable to make large shipments before late spring, when the rivers flowing to these ports became free of ice. For example, the first inland shipment of grain to Riga by river traffic arrived on April 19, 1817. Even grain ordered from Russia as early as August, customarily failed to arrive in Germany before the following summer; only in countries like Italy and Spain, where the outcome of Mediterranean harvests can be determined as early as June, was it possible to order and receive grain from the Baltic ports before winter set in.[127]

A decisive change, however, had occurred since the famine and mortality crises of the eighteenth century. Although the massive flows of grain from the steppes of New Russia and the plains of North America still lay in the future, both the Russian empire and the United States proved able to export enlarged quantities of grain and flour to Europe. Furthermore, the famine of 1817 ushered in a shift of international grain demand from the Baltic to the new ice-free Black Sea port of Odessa. All Russian ports became the focus of an unprecedented speculation in grain purchases. As *The Times* expressed it: "It is a remarkable historical fact that as Europe four years ago found in Russia her deliverance from moral and political oppression, so now that quarter of the globe finds in her a protection from the almost universal calamity of famine."[128] The winter of 1816–17 initiated large grain exports from Odessa. Russian wheat exports from 1815 to 1824 averaged 2.1 million *chetverts;* Odessa in the year 1817 alone·exported 1.1 million. Wheat exports from Odessa equalled one-third of Russian cereal exports that year. Western Europe resorted to Odessa for grain as early as autumn 1816, when some 600 ships were dispatched from Mediterranean ports. Altogether, cereal exports from Russia during 1817 amounted to a value of about 125 million rubles.[129] The search for provisions also reached out to the Middle East, creating an extraordinary trade in grain at Trieste during the years 1816–18, which led to speculative imports not only from Odessa but from Smyrna, Alexandria, and the Levant.[130] Similar to Russia, the United States likewise found prosperity in the European demand for cereals and flour. The value of wheat, corn, rice, and flour exports rose from $11 million in 1815 to a peak of $23 million in fiscal 1817, before declining to $19 million in 1818.[131]

The responsiveness of European governments to grain import opportunities varied considerably, however, and this fact influenced not only the movement of cereal prices but ultimately the differential rise in mortality rates. Although the French government placed its first order for foreign food supplies in November 1816,[132] the bulk of the overseas grain purchases did not arrive until the summer months of 1817, and then these supplies contributed to the speculative losses of merchants who also had placed orders abroad.[133] Nonetheless, the government succeeded in moderating Parisian bread price increases, though the price of one franc for the two-kilo loaf in 1817 represented a significant increase over the customary price of 0.60 francs. Even then the price was prevented from rising higher by subsidizing the Parisian bakers; the royal government donated 19 million francs while the city appropriated 5 million francs. One million hectoliters of wheat out of the total of 1.460 million purchased by the French government were earmarked for Paris, while the balance was allocated to the other departments, mostly to those in the north and east.[134]

The French government expended about 70 million francs for grain imports; and since much of the wheat was sold at a price below cost rather than distributed free, this entire sum was not added to budgetary expenditures. Perhaps the net additional expense incurred by the central administration as a consequence of its relief measures amounted to 50 million francs.[135] In any event not a staggering amount, but nevertheless a fiscal burden that was magnified by other pressing demands, which require some notice if the full dimensions of the subsistence crisis are to be understood. To begin with, the installment payment of the war indemnity and the costs of military occupation already constrained the French ministry to find more than 300 million francs in order to balance the regular budget in 1817. More than merely financial responsibility or integrity was at stake; if the treaty payments were not made, the occupation would continue indefinitely and thus undermine the restored Bourbon dynasty. But any hope of economic improvement vanished in the face of the subsistence crisis. As one contemporary historian put it: how could the anticipated taxes be collected during a year in which bad harvests, dearth, misery, and mistrust had combined to suspend industrial enterprises and commercial transactions. Even if the expected tax receipts were to materialize, more than 300 million francs would still have to be found to meet anticipated expenditures.[136] The dearth also added a substantial amount to the occupation costs because of higher food prices during the three-year period; the annual occupation cost had been estimated at 150 million francs when the treaty was signed, but in fact the final occupation expenses amounted to 633 million francs, despite the unanticipated reduction in troop numbers negotiated in 1817 in order to ease France's financial crisis. As already mentioned, a foreign loan proved the only realistic solution to the fiscal emergency. A successful foreign loan promised not only that the Allies would be paid and the occupation army reduced, but French credit and the value of French securities would be raised and army contractors, as well as the new loan contractors, would profit. In the terms of the contract signed February 10, 1817, Baring Brothers of London and Hope & Company of Amsterdam became equal purchasers of French securities, in effect the foreign bankers discounted the *rentes* of the French government.[137] As a collateral benefit, the Allies reduced their occupation forces, which not only relieved pressure on the French budget but removed 30,000 consumers from the dearth-stricken departments of eastern France.

The royal government of the United Netherlands for related reasons also came to the realization that massive foreign cereal imports were essential to avert famine and perhaps even rebellion, particularly in the Belgian provinces. In spite of official estimates that grain inventories were more than adequate to meet consumption needs in 1817, the government departed from its free-trade policy and prudently decided to spend 6 million florins for public rye purchases in the Baltic markets.[138] This measure tended to allay the mounting social discontent as well as to dampen prices and avert famine. The government's rye was sold at a figure below the prevailing market price, not distributed free, and consequently the net public expense was reduced to about one million florins. At the time of the expenditure, however, 6 million florins represented more than 10 percent of the total public revenue. It proved a judicious measure, for the government rye eliminated the dangers of famine and revolt.[139] In addition, as the king reminded the states-general, the policy of free trade in overseas grain had kept the price of bread lower than in its neighboring states.[140]

The subsistence crisis also forced the newly enlarged Prussian state to seek enormous grain supplies in the Baltic and to face the unwelcome prospect of a considerable public outlay when trying to curb expenditures in order to improve a shaky credit rating.[141] Surplus grain stocks did not exist in the western Rhenish provinces, and the new province of Saxony in central Germany suffered from both dearth and industrial depression, which meant costly relief measures.[142] Berlin proved slow in responding to the Rhineland's needs, however; not even the fear of food riots in Cologne and Düsseldorf seemed to impress the central authorities. The price of rye in the Rhenish provinces was nearly double the price in Berlin by September 1816; and the *Oberpräsident* at Cologne informed the finance minister that the majority of the inhabitants were simply unable to pay the higher prices.[143] The Prussian state government at first clung to the policy that municipalities bore the responsibility for the needs of their inhabitants. Ultimately, however, after a special inquiry conducted from Berlin, the state government concluded that the western provinces faced a severe subsistence crisis during the four months (April to July) preceding the new harvest, and as a consequence the king authorized an expenditure of 2 million taler to purchase rye for the Rhineland. The crown nevertheless expected to be repaid either in money or in kind, and to insure reimbursement the district presidents were made personally responsible for payment. If needy individuals proved unable to pay for the rye, the municipalities were required to bear the expense. Moreover, the price of the government rye was fixed at 3 taler per bushel, and thus in fact calculated to return 2.5 million taler to the crown.[144]

The rye was purchased in the Baltic markets of Königsberg, Landsberg, Libau, St. Petersburg, Posen, Stettin, and Riga. As events worked out, the cereal shipments arrived in the Rhineland later than anticipated, which occasioned a scandal (some deliveries did not take place until late fall) and a royal investigation. Carl von Clausewitz accused Prince Hardenberg of protecting relatives who were implicated in the inquiry, and he remained indignant that the Prussian government never explained the delay satisfactorily.[145] The failure of the Baltic rye to arrive on schedule meant, of course, an increased level of distress for the Rhenish population. The first large shipment was not delivered until the end of July, which was the most critical month of the subsistence crisis. After that bread prices declined considerably.[146] Irrespective of the mistakes and perhaps even the corruption of Prussian officials,[147] the purchasing, storing, and transporting of such enormous quantities of grain on a fixed timetable presented a formidable challenge to the facilities of the time. Clausewitz believed that the involvement of Dutch contractors in the cereal transactions had resulted in higher prices and delays.[148] The Continental policy, rigidly adhered to in Prussia, of censoring all reports dealing with the causes, progress, or consequences of the dearth, in order to minimize social unrest and to dampen price increases,[149] obscured both the actual grain transactions and the subsequent inquiry. But it is clear that the cereal shipments were unavoidably delayed by the virtual absence of an east wind during the months of March, April, and May, which "greatly retarded the arrival of corn from the Baltic, and greatly protracted the distress of many parts of Germany."[150]

The majority of the southwestern and northern German states also imported grain to alleviate the subsistence crisis. The Bavarian government purchased grain in Holland to drive prices down in domestic markets, and prices were further dampened by the speculative grain purchases made abroad by urban merchant groups when commercial investment opportunities declined during the dearth.[151] The government of Württemberg purchased at least 73,000 Scheffel of grain abroad.[152] Neither Baden nor Hesse-Darmstadt nor Nassau seem to have made foreign cereal purchases, despite welfare measures that included the public distribution of food supplies.[153] In contrast, the west German municipal governments responded to the subsistence crisis by securing foreign grain. In Göttingen, for example, where a bread shortage became apparent as early as June 1816, the municipal authorities began to place orders abroad as a precautionary measure. After some delay and miscalculation, the Göttingen authorities purchased 1,300 Malter of grain in Riga and the Danish port of Flensburg, at a total expense of more than 20,000 taler.[154]

At the same time, the various Kornvereine of the west German towns, organizations underwritten chiefly by wealthy burghers, probably provided the most effective relief through their grain-purchase and distribution programs. The prototype and perhaps the most successful of these associations was established at Elberfeld in July 1816; subsequently it became the model Kornverein for the principal western towns, such as Cologne, Düsseldorf, Koblenz, Frankfurt. The Elberfeld burghers raised an original subscription of 55,000 taler to buy grain directly from the Baltic to provision the town's 22,000 inhabitants, but particularly to make lower-priced bread available to purchasers of the Verein's tokens. The association's cereal purchases exceeded 450,000 taler during the year of its existence. Bread prices were maintained some 20–30 percent below those prevailing in the free market.

The Elberfeld *Kornverein* proved highly successful in minimizing the level of distress in the town, and its achievement was by no means an exceptional case in Germany.[155]

The Swiss cantons among all Continental states had the most pressing need to buy substantial quantities of grain abroad if famine and social unrest were to be averted, but the limited success of their programs was in sharp contrast to the performance of the German towns. While the Swiss states ultimately avoided mass famine by supplemental cereal purchases in Russia, Egypt, and the Levant,[156] the effectiveness of the relief measures varied from canton to canton and hinged on the local severity of the food shortage. Relief programs were relatively successful in Bern, where the government expended 500,000 francs for grain purchases; in Zürich, where 700,000 francs were spent; in Waadt, where this figure exceeded 2.3 million francs; and in Basel, where public grain purchases inhibited any increase in the price of bread after January 1817.[157] In the canton of St. Gall, however, where a large population and a huge cereal deficiency necessitated the expenditure of nearly one million florins for grain purchases abroad, the public food program merely averted stark disaster; which was also the case in Appenzell. This result ensued in part from inability or unwillingness to carry public relief measures beyond the subsidization of millers and bakers. The small net "loss" of 61,000 florins recorded by the government of St. Gall would suggest that destitute inhabitants secured only minimal assistance.[158]

The imperial government of Austria made no substantial grain purchases abroad, despite the existence of famine conditions in some provinces. With scarcity present in every land of the vast Monarchy, the backward communications system, if nothing else, constituted an effective barrier to the transportation and distribution of grain supplies. In addition, since the international grain trade was carried on in gold transactions, the unsteady financial condition of the government was also an inhibiting factor. Efforts nevertheless were made to encourage cereal imports, and modest public grain purchases were effected in Egypt.[159] In Italy, where excellent harbors made considerable cereal imports possible, substantial grain and vegetable shipments at least inhibited price increases, even in the absence of public purchases. Trieste, Venice, Genoa, and Leghorn began to draw on cereal supplies in Odessa, Constantinople, Alexandria, and in America as early as September 1816.[160] These grain shipments, however, proved of scant assistance to the large number of destitute persons in the rural and mountainous districts, who lacked the means to buy food at almost any price.

The royal government in Britain did not find it necessary to make public grain purchases abroad. This result followed in part from the fact that British merchants imported some 2.5 million quarters of grain and flour during 1817. These imports included 700,000 quarters that originated in Ireland, which was faced with a severe subsistence crisis, a true famine, and in fact would have benefited from imported provisions.[161] Consequently, underdeveloped Ireland, like the backward states on the Italian and Balkan peninsulas, once again experienced the familiar sequence of famine and mortality characteristic of the old regime.

The importance of the willingness and ability of European governments to take advantage of the enlarged grain supplies now available from the Russian empire and the American midwest is difficult to overestimate in any assessment of the differential mortality rates observed in the subsistence crisis. It is true that insistence on free trade in provisions was partially effective in minimizing the famine in some districts straitened by serious grain deficiencies. But in Ireland, Italy, Switzerland, and the mountainous lands of the Habsburg empire, the per capita food needs of the harvest-sensitive fraction of the population could be met only by the acquisition of cereals abroad and by the distribution of those supplies at a price below the free market.

Thus European governments, once they had succeeded in acquiring public grain supplies, then faced the problem of distributing provisions to citizens no longer able to pay the higher dearth-level prices and also to those who were truly destitute. Although public policies and procedures varied, the programs that were adopted fell into similar patterns. As a generalization, the governments in northwestern Europe and the Habsburg Monarchy followed more or less a policy of internal free trade in grain; whereas, the states of southwestern Germany and the Swiss cantons attempted to control every aspect of the grain trade.[162] In either event, the grain supplies purchased and imported by European governments were not simply distributed to poor persons free of charge. For the most part, this grain was sold at prices below those in the marketplace in order to depress prices, or it was sold to bakers in urban locations to assure a supply of bread below market prices.[163] Municipal subsidies also helped to keep urban bread prices considerably below those found in the villages. To take Württemberg as a typical example, the government sold its emergency grain reserves at 12–14 florins per *Scheffel,* while free-market prices varied from 35 to 40 florins; the bakers in Stuttgart were provided with public grain to keep the price of a six-pound loaf at 46 kreutzer, while the same loaf of bread sold for more than 100 kreutzer elsewhere.[164] As already noted, the two-kilo loaf sold for 1.25 francs in Paris, Lyons, and Rouen, where bakers were subsidized, while rural inhabitants paid 3, 4, and even 5 francs.[165] Similar policies were followed in Nuremberg, where bread grain was purchased by the municipal government,[166] and in most of the other towns in Germany and the Netherlands.[167]

Bread subsidies alone were not sufficient to provide for the subsistence needs of the unemployed, however, and additional public programs were adopted. Large-scale public works projects, such as fortifications, highway construction, road repairs, and even make-work activities, were utilized to furnish work and bread for unemployed workers. The Ministry of Interior in

France promoted the repairing of roads not only to provide work and bread but to put the long neglected local roads into usable condition and also to prevent the popular disturbances that subsistence crises often spawned.[168] The government of the Netherlands began the fortifications along the Franco-Belgian border called for in the peace settlement; these constructions ultimately cost more than 80 million florins and contributed to social as well as economic stability during the subsistence crisis.[169] The Swiss cantons also initiated public works programs, including a successful land-reclamation project in Glarus.[170] Men were hired for public works projects in the Prussian Rhineland, while women were employed to knit clothes for the army, and public highway construction provided jobs for some of the numerous unemployed textile workers in the province of Saxony.[171] The Habsburg administration in northern Italy instituted a program to construct roads and canals, and it has been estimated that Austrian public works projects placed 5 million francs (2 million florins) into the hands of Italian workmen.[172] The British government made £500,000 available for public works relief measures in 1817, but apparently few projects were ever undertaken.[173]

The possibility of providing employment by public subsidy of private industry also received attention, though its success was limited. The provincial assembly of East Flanders worked out a plan to borrow 400,000 florins from the state to employ 15,000 cotton workers to manufacture products that could be sold only at a loss. It was understood that the cost of maintaining these workers on public welfare would be even greater and also would be demoralizing.[174] Similar plans proved less successful in the less-developed Austrian empire. Textile manufacturers suggested public loans, subsidies, and assistance to provide employment for dismissed industrial workers in Austria and the Czech lands. Although the emperor authorized a commission to report on the merits of the proposal, workers secured no benefits during the subsistence crisis. The provincial government of Bohemia recommended that linen production be subsidized by public funds in order to alleviate the desperate situation of the workers, but little tangible relief materialized during the famine, in spite of imperial approval.[175]

Measures to increase employment, even when successful, were far from adequate to meet the needs of the large number of destitute. As a correspondent pointed out to the Brussels Oracle, what effective relief would be provided by the one franc earned daily by those working on the Belgian fortifications, when a half million manufacturing workers were in desperate straits, and "add to them, the workmen of every kind whose employment ceases with the autumn, the beggars by trade, the old men and women, the infirm, and then tell us whether public works can supply them with subsistence."[176] Moreover, although the charitable-works program instituted in Ghent employed 1,100 indigents, the town counted 20,000 destitute persons, and this measure failed to prevent continued protests and widespread looting. Municipal authorities both in Belguim and virtually everywhere in Europe were required to support large numbers of inhabitants on public welfare. The procedures instituted in the Belgian towns were representative of those adopted elsewhere, making allowances for the fact that needs and levels of distress varied considerably. Public relief committees set up kitchens in the towns to distribute Rumford soups and bread to the destitute either at low prices or free of charge.[177] The dimensions of the relief program can be comprehended from the fact that 513,896 paupers received public assistance in Belguim in 1817, approximately 15 percent of the population.[178]

In French towns, governments provided food for those unable to pay market prices by establishing soup kitchens, issuing bread allowances, selling grain below cost, and by subsidizing bakers.[179] The Ministry of Interior instructed the prefects "to procure the means of existence for persons whose age or infirmities do not permit them to work."[180] Since the Prussian state government adopted a policy of municipal responsibility for the welfare of the indigent and destitute, the towns were forced to levy excise taxes to supplement private donations and subscriptions. Because of the severe distress prevailing in Cleves, however, a Central Relief Association was established by the provincial government, and the Berlin government placed rye in the military storehouse at its disposal. The association at Cleves distributed a half pound of bread daily to 15,000 destitute persons.[181] Nevertheless, the various *Kornvereine* still provided the most effective relief for the urban poor in the Prussian towns, and the same was true in the urban locations of northern Germany. Public outlays were still necessary, however; in Göttingen, for example, municipal bakers supplied 25,901 loaves of bread to the needy between June 26 and September 30, 1817, and a public soup kitchen served 6,180 portions at low prices during the same period.[182]

Public assistance on a larger scale was required in the southwestern German states, where the level of distress plunged deeper. Welfare committees were set up in all Bavarian communities and in large towns like Munich, Augsburg, and Nuremberg both public and private organizations distributed Rumford soups and bread rations.[183] In Nuremberg, for example, more than 1,600 families were supported by low-priced bread; and from November 1, 1816, to July 31, 1817, the really destitute inhabitants were supplied with wood for fuel, bread, potatoes, and more than 100,000 servings of Rumford soup, either gratuitously or at low prices.[184] In Württemberg, where the relative number of destitute was probably even higher, public and private organizations distributed soup, bread, and money to unemployed paupers, while the government supplied the middling population with 237,604 bushels of grain, potatoes, and vegetables at low prices.[185] Similar public policies and welfare services were instituted in Baden, Hesse-Darmstadt, and Nassau.[186]

If the welfare and relief programs of the German states achieved some success in mitigating the famine, the remedial measures adopted in Switzerland, where the subsistence crisis touched greater depths, produced more disappointing results. Municipalities established soup kitchens to avert starvation, and in one district of St. Gall alone, 400,000 portions of soup were served by October 1817. Cereals, clothing, and financial assistance were dispatched to unfortunate communities in an attempt to eliminate large-scale begging. Nonetheless, these efforts proved insufficient in the eastern cantons, and genuine alleviation was provided only by the harvests of 1817.[187] Welfare and relief measures failed substantially in Italy also, despite public soup kitchens, tax relief, and the private distribution of food, clothing, and money. In spite of these programs, and large sums of money contributed by the Austrian government for benefit of the destitute in Lombardy–Venetia, the depth of the subsistence crisis and the poverty of Italy was simply bottomless.[188] The government of the Papal States attempted to furnish the destitute with work and bread, and the remainder of the Italian states also instituted welfare measures to support paupers and the indigent.[189] But the limited success of these relief programs was reflected in the elevated mortality recorded in Italy during the subsistence crisis. In Italy, as in Switzerland and most of central Europe, the distress became manageable only when abundant local grain supplies returned.

The Habsburg government assisted the various lands in the empire by direct grants of money. Sums were allocated to Styria, the Tyrol, and Carinthia, as well as to Lombardy–Venetia. But if the complaints emanating from Carinthia, which also suffered from severe harvest deficiencies, were typical and justified, the amounts expended were inadequate.[190] By contrast, the large sum of 3 million florins was granted to the Military Frontier to avert famine.[191] Effective relief, nevertheless, depended largely on private assistance; and the emperor repeatedly reminded landowners of their obligation to assist subjects in times of distress.[192]

Public poor relief was well established in Britain, where the continuing distress through 1817 resulted in climbing parish expenditures and higher rates for property owners. The expenditure for poor relief rose from £5.4 million in 1815 to £7.9 in 1818, the highest figure reached under the old poor law. Advances made available for public works relief measures under the Poor Employment Act of 1817 were limited to parishes where the poor rate was double the average of the two preceding years.[193] The poor rates in some parishes in North Wales simply could not be collected from farmers who had become virtual paupers themselves.[194] As on the Continent, the cities and towns instituted soup kitchens and general relief programs. In Liverpool, for example, the merchants and tradesmen raised £10,000 for the construction of new docks to furnish employment for the poor; but 20,000 persons were maintained at the expense of the parish in the winter of 1817.[195] The committee for the relief of the poor in Manchester distributed 400,000 quarts of Rumford soup during the same winter, and furnished 7,000 families with coal at reduced prices.[196] Towns like Edinburgh instituted semicharitable public works projects that furnished paid employment. The Edinburgh program paid a weekly wage of 6s., with added allowances for children, and attracted 2,251 applicants.[197] The British welfare problem was accentuated by the recent release of upwards of 400,000 men from the armed services, and a considerable number of workers from wartime occupations, whose appearance in the labor market increased the unprecedented volume of applications for poor relief.[198] Even though the level of distress plummeted much deeper in Ireland, the resources allocated to welfare and relief were far less than in Britain, a fact which contributed to the failure to control both famine and epidemic disease.

A combination of special additional taxes, higher poor rates, and capital levies at the municipal level (supplemented by state contributions) financed the expense of the public welfare programs. To take several typical examples, in France, Abbéville and Boulogne each voted an extraordinary imposition of 60,000 francs in order "to come to the assistance of the indigent";[199] while Lyons financed a subsidy to the city's bakers with a special tax of 230,000 francs levied on those of comfortable circumstances.[200] In the German towns, where extensive relief measures were needed, municipal administrations borrowed money to supplement funds made available by the state and private contributions. Nuremberg, for example, was compelled to raise 80,000 taler on three separate occasions in 1817 and 1818. The parish poor relief accounts in Prussia ran into deficits in 1817.[201] Swiss communities made financial sacrifices that resulted in indebtedness far beyond their means. But even these sacrifices proved inadequate in the face of 40,000 paupers in the cantons of St. Gall and Appenzell alone (more than one-fifth of the total populations), and when nearly one-quarter of the population of Glarus lacked means of subsistence.[202]

The inadequacy of public welfare derived in part from the unwillingness of all segments of the propertied classes to accept the concept of state responsibility for relief. As a consequence, traditional appeals to private charity continued to be made. If contemporary accounts can be trusted, the outpouring of private funds constituted a major contribution in sustaining Europe's poor and indigent. Even though the severe distress in Switzerland discounted the success of all relief programs, an impressive amount of private charity prevented worse consequences. The dramatic appeal of Julie de Krüdener's chiliastic projects was distinguished by charity distributed with a lavish hand. Institutions to care for widows, orphans, dependent paupers, and sick children multiplied throughout the Swiss cantons.[203] A fund for the benefit of the indigent in Vienna raised more than 500,000 florins and was followed by a door-to-door canvass to assist an estimated 36,000 working men and dependents. Similar relief associations sprang up in Styria, Bohemia, and Lombardy–Venetia, which solicited cash subscriptions, food, and clothing.[204]

The press in northwestern Europe carried numerous accounts detailing private charitable contributions by individuals, corporations, and social organizations. In France, the Ministry of Interior also reminded the prefects of the long-standing tradition of *noblesse oblige:* "Doubtless you will not call forth the charity of the well-to-do inhabitants of your department in vain, . . . I know too well that in the present circumstances all fortunes find themselves impaired; but it is in the most critical conjunctures that the French have always demonstrated the most generosity and self-sacrifice."[205] The appeal for private assistance proved successful and made it possible for the French charitable committees to draw on both public and private funds.[206] The British propertied classes likewise found it necessary to assist the unemployed and destitute, and the British press memorialized the most striking instances of private benevolence. Those able to work were paid wages "so modest as to induce them to return to their former habits of independent industry as soon as the demand for labour should revive."[207] Varied measures were utilized; for example, the Marquis of Stafford employed workers on drainage schemes, the repair and construction of roads, and to reconvert land, while at the same time he asked his tenant farmers to take on as many workers as each individual poor rate dictated. Stafford also approved a private subscription to continue production at an iron works on his property for the express purpose of employing the poor.[208] Stafford and other proprietors offered coal to the poor on the condition that it be transported free of tonnage.[209] These examples of British private charity can be multiplied. The duke of Portland reduced the rents of his Ayrshire tenants by 20 to 40 percent because of the poor harvest of 1816; at Bishop Auckland all laborers unable to find work secured daily employment from the bishop of Durham, either on his land or in improving the town streets; the marquis of Stafford supplied his poor tenants in Scotland with meal and potatoes during the dearth, at a cost of £7,000.[210] Private subscriptions also paid for the distribution of food to the urban poor, as in Leeds.[211] Several private relief organizations, like the Spitalfield Association, to assist distressed silk workers, sprang into existence. By contrast, private charity, though not totally absent, remained on a modest scale in Ireland, and as a consequence the level of distress worsened drastically in 1817.[212]

Private charity in the United Netherlands was as extensive as in Britain and France. The King believed not only that public officials had met the challenge of the subsistence crisis at every level but that "private charity, the fairest trait in the national character, had kept pace with the increasing distress."[213] The welfare committees in the German communities seem to have enjoyed the greatest private support in Europe, though the precise amounts contributed are not systematically known. The inhabitants of Koblenz contributed such items as money, horses, jewelry, works of art, antiques, clocks, metals, pottery, books, and needlework. The Queen of Württemberg helped to found organizations like women's charitable guilds, savings banks, and community charitable institutions, which gives some indication of the evolving attitude toward the poor and poor relief.[214]

These remedial measures, public and private, and the extent to which they were available and called upon determined to a significant degree the ultimate toll that the subsistence crisis would claim. While it would not be difficult to document the many deficiencies of the public welfare programs, the most striking outcome was the relative success some states realized in keeping mortality rates within bounds, compared to the experience of past famines. Moreover, it will be shown that the correlation between food prices and death rates was not invariant. Instead of the two curves moving directly together in conformity with the expected relationship between undernourishment and illness, in some states the lines tended to separate. This uneven correlation between food prices and death rates derived in large degree from the differential effectiveness of governments in the execution of necessary relief measures.

None of these welfare and relief programs represented innovations; perhaps all of the measures that were instituted can be traced back to the old regime. But now administrative remedies and welfare services appeared on a more concentrated scale, and these steps proved instrumental in dampening the rise in mortality levels. The mortality peaks that accompanied the subsistence crises of 1709–10 and 1740–43 were avoided this time. The enhanced ability to transport grain supplies also contributed to this result, since no European area was now entirely dependent upon its own cereal output. Moreover, the advance of potato culture as a field crop eased the famine in some locations, but its progress can be exaggerated. In fact, the postwar subsistence crisis, like the earlier famine of 1770–72, gave a large impetus to expanded potato production.[215] The progressive rationalization of political administration was probably the critical variable; public officials proved able to cope more effectively with problems that had caused dislocations in the past. Effective administrative remedies had begun to appear on a broad scale during the last half of the eighteenth century, particularly in the German municipalities confronted with the famine of 1770–72.[216] Although parish poor relief had been instituted in Prussia as early as 1696, the poor laws were not observed and welfare measures remained inadequate before 1750.[217] Both public welfare and private charity in France were incapable of providing adequate assistance throughout the eighteenth century, though efforts in that direction began to increase after 1650, and the intervention of public officials in the distribution of available cereal supplies helped to prevent severe famines after 1750.[218] The policies and practices adopted by French authorities in 1816–17 had in large measure been pioneered by the imperial government during the dearth of 1811–12.[219]

The administrative response to the subsistence crisis of 1816–17 also evidenced a noticeable resolution to minimize the hardships as well as the casualties. The motivation for the advanced administrative efficiency can plausibly be traced to an amplified fear of popular disorder following the upheaval of the revolutionary period. Also a heightened degree of humanitarianism that seems to be concomitant with the process of modernization might have played a role. In any event, the increased expenditure of public funds and private charity derived from changed motivations as well as from the added resources made available by economic growth. In part at least, these efforts curtailed epidemic disease and also resulted in death rates that remained lower than was to be expected on the basis of past experience. Even though neither the volume nor the efficacy of the public and private relief measures is exactly known, and even though an autonomous element is always present in infectious disease, the contrast between the relative effectiveness of the welfare programs in France, Germany, Britain, and the Netherlands and the higher levels of distress and mortality in the less rationalized administrations of Ireland, Switzerland, Italy, the Habsburg Monarchy, and the Balkan peninsula suggests that this outcome was not merely fortuitous.

chapter
three

Popular Disturbances
and Social Protest

GRAIN AND BREAD RIOTS

The Western world's last great subsistence crisis also set on foot the last great wave of European grain riots, which were still the typical expression of preindustrial popular discontent both in the town and in the countryside. The peasant *jacquerie* now belonged to the past, even though the memory of this phenomenon lingered on, and the urban strike, though already on the scene, was still a future form of economic and political protest. Popular reaction to the famine of 1816–17 ranged from time-sanctioned demonstrations in grain markets or in front of bakers' shops to looting, rioting, and arson. Rural misery in some regions spawned a rebellious upsurge of pillage and rioting and, on occasion, ravaging vagrant bands attacked farms and even markets. But, as Richard Cobb and George Rudé have observed, as long as the majority of the peasant proprietors remained reasonably content no real danger of a genuine rural uprising existed. The peasant riots that followed the calamitous famine of 1709 in France represented the last of these periodic rebellious rural outbursts which had been so frequent in the seventeenth century; and in that instance the tax exactions of the War of the Spanish Succession had added to popular discontent. From that time until the French Revolution, European popular disturbances lacked the scope and the level of violence that charac-terized the social protests of the seventeenth century. Severe dearths still recurred, even if major European famines were absent after 1709, but hunger riots persisted as regional rather than national or international phenomena. Nevertheless, whenever grain harvests were deficient, or war needs resulted in food shortages, hoarding, undue speculation, or panic buying, and therefore urban workers and the majority of the rural population felt threatened with hunger, the working population mounted demonstrations in grain markets and resorted to violence and rioting.[1] These popular disturbances matched the years of high cereal prices in the eighteenth century; in France they included 1725, 1740, 1749, 1768, 1775, and 1785 before the revolutionary crisis of 1788–89; while in Britain food riots broke out in 1709–10, 1727–28, 1740–41, 1756–57, 1766–67, 1770–74, 1789, 1794–95, and 1799–1800.[2]

The grain riots of 1816–17 were marked by a level of violence not seen in European popular disturbances since the Great Fear of 1789 and the French subsistence crises of 1792–93 and 1795. They also included a less violent practice that involved the imposition of popular price control by collective action, in France referred to as *taxation populaire*. While this practice has been traced back to 1693 in England and was widely instituted in the British food riots of 1766–67, its most extended application occurred in France during the so-called "flour-war" (*la guerre des farines*) of 1775. Peasants and urban workers invaded markets and forced dealers to sell grain at a just or reasonable price. Bakers and farmers as well as grain merchants were victimized. On occasion, both in 1775 and 1817, these attempts at unofficial price control descended to indiscriminate looting, particularly if the sellers resisted. Also, on occasion, magistrates and officials invaded markets and fixed grain prices at the lower levels demanded, either out of sympathy for the distress of the poor or to avoid bloodshed. Widespread instances of *taxation populaire* took place in the great food riots of the French Revolution as well as in 1816–17.[3]

The course followed by the European grain riots of 1816–17 serves not only as an index of the relative severity of the subsistence crisis from region to region but also facilitates comparisons with past famines. The postwar popular disturbances exceeded those of the eighteenth century in geographical scale and in magnitude, if not always in intensity; the degree of distress reached the point where not even the increased measure of economic growth, the more rationalized political administration, nor the enlarged availability of overseas grain supplies could dampen the social protest. At the same time, since distress mounted as grain prices advanced, the early outbreaks of popular discontent tended to be moderate or to be restricted to districts where subsistence difficulties were untypically pressing. For example, the first major indication of the impending disturbances surfaced during May 1816 in the agrarian riots that broke out in the East Anglian counties of Norfolk, Suffolk, Huntingdon, and Cambridge. Although the prevailing agricultural depression was the predisposing factor, an increase in the price of bread precipitated the insurrection in East Anglia. While the good harvests of 1815 had instituted declining wheat prices in October of that year, the cold spring weather of 1816 reversed this trend in April, and in May wheat prices climbed

33 percent above those of March.[4] A series of sporadic acts of protest, such as the breaking of threshing machines and the destruction of barns and grain stocks by fire, had earlier taken place in Suffolk, but when the price of wheat advanced in mid-May without any improvement in either agricultural wages or employment opportunities, these incidents evolved into a general disturbance. Ultimately, some 1,500 discontented persons formed into groups and destroyed the houses of those whom they found obnoxious. The rioters were armed with long, heavy sticks that were studded with short, iron spikes, and they carried a flag inscribed "Bread or Blood." The demonstrators demanded a reduction in the price of bread and meat to a maximum they had fixed. Similar disturbances took place in Norwich, where the rioters smashed windows, looted a flour mill, and vandalized buildings. The appearance of the militia and the reading of the riot act, which threatened the death penalty, put an end to the disorders.[5] The advance of bread prices in May 1816 also triggered food riots in regions of England unconnected with the agrarian troubles of East Anglia, but of course these disturbances were related to the postwar depression. At Bridport, a crowd numbering upwards of 2,000 demolished the windows of the principal millers and bakers before being dispersed.[6] At Biddeford in Devonshire, a large armed crowd tried to prevent a cargo of potatoes from being shipped out.[7]

Then the price of wheat leveled off at 74s. per quarter during the summer months, and the number of popular protests declined in Britain; but when the deficient harvests of 1816 failed to bring the customary lower food prices, and instead bread prices advanced as the price of wheat rose 22 percent between August and October, a new wave of demonstrations and riots occurred in the autumn. At Guilford, after the price of the quartern loaf rose to 1s. 2 ¼d., a crowd of 400 persons smashed the windows and destroyed the property of a baker.[8] Popular disturbances became particularly common in the northern counties; grain offered for sale at higher prices was seized, and the homes of millers and tradesmen were attacked, often by crowds made up of women and boys.[9] At Dundee, after a sudden rise in the price of meal, a crowd numbering 2,000 plundered upwards of 100 food shops and then looted the house of a large grain dealer before setting it on fire.[10] Attempts to ship oatmeal from Dumfries led to its seizure from the docks, whence it was carried to the town's market for public sale, together with a quantity of oatmeal looted from nearby mills. The magistrates swore in 200 constables, but failed to reestablish order; the militia finally had to charge the crowd in order to restore calm.[11] The riot that ensued after the first of the famous protest meetings in Spa Fields was for the most part an attack on London's bakers and butchers. In the tradition of the food riot, a crowd of boys placed a loaf of bread on the top of a stick and then proceeded to smash windows and remove bread from some bakeries. Shops that offered cheap bread were spared, however. The police finally succeeded in dispersing the rioters with no further damage beyond the looting of meat from several butchers' stalls.[12] These accounts could be multiplied, but the British postwar popular disturbances are too well known for further review here.[13]

By contrast, in the northwestern region of the Continent, public disorders did not appear until the poor harvests of 1816, and then they intensified in scale as the price of grain advanced step by step. In fact, popular disturbances were confined mainly to France during the balance of 1816 and consisted chiefly of grain market incidents. The events that occurred at Poitiers in Vienne at the end of October were typical of the early public unrest. A crowd of demonstrators demanded that the magistrates impose maximum prices for wheat. When the national guard refused to disperse the protesters, it proved necessary to call on regular troops; this sequence of events took place more often than not in the suppression of French market disturbances. A few arrests followed the theft of several wagons loaded with grain. Similar minor disorders ensued in other districts of the department. Market disturbances and misdemeanors multiplied almost everywhere in France in the late autumn of 1816, particularly in the western departments, but none were too serious.[14]

The insurrection that excited Toulouse for several days in November was of more significance. Although the harvest yields in the department of Haute-Garonne had not turned out much below average, the price of grain rose sharply because large quantities of wheat were being shipped to Marseilles. When the price reached 34 francs per hectoliter in Toulouse, the population refused to pay that amount and prevented several shipments of wheat from leaving the town. At the same time, demonstrators in the market priced and carried away wheat at 24 francs. These actions were repeated for several days until dragoons dispersed the rioters. Calm was restored on November 13, but once again the national guard proved sympathetic to the demonstrators.[15] The Toulouse disturbances exemplify the riots that frequently occurred in districts where no serious grain shortage existed. These disturbances grew out of the fear that grain exports would create famine conditions or would drive prices beyond the levels warranted by supply and demand. The official policy of free domestic circulation of cereals was maintained to the end of the subsistence crisis,[16] but local authorities, faced with threatening food riots, at times violated the law. Moreover, insurgent bands in the Vendée and in western Brittany stationed themselves along the domestic trade routes and seriously hindered the free circulation of grain. The success of this resistence can be inferred from the fact that wheat sold for 30 francs in Poitou when the price reached 100 francs in Strasbourg and Colmar. Public disorders concerned with the price of grain, its scarcity, or its export increased in all regions of France during the last months of 1816.[17]

There were few popular disturbances and little social protest was manifested elsewhere in Europe during 1816. But in Switzerland and Italy, where the subsistence crisis was most severe, the rising levels of anxiety and distress were reflected in the increasing number of crimes against property and in the increasing number of beggars.[18] Some granaries and bakeries were looted in Italy, and there were assaults on persons suspected of speculating in grain, but, on the whole, protests were individual acts rather than organized demonstrations,[19] and when planned popular disturbances did take place, mixed motives were identifiable in almost every case. For example, in May 1816 thousands of peasants in the vicinity of Bologna assembled on the ringing of the tocsin and laid waste to the rice fields in the belief that rice cultivation infected the atmosphere. Rice culture had been introduced into this region of Italy only fifteen years earlier, and apparently the peasants still resented the unfamiliar inconveniences attending its cultivation enough to destroy a potential source of food in the face of impending famine.[20] The German lands also were spared the large-scale organized rioting encountered in northwestern Europe, but popular unrest and social protest were far from absent in 1816. Vagrant bands roamed rural Germany and left a record of theft, robbery, and arson in their wake.[21] Nonetheless, the majority of popular disturbances still centered on bakeries and grain markets; as early as June 1816 the shortage of bread in Göttingen occasioned many scuffles and brawls, which continued to occur here and in other German towns until the end of the subsistence crisis, but there were few serious riots.[22]

From the end of 1816 until the summer of 1817, however, popular disturbances were more violent and incorporated larger numbers of demonstrators; these protests ranged from simple food riots to conditions bordering on criminal anarchy and disguised rebellion. In Britain riots connected with subsistence anxieties continued to trouble the towns and the countryside until the new harvests.[23] Bread riots in Glasgow necessitated military force to control the crowds.[24] The turbulence became more extreme in Wales, where the well-known riot at Merthyr Tydvil had been suppressed with bloodshed.[25] The subsistence crisis was more acute in North Wales, however. On the island of Anglesey, where the oat harvest was small, apprehension developed into fear of hunger when the price of bread reached a figure that few laborers could afford. The population of Amlwich refused to allow a ship carrying oatmeal to embark. An army detachment was called in to restore public order, and nighttime security patrols continued for six months.[26] The year 1817 proved to be a period of famine for virtually all North Wales, and while popular disturbances seldom duplicated the events in Amlwich, violence and social protest became endemic.[27]

The subsistence crisis grew still more acute in Ireland, and as a result public disorders multiplied to the point of social anarchy in the countryside. The Insurrection Act of 1814 had been withdrawn from the last two Irish counties only in April 1816, but the tranquillity of Ireland was disturbed again before the end of the year. Louth, Tipperary, and Limerick were once again placed under the military supervision of the insurrection acts in early 1817. The

scope and magnitude of the popular disturbances turned out less than anticipated, however; because of the severe distress, the poorest classes were forced
to be concerned with survival itself.[28] Organized riots were rare in the
hardest-hit famine districts everywhere in Europe. But social disorder became
extensive in Ireland during 1817 and, as on the Continent, popular unrest and
protest reached a peak in the early summer months. Central Ireland was the
scene of a series of attacks on homes and businesses where provisions were
stored, and grain barges bound for Dublin were intercepted on the canal. A
series of attacks on grain barges in northwestern Ireland ended in bloodshed
when a crowd attempted to prevent the shipment of oatmeal from Ballina to
Sligo; a military detachment fired on stone-throwing rioters, killing three and
wounding twenty persons.[29] Repeated acts of violence took place in
Limerick, in the counties of Kerry, Clare, and Kildare, in Londonderry,
Mayo, and Westmeath; the motivation for these disturbances clearly derived
from the mounting distress and want.[30] Armed bands searched the countryside
of Limerick for food and even broke into homes at night.[31] On balance,
however, the episodes of public disorder in Ireland did not approach the scale
reached in France and Belgium; rather, they amounted to an unending series
of spontaneous minor disturbances.[32]

Even when the degree of violent protest more than kept pace with the rise of
grain prices, the disturbances did not always evolve into borderline rebellion
or insurrection; the public disorder in the Norman departments of Eure and
Seine-Inférieur offers just such a case. The number of crimes committed in the
early months of 1817 was beginning to outstrip the local capacity to maintain
public security; at first it was mainly a case of petty thefts and misdemeanors
everywhere in France, but armed bands victimized travelers in some departments. As winter deepened and economic distress intensified, new segments
of the population resorted to crime, and the number of thefts reached the point
where magistrates no longer troubled to look for offenders. The Norman
departments experienced a high measure of theft. The prefect of Eure had
anticipated a critical situation, since grain prices not only failed to decline
after the harvests but contrary to normal traditions increased in the middle of
November (to 35 francs per hectoliter). The local administration feared especially the social emergency that would arise when the agricultural day-
laborers had consumed the grain received as harvest wages and would have to
face the prospect of buying bread at advanced prices.[33]

It should be noted, moreover, that even in the absence of exceptional
subsistence problems, each winter invariably brought on a crisis of some
magnitude in preindustrial societies like Normandy. Almost all agricultural
work stopped, with the exception of the limited employment provided by
threshing. Manufacturing stagnation followed the freezing of the streams,
which, of course, interfered with the operation of the paddle-wheels that
powered the mills. The inevitable result was unemployment for the village

poor, who then had to be supported by such public works as road-mending. The recurring winter crisis in Eure was further aggravated in 1816–17 by the prevailing depression in the manufacturing sector, so that those rural artisans who worked for the larger industrial concerns commanded even less purchasing power than usual. For example, when the price of a hectoliter of wheat reached 40 francs in early January, the textile manufacturers in the town had just lowered wages by one-third. Industrial workers, now unable to buy food in the town's market, began to form into bands for the purpose of searching for wheat at night in the surrounding countryside. When the price of wheat climbed to 45 francs on January 19, the prefect and the municipal council instituted a weekly distribution of five pounds of bread to all indigents, but this quantity was often insufficient to satisfy family nutritional needs. Public disorder mounted in Eure during the winter and spring months, taking the form of forced taxation, theft, demands on bakeries, and threatening demonstrations in grain markets. Although local police measures were strengthened, military units had to be despatched from Paris to maintain order.[34]

Even though the scale of violent protest was kept under reasonable control in Normandy, at least in comparison with events elsewhere in France, normal commercial routines were interrupted by the unwillingness of producers to risk transporting grains to market. Sales were consummated at farms instead, and grain purchasers were forced to accept the risk of transportation. As a consequence, flour became so scarce that the weekly food allowance in towns like Evreux had to be reduced from five to two pounds of bread at the end of February; the deficit was made up to some extent by substituting six pounds of potatoes. However, welfare programs existed only in the important French towns, such as Evreux, which was the capital of the department of Eure. Charitable assistance in the villages depended chiefly on the sympathetic generosity of local persons of consequence. At the end of April, when the price of bread jumped to 0.29 francs per pound and began its uninterrupted rise to 0.48 francs on June 8, the scale and gravity of public disorder mounted in Eure. Agricultural laborers were now wholly at the mercy of the unprecedented bread prices. Armed bands roamed the countryside soliciting food by intimidation and threats of violence. Controlling public order was made more difficult in Eure because of its proximity to Rouen. A substantial quantity of the grain that the government had imported from eastern Europe to maintain low-priced bread in Paris was stored in Rouen, from whence it was convoyed to the capital via the Seine. This procedure contributed to the already existing preconditions for riot in the Norman countryside. Still, it was the armed bands seeking food directly at farms who constituted the gravest danger to public security. For example, a band numbering 500 made up mostly of former soldiers invaded Eure from Seine-Inférieure on June 11; although the local police reinforced by cavalrymen were finally able to disperse them, it was not before the group had secured a large quantity of wheat by threatening to burn down farms and to hang resisting farmers. More frequently, however, the bands did not go beyond demanding wheat at a price of 20 francs a hectoliter. Nevertheless, the vagrant bands created terror in the countryside and deep concern among the administration. Local law enforcement was hindered by the unwillingness of juries to convict defendants charged with looting, a crime which carried the harsh punishment of five years penal servitude at hard labor.[35]

The scale of public disorder followed a similar upward curve in central Europe, but popular disturbances were few in number and lacking in violence compared to the rebellious riots in northwestern Europe. In Germany the majority of disturbances centered on bakeries and grain markets, although looting in the countryside by vagrant bands also infringed public security.[36] Grain riots of some concern broke out in the Bavarian towns of Memmingen, Augsburg, and Ratisbon at the end of 1816.[37] In 1817 Munich witnessed a market disturbance directed mainly against grain forestallers,[38] and the population of Ratisbon pillaged its bakers' shops.[39] Popular excesses also took place in other towns located in southwestern Germany.[40] Significantly, almost all of the riots occurred after the threat of famine had passed, but before grain prices had returned to customary levels. The market disorders at Mainz in Hesse-Darmstadt took on a more grave aspect; these outbursts, which also occurred after the danger of famine had passed, were directed against grain monopolists and, in addition, evidenced a note of anti-Semitism. The violence lasted several days, "houses were attacked, windows broken, and many persons ill-treated"; the troops of the garrison were required to reestablish public order.[41] The Prussian towns, on the other hand, avoided popular disturbances, with the exception of some minor scuffles in Koblenz and elsewhere. Why, then, did Germany remain so relatively calm compared to the scope and intensity of public disorder in northwestern Europe? Passing over a contemporary observation that the "natural good nature of the German people"[42] minimized riot and rebellion, two possibilities suggest themselves. Where the famine was most severe, i.e., in the states of southwestern Germany, the depth of the distress dictated an overriding concern with survival itself and thus tended to inhibit organized demonstrations. Organized social protest was also absent in the eastern departments of France, where once again the threat of famine was unmistakable. Food riots, in particular, were more the outcome of the danger of hunger than of famine itself. This generalization held true almost without exception in 1816–17, and, as George Rudé has noted, the great famine year of 1709 in France witnessed fewer popular disturbances than the moderate dearth of 1775.[43] Second, where the subsistence crisis did not progress beyond a severe dearth, i.e., the towns of the Prussian Rhineland and northern Germany, a measure of public welfare and private charity tended to dampen violent protest.

The first of these explanations operated even more categorically in Switzerland, where practically no riots or organized protests occurred. Because true famine conditions prevailed, the ensuing social upheaval followed a somewhat different pattern; want and misery produced numerous beggars and vagrancy on a massive scale rather than riot and rebellion. The one exception in Switzerland was a series of food riots in Geneva, where not only did the subsistence crisis remain moderate but also the demonstrations took place in the autumn of 1817, after the price of grain began to decline. Stores were looted and peasants were forced to sell provisions for less than the market price. As so often happened elsewhere in Europe, the town guard merely stood by and watched; but when the rioters increased in number and the demonstration took a seditious turn, the Genevan magistrates called in a squad of grenadiers who restored order after repulsing a stone-throwing crowd of men and women with their rifle butts.[44] Since the riots broke out after the dearth was essentially over, the protest probably also reflected a degree of unfocused social and political discontent.

The Habsburg Monarchy likewise escaped collective, violent demonstrations, and in part for the same reasons as Switzerland. But in addition to the tendency of the severe subsistence crisis to inhibit organized public disorder, the Habsburg empire also retained the advantage of extensive manorial obligations, which had the effect of dampening fears of hunger. Nevertheless, like Switzerland, the empire was inundated by swarms of beggars and vagrants, who were found everywhere from the streets of Vienna to the remote highland districts.[45] Granaries and bakeries were looted in Italy, both in the Habsburg domain and elsewhere, but these food riots were small matters indeed compared to the enormous demonstrations in northwestern Europe.[46] Popular disturbances also took place in European states where the dearth remained moderate but where political disaffection was rife. In Norway, for example, then a part of the united kingdom of Sweden and Norway, the peasants of Christiania pillaged grain warehouses and imposed popular price-fixing. The dearth promoted enmity toward the merchant groups who controlled the southern ports and toward the Diet, and, together with the almost total economic stagnation in Norway, convinced the rural population that even closer union with Sweden was desirable.[47] The food shortage in Catalonia apparently facilitated a political rebellion in the spring of 1817.[48] Finally, Tunis experienced a sequence of dearth, riot, and rebellion in 1817, but of course longer-range political factors were also present in the Barbary states.[49]

The popular disturbances in northwestern Europe tended to move beyond the riot stage and in the direction of rebellion as the subsistence crisis became more acute in the late spring of 1817. This progression was especially noticeable in the United Netherlands, where a significant fraction of the population, 15 percent in the Belgian provinces, was reduced to destitution.[50] The anxieties generated by the scarcity of food and employment opportunities were displaced into acts of pillage, riot, and arson. The urban riots and attacks on farms were motivated both by frustration and malice. The assaults on large farms, which often terminated in arson, reached a peak during June 1817, the same month in which cereal prices reached their highest level. The landowners in the rural countryside of Ghent slept fully clothed with weapons at hand in order to defend themselves againat ravaging bands of vagrants.[51] Large-scale attacks on urban bakeries and markets also broke out in June. Bakers' shops were looted in Bruges, Courtrai, and Louvain, but military force prevented the pillaging of grain storehouses. A military detachment numbering 5,000 was necessary to prevent the looting of the market hall at Namur.[52] At Mons, after a crowd had looted the market and threatened to pillage the grain storehouses, the town was forced to shut its gates and to train its cannon at several thousand workmen who had deserted their jobs on the nearby fortifications and approached the gates. Whether the men actually intended to invade the town is problematical, but the account received wide circulation in the European press. Market disorders multiplied at Bruges, Ghent, and Antwerp; the latter town had to call out the military garrison to restore order when crowds of rioting women looted bakeries and potato storehouses.[53]

The anniversary celebration of the battle of Waterloo turned out to be an occasion for extensive food rioting in Brussels. Apparently, the Belgian population used this event as an opportunity to register public protest. After a series of market disturbances had broken the peace, the prince of Orange appealed to the crowd for restraint and promised the demonstrators the bread that they demanded. While the speech had some effect in reducing the scale of the rioting, the army still proved necessary to protect the larger bakeries in the city. The disturbances ceased only when the promised grain arrived in Brussels to be offered for sale at a price below the market.[54] There is no question that political discontent was also present in the Belgian riots, but neither did the Dutch towns of Rotterdam and The Hague escape riots, looting, and popular price-fixing, which in turn necessitated military force to restore and maintain order.[55] Again, lower food prices proved to be the only effective solution. Almost all of the rioting ended in the Netherlands when grain prices declined as large cereal shipments arrived from the Baltic in the early summer of 1817. The last significant popular protest occurred at Brussels on July 14.[56]

While the popular disturbances in the Netherlands correlate with the rise and fall of the price of grain, and in a way can be explained by the subsistence crisis, it is clear that the food riots of 1817 contained not only a measure of political discontent but also reflected the timeless grievances that were common to all preindustrial societies. Political and social dissatisfaction was particularly rife in the Belgian provinces, where by far the most serious public disorder was found. Belgians opposed to union for either political, religious, or cultural reasons made use of the subsistence crisis to advance their opposition. They accused the Dutch royal ministers of conspiring with the merchants of Amsterdam and Rotterdam to forestall the grain market and, in the process, to starve the Belgian population. Although the King attempted to minimize the political dangers in his public statements, public disorder reached a scale where foreign diplomats regarded the social protest as a test of the government's ability to maintain the union.[57] In retrospect, the inability to avert serious riots in the Belgian towns did not augur well for the future of the united kingdom of the Netherlands.

The wave of European popular disturbances reached a crescendo in France during the month of June. As in Belgium, the disorders incorporated a measure of rebellion, in this case founded principally on nostalgia for the recent imperial past. Armed bands ravaged the countryside in the Ile-de-France, Champagne, Burgundy, Nivernais, and Orleanais, forcing communes to arm in self-defense. A veritable *jacquerie* unfurled on the markets and then spread into the rural districts to pillage farms. Observers did not fail to allude to the atmosphere of the Great Fear of 1789.[58] In eastern France, the price of provisions advanced to levels that became inaccessible to a majority of the working population. But there was no invariant correlation between the local severity of the subsistence crisis and the degree of social protest. For example, even though the departments located in Alsace and Lorraine experienced the most threatening famine conditions, this region witnessed few serious riots; either the desperate food shortage or the presence of a foreign army of occupation dampened popular disturbances. Relative proximity to Paris seems to have been the major variable that determined the nature of the demonstrations. Provisions had to be transported into Paris in order to maintain the precautionary policy of low bread prices in the capital; and this considerable operation could not be concealed from the anxious inhabitants of neighboring departments. At the same time, the decision to accord Paris privileged treatment aggravated the security problem created by the vagrant bands, since it attracted provincials who lived within traveling distance of the capital.[59] Faced with unappealing alternatives, the government concluded that the Parisian population represented a greater potential danger to public security than the vagabonds. Nonetheless, the dearth promoted a large enough influx of migrants into the capital to create the threat of famine in Paris itself. This immigration was responsible for the general Parisian census that was taken in 1817.[60] This count returned a total population of 713,966, among which 84,461 persons, or 11.5 percent, were classified as destitute.[61]

The vagrant bands that operated in the region surrounding Paris merged into still larger groups and then pursued activities which came close to insurrection. On June 3, a band numbering 5,000 persons seized control of the town of Château-Thierry in the department of Aisne, and once again the national guard refused to intervene. The rebels emptied the food storehouses and then intercepted the grain boats moving on the Marne River. After the government forces regained control of the town, the insurrection spread into the countryside. Communes within a three- to four-league radius of Château-Thierry likewise rose in rebellion, and peasants armed themselves with sticks, bayonets, and sabers. A military force called into action fired on the insurgents only with reluctance; several peasants were killed and wounded, but the remainder withdrew and carried on a campaign of plunder and murder in the countryside. In an attempt to ease the crisis, on June 7, the subprefect at Château-Thierry made it mandatory for every farmer and grain merchant to turn over a given quantity of wheat, otherwise he threatened to place the grain trade under military control. Identical disturbances took place in the northern districts of the department, where the prefect also violated the law by requisitioning grain from the markets, in the hope of heading off a general rebellion in the *arrondissements* of Saon and Soissons. A series of riots and demonstrations ensued nevertheless, in which persons were killed, wounded, and arrested. All of the peasant bands were finally dispersed by June 13, but only a total of twenty-eight arrests were made.[62]

These popular movements were duplicated in the department of Aube, where 6,000 peasants rioted at the market of Bar-sur-Aube on May 31. Farms in the surrounding rural area were also attacked. Regular army troops were called upon to pacify the district when the number of police proved inadequate. Several armed clashes occurred near Troyes, and the national guard repulsed a direct assault against the town on June 5. The market at Sens in the neighboring department of Yonne was looted in a similar pattern on May 30; the rioters invaded the countryside and attacked farms after being driven from the town. An army garrison was stationed at Sens when the armed bands continued to threaten the market, and this force probably prevented further bloodshed by discouraging 3,000 armed peasants from invading the town.[63] These accounts of riot and rebellion in the rural districts around Paris could be multiplied.

Neither location along the grain transportation routes to Paris nor a shortage of provisions was principally responsible for the grave public disorder that became rife in the department of Seine-et-Marne. La Brie, as the region was called, was in fact a major wheat exporting district and was expected to assure the food supply of Paris and to provide cereals for Champagne and Burgundy. Wheat production in 1816 remained in excess of local consumption needs, even though grain yields declined. But in those departments where grain production was invariably below local needs famine conditions were inevitable. Consequently, the demand for wheat rose in Brie, not only because of the needs of anxious neighboring departments and the grain orders of the public authority responsible for supplying Paris, but in 1817, also from the needs of the general commissary attached to the army of occupation. As grain producers became aware that larger profits could be realized from sales outside the department, less wheat was sold in the Briard markets and more wheat was shipped out quietly at night. The poorer segment of the population, both urban and agricultural day-laborers, were well aware of the department's food resources, however, and had no intention of allowing their wheat to nourish strangers while they died of hunger. The subsistence crisis reached a critical stage in May 1817, when the price of bread in Brie advanced to 0.75 francs per kilo, which represented the culmination of a steady rise from 0.31 francs in January 1816. Consumers blamed farmers and grain merchants for the dearth and voiced demands for the expulsion of the agents serving the Paris grain reserve and the occupation forces; they also insisted upon grain requisitions, price controls, and government regulation of the market. The Paris ministry adhered to the policy of free trade in grain, nevertheless, and justified this position by recalling the failure of the price controls attempted under the empire. The government also maintained that a dearth was now an impossibility. Appeals were made for patriotic support of the free-trade policy and for loyalty to the king; but at the same time peasant producers were reminded of the ugly prospects that would ensue if the population found empty markets and filled barns.[64]

An increasing number of vagrants inundated Seine-et-Marne in 1817, and as in other departments they solicited charitable assistance in the agricultural districts. While some of the beggars were destitute urban workers, the majority were rural people from Brie who were being reinforced by country people from neighboring departments. After a period of peaceful begging punctuated only by minor market brawls, the public disturbances turned into grave incidents at the end of May. Riots broke out in the market towns of Provins, Donne-Marie, Coulommiers, and Ferté-Gaucher, and these events were paralleled by a violent assault on the countryside. Country people who were threatened with starvation and who hoped to find food somewhere made up the backbone of these bands. According to the prefect, the influx of destitute people into Brie "could only be compared to an invasion or perhaps the migration of an entire nation."[65] Force became commonplace; bands of vagabonds smashed down doors or scaled walls, carried away bread and flour, abused, terrorized, and even threatened to shoot victims. The disorders spread into every canton; some of which were described as being *en insurrection*. The subprefect at Meaux estimated that the pillaging bands numbered more than 8,000 members. The wheat country of Brie found itself, in effect, a besieged citadel.[66]

The Paris press could no longer ignore the mounting anarchy and sedition, but by no means were the true dimensions of the turbulence reported. The *Moniteur* and *Quotidienne* for the most part simply reprinted the accounts that appeared in the *Journal des Maires,* the official publication of the Ministry of Police. These accounts not only tended to minimize the gravity of the social upheaval but they also adopted a tone of unrealistic optimism concerning the possibility of an immediate end to the crisis. The reports also repeated the message that France expected every subject in fortunate circumstances to contribute toward that end. But an official policy that insisted on public secrecy and that continued to maintain that a dearth was an impossibility created, in fact, popular beliefs which were inimical to public order. The unmistakable evidence of the prevailing dearth in the face of government assurances led to popular belief in the existence of hidden exports going abroad and of vast, underground supplies at home; the evidence also led to the conviction that persons in public office were creating the shortage of grain, for purposes usually not made clear. The official position, which held that a subsistence crisis did not really exist, and that as long as everyone obeyed the law and followed instructions there would be no shortage of grain, could only encourage the population to look for the guilty ones when the assurances fell through.[67]

Public officials contributed to the social disarray with their unfounded suspicion that the popular demonstrations were, for the most part, politically inspired. The Bonapartists were indicted most frequently, but the ultra-royalists were not above suspicion. No doubt many of the rioters were animated by nostalgia for a happier past, as well as by present grievances and the hope of economic relief. Former Napoleonic veterans, for example, made use of these occasions to indulge their seditious inclinations. Moreoever, even if political considerations were in large part submerged under subsistence anxieties, the official dearth policies were bound to produce political reaction when the food shortage became undeniable. As Richard Cobb has pointed out, in 1795 the choice was between bread and the Constitution of 1793, on one hand, and bread and long live Louis XVII, on the other, while in 1816 the dearth went to the tune of bread and *vive l'Empereur*.[68] Bonaparte's name was in fact invoked in almost all of the riots.[69] And if, for example, the authorities in Seine-et-Marne were predisposed to discover a Bonapartist uprising, there were numerous episodes to confirm these expectations. In May, when rumors that the government was selling wheat to England were circulating, a genuine conspiracy was uncovered; the conspirators planned to seize control in Brie and then to march on Paris. But the subsequent judicial proceeding established that the conspirators' goals did not go beyond the institution of controlled bread prices, the right to work, and freedom, even though the account mentioned insults to the king and stated that the defendants were staunch Bonapartists. At the same time, the evidence indicates that the vagrant bands who attacked the grain convoys bound for the famine-struck eastern departments had strong Bonapartist loyalties. It seems reasonable that public officials might have become wary of the political implications of the massive disturbances in the Paris region, where insurgent bands moved from farm to farm, not only stealing and looting but burning and killing. Moreover, the countryside was not pacified until July, and then it proved necessary to organize mobile military columns for 30 leagues around Paris to assure public security.[70] But in retrospect it is clear that social rather than political protest was uppermost and, even though a trace of sedition can be found in the popular disturbances, that the rioters were urged on by the primary instinct of hunger.

An examination of the events that made up the most explicitly political movement, the Lyons conspiracy of 1817, supports this conclusion. The city of Lyons had been stirred up politically by the unsuccessful Rosset conspiracy of January 1816, by the execution of the Bonapartist General Mouton-Duvernet on July 25, and by the beginning of the Rosset trial on August 26. Public protests remained within bounds, however, limited to some angry outbursts and posters hostile to the king. The majority of the Lyonnaise officials, magistrates, and the national guard held ultra-royalist political views, as did the commander of the military forces and the *maire* of Lyons. By contrast, the moderate ministerial royalists were few in the department of Rhône, and they tended to side politically with those of liberal leanings, who were recruited among merchants, manufacturers, half-pay officers, and other persons discontented with the restored Bourbon monarchy. Lyons also harbored a political party that was staunchly Bonapartist and revolutionary.[71]

Rumors of Napoleon's impending return surfaced in the early months of 1817. The Lyonnaise authorities suspected a purposeful conspiracy and maintained an untiring surveillance. The population of Lyons suffered through the subsistence crisis in the midst of this political and psychological atmosphere. Bread was lacking or very expensive, and the food shortage grew worse from week to week. By May the price of bread had already doubled, and to avoid a further increase, the municipal authorities voted to subsidize the bakers by levying a capital tax on the propertied inhabitants.[72] This measure was dictated in part by fear of revolt, for Lyons was paralyzed by a general economic depression; a large majority of the textile workers found employment only three or four days a week, and wages now ranged from 1.50 to 2.00 francs, instead of the customary 3.00 francs per day.[73] Nevertheless, in contrast to the departments in the Paris region, Rhône remained relatively untroubled through the month of May. But, as in the Paris region, the low price of bread in Lyons (0.35 francs per pound) compared to the price in the surrounding villages (0.55 francs) became progressively intolerable to the rural population. The government found itself confronted by a rural insurrection on June 8, in large part because it was unwilling or unable to subsidize bread prices in the villages and to avert trouble as it had in Lyons. Two days earlier, on June 6, the subprefect had observed that "the excessive price of bread and of all kinds of provisions has been the principal cause that has set off the ill-will likely to spur on the agitation in the country."[74] The urban assistance that was supposed to come to the rural rebels from Lyons itself miscarried and never materialized.[75]

The "Conspiration de 1817" was not an especially menacing rebellion, but the events brewed a political storm in France. The ultra-royalists believed that they had successfully thwarted a Bonapartist conspiracy, while their opponents saw the matter as a plot engineered by the Ultras to dupe France and to victimize the department of Rhône. Liberals charged that no real danger had confronted the local authorities, who, in an attempt to convince the Paris government of the existence of a genuine threat, had perpetrated a horrible tragedy which had terrified and bloodied an entire region. According to the departmental provost, on the other hand, the political situation in fact paralleled the events of March 1815; in spite of proof of a Bonapartist conspiracy in 1815, no precautionary measures had been taken and Napoleon was successful in returning to France. As far as the provost was concerned, Lyons had become the center of a conspiracy that planned to get rid of the monarchy.[76] The prefect of Rhône, even though also convinced of the existence of a seditious conspiracy, recognized the primary role that the subsistence crisis played in the rural uprising.[77]

The Paris government interpreted the Conspiration of 1817 in a similar way. The versions of the insurrection that appeared in the *Journal des Maires* cited the subsistence crisis as instrumental to the conspiracy. "There was an attempt to persuade the peasants that the entire kingdom was in insurrection; that Paris had given the signal; that to have bread at three *sous* per pound it was only a matter of overthrowing the government; and that to overthrow it sounding the tocsin was sufficient."[78] Even though the Paris administration concluded that the disturbances stemmed primarily from the dearth, the authorities recognized that social agitation could easily acquire a political character. It was acknowledged that as the misery deepened, many rural workers (always more imbued with Bonapartism than their urban counterparts) would perhaps see no other remedy than a return of the emperor, who after all had lowered bread prices in 1812. Other observers simply believed that the ultra-royalist officials had overreacted to the threat.[79] While the minister of justice believed in a Bonapartist conspiracy furthered by the subsistence crisis, he also remained convinced that the proceedings before the provost court had resulted in too many convictions and in excessively severe sentences. The court tried 118 defendants and convicted 79 of them, 12 of whom were sentenced to death, 24 transported abroad, and 40 sent to penal servitude. The minister of justice was able to reduce some penalties the following year when spirits were calmer.[80]

Even if the subsistence crisis was fundamental in promoting the rebellious disorders, the political uneasiness of the royal ministry and the ultra-royalists seems justified by French history. Memories of the Hundred Days were still fresh, and some officials believed that a more precautionary policy in 1815 might have prevented the return of Bonaparte. Moreover, anxious officials were uncertain whether the disturbances represented a reenactment of the politically innocent food riots of 1775 or were a rehearsal of the events that took place during the winter of 1788. Further, as observed above, the memory of peasant *jacqueries* had by no means lost its terror. The communications at hand in 1817 offered no method of assessing the dangers realistically. Appropriately, the Paris ministry tried to maintain security and to preserve a semblance of order without driving anxious rioters into the camp of political rebels by resorting to excessive measures of suppression. Simultaneous popular disturbances in neighboring European states could only have added to the fears of political insurrection in France.

At the same time, the French disturbances help to place the postwar demonstrations in Britain in better historical perspective. While historians have recognized the correlation of public disorder with the subsistence crisis in Ireland, the postwar unrest in Britain has been almost exclusively connected with early industrialization and the unemployment that resulted from stagnation in trade and manufacturing. Some historians have emphasized the paramount influence of the political reform movement in the genesis of these disturbances, another milestone, so to speak, in the attempt of the British working classes to achieve fuller social equality. Not that the special position of the subsistence crisis is ignored, but the dearth is perceived as incidental rather than instrumental to the demonstrations.[81] It is undeniable that the more developed economy and the unique events of English history resulted in the precocious appearance of class consciousness in Britain. It is also true that Luddism and an embryonic political discontent among the working population cast the British disturbances in a somewhat different mold from those on the Continent. For all that, it is striking that public disorder and social protest in the United Kingdom bore a remarkable resemblance to the popular disturbances observed elsewhere in Europe.

The timing of the British demonstrations and disturbances also coincided with those on the Continent. When cereal prices began to decline at the end of June, *The Times* not only looked forward to the end of public disorder but made clear that the subsistence crisis was the essential driving force behind the protest movements:

It is not without reason that "peace and plenty" has been adopted by the common sense of mankind as a natural, and familiar, and undivided expression; for sure we are, that what it has now become the fashion to nick-name insurrection against the Government, is an affair much more of the stomach than the brain; and that a quartern loaf at 1s. 8d. is the most mischievous weapon that can be placed in the hands of the new militia, just regimented for home service during peace.[82]

But more than food rioting was involved, and the level of social protest became a grave political concern after the mass demonstrations at Spa Fields in November and December. Working-class distress coupled with the revival of political reform agitation convinced the officials responsible for public security that rebellion was in the wind. The government suspended the right of Habeas Corpus in February 1817, and adopted a series of measures aimed at potential sedition, but the menacing popular disturbances continued until the harvests of 1817. At the well-known meeting of 10,000 or more persons in Manchester on March 10, it was resolved that a part of their number should proceed to London to petition for relief. In effect, the protest turned out to be a hunger march of weavers, each man with a blanket on his back, to win the support of the Prince Regent for measures to alleviate the stagnation of the cotton trade. The petitions failed to mention political demands. Some six or seven hundred weavers began the journey; the majority of them were intercepted almost at once, however, and ultimately only one "Blanketeer" reached London. Still, the popular agitation continued; the climax occurred in June with the Derbyshire rising, the so-called Pentrich Revolution, an insurrectionary movement that planned to storm the town of Nottingham. This abortive rebellion took place at the peak of the subsistence crisis at a time of severe economic distress.[83] The Pentrich Revolution paralleled on a smaller scale the Conspiration de 1817 in the department of Rhône. Then, as on the Continent, the public disorder in Britain virtually ceased on the eve of the harvests. The political content of these popular disturbances has been exaggerated by bracketing them exclusively with the British working-class movement; the demonstrations were tied up with and cannot be understood apart from the European subsistence crisis.

The seditious elements of the postwar disorders have in fact been exaggerated almost everywhere in Europe. The Breslau "insurrection" of August 23, 1817, represents another case of misplaced emphasis; a rebellion threatened when municipal artisans refused to be bound by the Prussian militia oath. After the mutiny was put down, it was determined that the workers' resistance was based on the fear of destitution for their families in the event of active service, because of the high price of provisions.[84] The point can be made even stronger by examining all of the facets of the White Terror in postwar France. This program of political repression soon became involved in suppressing the popular disturbances engendered by the subsistence crisis. The special provost courts that had been instituted to foster the prosecution of political opponents also held jurisdiction over common law crimes. According to a study of the judicial aspects of the White Terror, no more than 265 of the 2,280 cases which came before the provost courts in a two-year period can be considered political prosecutions. Some 1,560 cases concerned only common law crimes, which had been within the jurisdiction of the special courts under the Empire. A total of 237 cases involved seditious speeches or writings and the display of the tricolor. An additional 28 cases of a political nature are included among the offenses clasified as "armed rebellion" and "seditious assembly." Except for the 28 cases that specifically involved political protest, the 243 cases classified as armed rebellion, the 173 cases charging defendants with seditious assembly, and the 65 cases of "murder by armed bands" were in fact concerned with such offenses as attempts at popular *taxation* of grain, resistance to tax collectors, attempts to prevent shipments of grain, and cutting wood in public forests.[85] Moreover, after 1816 few persons were the object of police measures for political reasons;[86] the provost courts evolved into an agency for dealing with crimes arising from the subsistence crisis.

Persons who were arrested in the market disturbances were invariably turned over to the provost courts for criminal prosecution.[87] The provost court at Besançon, for example, adjudicated far more cases arising under common law crimes than offenses involved with sedition. Moreover, it was not unknown to violate the sedition laws in order to be remanded to jail, where at least food was available. Rather than being an instrument of political reprisal, the provost court in Doubs became a kind of *cour d' assises* made necessary as a result of the crime wave peculiar to the subsistence crisis.[88] While political disaffection was not absent from the popular disturbances and protest movements that swept postwar Europe, the seditious element must be seen in perspective and relegated to a distant second place.

BEGGARS AND VAGRANTS

In the regions of Europe that escaped organized demonstrations and riots, the severity of the subsistence crisis nevertheless set on foot hundreds of thousands of beggars and vagrants, who were urged on by the demands of hunger. Instead of a case of anxiety being displaced into collective violent action, their fears were translated into begging and petty theft. Switzerland, southwestern Germany, Italy, Ireland, the Habsburg Monarchy, and the Balkan peninsula were inundated by beggars and vagabonds, whose numbers became monumental in the late spring of 1817. As mentioned, in central Europe the year 1817 was known as the year of the beggars. But the states of northwestern Europe also saw a considerable number of beggars and vagrants, particularly in those areas where the shortage of food was acute. Even when vagrants did not combine into large marauding bands, as in the Paris region, vagabondage was always an object of grave concern for preindustrial administrations whenever distress was widespread. A genuine vagrant who absented himself from the local workhouse became a virtual outlaw in France; vagrants were made the responsibility of the commune from which they originated, and in times of distress local authorities were required to furnish relief and work to keep them tied down to one location.[89] In 1817, however, the number of vagabonds in France proved too large for effective supervision, and, in spite of repeated administrative efforts, vagrants were able to form the ravaging bands which evolved into the most menacing of all the popular disturbances.[90]

The adequacy of relief measures and the severity of the food shortage, as well as the effectiveness of the police, determined whether the number of beggars and vagabonds grew to critical proportions in northwestern Europe.

Because the food shortage remained moderate in western France, the disturbances were limited chiefly to urban grain market scuffles. In the Dutch provinces of the Netherlands, where the shortage of grain was more severe, adequate public relief and stern security measures confined the public disorder to a few urban food riots. In the Belgian provinces, where the subsistence crisis was more pressing and where both relief and security measures were less effective, the urban demonstrations that focused on the high price of provisions were larger, more violent, and more threatening; but also the number of vagrants increased in the rural districts, where they carried out the pillaging of large farms and indulged in premeditated arson. England also witnessed large-scale urban demonstrations and rural arson, but on a less concentrated scale than in Belgium. On the other hand, the cities and large towns of northwestern Europe were more or less successful in furnishing adequate relief and sufficient work opportunities to keep their inhabitants tied down and thus to minimize the number of beggars and vagrants. This was the consequence of a higher level of economic development and the more rationalized administrations in northwestern Europe, which, at least in the urbanized locations, provided workhouses, public welfare, and private charity. To take Liverpool as an example, some 1,667 persons were counted in workhouses during the winter of 1817, and an additional 20,000 out of a population of 100,000 were being maintained at the expense of the parish.[91] Needless to say, relief resources of this magnitude were not available in the rural parishes and were wholly inadequate in rural Ireland.

But even when large numbers of industrial workers fell into destitution in London and Paris, a combination of public assistance and private charity eliminated the hordes of beggars and vagabonds that troubled cities in central Europe in 1816–17. The London silk-weaving center of Spitalfields, for example, counted from 20,000 to 30,000 unemployed weavers at the end of 1816, according to evidence presented to the Committee of Police.[92] Weavers were forced to sell or pawn their furniture, bedding, clothes, and even looms, and, as a last resort, to desert their homes.[93] While London no doubt had a considerable number of vagrants, the evidence does not indicate the extensive begging reported in continental cities during the subsistence crisis; in fact, neither London nor other English cities and towns saw large numbers of beggars and vagabonds. This problem was not absent, however, and it was apparently serious enough to prompt a correspondent of *The Times* to propose public dormitories as a means of alleviating the distress of homeless, destitute persons who were seen "wandering during these inclement nights in our streets, in our fields, and like the wretched Chinese, even in rafts upon our rivers."[94]

In the regions of the United Kingdom and France where the subsistence crisis was as severe as in central Europe, by contrast, the number of beggars and vagrants not only constituted a grave social problem but on occasion threatened public security, since vagabonds were compelled to live either by begging or by crime. Famine spawned enormous numbers of beggars in Ireland and in the eastern provinces of France. Begging and vagrancy also became rife in Scotland and Wales, but on a reduced scale. North Wales was somewhat of an exception, however; according to a farmer in Anglesey, "Beaumaris gaol and castle together would not have held the swarm of tramps and beggars had the Vagrancy Laws been strictly applied."[95] Vagabonds roamed through the countryside of Cardiganshire in the winter of 1817 begging for food and looking for work at farmhouses and at the homes of gentry. Beggars and vagabonds were numerous everywhere in North Wales.[96] In Scotland, the large number of poor Irish immigrants who made their way to Glasgow posed a serious vagrancy problem. Stockades in fact were erected at Glasgow in 1818, "in order to prevent Irish and other disorderly persons from going about." Later, a subscription fund was opened to deport Irish migrants. These steps were connected in part with a program to control the prevailing typhus epidemic.[97] The Council Chamber of Aberdeen also acted to suppress begging in order to prevent the spread of typhus into middle- and upper-class homes.[98]

British beggars were few in number, however, compared to Ireland and eastern France, where the rural scene resembled that of central Europe. Because of the severity of the dearth in eastern France, the relief measures that were in part aimed at minimizing begging and vagabondage had in fact an opposite result by encouraging the destitute to leave their communes in hope of doing better elsewhere.[99] Travelers reported swarms of beggars in Burgundy in 1817: "beggars, very numerous yesterday, have increased greatly; at every stage a crowd of women and children and of old men, gather round the carriage."[100] Thomas Raffles, traveling in France with his famous cousin, found the level of mendicancy less grim in Burgundy than in Ireland: "We have seen many beggars on the road, but certainly not so many as I expected, and by no means as many as besiege the traveler in Ireland." But when the party reached Franche-Comté, they found a greater number. "The only unpleasant circumstance in crossing the Jura and which bespoke the deep poverty of the people, was the great increase of beggars. They were chiefly children, and their number and their importunity were truly astonishing."[101] Begging continued to be a public concern in eastern France for the balance of 1817, but the number of beggars and vagabonds declined with the price of bread.[102]

Begging and vagabondage assumed higher proportions in Ireland, where the hardship caused by the subsistence crisis was appalling. In the northwest, peasants took to the shore to gather mussels and the remains of fish. Many hundreds of families with small holdings in the mountains of Tyrone were compelled to abandon their homes in the spring of 1817 in order to subsist by begging. The number of beggars and vagabonds increased as people began to search for nettles, wild mustard, and cabbage-stalks to stay their stomachs.[103] As Dr. William Harty summed it up:

... fuel scarce and dear; farmers generally failing in consequence of the change from war to peace; beggars passing through the country in crowds, seizing on provisions; great deficiency of employment, and scarcely any manufacture in their towns; the want of food so pressing, that seed potatoes were taken up from the ground and used for the support of life; nettles and other esculent wild vegetables *eagerly* sought after to satisfy the cravings of hunger; influx of strangers to such a degree that it was emphatically said, "the whole country was in motion," and female mendicants often carrying about in their arms children suffering from fever.[104]

The poor of the country, especially those in the districts where the well-to-do population was small, crowded to the towns in search of food and employment.

Many states in central Europe, however, witnessed an even higher density of beggars and vagabonds during 1817. Parallel to the experience in northwestern Europe, some German states saw more vagrants than others. In southwestern and central Germany, the incidence was so great that the press was aroused. Newspaper editors collaborated to put pressure on public officials to end "the immense degree of begging" which had "reached disgraceful proportions" in every state where it was tolerated.[105] German communities that instituted effective relief programs to feed their destitute found, like those in France, that they also ran the risk of attracting hordes of beggars from the countryside. Beggars began to appear in Munich, for example, before the end of 1816: "Already the advance guard of the approaching enemy manifested itself; beggars appeared from all directions, as if they had crawled out of the ground."[106] The Bavarian government reacted by instituting compulsory workhouses on November 17, 1816; and a few days later ordered strict procedures for dealing with native beggars and vagrants. First offenders were threatened with fourteen days of detention or with corporal punishment. For second offenders the penalty could be increased to four weeks' incarceration and more severe corporal punishment. Nonindigenous beggars apprehended within the kingdom were to be whipped and then confined for at least four months and possibly as long as a year.[107] The enormous number of beggars and their seemingly outrageous behavior dictated analogous measures in nearly all west German jurisdictions. Beggars not only stationed themselves at church doors, marketplaces, and other locations where the public passed, they combined into groups, knocked on the doors of homes, and even entered houses without permission.[108]

In fact, begging became a security problem in those states where the shortage of food produced genuine hunger; for example, in Württemberg, "One saw wandering around in the towns and villages persons who looked like cadavers, and among them multitudes of children crying out for bread. Hunger and unnatural food produced wretched and chronic ill health among some, outbreaks of frenzy among others; those in the most desperate condition deemed themselves no longer bound by the laws that are adopted for the protection of private property.''[109] Starving beggars and vagabonds often resorted to theft in desperation during 1817, and the complaints against them were universal. Beggars were as common in Baden as in eastern France;[110] and the grandduchy, like the Swiss cantons, also had to cope with the inevitable disorder that followed in the wake of Madame de Krüdener's chiliastic activities. Processions of pilgrims and unemployed workers flocked to her residence in Baden, where they added to the already huge population of beggars and vagrants.[111] The thousands of German, Swiss, and Alsatian emigrants traveling to the Netherlands by river and highway increased the number of beggars in Hesse-Darmstadt, since many lacked resources and sooner or later were reduced to begging. Mainz was a focal point in this movement, and as a result the burdens fell disproportionately on the town. By May 1817, one-third of the population of Mainz, or 8,000 persons, were in need of public assistance.[112]

The provinces of the Prussian Rhineland also adopted ordinances that prohibited begging, but, as elsewhere in west Germany, the number of beggars increased nevertheless. Communities like Cologne were reluctant to enforce the regulations in the midst of the subsistence crisis; instead they practiced such expedients as giving tokens rather than money to beggars; the tokens entitled the bearer to food that was distributed at designated stations. Cologne supported 1,030 indigent inhabitants by resorting to this camouflaged begging. After the worst months of the famine passed, however, public opinion demanded an end to mendicancy. The district of Cleves threatened to confine beggars in workhouses, and the other Rhineland districts also tightened up on regulations that prohibited begging.[113]

Begging and vagabondage were not a threat to social order either in northern or eastern Germany, where the subsistence crisis remained moderate. Effective municipal relief programs and the absence of rural overpopulation also contributed to this different result. Moreover, the northern and eastern German towns escaped much of the popular disorder that became so rife in Europe by adopting the necessary preventive measures as well as adequate relief programs. This generalization is less valid for the rural districts, however.[114]

The Austrian empire, by contrast, failed to escape the proliferation of beggars and vagrants, despite its manorial institutions. Thousands of families were reduced to begging by 1817 as the result both of the subsistence crisis and industrial stagnation, but numbers varied from province to province.[115] Begging became a chronic problem even in Vienna, where the authorities maintained police control by expelling outsiders and putting indigenous beggars on the public works projects.[116] Large numbers of artisans migrated from the highland to the lowland districts in search of work and bread during 1816. Moreover, these journeymen were described as merely the "forerunners of a far more numerous troop of beggars who sprang from the highlands."[117] The Hungarian lands were also "overrun with bands of beggars," particularly in Transylvania, where famine conditions were severe. It proved almost impossible to send relief to the remote districts, which were isolated by the Carpathian mountains.[118]

Beggars and vagrants were just as numerous in Italy, where roving crowds of destitute persons were believed to be chiefly responsible for the diffusion of epidemic typhus.[119] Roman authorities, like those in Vienna, mounted periodic campaigns to sweep the city of beggars and vagabonds.[120] Severe famine conditions and backward administrations both were responsible for the enormous number of beggars in Italy and Hungary; but in eastern Switzerland, the depth of the subsistence crisis itself gave rise to the even higher level of vagrancy, despite the fact that in contrast to Italy, Hungary, and Ireland this region boasted a measure of economic development and administrative modernization. The testimony of anxious onlookers leaves no doubt as to the unprecedented number of Swiss beggars.[121] The degree of social disintegration was unmistakable in the eastern cantons in the spring months of 1817:

... the perpetually increasing crowd of mendicants and vagabonds who menace the rights of property, and endanger the public health and safety, are to be every where expelled from those communes to which they do not rightly belong.... The general impression, however, is that the mass privation seems in no wise to diminish, and that hardships and sufferings may fairly be anticipated more grievous than have been experienced by the poor.[122]

This observation proved to be prophetic: A foreign traveler sojourning in Appenzell in June reported that "the number of beggars, mostly women and children is perfectly shocking,... manufacturers are without work, and it is impossible for them to procure food: they are supported by private and public charities, and distributions of economical soup."[123] Social and economic tensions were as drawn in St. Gall, where the stagnation of the cotton industry had left more than 30,000 women unemployed.[124] At the same time, beggars and vagabonds were relatively uncommon in the cantons of Zürich and Bern.[125]

By contrast, multitudes of people invaded the towns and villages of eastern Switzerland in search of food. Highways were clogged with hordes of destitute vagrants who were numerous enough to be mistaken for armies. Door-to-door beggars carried the stamp of famine; as Ruprecht Zollikofer expressed it, "the paleness of death in their cheeks," and a wild, benumbed look of desperation in their eyes.[126] Two-thirds of the 30,000 paupers counted in St. Gall and

Appenzell lived by vagrant begging. The instinct of self-preservation apparently eliminated any fear of criminal prosecution. "Neither sentries nor bailiffs nor policemen nor begging-ordinances were any longer respected; not even severe penalties were feared;—hunger and misery, instinct of self-preservation, and gross, often base temper engendered a far stronger command, which despised harsh measures as mere child's play."[127] Occasionally parents who were no longer able to provide food for their children cast them adrift to fend for themselves, in a nineteenth-century reenactment of the tale of Hansel and Gretel.[128]

Swiss observers commented on the number of crimes committed by beggars and vagabonds, and a rising rate of criminality has always been a concomitant of economic crisis. Systematic global crime statistics are scarce for this period, and the widespread social upheaval must have increased the percentage of undetected and unrecorded crimes; nevertheless, both the impressionistic and fragmentary statistical evidence indicate that a wave of crime ran parallel to the popular disturbances. The zeal with which offenders were prosecuted varied considerably from jurisdiction to jurisdiction, however. In Switzerland, where the severe famine gave rise to a great number of crimes, public officials seemed to make little allowance for exigencies. The most rigorous measures "against criminals of all classes" were reportedly "seconded by the affluent members of society, if any man can be really called affluent who is threatened with plunder from day to day."[129] This view was based on the conviction that Swiss society was beset by "increasing depravity, frauds, embezzlements of all kinds, pilfering of houses."[130] Offenders convicted of arson or robbery were beheaded in Appenzell, while those found guilty of lesser crimes against property were whipped. The accounts are similar for St. Gall, where it was reported that "crimes multiply with wants, the prisons are full, and executions frequent." Not even acts of human desperation were deemed to be extenuating, for three women were decapitated for the crime of infanticide.[131] Criminality kept pace with the rising price of subsistence in eastern Switzerland, but the number of suicides increased, as well as the executions for infanticide.[132]

A similar increasing level of criminality and violence is reported for Italy as the subsistence crisis deepened. Theft, robbery, burglary, assault, and homicide: crimes against property and crimes against persons multiplied. Accounts of the mounting danger confronting travelers in Italy circulated in western Europe. Bandits were so numerous in the Papal States that it was no longer possible to ensure the safety of travelers; and conditions were not much better in the Austrian provinces of Italy, where bandits attacked travelers and couriers in the environs of Milan. The Austrian countryside was also plagued by bandits.[133] In an attempt to reduce violent crime in Italy, the Austrian administration prohibited and attached severe penalties to the manufacture, sale, or possession of dangerous weapons in Lombardy–Venetia.[134]

In the German lands, according to Franz Schnabel, the postwar years witnessed a lack of public security that had not been seen since the seventeenth century.[135] But this public disorder neither began with the onset of the subsistence crisis nor ended with the return of lower food prices; nevertheless, crimes againat property multiplied during the period, and the crime rate increased with the incidence of vagrancy. Begging and vagabondage were tolerated in Germany in part on the assumption that they would subside with the subsistence crisis. As the disorder continued into 1818, however, propertied persons demanded harsher public action. These complaints were prompted by the wave of crime and intimidation which threatened the security of the rural villages and isolated farms.[136] As elsewhere in Europe, the subsistence crisis was accompanied by an upsurge of arson; and as early as May 1816, reportedly some fifty villages in Brunswick had been damaged by fires of malicious origin. A number of vagabonds were subsequently arrested and charged with arson.[137] Accounts of suspected arson continued through 1817; numerous dwellings were burned down in Franconia, for example, by bands of incendiaries.[138]

Arson, in fact, developed into an endemic European phenomenon during the subsistence crisis. Fires of suspicious origin also troubled the Belgian provinces, particularly during the spring of 1817. Substantial farms were reduced to ashes in the countryside near Brussels, Hermelgein, Grammont, and Ninove.[139] The incidence of arson which accompanied the subsistence troubles in England seems to have caused more anxiety than the food riots. The British press carried repeated accounts of incendiarism in England and France during 1816–17. The initial outbreak in England coincided with the East Anglian agrarian disturbances of May 1816, which elicited from *The Times* an observation that arson seemed to be motivated by "gratification of an unreflecting vengeance."[140] This generalization had some validity both for Britain and the Continent, for despite the shortage of grain in the markets, wheat stacks and grain barns were often put to the torch instead of being plundered. Other farm buildings and even dwellings were burned down. There was a sufficient number of victims in Britain to prompt a major insurance company to consider offering specific protection against loss from arson.[141] Before the wave of incendiarism subsided in the summer of 1817, suspicious fires had been reported in nearly every area of Britain.[142] Some rough quantitative measure of the increasing incidence of arson in Britain can be derived from the number of judicial commitments for this crime, which rose from 13 in 1815, to 33 in 1816, and to 30 in 1817, before dropping off to 21 in 1818.[143]

While it is difficult to construct systematic figures reflecting the increase in criminality, some quantitative measures are available because observers were struck by the rise in the crime rate. In Baden, for example, the number of criminal accusations for theft more than tripled from 1815 to 1817. Convictions for theft had increased everywhere in Europe.[144] *The Times* in Britain was impressed with the huge increase in the number of criminal commitments and observed that "at no modern period of British history, have the county gaols been crowded with so many prisoners of every description, or the labours of the Judges been so heavy, as during the circuits just terminated." Even if the statement that "the number of criminals tried and convicted has been three or even four times larger than usual"[145] seems to be exaggerated, the number of criminal commitments for simple larceny and larceny by servants did rise from 5,409 in 1815, to 9,396 in 1816. Total criminal commitments in England and Wales rose from 7,818 in 1815, to 13,932 in 1817, or an increase of 53.2 percent. This higher rate of criminality was reflected in nearly all crimes, including commitments for assault and riot. Finally, after a new rise of 5.1 percent in the number of criminal commitments during the depression year 1819, a moderate but steady decline in the crime rate established itself during the years of low food prices in the early 1820s.[146]

Observers in France also were struck by the increase in the crime rate during the subsistence crisis. Reportedly, the prisons of riot-torn Seine-et-Marne were bulging with accused persons in 1817. Yet, only thirty persons finally received prison sentences, usually running from five to ten years, though four defendants were sentenced to death.[147] This disparity between the number of arrests and the number of prison sentences was typical of the leniency of French officials toward crimes committed during the dearth. Moreover, this policy stands in sharp contrast to the harsh criminal justice dispensed in Switzerland. In the department of Eure, for example, where theft and looting had been commonplace, only 243 persons were indicted and tried before the courts; and then the majority of the penalties meted out were surprisingly light, ranging from one week to one year in jail. The harshest punishment, five years' imprisonment, was reserved for those defendants convicted of resisting authority with armed force.[148] In Doubs, where many cases of theft were simply not pursued, not every magistrate turned the other way, however. According to a count taken on March 3, 1818, 355 convicted criminals were serving penal sentences in the Besançon prison, which was an unusually high figure.[149] Inasmuch as the departments of Seine-et-Marne, Eure, and Doubs were the scene of extensive popular disorder, a large number of arrests might have been anticipated. But the rate of criminality also rose in the department of Meurthe, where popular disturbances were few. The monthly number of crimes scarcely varied from January 1816 to April 1817; however, when grain prices reached their peaks in the late spring of 1817, a noticeable increase in the cases of theft occurred. The prosecutions for theft brought before the courts climbed from 31 in 1816 to 184 in 1817, of which 127 represented arrests made from May to August 1817. Unlike the practice in Eure, the courts in Meurthe handed out harsh sentences for cases involving the theft of food, probably because of the critical shortage of grain in eastern

France. Convicted defendants often received prison sentences of five to seven years at hard labor, and even a term of solitary confinement.[150] Generalizations cannot be made from the experience of a handful of departments; but the global figures issued by the Ministry of Interior point unmistakably to a high correlation between the rate of crime and the course of grain prices. The annual number of defendants tried before the French courts in the postwar years increased as follows:[151]

1814	5,785
1815	6,551
1816	9,890
1817	14,084

These figures include only those cases brought before the regular *cours d'assises*, not the sentences pronounced by the special provost courts.

While it is true that the rising rate of criminality was a sign of social pathology, the French administration nevertheless followed a policy of limiting the number of arrests and the severity of penal sentences. Aside from the harsh sentences meted out in the Lyons' conspiracy, in which case it was believed that the crimes were politically inspired, criminal justice was dispensed as if the famine itself absolved the crimes it occasioned. On August 14, 1817, after the subsistence crisis was surmounted, the king pardoned all persons who had been convicted of crimes arising from the dearth, which was considered to have begun on September 1, 1816:

The zeal and firmness which our courts and tribunals have brought to the maintenance of public order has merited our approval; but our heart has groaned from the severities that justice and the law have commanded against a too large number of persons, who, in several parts of the kingdom, have been involved in criminal disorders through the scarcity and dearness of provisions. We feel the need not to confuse these unfortunates with the vicious men who would have tried, in some places, to push them into excesses whose most certain result was to aggravate their distress and to increase the ills of the state.[152]

The amnesty was consistent with the paternalistic view of justice held by old regime administrations; but despite the lingering traces of an old regime mentality in postwar France, the pardon also represented another gesture of conciliation on the part of the restored Bourbon Monarchy. Even though the press gave extravagant publicity to persons released under the law, the amnesty was still a genuine act of compassion.[153]

The subsistence crisis also kindled religious commotion in the Western world. Religious enthusiasm has been another indicator of social pathology, and in 1816–17 the more severe the distress the more intense the religious excitement, which evolved into chiliastic movements in central Europe, where tensions were highest. But wherever the popular disturbances engendered by the subsistence crisis stayed within bounds, the religious revival tended to be moderate. Not a hint of chiliasm appeared in America, for example; however, some measure of religious enthusiasm broke out in New England, where weather patterns were most anomalous and food in shortest supply. "An improved state of religious society became strikingly evident" in New Hampshire.[154] In fact, a heightened interest in religion accompanied by larger church attendance was observed throughout New England and New York. Deficient harvests generated an atmosphere of depression, particularly in the northern districts. Many towns "were received about the same time on the West side of the Green Mountains. In 1816 an uncommon gloom spread over the whole state . . . yet nothing appeared to promise a revival until September." The state of the harvest was responsible for the change of heart in September; and, then "in October 1816 an unusual earnestness in prayer was manifested among the members of the churches." These accounts can be multiplied for the villages of Massachusetts and New York.[155]

In Austria, by contrast, a chiliastic religious movement reflected the degree of social protest. A sect that advocated equality and community of property formed in Upper Austria; its prophet was a Roman Catholic priest named Pöschl, who preached the coming of the thousand-year *Reich*. The most lurid accounts of the sect's activities circulated in western Europe. Even *The Times* reprinted a report "that this sect sacrificed during Passion-week several men who died in the most horrible torments. A girl of 13 was put to death . . . on Good Friday."[156] Needless to say, none of these details had any basis in actuality. Nonetheless, Pöschl and eighty-six of his followers were arrested, and a military detachment was quartered in the disaffected villages. The German press also circulated exaggerated accounts of the social upheaval caused by the sect, claiming that "the Austrian Government has been obliged to send troops against the tumultuous assembly of the peasants, who are said to have formed a sect amounting to 10 or 12,000 persons."[157] In fact, Pöschl had encouraged the peasants to refuse to perform the traditional corvees.[158] The religious enthusiasm, which was called "Pöschlianismus," then spread its contagion into famine-stricken southwestern Germany.[159] This chiliastic movement, as has been true of the majority of such movements in European history, was inspired by the fusing of religious excitement with economic distress and social disaffection.

Accordingly, the famine in Switzerland proved a fruitful environment for the remarkable chiliastic projects of the famous Julie de Krüdener. The baroness had been expelled from Baden in January 1817 on the grounds that her religious activities constituted a threat to public order. The letter of protest which she directed to the official who had put an end to her work in Germany sums up the tenor of her religious message: "The time is approaching when the Lord of Lords will reassume the reins. He himself will feed his flock. He will dry the eyes of the poor, He will lead his people, and nothing will remain of the powers of darkness save destruction, shame, and contempt. . . . The Rhine rots with corpses; people, contrary to the law, are buying blood at butcher shops. Misery is rampant and menaces all our security.''[160] The Lady of the Holy Alliance soon became the center of a great uproar in Switzerland. The frightful distress helps to explain the missionary zeal of Julie de Krüdener, and her message was even more convincing because she could point to the widespread misery as an infallible sign of the imminent coming of Christ. She increased her persuasiveness, moreover, by distributing charity with an open hand. Her jewels were converted into a considerable fund, and this resource was supplemented by contributions from friends in Livonia, by the income from her own estates, and by large gifts from Swiss converts.[161]

A marked tendency toward religious enthusiasm, mysticism, and prophecy had already become commonplace in Switzerland;[162] thus Swiss authorities were concerned that the baroness' activities could only stimulate this predisposition. ''Krudianismus,'' as the movement was called, found the majority of its followers in the eastern cantons, where the famine was most severe; Madame de Krüdener combined public sympathy for the plight of Swiss paupers with predictions of the imminent end of the world. Because of the intense religious excitement, which was probably enhanced by malnutrition, an account of the baroness' success in feeding 900 persons with 19 loaves of bread was believed. In addition to performing seeming miracles, she also challenged the social order by protesting the harsh treatment meted out to Swiss beggars.[163] Not least of all, her charitable activities occasioned a popular uproar almost everywhere. ''The continually increasing number of idle and licentious vagabonds, who flocked partly from the neighboring cantons, partly from the more remote, to Madame de Krüdener, made it impossible for the police of Lucerne longer to suffer the disorder.''[164] A series of comparable experiences led to her banishment from Zürich, Schaffhausen, and other Swiss towns. By September she was back in Baden, where she was kept under close surveillance; her work was also curtailed by the exhaustion of her resources.[165] Julie de Krüdener continued to increase her unpopularity among Swiss officials by offering the poor and oppressed a sanctuary in the Caucasus, where Tsar Alexander was to establish a kingdom ordained by God.

EMIGRATION

The European subsistence crisis in fact revived large-scale emigration. Several hundred thousand desperate, or adventurous, Europeans responded to the increasing distress by seeking more favorable opportunities abroad, either in

America or in eastern Europe. The movement of tens of thousands of men, women, and children down the Rhine to Holland was the most conspicuous aspect of this exodus. Even though figures for international migrations are not available for these years,[166] it is nevertheless possible to determine the approximate number of emigrants from the fragmentary evidence. The evidence demonstrates also that the harvest failures of 1816 were the major variable which induced the new wave of European emigration in 1816–17. While it is true that the end of a quarter century of war had released pent up pressures for emigration, it is also clear that the rate of emigration fell off sharply when low-priced bread and ample harvests returned in the autumn of 1817.

The pattern of emigration from Switzerland shows these relationships in a distinct way. Two-fifths of the natural population increase had left Switzerland in the eighteenth century; but as the Swiss economy developed in the course of the century the flow of emigration slackened.[167] The new hope, stated bluntly, was to export textile manufactures and watches in place of Swiss soldiers. Because of this hope and because of the fear that artisans would disseminate abroad secrets essential to Swiss industrial competitiveness, a widespread hostility to emigration had developed by 1815.[168] Nevertheless, as the crisis deepened in 1817, the industrial cantons like Appenzell, St. Gall, Glarus, and Zürich were forced to bow to the inevitable. Moreover, the federal council accepted emigration, including mercenary service, as a necessity in 1817, in order to alleviate increasing pauperization. Glarus, for example, was supporting a quarter of its 28,000 inhabitants on public welfare in this year.[169]

America was the principal destination of the postwar Swiss emigrants and their main route was to travel down the Rhine to Holland.[170] But Tsar Alexander, who was interested in migrants as settlers in southern Russia, was successful in attracting a small number of Swiss emigrants to the Russian empire. Julie de Krüdener's promises to potential Swiss settlers remained vague because she had actually lost communication with Alexander by 1817; the tsar, however, employed her son-in-law, Baron Berckheim, as his agent in Switzerland. A small group of Swiss emigrants ultimately did settle in the neighborhood of Tiflis. An attempt to attract Swiss settlers to Poland proved no more successful. In his capacity as king, Alexander promised newcomers a six-year exemption from all public burdens and other concessions. Jews were explicitly excluded from this invitation. Despite cautionary statements issued by Swiss officials, hundreds of emigrants were attracted by the promises and crossed the frontier into Baden to begin the long journey. Because of the nearly insurmountable difficulties that eastward migrants faced, however, Swiss settlement in Poland remained numerically insignificant.[171]

Even the approximate numbers who made up the new wave of Swiss emigrants and mercenaries are difficult to ascertain. Among the considerable number who migrated from St. Gall and Appenzell, Zollikofer mentioned "a few thousand" youths who enlisted in French and Dutch regiments.[172] Between March 1 and May 28, 1817, the town of Mainz counted 14,385 emigrants who had originated from Baden, Alsace, Switzerland, and Württemberg, but the number of Swiss is not known.[173] In 1818 the Brazilian government approached Switzerland for settlers of the Catholic faith. Several cantons, in particular Freiburg, utilized this opportunity to drain off paupers. An emigration numbering 2,000 persons was organized to settle near Rio de Janeiro; but this New Freiburg enterprise eventually failed. The flow of Swiss emigrants subsided after 1819.[174] It is safe to conclude that Swiss postwar emigration numbered in the thousands, but it is doubtful if the figure reached as high as 20,000.

While the data on which French emigration for this period rest are also uncertain, figures of a kind are available for some eastern departments and they indicate extensive emigration after the harvest failures of 1816. In four departments located in Alsace and Lorraine, the number of passports requested in 1817 surpassed 20,000. But this figure underestimates French emigration, especially to continental destinations such as Prussia, Spain, and Russia.[175] Not only are the passport statistics incomplete for 1817; numerous persons, in addition, attempted to leave without any authorization.[176] For what it is worth, the British press claimed that 30,000 French migrants had arrived in the United States alone by the summer of 1817.[177]

The passports requested in the departments of Meurthe, Moselle, Bas-Rhin, and Haut-Rhin numbered 13,016 for the first half of 1817, the peak period of the subsistence crisis. The most frequent destinations listed were the Russian empire and North America. Agents for American emigration, who were commissioned by shipping firms in Amsterdam, offered French settlers not only transatlantic passage but the opportunity to become landowners as well. Competing Dutch shipping firms offered passage to French emigrants who were bound for eastern Europe.[178] French settlers also migrated to Germany; for example, some 4,000 passports were issued to Alsatians alone for emigration to the Rhine cantons of the Palatinate.[179] For the most part, the French emigrants did not leave urban occupations but were made up of agricultural day-laborers.[180]

At the same time, a significant number of French emigrants never reached their destinations. Some were forced to return from Amsterdam when they could no longer support themselves; some turned back when they learned of the deplorable conditions awaiting them in Amsterdam; others died during the journey, often undertaken in carts filled with children and oldsters. Returnees were generally destitute, and thus added to the burdens of local officials, who often had reservations about taking them back.[181] Then, the prospect of better harvests in 1817 reduced the number of passport applications after the month of June, and the number of departures dropped off accordingly. French emigration subsided in 1818; the subsistence crisis had prompted the migrations and favorable harvests terminated them.

The pattern of emigration from the United Kingdom followed the course of the postwar crisis in a more continuous way. An indication of the number of emigrants can be obtained from the record of British passengers from United Kingdom ports to extra-European states. These figures show a noticeable increase in 1816, and then continue to rise through 1819, which was of course a year of severe commercial depression in Britain. A decline did not appear until 1820, as the following table indicates:[182]

1815	2,000
1816	13,000
1817	21,000
1818	28,000
1819	35,000
1820	26,000
1821	18,000

British migration on balance was directed toward America and South Africa. Reportedly, "tens of thousands" of Englishmen migrated to the United States between 1815 and 1819, many of them originating from Yorkshire.[183] Thousands of demobilized veterans, moreover, migrated to Latin America to join insurgent groups; Simon Bolivar's forces were strengthened by at least 6,000 British volunteers before the end of 1818.[184] Also, a group of Scots' shepherds and small farmers accepted Tsar Alexander's liberal terms and settled in Poland.[185] Irish emigration to the United States and Canada rose from 6,500 in 1816, to 7,500 in 1817, and then to 20,000 in 1818, or a three-year total of 34,000. In 1816 and 1817 as many as two-thirds of the emigrants originated from Ulster, but in 1818 the majority came from the south of Ireland.[186] In Britain at least, the subsistence crisis as distinct from the general postwar depression was not so critical a variable in promoting emigration.

On the other hand, the subsistence crisis played a primary role in the wave of emigration from the Rhineland region of Germany. The revival of large-scale emigration also resulted from overpopulation and a tendency to religious separatism in southwestern Germany, but the timing of the movement points to the paramount influence of the famine. The majority of the migrants were fleeing from a worsening economic outlook. Informed contemporary observers, such as Hans von Gagern, who tried in vain to persuade the German *Bund* to take federal action to counter the social and political dangers inherent in the migrations, underscored the importance of the subsistence crisis in the sudden revival of emigration fever: "Owing to the harvest failures of 1816, the year 1817 was the last one in which the human race was afflicted by famine. Misery, want, and alarm appeared in many forms in all European lands, especially in Germany. Even though Germans had frequently been seized with the desire to emigrate in the past two centuries, now in 1817 it was on a much more intensified scale; but because of the cause there was less desire among the well-off and better classes."[187]

Predisposing causes also contributed to the new wave of emigration. As mentioned, rural overpopulation had become a basic difficulty in Baden, Württemberg, the Bavarian Palatinate, and the Prussian Rhineland. But this high population density vis à vis the productive capacity of the land was still manageable when harvest yields were favorable. Not even the combined impact of demobilization and the below-average harvests of 1815 collapsed the delicate balance between population and production.[188]

Nevertheless, as Mack Walker has pointed out, the margin for safety had become too precarious for persons engaged in subsistence agriculture. The progressive fragmentation of arable lands in southwestern Germany had resulted in holdings that were too small to support families. As a consequence, peasant families increasingly devoted more effort to domestic industry, particularly to weaving and the manufacture of wooden articles, in order to compensate for the deficiency of land. But this expedient lost much of its effectiveness when the postwar years brought commercial depression, as well as the competition of factory products. On the other hand, if the slump in the industrial market could be offset only by added peasant dependence on agriculture, it is clear that the harvest failures of 1816 came at an unpropitious time. For the majority of peasants the harvest deficiencies did not translate into windfall profits, rather they dictated entering the grain market as consumers at a time when prices were high and income opportunities low. Trapped between the inadequacies of agriculture and manufacturing, thousands of German families saw no solution but emigration.[189]

German emigration was part of the regional movement that gathered momentum in the Rhine valley at the end of 1816. As was the case in France and Switzerland, the migrants came from districts that were hit hard by the subsistence crisis. Geographical and political variables were also important, however; successful emigration depended on the availability of transportation and the concurrence of political authorities as well as economic means and the willingness to leave. Although the precise number of Germans who attempted to emigrate during the subsistence crisis is not known, it is clear that the majority originated from Württemberg and Baden, and that smaller numbers also left from the Palatinate, Rhenish Prussia, Nassau, and Hesse-Darmstadt.[190]

The total number of Germans who left permanently for North America during 1816–17 probably amounted to 20,000.[191] Including those who migrated to the Russian empire, the total figure exceeded 35,000—some 20,000 from Württemberg, 15,000 from Baden, and several thousand more from the Rhenish areas to the north.[192] Emigration from Württemberg in fact totaled 20,491 during 1816–17, exclusive of the period from August to October 1817, for which the records are missing.[193] It is also known that some 16,000 to 20,000 emigrants received permission to leave Baden.[194] No quantitative estimates are available for the other Rhineland states except for Nassau, where the number of emigrants amounted to 406 families and individuals.[195] But in measuring social upheaval, the number of Germans who *attempted* to emigrate is the more significant figure. Those who succeeded in leaving Germany permanently created fewer social and political problems than those who tried and failed. The latter either turned to begging and stealing, became stranded in foreign states, or returned home destitute—if they did not die en route. To take the case of Baden as an example: while 15,000 emigrated successfully, some 50,000 persons applied for permission to emigrate or simply tried to leave;[196] this latter figure represented nearly 5 percent of Baden's population. Although the number of unsuccessful migrants who actually reached Holland either by river or by highway is not known, reportedly, 30,000 Germans, Swiss, and Alsatians were stranded in Amsterdam alone in May 1817.[197]

Needless to say, the many thousands of migrants traveling down the Rhineland to Dutch ports caused a crisis in the Rhenish states, as the press accounts indicate:

Although a great number of emigrants from different Rhineland areas who wanted to make their way to America, but, who, devoid of all resources, have been unable to find any place on the ships in the Dutch ports and are now returning home by begging and are in the most deplorable state; and even though from all sides the most accurate information is being received concerning the tragic fate to which these unfortunates expose themselves even when they succeed in reaching the destination of their voyage; nevertheless, since the end of last month [i.e., April 1817] whole multitudes of emigrants with their families, especially with an unbelievable number of small children, have been leaving from the Rhineland to proceed to the New World.[198]

Mainz, owing to its location, was the first German town to experience the full onslaught of the migration. Many of the destitute migrants who made their way on foot pushed carts loaded down with family possessions. Because they lacked the money to pay for overseas transportation, poor migrants had no prospect of reaching America except as indentured servants. Indeed, they could not hope to reach Holland except by begging or stealing. By late spring the migration became a threat to public order, public security, and even to public health, particularly in the Prussian Rhineland.[199]

The disturbances occasioned by returnees proved even more menacing than the migratory movement down the Rhine. Thousands of poor German families had already accumulated in Amsterdam and other Dutch ports at the beginning of 1817. Since shipowners could not even accommodate emigrants with passage money, the destitute began to jam the poorhouses and streets in Holland.

Moreover, the long waiting period often exhausted the funds of emigrants who arrived with money for passage. Long before the emigration became a flood in the spring months, thousands of penniless Germans began the homeward trek, and in the process discouraged some of their countrymen who passed them on the way. The Dutch police, who were concerned with maintaining order and security, began to deport the destitute and to turn new arrivals back at the frontier. The majority of the returnees had to resort to begging in order to make their way home. The Prussian Rhenish provinces bombarded the Berlin government with complaints against the thousands of vagrant and stateless persons, who were now a threat to public security in the Rhine valley. Officials at Cleves suggested restricting all outsiders to designated highways as a method of preventing vagrants from wandering into the countryside.[200]

Despite the many hazards, returnees arrived back in their native states in numbers large enough to raise additional social and economic issues. The thousands of migrants who returned to Baden had to be supported by state welfare programs until they found a place for themselves, either in their old or in new communities. Returnees were not always restored to their former civic rights during the interim period, but remained dependents of the state.[201] In Nassau, however, the government insisted that returnees be accepted back by their former communities, in order to prevent them from falling into vagabondage.[202] While the number of emigrants who failed to reach America was larger than those who were successful, not all of the former became returnees. The mortality rate among the impoverished was high; for example, it was not unusual for 10 percent or more of a ship's passengers to die from typhus and other contagious diseases between embarkation in Holland and safe arrival in America. The *Zeeploeg*, which sailed from the Texel at the end of July with 500 German emigrants aboard, reported sixty deaths.[203] Even successful emigrants were described as "miserable wretches," and by one observer as arriving in America "in a more lamentable condition than that of the Lazaroni at Naples."[204]

The instrumental role of the subsistence crisis in promoting German postwar emigration can be documented from the evidence available for Württemberg. To begin with, despite a larger population and also a larger number of emigrants, Württemberg played a subordinate role to Baden in the account of Rhineland emigration to America. The majority of migrants who left Württemberg traveled to Russia; a glance at the destinations of 17,383 emigrants in 1817 indicates this eastward movement:[205]

Russian empire	9,233
North America	6,009
Austria	1,559
Prussia	43
Other German states	539

The migration to Russia stands in contrast to the Baden experience, in which no more than thirty-four persons joined the German settlements of 1816–17 along the Black Sea coast of the Caucasus region. Also, a thousand or so German emigrants settled in Poland.[206] Three principal reasons prompted Württembergers to migrate eastward. First, a tradition of Swabian emigration to southern Russia had taken hold in the eighteenth century. Second, the Romanov dynasty was connected with the ruling house of Württemberg, a relationship that facilitated Tsar Alexander's plans to populate his new lands with German settlers. Third, the Württembergers who had already emigrated to Caucasia maintained a special religious bond, which was grounded in a pietist separatist movement.[207] At the same time, the social and economic hardship produced an atmosphere that was propitious for chiliastic movements. The message of Baroness de Krüdener contributed to the religious enthusiasm; and the sect called ''Pöschlianer,'' which caused such commotion in Austria, won the largest number of its German converts where the borders of Bavaria, Württemberg, and Baden meet.[208] Economic motivations, nevertheless, outweighed religious enthusiasm as the reason for emigration. Mack Walker has suggested that famine made religious excitement more plausible and more substantial.[209] In any event, the reasons stated by the same 17,383 emigrants are available and they clearly indicate the paramount importance of economic discontent:[210]

> Economic 15,477
> Religious 963
> Marriage 623
> Kinship 320

Finally, it should be noted that the emigration to Russia, similar to the emigration to America, was attended by a large share of misfortune and failure.

Thus, the chief impetus for German emigration came from the subsistence crisis, fueled also by religious and political discontent.[211] Local officials and village authorities recognized that the exodus was a direct response to economic distress and the fear of hunger and, accordingly, recommended a policy of encouraging emigration; but policy-making officials continued to suspect that the real causes were to be found among foreign shipping agents, swindlers, and demagogues. State governments therefore pursued an ambivalent course, neither prohibiting nor promoting emigration, and also concerned themselves unduly with police action against agitators and dissemblers.[212] But as popular disorder mounted in spring 1817 nearly all German states tightened up on their willingness to issue emigration permits. Baden officially forbade further emigration after May 23; however, in most states the restrictions assumed the form of a financial means test. The Prussian government of Lower Rhine, moreover, closed its borders in May to all emigrants who lacked passage money. Further, the Russian government restricted emigration to settlers who held visas from Russian ambassadors. Finally, after June 15 the Dutch authorities refused admission to emigrants bound for the United States unless sponsored by an inhabitant of the Netherlands.[213]

In fact, mass German emigration ended more from the combined effect of lower food prices in the summer of 1817 and the spectacle of destitute returnees than from government prohibitions. Emigration fever died out after 1817 and failed to revive during the 1820s, a decade of low grain prices and higher real incomes. An appropriate emigration policy was simply not possible at this time in view of the large number of migrants. While local officials urged policy-makers to foster emigration as a means of easing public burdens, and also as a way to prevent crime and riot and to minimize begging, the central governments did little more than to temporize and improvise. Since adequate transportation was lacking and the majority of those hoping to emigrate were impoverished, state officials were uncertain of the outcome and also believed that any attempt to facilitate the movement had little chance of success.[214] Given the historical circumstances, subjects and governments alike were still at the mercy of all the elements of a preindustrial world.

Not even the New World escaped the migration fever that was inspired by the harvest failures. The United States witnessed a large-scale exodus from New England and a westward movement that paralleled the European migrations. This phenomenon has generally been perceived as an American episode, unrelated to the Western world's last great subsistence crisis. The westward movement has been accounted for by a combination of the well-known "pull" and "push" factors, the most common of the latter being overpopulation and soil exhaustion in the Atlantic states. But these two push factors offer no more than partial explanations, for they fail to account for the ebb and flow of westward migration during the postwar decades. After all, the 1820s saw the virtual cessation of westward migration, and unless it is claimed that the population of the coastal states declined or that the soil improved its fertility, explanations of this kind can be carried only so far. The postwar wave of westward migration can be more adequately accounted for by the anomalous weather patterns and their effect on agricultural productivity and commodity prices. This suggestion is not entirely new. Joseph B. Hoyt broached the possibility that long-run weather conditions have been overlooked in the history of American internal migration.[215] Earlier still, Arthur C. Boggess identified the postwar depression and crop failures, together with the cold weather, as major ingredients in the settlement of Illinois.[216]

Evidence supporting these conclusions can be found in numerous contemporary historical accounts. The westward migration from Maine was significant as early as 1815, and was traced to the scarcity and high price of provisions and the principal necessities of life. Then after the "uncommonly cold and unpropitious" springs of 1816 and 1817, the fear of famine gave "a fresh impulse to the enchanting spirit of emigration. Hundreds who had homes, sold them for small considerations, and lost no time in hastening away into a far country." Although a favorable change in the seasons delayed further removals, and in 1818 more returned than emigrated, Maine lost some 10,000 to 15,000 inhabitants to westward migration.[217] A contemporary historian of New Hampshire related a similar sequence of events. "A scanty harvest and a general scarcity of Bread, the natural results of a season of such unusual rigors, gave a new impulse to westward migration. Hundreds of farmers, discouraged by the small returns, gave up their farms," and "sought, in the fertile wilds of a distant land, for that bright sunshine of prosperity." For many it seemed impossible to raise their bread "on the cold hills of New-Hampshire, and that they must hasten to the remote *West*."[218] The Decade 1811–20 also proved a period of slow population growth for Vermont. The population of the United States increased 32 percent in this decade, while the increase in Vermont only amounted to 8 percent. More than sixty Vermont towns lost population between 1810 and 1820, and as many more experienced no population growth. An earlier population boom was wiped out by a series of events beginning with the national embargo of 1808 and the War of 1812. However, the heaviest blow that struck Vermont was the adverse weather of the decade 1811–20, particularly the cold seasons of 1816.[219] In fact, the cold weather of this decade depopulated the upland settlements throughout northern New England. The pause in immigration was paralleled by increased migration to the west.[220] The population of all New England states, with the exception of Connecticut, grew at a slower rate during the decade 1811–20 than had been the case in the previous decade. Every state but New Hampshire reversed this trend during the milder decade of 1821–30. Southern New England had already become relatively overpopulated by 1810; the significant change was that migration had gone north before 1810 but after 1810 the flow went west.[221]

The flow of New Englanders westward became a flood during 1816–17. One description of this movement depicts the majority of migrants as almost as destitute as their counterparts traveling down the Rhine valley:

In the pressure of adversity, many persons lost their judgment, and thousands feared or felt that New England was destined, henceforth, to become a part of the frigid zone. At the same time, Ohio—with its rich soil, its mild climate, its inviting prairies—was opened fully upon the alarmed and anxious vision. As was natural under the circumstances, a sort of stampede took place from cold, desolate, worn-out New England, to this land of promise.

I remember very well the tide of emigration through Connecticut, on its way to the West, during the summer of 1817. Some persons went in covered wagons— . . . some on foot and some crowded together under the cover. . . . Others started in ox-carts, and trudged on. . . . Many of these persons were in a state of poverty, and begged their way as they went. Some died before they reached the expected Canaan; many perished after their arrival, from fatigue and privation.[222]

Westward migration originated from eastern states other than New England. Crop failures in 1816 prompted migrations from both North and South Carolina.[223] A considerable number of migrants found their way to the southwest as well as to the northwest, many of them being "driven there from different parts by the failure of their crops."[224] Seemingly, however, the economic hardships were less severe in the south. But the description of New Englanders fleeing westward is reminiscent of accounts of the exodus from the Rhineland. The majority of the migrants on both continents were attempting to escape from hunger, unemployment, and an uncertain economic future.

chapter
four

Demographic Aspects and
the Role of Epidemic Disease

DEATHS, BIRTHS, AND MARRIAGES

The old biological regime was shattered almost everywhere in Europe during the second half of the eighteenth century; from that time onward subsistence crises ceased to produce calamitous mortality peaks.[1] The early 1740s marked the last period when famine and a concomitant surge in the number of deaths reduced the population growth generated by the excess of births over deaths in years of good harvests. While death from natural causes has never again taken a drastic toll in Europe, nevertheless some regions continued to experience steep increases in mortality rates. The famine of 1816–17 was the last great subsistence crisis not only because dearth touched almost all of Europe but also because it produced the demographic effects characteristic of preindustrial crises. Although the number of births and marriages declined only moderately in comparison to Old Regime famines, the death rates rose in some states to levels above those recorded in the subsistence crises of the eighteenth century. The old biological regime had not completely disappeared in Europe; moreover, even after 1817, subsistence crises were still capable of doubling the death rate in restricted areas, as the Irish famine of 1845–47 demonstrated.

Old Regime demographic crises generally lasted no more than a year or two, but the population effects were powerful and were not limited to a sudden rise in mortality. The doubling or more of the death rate was paralleled by a birth rate that could be cut in half and by a steep decline in the number of marriages.[2] In addition, the number of beggars and vagrants multiplied, as was still the rule in 1816–17. Jean Meuvret seemed to demonstrate that preindustrial demographic crises were connected with high cereal prices; however,

Pierre Goubert has implied that the crises were caused neither "by the high price of food, nor by any kind of dearth or starvation but by epidemics."[3] Despite the explicit language, it appears that Goubert intended only to qualify not to deny the validity of Meuvret's findings. But Goubert's position also needs refinement. While this study support's Meuvret's contention that preindustrial demographic crises resulted principally from high cereal prices, the relationship between the two phenomena was less direct and the role of epidemic disease more complex than thought. For example, the differential movement of death rates in 1816–17 did not necessarily follow the differential movement of food prices, but neither was the relationship between the two variables unconnected. Thus, the major question surrounding preindustrial mortality crises is whether famine progressed automatically to mortality, so to speak, or whether famine and epidemic disease operated essentially independently of one another.

In order to confront this issue, however, it is necessary to consider the comprehensive relationship between economic cycles and population movements. It is well established that birth, death, and marriage rates fluctuate with changes in the economic outlook. At the same time, since this relationship was particularly sensitive in preindustrial Europe, the severity of a subsistence crisis can be gauged from the indexes provided by the rise and fall of vital rates. Other factors may, of course, exert a simultaneous influence; a postwar marriage pattern comes immediately to mind in the aftermath of the Napoleonic wars. Nonetheless, harvest failures in Europe induced marriage postponements prior to the twentieth century, which in turn resulted in a decline in the number of births. While an economic crisis accompanied by famine might lower effective fertility by increasing the incidence of spontaneous abortion or by inducing temporary amenorrhea and sterility, birth rates like marriage rates reflected mainly voluntary adjustments to economic prospects. The death rate, by contrast, changed involuntarily, governed chiefly by the level of nutrition and of real wages.[4]

European population statistics are neither comprehensive nor precise for this period, but in some jurisdictions the figures are adequate to follow short-term population movements. Annual vital statistics are available in France for the entire nineteenth century and thus present an opportunity to examine postwar trends in broader perspective; the population movements are reasonably accurate, even though the censuses taken in 1811 and 1816 were defective.[5] The number of births, deaths, and marriages during the first postwar decade are reproduced in Table 12. The most untypical year of the period was 1814, in which the figures reflect the continuing influence of the war. The record high number of births in 1814 was the consequence of the numerous marriages contracted in 1813 to avoid conscription, newly-weds having been made exempt from military service. The abnormally low marriage figure in 1814 resulted from many unions having been anticipated the previous year.[6]

Table 12. Annual Population Movements France, 1814–
23 (in thousands)

Year	Births	Deaths	Natural increase	Marriages
1814	994.1	873.0	121.1	193.0
1815	953.1	762.9	190.2	246.0
1816	968.9	723.7	245.2	249.2
1817	944.5	750.6	193.8	205.9
1818	914.6	755.5	159.0	213.3
1819	987.6	786.0	201.6	215.3
1820	960.0	769.3	190.2	209.0
1821	965.4	741.3	224.1	222.7
1822	972.6	777.0	195.6	235.8
1823	963.3	743.4	219.9	261.8

Source: France. Statistique générale, *Statistique de la France: Territoire, population* (Paris, 1837), pp. 316–34, 380.

The high death rate in 1814, estimated at 29.4 per 1,000, also derived from wartime conditions; the Empire collapsed in military defeat and invasion, which triggered a serious typhus epidemic.[7] In spite of the Hundred Days and Waterloo, 1815 was the first normal year insofar as the death rate was concerned; but the high number of marriages that year reflected the process of demobilization. The largest surplus of births over deaths during the entire period was recorded in 1816. The estimated death rate of 24.7 per 1,000 in 1816 proved to be the lowest in France until 1836; and the natural population increase of 245.2 thousand was the greatest net gain during the postwar decade. The number of marriages contracted in 1816 was the largest until 1823. Then, the movement of the population echoed the effects of the subsistence crisis for the next two years. The birth rate fell in 1817, despite the many marriages in 1816, and in 1818 the number of births declined further. Marriages declined by 18 percent in 1817 and initiated a trough that persisted until 1821. Mortality, on the other hand, rose during the years 1817–19. If the war year 1814 is ignored, the natural increase of 159.0 thousand in 1818 was by far the smallest population gain of the postwar decade.

The subsistence crisis induced a fall in the number of births and marriages everywhere in western and central Europe. Table 13 displays the available figures for the number of births during the years 1815–20. With the exception of Prussia, each state recorded fewer births in 1817 than in 1816, and this trough in fertility continued into 1818. But the fall in the number of births was modest compared to earlier famines. Counting 1816 as the base year, and excluding states where the statistics are incomplete, the birth rate declined approximately 3 percent in 1817, and remained at the lower rate in 1818. However, southwestern Germany, Switzerland, and Italy, the regions that

Table 13. Annual Number of Births, 1815–20 (in thousands)

	1815	1816	1817	1818	1819	1820
France	953.1	968.9	944.5	914.6	987.6	960.0
United Netherlands	195.4	196.6	177.6	183.8	205.3	195.9
Prussia	n.a.	448.0	454.6	463.9	492.8	484.4
Hanover	45.4	50.3	47.9	48.8	51.6	n.a.
Württemberg	54.8	55.0	47.8	43.2	57.8	57.2
Baden	n.a.	n.a.	35.4	35.3	42.0	40.6
Switzerland[a]	24.0	23.0	18.9	16.7	22.9	23.4
Lombardy	80.0	86.0	82.0	86.0	92.0	92.0
Tuscany	45.2	42.2	37.9	46.5	54.8	55.6
Apulia	39.4	36.0	31.3	41.1	46.1	46.2
Bohemia & Moravia	209.9	209.4	208.3	204.2	239.0	232.3
Vienna	12.3	11.6	11.2	11.5	12.6	12.8
Styria	25.9	24.7	24.5	25.6	31.3	30.2
Tyrol & Vorarlberg	n.a.	23.7	21.6	26.1	26.3	26.0
Carniola	n.a.	12.4	11.5	10.5	16.0	14.6
Sweden	85.2	87.7	83.8	85.7	84.2	84.8
Norway	27.7	32.2	30.3	29.1	30.5	32.3
Totals[b]		2,307.7	2.233.7	2.237.3	2,450.8	2,388.3

[a]Includes the cantons of Luzern, Unterwalden, Glarus, Solothurn, Basel, Appenzell, St. Gall, Thurgau, Waadt, and Neuenberg.

[b]Total births for 1816, 1817, 1818, 1819 do not include incomplete series for Baden. Total births for 1815 are omitted because the figures are too incomplete to be comparable.

Sources: France, Statistique générale, *Statistique de la France: Territoire, population* (Paris, 1837), pp. 316–34; Adolphe Quételet, *Sur l'homme et le développement de ses facultés* (2 vols.; Paris, 1835), 1: 94; Robert Demoulin, *Guillaume Ier et la transformation économique des provinces belges, 1815–1830* (Liège, 1938), p. 399; J. Marshall, *A Digest of all the Accounts* (London, 1833), p. 80; Prussia, *Preussische Statistik* 48, A (1879): 2, 4, 33; Johann Hoffmann, "Uebersicht der in Preussischen Staate im Jahre 1841 vorgekommenen Geburten, Trauungen und Todesfälle. . . ." in *Sammlung kleiner Schriften* (Berlin, 1843), pp. 2–4, 11–12; Hermann Losch, "Die Bewegung der Bevölkerung der Württembergs im 19. Jahrhundert und im Jahre 1899," *Württembergische Jahrbücher für Statistik und Landeskunde* (1900), part 2: 56, 58; *Vaterländisches Archiv des Königreichs Hannover* 3 (1820): 92–93, 101, 109, 326–27; A. J. V. Heunisch, *Das Grossherzogtum Baden* (Heidelberg, 1857), pp. 231, 248, 252; Eidgenössisches Statistisches Amt, *Schweizerische statistische Mitteilungen* (Bern, 1862–1919), Lieferung No. 128 (1901), p. 195; Mario Romani, "Il movimento demografico in Lombardia dal 1750 al 1850," *Economica e Storia* 2, no. 4 (1955): 415–28; Pierfrancesco Bandettini, *La popolazione della Toscana dal 1810 al 1959* (Florence, 1961), p. 11; Franca Assante, *La Puglia demografica nel secolo XIX°* (Naples, 1967), pp. 76–77; Pavla Horska, "L'État actuel des recherches sur l'évolution de la population dans les pays tchèques aux XVIIIe et XIXe siècles," *Annales de démographie historique* (1967): 183; G. A. Schimmer, "Die Bewegung der Bevölkerung in Wien seit dem Jahre 1770," *Statistische Monatschrift* 1 (1875): 132; J. V. Goehlert, "Die Entwicklung der Bevölkerung der Steiermark vom Jahre 1754 bis auf die Gegenwart," ibid., 5 (1879): 64; idem, "Die Entwickelung der Bevölkerung von Tirol und Vorarlberg," ibid., 6 (1880): 63; Vincent Goehlert, "Die Entwickelung der Bevölkerung Krains seit dem vorigen Jahrhundert," ibid., 8 (1882): 189; Sweden, Statistiska Centralbyrån, *Historisk Statistik för Sverige, I, Befolkning 1720–1967* (Stockholm, 1969), p. 92; Michael Drake, *Population and Society in Norway 1735–1865* (Cambridge, 1969), pp. 169–75, 182.

experienced the most severe subsistence crisis, recorded a decline in births of nearly 15 percent in 1817. At the same time, strong birth rates were the rule almost everywhere in Europe during this decade, and they dampened any tendency toward falling fertility. This was especially true in the German lands, where the last phase of the Napoleonic wars had interfered with normal family formations.[8] No state experienced a calamitous decline in the number of births in 1817–18, although a definite fall in the birth rate is noticeable in Württemberg, Switzerland, and France. Wilhelm Roscher claimed that the military conscription classes that corresponded to the birth cohorts of 1817–18 proved to be 25 percent below average in numbers in Germany, but since fertility figures are not available for Bavaria, Baden, Saxony, and most small German states, this statement cannot be verified.[9]

The end of the subsistence crisis ushered in a buoyant recovery of fertility rates during 1819. Every state except Sweden recorded a marked rise in the number of births in 1819, and the aggregate figures rose by 8 percent. The number of births rose 33 percent in Württemberg, 38 percent in Switzerland; both states had experienced depressed fertility in 1817–18. In the Italian states, where the aggregate number of births increased by 27 percent over the low points of 1817, the birth rate in Tuscany rose from 28.9 per 1,000 in 1817, to 41.8 in 1819; and in Apulia the birth rate climbed to an even higher 50.8 per 1,000 in 1819. The greater fluctuations in Italy resulted in part from the fact that the peninsula had suffered three consecutive bad harvests. In the Czech lands of Bohemia and Moravia–Silesia the birth rate soared 15 percent to a figure of 46.9 per 1,000, the highest fertility rate recorded from 1785 to 1918. While the total figures are small, the Habsburg province of Carniola witnessed an increase of more than 50 percent in the number of births. The decline of fertility rates in 1820 is traceable to a normal cyclical downturn and to the dampening effect which the commercial depression of 1819 had on the number of births in the states of northwestern Europe, including Prussia, where the trend of rising fertility was reversed.

The annual movement of marriages, not unexpectedly, followed a course similar to the fluctuating birth rate, as the figures in Table 14 indicate. The aggregate number of marriages peaked in 1816, declined a drastic 42 percent to a low point in 1817, recovered in 1818 to a rate 31 percent above 1817, continued to rise in 1819 to a level almost equal to 1816, and then declined slightly in 1820. The recovery apparently was cut short by the commercial depression of 1819. Despite the more fragmentary data, a strong inverse correlation between marriage rates and grain prices is evident, with an amplitude noticeably larger than was the case in the birth rate.

While the magnitude of the decline in the number of births and marriages is an index of the severity of a subsistence crisis, the steepness of the rise in the number of deaths is a more accurate indicator. A fall in birth and marriage rates might result as much from a darkening economic horizon as from an impending shortage of food; but a rise in death rates signals a decline in

Table 14. Annual Number of Marriages, 1815–20 (in thousands)

	1815	1816	1817	1818	1819	1820
France	246.0	249.2	205.9	213.3	215.3	209.0
United Netherlands	48.9	40.8	33.9	39.2	42.4	43.2
Prussia	n.a.	117.4	112.3	111.5	111.0	109.6
Baden	n.a.	n.a.	6.7	7.4	7.4	7.2
Switzerland[a]	5.0	5.0	3.6	4.1	5.2	5.7
Tuscany	8.3	7.0	6.9	11.2	14.3	14.2
Apulia	n.a.	7.0	8.6	n.a.	14.2	9.3
Bohemia & Moravia	33.8	39.8	40.8	42.2	45.7	49.2
Vienna	2.4	2.9	2.2	2.4	2.6	2.7
Styria	5.1	5.3	5.0	5.4	6.0	6.0
Tyrol & Vorarlberg	n.a.	4.6	3.3	4.4	5.4	5.2
Carniola	n.a.	n.a.	1.6	2.1	3.0	2.9
Sweden	23.6	23.0	21.0	21.4	20.8	21.7
Norway	9.2	9.4	8.0	7.7	7.7	8.7
Totals[b]		511.4	353.1	464.9	493.6	494.6

[a]Includes the cantons of Luzern, Unterwalden, Glarus, Solothurn, Basel, Appenzell, St. Gall, Thurgau, Waadt, and Neuenberg.

[b]Total marriages for 1816, 1817, 1818, 1819 do not include incomplete series for Baden. Total marriages for 1815 are omitted because the figures are too incomplete to be comparable.

Sources: See sources listed in Table 13.

Table 15. Annual Number of Deaths 1815–20 (in thousands)

	1815	1816	1817	1818	1819	1820
France	762.9	723.7	750.6	755.5	786.0	769.3
United Netherlands	137.6	136.1	152.6	140.4	148.4	145.1
Prussia	n.a.	287.1	307.0	314.0	334.4	297.0
Hanover	28.3	32.3	32.0	33.0	38.3	n.a.
Württemberg	44.8	42.1	50.7	39.7	43.2	42.8
Baden	n.a.	n.a.	30.4	31.2	28.9	27.9
Switzerland[a]	16.9	18.2	26.4	21.0	18.9	16.9
Lombardy	78.0	90.0	108.0	77.0	72.0	74.0
Tuscany	40.2	48.1	67.9	38.4	36.6	37.1
Apulia	31.5	46.0	58.6	31.1	27.4	23.9
Bohemia & Moravia	146.8	143.9	160.7	152.7	164.0	137.9
Vienna	11.5	12.3	12.7	11.0	11.5	10.8
Styria	26.3	26.6	28.0	23.5	21.2	19.5
Tyrol & Vorarlberg	n.a.	20.0	25.3	20.2	19.4	19.1
Carniola	n.a.	10.0	15.3	10.3	9.1	8.7
Sweden	57.8	56.2	60.9	61.7	69.9	62.9
Norway	18.0	17.8	16.5	18.0	18.9	18.3
Totals[b]		1,710.4	1,873.2	1,747.5	1,819.2	1,711.2

[a]Includes the cantons of Luzern, Unterwalden, Galrus, Solothurn, Basel, Appenzell, St. Gall, Thurgau, Waadt, and Neuenberg.

[b]Total deaths for 1816, 1817, 1818, 1819 do not include incomplete series for Baden. Total deaths for 1815 are omitted because the figures are too incomplete to be comparable.

Sources: See sources listed in Table 13.

biological well being. Moreover, rates of mortality must be matched with the movement of grain prices to ascertain the degree of correlation between famine conditions and the outbreak of epidemic disease. Table 15 displays the annual number of deaths for the years 1815–20, where the figures are available.[10] In the aggregate, the number of deaths rose 9 percent in 1817, and then declined slightly less than 7 percent in 1818. An approximate correspondence between the grain price curve shown in Table 7 and the movement of mortality rates in 1817 and 1818 is noticeable, but the same relationship between the two variables was not repeated in every European state. The price of grain increased by the smallest percentage in France, the Netherlands, Prussia, Hanover, Britain, Norway, and Sweden; and the moderate rise of food prices in these states, all located on the littoral of the North and Baltic Seas, was paralleled by a moderate rise of mortality rates. The remaining states included in Table 15 saw grain prices reach famine levels in 1816–17; the largest increases were recorded in Switzerland, the states of southwest Germany, and in the provinces of the Habsburg Monarchy. Although grain prices did not rise so sharply in Italy, the price of food advanced beyond the reach of the impoverished working population, and in fact a genuine shortage prevailed in most Italian districts. This statement can also be applied to Ireland, which, like Italy, was an underdeveloped land with an impoverished working population. While mortality rates rose higher in these central European states and in Ireland, the number of deaths in southwestern Germany and in several Habsburg provinces failed to increase proportionately to the rise in grain prices during 1816–17.

Examining each state, mortality in France rose less than 4 percent in 1817; in the United Netherlands, where cereal prices climbed higher than in France, the number of deaths increased by 12 percent. In Prussia, where average grain prices rose least, the rise in mortality during 1817 amounted to a more moderate 6 percent; the higher increase of the death rate compared to France is explained in part by the severe dearth in the western Rhineland provinces.[11] In Sweden the number of deaths increased 8 percent; whereas in Norway and Hanover the death rate declined slightly in 1817.

The sharp rise of grain prices in Switzerland, Italy, the Tyrol, and Carniola was matched by a corresponding increase in mortality rates. Also, in contrast to northern Europe, the poor harvests of 1815 had induced a rise in the number of deaths in Italy, Switzerland, and elsewhere in central Europe during 1816. The number of deaths rose 8 percent in Switzerland in 1816, and then in 1817 jumped to a figure 56 percent above 1815. In the province of Lombardy, the number of deaths rose 15 percent to a rate of 41.0 per 1,000 in 1816, and then increased to a rate of 50.0 per 1,000 in 1817, or nearly 39 percent above the 1815 figure. In the grandduchy of Tuscany, the number of deaths rose 18 percent to a rate of 35.5 per 1,000 in 1816, and then increased to 52.0 per 1,000 in 1817, or more than 68 percent higher than 1815. Mortality levels fluctuated more in Apulia, where the death rate rose from 36.7 per 1,000 in 1815 to 65.6 per 1,000 in 1817, an increase of 78 percent. These elevated death rates were exceeded in other Italian locations. In Bologna in the Papal States, for example, the death rate reached 81.8 per 1,000 in 1817; the 5,085 recorded deaths were twice the 2,531 registered births.[12] In the Venetian province of Padova, the number of deaths climbed from 11,079 in 1815 to 19,374 in 1817.[13] A drastic rise in the death rate also occurred in eastern Switzerland, where the number of deaths recorded in Appenzell and St. Gall nearly doubled from 6,235 in 1815, to 11, 675 in 1817.[14] Mortality levels likewise rose sharply in the southern provinces of the Austrian empire; the number of deaths recorded in Carniola was 53 percent higher in 1817 than 1815, while in the Tyrol this increase amounted to 26 percent. The fragmentary data available for Dalmatia and the Military Frontier suggest that both provinces counted more deaths than births in 1817.[15] Annual vital statistics are not available for the Hungarian lands either, but reportedly more than 50,000 persons died of starvation in the eastern counties of Arad, Szatmár, Krassó Bihar, and Bereg. The combination of deficient crop yields and poor communications converted want into famine in Transylvania and in some Slavic districts.[16]

The number of deaths also increased significantly in the balance of states that experienced famine food prices; but mortality rates stayed far lower than the peaks recorded in Switzerland, Italy, and the Alpine–Carpathian–Balkan region. The severe subsistence crisis that prevailed in southwestern Germany is reflected in the experience of Württemberg, where the figures in Table 15 show that the number of deaths in 1817 was 20 percent higher than in 1815. Bavaria and Baden likewise witnessed elevated mortality rates in 1817, but apparently the increase was smaller than in Württemberg.[17] This same disproportionately moderate rise in death rates occurred in the Czech lands and in Austria. The death rate in Bohemia and Moravia–Silesia rose about 10 percent in 1817, while mortality increased less than 6 percent in Styria and less than 4 percent in Vienna.

The annual movement of the natural increase of the population exhibited trends similar to fertility and mortality, both in the aggregate and on a state-by-state basis. This measure, which represents the net result of annual changes in mortality and fertility levels, is a more telling index of the impact of a subsistence crisis because of its double sensitivity. As Table 16 indicates, the natural increase declined 40 percent in 1817, and in 1818 remained 19 percent below the figure for 1816. The states of northern Europe showed the smallest decline in the natural increase of the population, except for the Netherlands (where grain prices in these regions climbed highest), which saw a drop of 59 percent in 1817. Switzerland, the Italian states, Carniola, and the Tyrol, the states that recorded the most significant increases in the death rate, all returned natural decreases of the population in 1817. The Italian states,

Table 16. Annual Natural Increase of the Population, 1815–20 (in thousands)

	1815	1816	1817	1818	1819	1820
France	190.2	245.2	193.8	159.0	201.6	190.2
United Netherlands	57.8	60.5	24.9	43.3	56.9	49.8
Prussia	n.a.	160.9	147.6	149.9	158.4	187.5
Hanover	15.6	16.3	14.1	14.0	11.5	n.a.
Württemberg	10.0	12.9	− 2.9	3.5	14.5	14.4
Baden	n.a.	n.a.	5.0	4.1	13.1	12.5
Switzerland[a]	7.1	4.9	− 7.6	− 4.4	4.0	6.6
Lombardy	2.0	−4.0	−26.0	9.0	20.0	18.0
Tuscany	5.0	−5.9	−30.0	8.1	18.2	18.5
Apulia	7.9	−10.0	−27.3	10.0	18.7	22.3
Bohemia & Moravia	63.0	65.5	47.6	51.5	75.0	94.3
Vienna	0.8	− 0.8	− 1.5	0.5	1.1	2.0
Styria	− 0.4	− 1.9	− 3.6	2.1	10.2	10.7
Tyrol & Vorarlberg	n.a.	3.7	− 3.7	1.5	6.9	6.9
Carniola	n.a.	2.3	− 3.8	0.3	6.9	5.9
Sweden	27.4	31.4	23.0	24.0	14.4	21.9
Norway	9.7	14.4	13.8	11.1	11.6	14.0
Totals[b]		595.4	358.4	483.4	629.9	675.5

[a]Includes the cantons of Luzern, Unterwalden, Glarus, Solothurn, Basel, Appenzell, St. Gall, Thurgau, Waadt, and Neuenberg.

[b]Totals for 1816, 1817, 1818, 1819 do not include incomplete series for Baden. Total for 1815 is omitted because the figures are too incomplete to be comparable.

Sources: See sources listed in Table 13.

moreover, counted more deaths than births in 1816, as was the case in Switzerland in 1818. The states that experienced a middle-range increase of mortality, such as Württemberg, also registered a net decrease in 1817; which was similarly true in Austria, where the rise in death rates was moderate but where grain prices reached famine levels. Bohemia and Moravia–Silesia, on the other hand, recorded a natural increase of the population each year, though the numbers declined significantly in 1817 and 1818.

The European subsistence crisis ended in 1818 and the demographic movements reflected this economic improvement straightforwardly; the fertility rate rose nearly 10 percent, the mortality rate declined 12 percent, and the natural increase of the population rose a strong 35 percent. However, not all states participated in the demographic recovery to the same degree. A continuing decline in the French birth rate in combination with a small increase in the number of deaths resulted, as mentioned, in the smallest natural increase in population during the postwar decade. In Switzerland also, where the subsistence crisis had been so calamitous, the birth rate continued to decline in 1818 and in conjunction with an elevated death rate produced a net decrease in the population. Nonetheless, on balance, the movement of the population was notably positive in 1818, even the Italian states registered a natural increase after two consecutive years of significant losses.

The natural increase of the population rose a further 30 percent in 1819, the last year in which the demographic effects of the crisis were discernible; nevertheless, 1819 was also a year of higher mortality rates. The number of deaths rose nearly 5 percent, which was more than offset by a 9 percent rise in the number of births. Two distinct patterns are noticeable. First, the death rate rose in every state located in northern Europe; second, the death rate declined in Switzerland, Italy, and in the Habsburg empire. At the same time the number of births increased in every state, except for an insignificant decline in Sweden. Two factors will account for most of the increase in the death rate. First, the large increase in the number of births was responsible for more than half of the increase in the number of deaths, as a consequence of high infant mortality rates. Although infant mortality levels are not available for most states, a rate of 200 per 1,000, or 20 percent, seems a reasonable estimate for this period. Infant mortality rates are known in the Czech lands, and the figure measured a high 268.7 per 1,000 in 1819.[18] In Sweden, however, the infant mortality rate in 1819 amounted to a much lower 183.1 per 1,000.[19] If a rate of 200 per 1,000 is used, then some 42,000 of the 71,000 added deaths in 1819 can be explained (in a rough calculation) by the 213,000 added births. The second factor inducing higher mortality rates was the commercial depression of 1819, which struck the more developed northern states more severely, and could account for the residual number of additional deaths. A more precise answer awaits the availability of vital statistics on a monthly basis and further research into the history of infectious disease.

As indicated, the demographic evidence discloses two critical points that must be resolved to understand the relationship between famine and epidemic disease. First of all, the rise of European mortality rates was moderate compared to the experience of past famines, despite the extraordinary high level of food prices. Second, the movement of the death rate did not exhibit an invariant correlation with the movement of grain prices. In some locations, instead of both curves moving directly together in accordance with the expected relationship between nutritional levels and disease, the two lines tended to separate. For example, cereal prices climbed threefold in southwestern Germany and higher still in Austria and Bohemia, but the number of deaths rose only marginally compared to the high death rates in Switzerland and Italy. In northern Italy, by contrast, where the number of deaths nearly doubled between 1814 and 1817, the average price of wheat rose less than 75 percent during the same period.[20] Before dealing with these issues, however, an examination of the fragmentary statistics and the impressionistic evidence available for the two major subsistence crises of the eighteenth century will lend some perspective to the matter of differential mortality rates and to the central question of autonomous or dependent epidemic disease.

The earlier subsistence and mortality crisis occurred in 1709–10, and while the statistical data are thin, the literary evidence conveys a conclusion of much higher mortality than was the case in 1816–17. This statement is particularly true for northern Europe, where death rates rose drastically in 1710–11, primarily from epidemic disease. Since the Great Northern War spanned these years, the higher mortality rates ensued in part at least from wartime conditions. A large number of the deaths resulted from an outbreak of epidemic bubonic plague in 1709–11. It seems probable that the war was responsible for the epidemic, since military operations gathered large numbers of men, material, and food supplies from eastern as well as northern Europe and brought them together in unsanitary camps.[21] Plague had already become epidemic in Constantinople as early as 1707, from where the contagion spread to Thrace, Serbia, Rumania, Hungary, Poland, Livonia, Denmark, Sweden, Germany, Austria, and Spain by 1708. The death toll was enormous in Danzig and its suburbs, which supposedly lost more than 32,000 inhabitants to this disease between November 1708 and January 1710. Reportedly, Prussia and Lithuania combined lost more than 280,000 victims to plague in 1709–10. The epidemic spread to Sweden in 1710, where 21,000 persons died from plague in Stockholm and 16,000 more died in Karlskrona. Copenhagen recorded more than 20,000 deaths attributed to plague in 1711. The toll was enormous in northeastern Europe; some 200,000 persons are said to have died from plague in Livonia and Kurland during 1710, and 215,000 died in Brandenburg the same year. In the Habsburg Monarchy more than 300,000 persons were reported to have died from plague. The epidemic continued to claim lives in Germany and the Habsburg Monarchy from 1712 to 1714, but the number of victims was smaller, with the notable exception of Prague, which lost 48,000 inhabitants. Plague continued to break out in Poland and the Ottoman empire until 1720, from where no doubt the infection spread to Marseilles in 1720.[22] Whatever the accurate number of plague victims in northern and eastern Europe, the death rate must have been remarkably high; but given the crushing impact of the epidemic, it is problematic what percentage of the deaths were in fact attributable to the severe weather of 1709 and the subsequent famine, rather than to plague.

Despite the many references to a major mortality crisis in northwestern Europe, which escaped the epidemic of bubonic plague in 1709–10, the quantitative evidence is too fragmentary to establish mortality rates. Charles Creighton has found that the "London fever of 1709–10" was instrumental in the rise of the London bills of mortality from 21,800 in 1709, to 24,620 in 1710, or a 16 percent increase in the number of deaths. The increased mortality resulted from a combination of the severe winter of 1709, famine, smallpox, and a sharp rise in the cases of "spotted fever," presumably typhus.[23] Thomas Short has included 1710 in his table of "sickly and mortal" years in England, but the level of mortality in this year is not conspicuously high compared to the other years in the series.[24] J. D. Chambers's study of

Nottinghamshire does not disclose a calamitous increase in the death rate; although the number of deaths rose in 1710–11, mortality had been higher in 1708.[25] Even if Britain escaped a major mortality crisis, no doubt the death rate rose more steeply than in 1816–17.

France experienced a more severe mortality crisis than Britain, but Jean Meuvret has cautioned that it is difficult to confirm the literary comment with an exceptional number of deaths in the village parish registers.[26] A study of mortality in Anjou indicates that the parish registers rarely showed a level of mortality commensurate with the famine grain prices of 1709–10.[27] The number of deaths in Beauvais rose noticeably in 1710, but the mortality peak occurred in 1712, when the death rate climbed above 70 per 1,000. While death rates did not rise drastically everywhere in France, some locations in northern France witnessed high mortality and the crisis was more severe there than in England.[28] The number of deaths rose sharply in Paris during the last half of 1709 and the first half of 1710; the death rate reached a point about 50 percent higher than the average of the eighteenth century.[29] Hainaut and Liège in the southern Netherlands saw a noticeable rise in the number of deaths in 1709–10, as a consequence of the severe winter and ensuing famine; several parishes recorded a threefold rise in mortality.[30] The limited demographic data available for the Dutch provinces, however, yield no evidence of a major mortality crisis in 1709–10.[31] Although 1709–10 were also years of subsistence crisis in west Germany, mortality rates apparently rose no more than marginally.[32] Neither does the evidence disclose a mortality crisis in Switzerland.[33] Final judgment must be reserved because of the paucity of demographic statistics, but it can be concluded that the mortality crisis of 1709–10 was centered in northern and eastern, not western, Europe. Further, the high mortality rates and excess deaths stemmed more from the bubonic plague epidemic than from either starvation or famine fevers such as dysentery and typhus.

The mortality crisis of the early 1740s, for which more statistical evidence is available, produced the last grievous rise in the death rates of northern and western Europe, and also produced the last major setback to population growth in these regions of Europe. The countries of northern Europe again witnessed the greatest rise in mortality rates, as the following figures indicate:[34]

Deaths per 1,000 population

Year	Norway	Sweden	Finland	Denmark
1739	22.8	30.6	31.9	27.2
1740	25.1	35.5	52.0	30.5

—Continued

Year	Norway	Sweden	Finland	Denmark
1741	40.8	32.2	31.6	31.1
1742	52.2	39.0	45.6	29.2
1743	28.4	43.7	38.1	26.9
1744	21.4	25.3	25.0	22.6

Death rates rose in all Scandinavian countries following the severe winter and crop failure of 1740, and mortality continued to rise in Norway until 1742 and in Sweden until 1743. Norway experienced a natural population decrease of 8.9 thousand in 1741, and 16.5 thousand in 1742; Sweden recorded a natural population decrease of 5.9 thousand in 1740, 0.7 thousand in 1741, 12.7 thousand in 1742, and a peak decline of 22.8 thousand in 1743; while Finland saw a decrease of the natural population in 1740, 1742, and 1743.[35] Unlike the mortality crisis of 1709–10, the drastic rise in Scandinavian death rates ensued primarily from epidemics of dysentery and typhus, the classic European famine fevers.[36] Bubonic plague epidemics had again swept through southeastern Europe in 1738–39, but this time northeastern Europe escaped the contagion.[37]

Systematic mortality statistics are not available for Britain; nonetheless, the fragmentary data point to a noticeable rise in death rates, but not to the degree seen in the Scandinavian countries. The death rate in 17 Shropshire parishes rose from 22.3 per 1,000 in 1739, to 38.5 in 1741, before declining to 34.0 in 1742, and returning to 22.3 per 1,000 in 1743. Small natural decreases in population occurred in both 1741 and 1742. These years also witnessed a rise in adult and a decline in child burials,[38] a mortality pattern that is consistent with an epidemic of typhus. Creighton has reported a mixed epidemic of typhus, relapsing fever, and dysentery—all famine fevers—in Britain during 1741–42, especially in the southwestern counties. The number of fever deaths in London reached 7,528 in 1741, the highest total recorded in the bills of mortality; moreover, the total of 32,119 deaths that year amounted to the largest figure from the great plague of 1665 until civil registration in 1838. The death rate in the western weaving town of Tiverton exceeded 70 per 1,000 during the typhus epidemic. In Norwich burials were greater than baptisms in each year from 1740 to 1742. The number of fever deaths in Edinburgh more than doubled from 1740 to 1741, and the death rate approached 50 per 1,000. Descriptions of the epidemic fever of 1741–42 in Britain are consistent with the symptoms of typhus.[39] Thomas Short's examination of twenty-seven parish registers in provincial towns disclosed a surplus of burials over baptisms each year from 1740 to 1742, before the balance changed in 1743.[40] In the Vale of Trent, burials rose above baptisms in the Nottinghamshire villages for the last time in 1741 and 1742; the elevated mortality was induced by the combination of wet, cold weather, food shortages, and epidemic typhus.[41] All

British parish registers seem to attest to a population setback in 1740–42, caused by harvest failure and epidemic disease; this time followed by a quick and final recovery from such demographic shocks.[42]

Neither are aggregate mortality statistics available for France, but the fragmentary evidence indicates that the northern and western provinces passed through a mortality crisis of the same magnitude as in Britain. The number of deaths recorded in the rural communes of Brittany and Anjou exceeded the number of births by 52 percent in 1741, and the region failed to show a natural population increase until 1743. Some 80,000 deaths have been attributed to a mixed epidemic of typhus and dysentery that raged in Brest and in parts of Brittany in 1741.[43] The epidemic diseases that broke out in Anjou are difficult to identify; contemporary accounts of symptoms suggest influenza and enteric fevers, as well as typhus.[44] The death rate also rose noticeably in Beauvais during the years 1741–43, doubling in some parishes.[45] While the mortality crisis in Paris remained at a lower level than in 1709–10, the death rate nevertheless rose between 1739 and 1742, with a peak number of deaths in 1740.[46] The mortality crisis that occurred in northern France in the years 1739–43, as in 1709–10, originated in a subsistence crisis.[47] The same was true in the Belgian provinces of the Netherlands, where the harvest failures of 1740 gave rise to a mortality crisis, with a great number of deaths from dysentery.[48] But again as in 1709–10, the Dutch provinces of the Netherlands seem to have escaped more lightly.[49] Germany, Switzerland, and Italy apparently also experienced no more than a marginal increase of mortality rates in the early 1740s.[50]

By contrast, the mortality crisis in Ireland may have been more severe than the great famine of 1845–47. Since virtually no demographic statistics are available for the 1740s, however, it is necessary to rely on contemporary impressions and estimates. Epidemics of typhus, relapsing fever, and dysentery combined with famine to drive up mortality rates.[51] The increase in the number of deaths was not confined to the poorer classes. Contemporaries estimated that from one-fifth to one-third of the "common people" perished in 1740–41; the numbers mentioned varied between 200,000 and 400,000 deaths from starvation and epidemic disease. These figures are probably too high; a physician who practiced in Cork and saw the mortality crisis at its worst estimated the number of added deaths at 80,000, the same total arrived at by the physician and historian John Rutty.[52] Michael Drake, nevertheless, believes that 80,000 is too low and has suggested a figure of 300,000.[53] If a population of 3 million is an accurate figure for Ireland in 1740,[54] then the death rate reached at least 50 per 1,000 for the two-year period. Although these years marked the last mortality crisis for northern and northwestern Europe, this was not to be the case in Ireland until another century had passed.

These two earlier mortality crises yield some comparative knowledge concerning the relationship between famine and epidemic disease, but because the demographic statistics are sparse and the contemporary grasp of the nature of epidemic disease uncertain, the central issue of the autonomous or dependent occurrence of dysentery, typhus, and plague epidemics remains unsettled. Also it is unclear why some northern European states suffered higher mortality rates than others, even though the entire region experienced the same weather and crop failures. A closer look at the subsistence crisis of 1816–17 makes a useful contribution to the resolution of these questions, because the quantitative evidence is more systematic and the historical record of epidemic disease is more complete. This set of unresolved problems was alluded to by Louis Henry in his summary observation: "We still do not know whether this reduction in disasters was produced by man, the result for instance of economic progress, or whether it was just a piece of good luck."[55]

FAMINE AND EPIDEMIC DISEASE

The experience of the majority of the northwestern European states indicates that famine did not always progress automatically to mortality. The uneven correlation between the movement of European grain prices and death rates in 1816–17 also suggests that some states were able to escape the demographic effects of famine earlier than others. In northwestern Europe, as outlined above, the rise in death rates was curbed by programs which kept staple food prices within reach of the poorest segment of the working population and provided welfare and relief for the unemployed and destitute. On the other hand, death rates rose sharply in Switzerland, Italy, and in the southern provinces of the Habsburg Monarchy, despite similar governmental attempts to prevent hunger and starvation. These mortality peaks ensued from the combined inroads of famine and epidemic disease. It has already been suggested that the differential success in keeping death rates low resulted primarily from the differential effectiveness of political administration. However, the unresolved issue is whether the epidemics were mainly fortuitous and occurred independently of the subsistence crisis, or whether the famine was responsible for their diffusion.

Jean Meuvret questioned the progression from famine to mortality, summed up in the oft-repeated formula "first dearth and then plague," and pointed out that in some cases famine and epidemic disease have operated independently of one another.[56] Chambers adopted an extreme view, insisting that preindustrial death rates were relatively autonomous, and admonished historians to recognize that epidemic cycles frequently overrode Malthusian factors. He spoke of the "fortuitous" nature of epidemic disease, and even questioned whether undernutrition and malnutrition interfere with the ability to resist infectious disease, except in illnesses like tuberculosis, in which the relationship has been established.[57] Famines in Europe were not invariably followed by serious epidemics, and it is possible that crises of public health were essentially autonomous in origin and not directly related to problems of subsistence. As Meuvret expressed it, there is the possibility that two distinct mortality crises have been confused.[58] Fernand Braudel has written that "every disease has its own autonomous life, independent of the endless correlations" suggested by historians; that correlations with economic crises are "at most only minor accidents in a history linked with other factors: rodents, parasites, bacilli, viruses, or some form of merchandise."[59] E. A. Wrigley has spoken of the "apparently fortuitous incidence of epidemic disease" in connection with the European typhus epidemic during the subsistence crisis of 1741.[60] Finally, it has frequently been suggested that the decline of mortality from epidemic disease has resulted either from an increase in the natural immunity of European populations long exposed to the infection, or from changes in the ecology of disease-carrying animal vectors, such as rats.[61] However, the findings of this study lead to the different conclusion that the progressive rationalization of political administration and improved economic productivity, which together brought about the abatement of famines and erected structural barriers against vectors, were the factors mainly responsible for the taming of severe epidemic disease.

To begin with, it is difficult to establish a direct cause-and-effect relationship between famine and an increase in the number of deaths, even though death rates depend primarily on the levels of nutrition and real income. Despite numerous references to death from hunger in all European subsistence crises up to and beyond 1817, medical opinion today believes that starvation is rarely an ascertainable direct cause of death.[62] Rather than death resulting from starvation, malnutrition alters the resistance of the host to potentially fatal infection, and infectious disease in turn aggravates existing malnutrition.[63] Nonetheless, the experience gained from World War II, particularly in German concentration camps, indicates that death can occur from "famine disease" apart from starvation in association with complicating infectious diseases. Emaciation, edema, and diarrhea are the cardinal symptoms of famine disease. However, morbidity during famine is characterized by a mixture of the symptoms of starvation and of various infectious diseases, particularly dysentery. Diarrhea, for example, was not only widespread in all German concentration camps, it was the most common cause of natural death among the prisoners. In view of the unhygienic conditions in the camps, one would assume that the majority of the cases of diarrhea were of an infectious type, like dysentery. But most cases were a direct result of starvation not of a contagious disease that might result from an increased risk of infection and from lowered resistance. In the majority of the cases observed, the diarrhea was a symptom and not a complication of famine disease. Moreover, hunger diarrhea was never observed until the prisoners had been subjected to starvation for several months. The loss of weight accelerated in the later stages of starvation, and the diarrhea became increasingly severe; most of the patients died in a state of extreme emaciation (marasmus).[64]

These biological relationships will account in part for the higher mortality rates during the subsistence crisis of 1816–17; but the incidence of epidemic disease depended more on the social conditions created by the famine and the administrative response to the consequences of these conditions. Famines have been accompanied by serious epidemics because standards of hygiene are lowered, because the resistance of the population to infection is reduced by under- or malnutrition, and also because the diffusion of contagious disease is promoted by the migration of the population in search of food. The symptoms of starvation and of infectious disease, however, become interwoven and difficult to separate. During World War I, for example, medical investigators tried to find a specific microorganism causing the "war edema," because edemas often appeared in association with acute fevers.[65] Similarly, the presence of widespread diarrhea in preindustrial famines has led observers to a conclusion of infectious disease such as dysentery. Although a valid differentiation of these two groups of ailments demands a knowledge of pathology which was not available in the nineteenth century, it is nevertheless possible to distinguish in a rough and ready way whether the rise of mortality rates in 1816–17 derived primarily from hunger or from uncontrolled epidemic disease.

Typhus fever, a contagious disease that is promoted by famine conditions, was the most widespread epidemic disease during the subsistence crisis. Typhus, however, did not become a national health problem in France, the Netherlands, or Germany,[66] the states where the rise in death rates remained marginal. The incidence of typhus climbed in some German locations, like Westphalia, Upper Silesia, and Bremen, but not alarmingly.[67] Even in southwestern Germany and eastern France, where death rates rose more noticeably, the higher mortality did not result from "famine fevers." Neither was an outbreak of epidemic diseases unrelated to nutritional levels responsible for the elevated death rates in this region of northwestern Europe. While an increase in the number of deaths from smallpox became evident in some European countries during the postwar years, the evidence fails to indicate a serious epidemic in 1816–19.[68] The number of smallpox deaths in Paris, for example, rose from 251 in 1816, to a peak figure of 993 in 1818, and then declined to 105 in 1820.[69] Belgium experienced a smallpox epidemic in 1817, with Ghent reporting an outbreak among children, which claimed 48 lives in one commune.[70] The smallpox epidemic was apparently more serious in Ireland, particularly in Ulster during 1817–18; and when the epidemic broke out in the eastern counties of England in 1819, it occasioned 193 admissions to the London smallpox hospital, the highest figure since 1805.[71] In Moravia–Silesia, where the number of cases of contagious disease is known, and where the rise in the death rate was also marginal, the number of deaths attributable to typhus, smallpox, and other epidemic illnesses increased during the subsistence crisis. But, as the following figures indicate, this increase was not devastating:[72]

1815	1,284
1816	1,800
1817	3,106
1818	1,939
1819	900

No evidence of widespread epidemic disease has survived for northwestern continental Europe, except for scarlet fever epidemics in France and Germany, in which the death toll was not high.[73]

Although the increase in the number of deaths from smallpox and typhus cannot be ignored, in all probability the death rate rose in these northwestern countries primarily because the combination of malnutrition and abnormal diet multiplied the fatal cases of diarrhea and tuberculosis. Tuberculosis is an infection which is especially fostered by protein, vitamin, and mineral deficiencies.[74] Early childhood infection often shows no symptoms, and the lung heals; but young adults infected as children carry the tubercle bacillus, and reactivation of this infection is brought about by severe distress, such as undernutrition.[75] Not unexpectedly, a pronounced increase in the incidence of tuberculosis occurred in all countries devastated by the two world wars, in spite of the fact that tuberculosis morbidity had begun to fall. Undernutrition, together with poor sanitary conditions, greatly enhances the possibility of infection. In German concentration camps, the morbidity from tuberculosis was very high, and tuberculosis was one of the most important causes of death. Clinical evidence indicates that pulomonary tuberculosis tends to develop in the more exhausted patients, who are likely to have a lowered resistance to the infection.[76]

Morbidity from dysentery or diarrheas developed into a health problem throughout western Europe in 1816–18.[77] The consumption of indigestible foods and decomposing flesh of dead animals became commonplace during the subsistence crisis, particularly in rural districts. Reportedly, entire villages in eastern France were reduced to eating herbs, roots, grass, and fungus growths.[78] Travelers from France to Switzerland related that the beggars were ravaged by famine.[79] "Many individuals have died, if not of hunger, at least of the insufficiency and bad quality of the food. . . . such vegetables as grow wild in the fields at this season might afford great relief; but the idea of eating grass like animals appears dreadful to these people."[80] In rural Bavaria, horses and watchdogs as well as roots and fungus growths served as nourishment.[81] The destitute in Württemberg were compelled to eat grass, roots, and bread baked from mixtures of bran, straw, and sawdust.[82] In the Prussian Rhineland, a forced diet of herbs and milk was blamed for an illness that produced swollen and yellowed features.[83] The subsistence of large numbers of the population of Nassau and the Palatinate also depended on unwholesome diets.[84] Analogous conditions prevailed in the Habsburg lands; persons reduced to desperation were forced sooner or later to eat indigestible and unwholesome foods, such as nettles, spoiled cereals, and carrion meat.[85] Whether these diets promoted dysentery or whether the majority of diarrheas resulted from famine disease cannot be determined, but in any event the consequences might either be fatal in themselves or weaken resistance to fevers. Enteritis caused by undernutrition must have been especially malignant among young children. Moreover, the conditions that lower the barriers for one type of infection often admit the pathogenic agents of others.[86]

To the surprise of contemporaries, the public health problems and widespread epidemics that were anticipated in 1817 failed to materialize north of the Alps, except in the United Kingdom.[87] *The Times* believed that "France will be fortunate if serious epidemic distempers are not the consequence of the present misery."[88] It was observed, typically, in Württemberg that "despite so many unusual kinds of nourishment, the health of the people did not become imperiled. While as a rule diseases and plague were the ultimate consequence of want and dearth, this time the state of public health remained better than at any other time."[89] Comparable statements were made in the Prussian Rhineland.[90] Effective welfare and relief measures were credited with preventing the mass epidemics that had accompanied past dearths in southwestern Germany.[91] Staatsrath von Hazzi believed that improved public health facilities and administrative procedures were also responsible for containing epidemic disease in Bavaria.[92]

The prevention of outbreaks of ergotism was one example of the way in which administrative procedures contained famine fevers, particularly in the German states. Ergot poisoning results from eating grain, usually rye, that has been infected by a toxic fungus. A heavy infection of rye, such as caused the severe epidemics in France and Switzerland in 1709–10, is rare and only arises when the meteorological conditions are ideal. Cold, wet springs, as in 1816 and 1817, have been the chief factor in European epidemics. However, after infection of the rye has taken place, wide dissemination of the spores is favored most by hot, dry, and windy weather, which was relatively absent in the summer of 1816.[93] The last major epidemic of ergotism in western and central Europe occurred in eastern France during the years 1814–16.[94] Even so, because of the excessive precipitation in spring 1816, rye infected with the ergot fungus was commonplace in Germany.[95] Ergotism becomes a particular hazard during times of famine, when there is a reluctance to discard even diseased grain; and famine diseases like ergotism were still a threat to public health in the absence of prophylactic administrative measures. After the great European outbreak of ergotism in the subsistence crisis of 1770–71, German governments especially began to supervise the cleaning of rye and also to confiscate rye that was insufficiently cleaned. The Hanoverian government exchanged sound rye for ergotized rye in 1771.[96] The consumption of diseased rye in Germany and Austria during 1816–17 was effectively prevented by an educational program and by a series of public inspections at the marketing, milling, and baking stages.[97] Ergotism also became less common between 1771 and 1816 because of economic development; improvements in agriculture such as drainage reduced the level of ergot infection, and the increased cultivation of the potato, especially in northern Germany after the subsistence crisis of 1770–71, reduced peasant dependence on rye during the late summer in years of famine.

Whereas more efficient administration and economic development were in large part responsible for keeping mortality rates below calamitous levels in this area of northwestern Europe, the combination of low standards of public health, relative poverty, backward administration, and poor communications permitted serious epidemics in Italy, Switzerland, Ireland, and in the Habsburg Monarchy south of the Alps. The number of beggars were able to reach enormous proportions in Italy, Switzerland, and Ireland; in addition, the number of destitute persons made up a larger percentage of the population than was true elsewhere in western and central Europe. The drastic death rates experienced in these countries during the subsistence crisis were as much the result of typhus and epidemic disease as of famine and hunger.

The European typhus epidemic of 1816–19 can be traced to the weather patterns, the famine, and economic distress. Wherever typhus appeared, the contagion had been preceded by hunger and want.[98] Typhus fever broke out on both sides of the Adriatic during 1816, and then spread into the Alpine area.[99] Famine conditions were extreme in both the Alpine and Italian lands of the Habsburg Monarchy. Scurvy and pellagra, nutritional deficiency diseases, preceded typhus in Lombardy, where the inhabitants of the mountain districts of Brescia and Bergamo were forced to eat grass and roots as early as 1816. By June of that year, nearly three hundred cases of scurvy were counted in the hospitals of Brescia alone.[100] The Habsburg emperor, in a memorandum addressed to his chancellor, Metternich, dated in August, related that "in Gorizia the distress had become so severe that the population was reduced to a diet of lettuce and soup made from herbs, and on very many days had nothing to eat at all."[101] By January famine gripped the Lombard valleys and highland districts; not only had many persons already died of hunger, now also typhus fever threatened to spread. The emperor instructed Metternich to redouble the precautionary steps already taken to control the epidemic,[102] but whatever additional measures were taken proved ineffective.

Poverty, outdated administration, and the subsistence crisis together rendered precautionary or remedial measures problematical in Italy. For example, a British physician who visited the Lunatic Hospital at Milan in 1817, found that more than one-third of the five hundred patients were pellagrous, and also that the public hospitals of Lombardy were wholly incompetent to treat the vast number of persons affected with pellagra. "The greater proportion of these unfortunate people perish in their own habitations, or linger there a wretched spectacle of fatuity and decay."[103] He concluded that pellagra appeared to have increased "in a tenfold ratio, during the last two years; the effect of bad harvests added to the preceding wars."[104] No large district of the Italian peninsula escaped famine or typhus. Epidemic typhus raged from Rome to Ragusa in 1817.[105] Although famine spared Sicily, the island was not exempt from typhus; vessels entering Genoa, the Roman states, Tuscany, Messina, and Palermo were placed in quarantine because of the "contagious spotted fever."[106] Piedmont was least affected by the famine, but the Savoy districts were ravaged by both typhus and hunger.[107] It is not possible to estimate the percentage of deaths that resulted from typhus and the percentage from famine disease; but the elevated death rates in Italy, in some states higher than those in Scandinavia in the 1740s, proceeded from the combined inroads of typhus, deficiency diseases, and hunger.

By contrast, the evidence in eastern Switzerland helps to throw considerable light on the relative weights to be assigned to the causes of elevated mortality in 1817. A significant number of Swiss apparently died from famine disease; there seems to be no other explanation for the high death rates recorded in eastern Switzerland. The press observed that "many of these had literally died of hunger, the majority at least from illnesses occasioned by distress, want, and noxious foods."[108] The practice of consuming unnatural food received abundant comment in Switzerland. One observer noted: "It is horrible to see emaciated skeletons with voracious appetites gulping down the most loathsome and unnatural foods—carcasses of dead animals, cattle fodder, leaves of nettles, swine food and so forth."[109] According to Ruprecht Zollikofer: "Hunger and want sowed the seed of death; harmful, unnatural food and unspeakable misery expedited it"; he added that "carrion, horses, dogs, and cats were delicacies for many."[110] Moreover, some who survived starvation succumbed when food became available again. "After supporting for some time a miserable existence, on scarcely any thing but boiled nettles and other herbs, their organs became impaired, and when too late assisted by better food, they could not digest it; their extremities swelled, and they perished in a few days."[111] The added knowledge of famine disease acquired during World War II suggests that thousands of persons died of starvation in eastern Switzerland. In addition to the evidence of extreme emaciation and famine edema, the perilous consequences of rapid change in diet when food became available also anticipated the experience in German concentration camps. After the liberation of the camps, many deaths occurred as the result of wrong dietetic treatment, which produced an "alimentary" diarrhea. Moreover, famine edema was frequently accentuated in patients when their food situation was substantially improved.[112]

Zollikofer estimated that at least 5,000 of the 12,600 deaths registered in St. Gall and Appenzell in 1817 resulted from the famine. The most numerous cause of death recorded in St. Gall was *Auszehrung und Lungensucht,* which accounted for 2,024 in a total of 8,067 deaths. Although the term lacks clinical precision, the words imply a wasting disease like tuberculosis; but the terminology would apply equally to the symptoms of famine disease. *Faul-, Nerven- und Gallenfieber* accounted for 668 deaths in 1817, or less than 9 percent, and presumably these terms refer mainly to typhus.[113] Of the 5,870 deaths in St. Gall in 1818, 1,820, or 31 percent, were recorded under *Faul- und Nervenfieber,* while 1,045, or 18 percent, were classified under *Auszehrung.*[114] These figures indicate that starvation was the principal cause of high mortality in 1817, whereas typhus became more dangerous in 1818. This conclusion is supported by the knowledge that the case-fatality rate of typhus was low in Switzerland in 1817, and also by the fact that the incidence of typhus was lowest in the spring and summer months when the number of deaths was greatest. The monthly mortality rates in Appenzell also peaked in July and August, with 496 and 532 deaths respectively, followed by a sharp decline to 299 deaths in September and a continuing decline until December, when the number of deaths climbed to 296. This pattern is consistent with the knowledge that the typhus epidemic reached its peak in the Alpine region only in the winter of 1817/18.[115]

The United Kingdom also witnessed a typhus epidemic following the harvest failures of 1816. Cases of typhus fever appeared simultaneously among the Spitalfields silk workers in London and among the Irish peasantry in the autumn of 1816. However, the contagion first assumed epidemic proportions in Ireland. Contemporary physicians who observed the diffusion of typhus fever in Ireland proved remarkably accurate in detailing the epidemiology of the disease:

I consider the predisposing causes of the present Epidemic to have been the great and universal distress occasioned among the poorer classes, by the scarcity which followed the bad harvest of 1816, together with the depressed state of trade and manufactures of all kinds. The low condition of bodily health arising from the deficiency and bad quality of the food; the want of cleanliness both in the persons and dwellings of the poor, . . . I consider the contagion to have been rapidly spread by the numbers wandering about in search of subsistence, and also by the establishments for the distribution of soup and other provisions among the poor where multitudes were crowded together, many of whom must have come from infected houses, or were perhaps even laboring under the early stages of the disease.[116]

The human body louse is the main vector of typhus. The cold spring, summer, and autumn weather in Ireland during 1816, and the constant precipitation, which made peat and wood for fuel either unavailable or expensive, maximized the preconditions for a typhus epidemic.

The disease is spread through the feces of the louse; feces' dust, moreover, remains infectious for years, and can be inhaled or even enter through the conjunctiva of the eyelid. Desiccated infected louse feces shaken out as dust from winter or cold-weather clothing explains in part the seasonal incidence of typhus. The inability to keep warm and clean increases the number of lice, and then the propensity of families to huddle together under heavier textiles, possibly infected with louse feces, or merely wandering in crowds, facilitates the spread of the disease. Those exhausted by hunger are not likely to take great pains about personal cleanliness. Clothes that had any market value were often sold or pawned in subsistence crises. Neighbors in Ireland crowded into any cabin where a fire was burning. More often, the lack of fuel made a fire or hot water impossible, so that windows and crevices were stopped up and the washing of both clothes and persons ceased. Fever patients admitted to hospitals in Ireland were frequently bronzed with dirt, their hair infested with lice, and their clothes in rags.[117] To take a concrete example, the typhus epidemic that broke out in the Strabane district of western Ulster in May 1817, reportedly began in a large house that had been occupied during the winter by families from the mountains. They brought no furniture and no bedding, except blankets. Each room was rented at a shilling a week, and the tenant of a room made up the rent by taking in beggars at a penny a night. The straw bedding was never renewed, merely thrown into a corner during the day to be spread again at night. More than a quarter of the one thousand inhabitants of Strabane were being fed by a soup kitchen opened in the spring of 1817. This charitable measure attracted crowds of people from the surrounding countryside. The fever began among the houseful of vagrants in May, spread throughout the town in June, and developed into a serious epidemic by the autumn. The soup kitchen was closed down for lack of supplies, and the country people returned to their cabins carrying typhus with them.[118]

The number of persons who died in the famine is not known, as was the case in 1740–41, because of the continuing absence of parish demographic statistics. The estimates for 1817–18 are no doubt more accurate, however. Dr. William Harty compiled morbidity and mortality totals for the Irish epidemic and concluded that 800,000 persons were infected and that more than 40,000 "perished by the joint ravages of Famine, Dysentery, and Fever." Harty believed, moreover, that he had by no means exaggerated either the morbidity or mortality, and that the total deaths from the epidemic probably reached 44,300.[119] Since his figures return a case-fatality rate of approximately 6 percent, they may represent underestimations. In typhus fever, the case-fatality rate increases rapidly with age. Among hospitalized patients between sixteen and twenty years of age, the mortality may be as low as 10 percent; whereas in patients of forty to fifty years, a mortality of 40 percent is not uncommon; and among the oldest age cohorts the case-fatality rate can reach 100 percent.[120] Another contemporary estimate placed morbidity from fever and dysentery at 1.5 million cases, and the additional mortality in 1817–18 at 65,000.[121] Since a percentage of the cases of "fever" were relapsing fever and not typhus, however, the case-fatality rate would be somewhat lower.[122] Cases of famine dropsy (presumably famine edema) and dysentery were more common than cases of fever in the early months of the famine; but what percentage of the dysentery cases were in fact bacillary dysentery, with its high case-fatality rate, and what percentage were confused with famine diarrhea is problematic.[123] In any event, K. H. Connell has suggested that Harty's totals should be inflated to 850,000 fever cases and to 50,000 deaths.[124]

A long period of comparative immunity from typhus came to an end in Britain with the postwar depression and the harvest failures of 1816. Both typhus and relapsing fever, also conveyed by the human louse, became epidemic in England, Wales, and Scotland. The Glasgow Royal Infirmary treated 1,371 fever patients in 1818, a figure that had increased each year from a total of 90 patients in 1814. Furthermore, as a result of the inability to handle the inflated number of typhus cases, two temporary fever hospitals were opened in 1818, one of which treated 1,929 patients before it was closed in July 1819. The number of fever patients treated at the Royal Infirmary declined to 630 in 1819.[125] Mortality statistics for Glasgow are not available for these years, but it has been estimated that among a population of 130,000 there were some 32,000 cases and 3,500 deaths from typhus in the year 1818 alone.[126] Epidemic typhus and relapsing fever also visited the Scottish towns of Aberdeen, Carlisle, Paisley, and Edinburgh.[127] No systematic basis exists to allow global estimates either of the morbidity or the mortality from fever in the Scottish epidemic. An Edinburgh journal deemed the postwar epidemic a national tragedy;[128] but in all probability the number of cases should be measured only in thousands, not hundreds of thousands, as in Ireland.

The typhus epidemic visited almost every town and village in England, as well as in Scotland and Ireland. The manufacturing towns of Yorkshire and the eastern districts of London were hit particularly hard.[129] The London outbreak that began in autumn 1816 among the Spitalfields silk workers spread in 1817 to the poorhouses and to the private dwellings of the poor in the crowded districts. The fever was especially rife in the many poorhouses that were overflowing with "half-starved beings, many of them deriving their sole claim to relief from having slept in the streets of the parish, and who were already seized with fever."[130] Thomas Bateman, the medical superintendent of the London House of Recovery, believed that fever had become an index of economic conditions in Britain and also "that deficiency of nutriment is the principal source of epidemic fever."[131] A parliamentary select committee was established to investigate the epidemic when the contagion continued to spread in 1818. However, the committee was unable to determine to what extent fever was more prevalent than in previous years, despite the evidence presented by the medical superintendents and by the dispensaries. Physicians reported an increase in the number of cases compared to past experience, and told of threefold to sevenfold more patients than in past years. The committee found evidence of an "alarming increase of contagious fevers in the hospitals of the Metropolis," and learned that in all the hospitals of London a large number of patients were refused admission "for want of room."[132] But not even an approximate figure for the number of cases of typhus fever can be derived from the committee's report. Concerning mortality, Bateman computed a case-fatality rate of 10 percent for the years 1817–18, with extremely high mortality for those over fifty years old and very low mortality for patients under seventeen years.[133] While it is known that Bristol recorded 2,213 cases of epidemic fever, with a case-fatality rate of 13.5 percent, on the other hand, some London hospitals lacked even a register of diseases.[134] From all the evidence an estimate of 100,000 cases of epidemic fever in England cannot be too far wrong.

In any event, it is difficult to speak in terms of a "fortuitous" outbreak of epidemic typhus, either in the United Kingdom or on the Continent. At the same time the low case-fatality rate may be accounted for by a lowered susceptibility to the infection. It has long been observed that locations where typhus is endemic suffer less severely from the disease than populations that have lacked exposure. Where typhus is endemic, a part of the population at least will develop some degree of immunity as the result of mild cases contracted in childhood. Although such immunity is insufficient to protect against a subsequent severe infection, it is nevertheless sufficient to lessen the virulence of the attack and thus lower the case-fatality rate.[135] While infectious disease was surprisingly absent in German concentration camps, typhus was the one severe epidemic disease encountered and it raged violently when introduced into the Dachau camp. The infection apparently was brought into the camp by a draft of Hungarian prisoners and spread rapidly among the other internees. Both the morbidity and mortality rates were higher among the west-European than among the east-European internees. The case-fatality rate among the nursing staff, moreover, was close to 100 percent. The east-European internees, originating from a region where typhus was still endemic in the twentieth century, exhibited on balance a greater resistance to the infection.[136] Following the general rule governing infectious disease, typhus fever is far milder in children than adults,[137] and in endemic locations in the United Kingdom and on the Continent a degree of immunity no doubt had developed from childhood exposure.

PLAGUE AND PUBLIC HEALTH

The bubonic plague epidemic that moved into southeastern Europe suggests different epidemiological relationships, however. Unlike the history of typhus, the evidence on plague fails to support a view of increasing natural immunity among European populations. Neither does the historical record confirm the supposed linkage of plague and malnutrition. Those historians who have advanced a case for autonomous plague epidemics seem to be justified in this position. What limited knowledge there is indicates an antagonistic rather than a synergistic relationship between protein deficiency and resistance to infection from the plague bacillus.[138] Nonetheless, the connection between famine and plague was not fortuitous; the repeated concomitance of the two phenomena was more than coincidental. A brief survey of the epidemic that reached Europe during the second decade of the nineteenth century will indicate an *indirect* connection.

The epidemic appeared first in central and northwestern India in 1812, where it had been preceded by famine and by high mortality among the rats. Bubonic plague broke out in Constantinople in the summer of 1812, from where it spread to Greece, Cyprus, and the Crimea the same year. Supposedly, plague was brought to Odessa from Constantinople in clothes smuggled past quarantine restrictions; from there the infection spread into the neighboring villages and into Podolia and Transylvania. During 1813 plague reached Egypt, the Ionian Islands, and also Malta, which had been free of the disease for 137 years, owing to its effective quarantine laws. Serious plague epidemics raged simultaneously in the Balkan lands of Thessaly, Bulgaria, and Wallachia. Plague reportedly claimed 25,000 to 30,000 lives in Bucharest, which had a total population of about 80,000 inhabitants. Epidemics continued in Constantinople and Alexandria during 1814, but more serious outbreaks of plague occurred in Smyrna (35,000 deaths) and Bosnia (105,000 deaths). A murderous epidemic broke out in Arabia in 1815; and in the same year plague deaths were recorded in the Adriatic districts of the Austrian empire—Dalmatia, Fiume, Istria, and along the military frontier. Apprehensive press accounts began to circulate in Vienna, Paris, and London, and in 1816 drastic orders of quarantine were issued in Adriatic and Mediterranean ports.[139]

Western press interest centered on an outbreak of epidemic bubonic plague in Noja, a coastal town on the Italian side of the Adriatic in the kingdom of the Two Sicilies.[140] Noja, a community of 5,413 inhabitants, located in Apulia near Bari, apparently imported the infection from its sea traffic with the plague-ridden Dalmatian islands.[141] The first case of plague was confirmed in November 1815. Since some inhabitants had fled from Noja before a drastic military *cordon sanitaire* sealed off the town, plague epidemics were also anticipated elsewhere in Italy. The pestilence attacked only the poor in the miserable parts of Noja until the middle of January, then the disease also struck down the well-to-do and continued to rage in February and March. The level of mortality moderated in May, and the last plague death was recorded June 7, 1816. A total of 921 inhabitants contracted plague and of that number 721 died, which amounted to one-seventh of the population. In an attempt to disinfect the town, 192 houses of the poor were burned to the ground. The Noja epidemic was attributed to three successive harvest failures and the prevailing famine in Apulia, even though the other towns in the province escaped the epidemic. A few sporadic cases of plague were reported in Naples, but they produced no epidemic consequences. Isolated cases of plague also broke out in all the quarantine lazarettos of the Mediterranean. Plague persisted in Constantinople, Smyrna, Cyprus, Crete, Alexandria, Salonika, the Morea, and Albania during 1816. In 1817 plague epidemics ravaged Belgrade, Scutari, Mecca, Algiers, Tunis, Tripoli, Bone, and Tangiers. The Barbary states were not free of bubonic plague until 1822. The Balearic Islands in the western Mediterranean labored under a severe epidemic in 1820 that resulted in 12,000 deaths. Finally, the contagion appeared somewhere in the Turkish provinces until 1850, from where it often spread into southern Russia, Bessarabia, and present-day Rumania.[142]

Surprisingly, the major European Mediterranean ports passed through the plague epidemic unscathed. After the devastating outbreaks at Marseilles in 1720 and at Messina in 1743, the large ports in Christendom maintained a system of maritime quarantine, with lazarettos, which provided effective protection by this time. Venice had not only worked out a system of quarantine centuries earlier, the city-state also had introduced the system of Bills of Health carried by ships. When the epidemics in Italy began to produce anxieties in Marseilles, the *Journal de Marseille* predicted that the public health measures adopted by the administration would safeguard the population of southern France and contended that "Marseille, especially, had nothing to dread from this pestilence: a city that has secured itself from the contagion of Egypt and the Levant should know no fear."[143] Quarantine also proved effective in the major Italian ports. British ships with a foul bill of health engaged in the grain trade of the eastern Mediterranean had to spend 60 to 65 days in quarantine at Stangate Creek. Scotland had even more stringent quarantine regulations, which may explain its escape from the epidemic of bubonic plague that ravaged northwestern Europe in the 1660s. By contrast, Turkish bills of health were still unreliable, and the same was true of the quarantine procedures in force in the small towns of the Adriatic.[144]

With effective maritime quarantine, land-borne epidemics of bubonic plague represented the most serious threat to central Europe. Plague was rife in Bosnia, Serbia, Transylvania, and Dalmatia by 1815, and by November of that year the disease had broken out among the Austrian soldiers on the military border, and also in a few Hungarian districts.[145] While it is true that the effectiveness of the quarantine line along the Austrian–Turkish border should not be overrated,[146] when the control of bubonic plague became the principal function of the Military Frontier, its significance seems to have increased. Epidemic plague had penetrated into Hungary in 1739, as in 1710, despite the sanitary cordon. But the thousand-mile military border was not established along the entire frontier with the Ottoman empire until 1770. Then, when Russia, Moldavia, and Wallachia were ravaged by plague epidemics in 1770–72, the spread of the disease into Transylvania was contained. This success in preventing plague epidemics in the Habsburg lands protected by the Military Frontier was even more complete in 1813–17. Moreover, in spite of continued outbreaks of bubonic plague in the Balkans, Russia, and the Middle East, the contagion no longer spread into central Europe after the consolidation of the Austrian *cordon sanitaire*.[147]

Thus, the relative absence of epidemic plague in central Europe during 1813–17 in contrast to the experience of the Ottoman lands was no mere accident. Modernized public health administration helped to protect Christendom, while the more traditional Ottoman societies remained at a disadvantage. A system of maritime quarantine comparable to those operating in Western ports was established at Constantinople only in 1839, whence the procedures were adopted in other Ottoman ports. The relaxation of quarantine regulations because of the special religious status of pilgrims was responsible for the spread of plague from Mecca to Tangiers in 1818,[148] and no doubt on other occasions also. Neither was the advance of bubonic plague to several south European outposts essentially a fortuitous event. While the original outbreak of the disease in central Asia among rodent reservoirs of infection may be explained only by the biology or ecology of microorganisms, fleas, and animal hosts, nevertheless historical events facilitated the advance of plague from endemic locations in the Middle East to southeastern Europe and the Mediterranean.

To begin with, the successive years of harvest failure and famine in central and southeastern Europe attracted grain shipments from the ports of Constantinople, Smyrna, Odessa, Alexandria, and the Levant. The shipping of grain was found to be the most important vehicle of plague infection in the diffusion of the disease throughout the world during the 1890s and subsequent decades. It is not a question of contamination of the surface of the grain, rather, grain is the preferred food of the black (house or ship) rat, the major reservoir of plague infection. Moreover, the rat's most common flea, *Xenopsylla cheopis*, not only breeds best in the debris of cereal grains but is also the most dangerous vector of the plague bacillus.[149] Although the details are vague, the last major plague epidemic in northwestern Europe has been traced to Dutch ships returning to Amsterdam from Smyrna and the Aegean islands in 1663, which was a year of subsistence crisis in France and the Netherlands.[150] The plague and quarantine commission in France noticed not only the correlation between dearth in Syria and plague cases in the lazarettos of Venice, Trieste, Leghorn, Genoa, and Marseilles from 1721 to 1830, but also that plague broke out in Syrian ports during years of scarcity not from undernutrition but as the result of grain imports from endemic plague locations.[151] It is well established that plague has also been introduced by flea-infested cotton, wool, hides, and furs.[152] The spread of bubonic plague through either the transportation of grain and fodder or clothing and textiles has been traced to troop movements during times of war. Turkish troops were said to have brought bubonic plague into Bucharest in 1813 and into Novi Bazar in Bosnia in 1814.[153] Because of military operations in the Balkans, these years witnessed extensive Turkish and Russian troop movements. The outbreak of bubonic plague during 1738–39 in Transylvania, Hungary, and the Ukraine has also been attributed to the military operations of those years,[154] and no doubt the Great Northern War played a major role in the great epidemic of 1709–14.

The history of bubonic plague in eastern Europe fails to support the view that the disease disappeared from Europe as a consequence of acquired natural immunity. Moreover, it is unlikely that human populations could develop immunity based on genetic insusceptibility, for plague not only is a highly virulent infection but also the disease appeared only sporadically in Europe, and not under conditions of continuous infection that touched generation after generation.[155] Even with respect to specific immunity acquired in childhood, the evidence indicates that recovery from an attack of bubonic plague did not protect an individual from a subsequent infection.[156] The suggestion of an autonomous reduction in the virulence of plague infection also seems untenable. Not only did several hundred thousand Europeans succumb to bubonic plague during the second decade of the nineteenth century, more than 10 million persons in India died from plague during the two decades from 1898 to 1918.[157] In the Noja epidemic, where statistics are available, the morbidity rate approximated 15 percent of the population, and the case-fatality rate bordered on 80 percent; these figures do not deviate appreciably from the average western European experience of the seventeenth century.[158]

An ecological revolution among rats has been most often advanced as the factor responsible for the disappearance of bubonic plague from Europe. A decrease in the relative number of indoor rats (*Rattus rattus*) brought about a decline in the density of the indoor rat flea (*X. cheopis*), the most dangerous vector of plague.[159] It seems certain that the partial displacement of the black house rat (*R. rattus*) by the brown field rat (*R. norvegicus*) reduced the likelihood of plague epidemics in Europe; moreover, the introduction of plague into a healthy area may be possible only where black rats exist.[160] But it seems doubtful that this change can be traced to the reported migrations of the Norway rat from central Asia to Europe in the eighteenth century and the subsequent ousting of the black rat from Europe. Norway and black rats often coexist in the same vicinity, as, for example, in some northern European cities and in the Mediterranean and Balkan countries today.[161] Even if the late arrival date of the Norway rat is accepted, both the timing and the direction of its migration are out-of-phase with the northwest-to-southeast retreat of plague from Europe, and also with the continuing Russian plague epidemics of the eighteenth century. The traditional account contends that the brown

Norway rat appeared in Astrakhan in 1726, and by 1728 had advanced as far west as Hanover. Yet, an epidemic of bubonic plague claimed more than 50,000 lives in Moscow in 1770–71, and also spread into Poland and Rumania, not to mention the outbreak of plague in Astrakhan itself as late as 1877.[162] Presumably, the Norway rat would have invaded and colonized eastern Europe in the course of its movement from the Volga River to western Europe in the eighteenth century; yet, serious epidemics of bubonic plague continued to occur in eastern Europe and in the Balkan peninsula well into the nineteenth century.

More likely, the transformation of material life and human ecology that is coincident with modernization was the principal factor responsible for the retreat of plague from Europe in a southeasterly direction. To begin with, human infections can be grouped into two major categories. One, those infections derived from the external environment and from other species, like bubonic plague. Two, those infections caused by primary human pathogens, like smallpox. Infections falling into the first category can be prevented in most instances by environmental sanitation and by control of vectors. This kind of control raises more economic and administrative than scientific problems. Plague strikes those at risk, and, therefore, measures that block contact of the vector with humans effectively prevent infection. Bubonic plague depends mainly on flea-bite; if infective fleas are not present, there will be no epidemic. The weight of scientific opinion and the results of clinical study point to the rat flea as the principal vector of plague;[163] nonetheless, evidence exists to implicate human ectoparasites as well, particularly the flea (*Pulex irritans*) and possibly the louse.[164] A study of a sixteenth-century epidemic in Venice has concluded that the human flea was a major vector of plague in the sixteenth and earlier centuries.[165] Twentieth-century studies of plague in Morocco and in Iran, where apparently rats are not found, have suggested that plague can become truly epidemic only where there is interhuman transmission by the human flea, otherwise the number of cases caused by the bites of rodent fleas tends to remain below epidemic levels.[166]

In both cases, housing and vector control, not nutrition, are the key variables in the prevention of plague epidemics. Bubonic plague is chiefly a disease of underdeveloped traditional societies. Plague failed to produce widespread epidemics in western and central Europe during the early nineteenth century because of effective quarantine measures and because of critical improvements in domestic hygiene. By this time structural materials such as masonry, brick, and tile were replacing wood, earth, and straw in the dwellings and commercial buildings of European towns and cities. The fear of fire rather than protection against epidemic disease furnished the early motivation for improved housing; nonetheless, the transformation helped to reduce both hazards. Before brick and masonry houses became widespread in Britain during the eighteenth century, the dwellings of the well-to-do were made of timber, half-timber, or timber framed, while the dwellings of the poor were often mere hovels made of unseasoned wood. This was true not only in London but in large towns such as Bristol, York, Liverpool, and Manchester.[167] Although the contribution of the great fire of London (1666) to the elimination of plague has long been debated, the fact that 13,200 houses built mainly of wood were destroyed and replaced by 9,000 brick houses,[168] if nothing else, resulted in less favorable breeding sites for fleas and rats. A similar development occurred in Berlin and the towns of Brandenburg in the interest of fire protection. As late as 1650, the majority of houses were covered with straw or wood shingles. A new fire ordinance in 1672 set the future pattern for Berlin and Brandenburg by requiring fireplaces, ovens, and chimneys to be built of stone or tile, and calling for masonry firewalls to separate them from wood structural material. In addition, all storage sheds used to hold unthreshed grain had to be removed from within the city walls. A revised ordinance in 1707 insisted on brick and stone construction where fire hazards were high; moreover, firewalls were ordered at frequent intervals, and were to pass completely through a city block, two feet above the height of the roofs.[169] Similar transformations of building materials and building codes took place in almost all major cities, especially ports in western Europe.[170] But this transformation had not taken place in Moscow at the time of the plague year 1771, when wood buildings outnumbered stone buildings by 11,825 to 713, and many were still covered by thatched roofs. Even in 1775, after thousands of small wood dwellings had been burned to the ground as an antiplague measure, a total of 7,653 wood buildings remained standing.[171]

These structural changes were of critical significance in Europe's escape from bubonic plague. The comparative frequency of the two rat species in the areas of their coexistence is in a state of constant flux, depending upon building conditions. Pollitzer has suggested that these ecological factors became unfavorable for the house rat in the nineteenth century; but the transformation of building methods in the twentieth century has been propitious for this species, which explains the increasing frequency of black rats in Europe.[172] Inasmuch as the black rat lives and breeds in human dwellings, the new brick houses, masonry firewalls, shingled or tiled roofs, all combined to offer less favorable harborage to this "domesticated" rat. Floors covered with straw as well as other favorable breeding-grounds for fleas also disappeared. A flea can live as long as a year, and it can be a reservoir of infection whether it lives in the fur of a rodent or in the dust and soil of flooring. If the human flea was a major vector of plague, the gradual disappearance of timbered structures, in particular rotting and unseasoned wood, likewise reduced the risk of plague. In fact, the human body flea spends part of its life in the dust and dirt of human sleeping quarters. Finally, public as opposed to domestic storage of grain meant that house rats and fleas were less likely to share human habitations.[173]

It was the housing contrast between Western and Ottoman lands that was primarily responsible for the continuing epidemics of bubonic plague in the Balkan peninsula and the Middle East. This sharp contrast was still apparent in the 1840s, when the French plague and quarantine commission published its report. At Erzurum, for example, an Armenian city with 50,000 inhabitants, which was surrounded by heavily populated villages and had been identified as a major inveterate focus of plague, the homes of the majority of the population both in the city and the country were made of earth. Not only were the houses described as "low, narrow, damp" but also "in the winter all members of the family and all the animals lived together indiscriminately in these kinds of foxholes (*tanières*)."[174] While this description refers to the 1840s, the housing conditions had not changed for centuries. Moreover, the same description applied to the housing found in all Turkish possessions, "whether in Europe or in Asia."[175] The principal towns on the Turkish side of the Danube were dominated by buildings that were no more than sheds (*hangars*) and by houses that were merely huts (cahuttes). The homes in Vidin, in present-day Bulgaria, were said to be "almost completely buried in the ground; they are burrows (*terriers*) rather than human habitations."[176] It is not surprising to learn that today bubonic plague is a disease of rural not urban populations.[177] In the decade of the 1960s, nearly 5,000 cases of plague were reported in rural South America, the majority in locations where villages are expanding and land is being settled or cleared. The contact between humans and rodents becomes more intimate, and the same relationship is true of rats and indiginous rodents and their ectoparasites.[178] Escape from bubonic plague in Europe demanded a set of structural sanitary barriers, which was provided by quarantine, public hygiene, and above all by the clean, rat-free dwelling.[179] Underdeveloped southeastern Europe, as well as the Middle East, lacked such safeguards in the early nineteenth century. Consequently, epidemic bubonic plague was still rife in the Balkan peninsula and in the Ottoman empire. Neither medical advance, nor greater agricultural productivity, nor the advance of the Norway rat were the salient conditions for the conquest of plague in Europe. This result ensued from the structural and functional improvements effected by modern governments and their citizens.

The evidence suggests that any model of explanation covering famine, mortality, and epidemic disease cannot be reduced to the simple interaction between nutrition and infection. Either in the case of an autonomous zootic disease like bubonic plague, or in a communicable human disease like typhus, social, economic, and political conditions as well as biological and meteorological factors are inevitably involved. Nor is escape from plague or epidemic typhus quite as automatic as the French plague commission contended in its conclusion that "the progress of civilization" and the application of the rules of hygiene would prevent epidemics.[180] The United Kingdom and Switzerland, both modernizing societies, as well as backward Italy failed to control severe typhus epidemics. Yet Britain and Switzerland were as developed as France and the Netherlands, and more so than Austria and the majority of German states. Switzerland failed to minimize the rise in mortality rates because political decentralization reduced the resources that could potentially have been allocated to those cantons in which the subsistence crisis developed into famine—decentralization led to administrative competition instead of cooperation. The United Kingdom failed to control famine and epidemic disease in Ireland chiefly because administrative guidelines based on the principles of early liberalism created blind spots. A similar administrative policy permitted both the typhus epidemic and social distress to assume major proportions in England, Scotland, and Wales. In Britain, however, unlike Ireland and Italy, economic development produced a modicum of relief and, together with the sanitary barriers found in a modernizing society, prevented a drastic increase in the death rate. Even though the relationship between famine and epidemic typhus or dysentery cannot be reduced to the straightforward interaction between nutrition and infection, as in the case of scurvy or pellagra, the subsistence crisis provided the necessary connection through the economic and social turbulence that it engendered.

chapter
five

The Harvest Failures and
the Postwar Trade Cycle

GRAIN OUTPUT AND THE LABROUSSE THESIS

The Western economy of the early decades of the nineteenth century was still primarily agricultural and the level of grain output continued to generate the single largest impact on economic activity. As indicated, however, the postwar trade cycle was also affected by readjustments in trade and industry in the wake of wartime dislocations and the return of peace in 1815. Abrupt changes in inventory investment, contractions and expansions of the money supply, fluctuations in industrial production and employment were among the economic variables that led to brief periods of expansion to be followed by depression or stagnation almost everywhere in the Western world between 1815 and 1819. The dominant factor in the postwar trade cycle, however, was the violent fluctuation of agricultural productivity and consequently of the price of foodstuffs, which exercised the primary influence on the entire Western economy.

The contraction of 1816–17 and the following commercial boom were governed in large part by the varying annual levels of agricultural output. Agriculture not only made up the largest component in the national income, it was also the largest industry if measured in terms of capital and labor force. Within the agricultural industry, cereal culture was the leading sector. The concentration on grains and the undue dependence on fluctuating yields was an economic as well as a social hazard. The demand for wheat, rye, barley, and oats, which was expressed primarily by the need for bread and fodder (needs for which no alternatives existed at this time), caused the demand for grain to continue to be inelastic and thus unresponsive to price changes.

Though potatoes were becoming a supplement to the grain supply, the importance of this plant as a field crop still lay in the future. On the supply side, the quantity of grain brought to market varied significantly from year to year, mainly as a consequence of weather conditions, a fact clearly apparent from the experience of the years from 1815 to 1820. If the impressionistic evidence presented above is trustworthy, grain yields in severely affected districts might fall to a level barely half of the volume of the better years. Consequently, the economic foundations of preindustrial society rested on a narrow and unstable base.[1] Economic well-being, it bears repeating, still varied decisively with the outcome of the harvests, and real income moved inversely to the price of grain.

The entire economy, moreover, remained susceptible to the rhythm of the seasons; the weather not only determined food consumption, it also governed the supply of raw materials to industry. The volume of the grain harvest, beyond its bearing on consumer purchasing power, influenced the quantity and price of materials for such industries as brewing and distilling, and even starch-making. Employment was also affected, since the typical industry still processed the output of the land. A decrease in the labor needed to harvest a smaller crop was paralleled by a reduced demand for labor at the grain mills, breweries, and distilleries. Since the flow of money wages diminished, while the price of food rose, the demand for clothing, footwear, beverages, and the small conveniences within reach of working-class budgets declined. These economic effects tended to reinforce each other; for example, a poor grain harvest produced high barley prices and resulted in a lower output of malt and beer, and at the same time the higher price of bread forced the laboring population to reduce its consumption of beer. Since employment tended to contract in times of dearth, the demand for manufactured products could fall off sharply.[2]

While the effects of harvest fluctuations on aggregate money income and effective demand were of major cyclical significance, the effects on real income and on the distribution of incomes were probably even more important.[3] Expenditures for bread still occupied first place by far in popular budgets, and, accordingly, when grain prices doubled, the decline of real income was substantial. Bread consumed half of a poor laboring person's budget when cereal prices stood at customary levels; and even in England food and drink claimed nearly two-thirds of a laboring family's budget.[4] The majority of Europe's population was made up of wage-earners and agricultural workers who were compelled to purchase bread or cereals at market prices.

Although it is clear that fluctuations in harvest yields shifted demand curves for industrial products, these shifts are not traceable in detail. A severe harvest deficiency should redistribute income not only to the agricultural sector but in favor of large grain producers and grain dealers and away from subsistence peasants and day-laborers. Thus, while it can be surmised that rural income is transferred from a large low-spending peasantry to a smaller high-spending agricultural class, it is not known which group had the higher marginal propensity to consume. As far as contemporary understanding was concerned, the net effect of a severe harvest failure was to reduce rather than to increase the demand for industrial goods and services. Some commentators were convinced that the economic crisis of 1816–17 had resulted from the crop deficiencies and that the distress would pass with the appearance of the improved harvest yields that were anticipated in 1817.[5]

A case can be made that good harvests increased the demand for labor, increased real wages because of the decline in the price of bread, and also increased the demand for industrial products and services. Contemporary observers assumed that the income elasticity of demand for clothing, textiles, footwear, and drink was extremely high. Conversely, a case can be made that poor harvests lowered real wages through higher food prices, reduced investment in agriculture, and led to a decline in the demand for nonagricultural goods. But it is also possible that an abundant harvest with its ensuing loss of revenue to the agricultural sector might result in a reduction in farm investment, the dismissal of farm labor, and, because of the controlling size of the rural community, lead to a decline in the demand for industrial goods and services. The resolution of these issues depends on multiple variables, such as the severity of the crop deficiencies, the structure of the agrarian community and the distribution of land holdings, the relative product of the agricultural and industrial sectors, the marginal propensities to consume, and other empirical data not readily available.

The evidence that is at hand, nonetheless, leads to the conclusion that the harvest deficiencies of 1816 produced a sharp decline in real income, and because the economy was still dominated by a subsistence agricultural sector the fall off in output had an impoverishing effect. To begin with, the large increases in the price of grain which are reflected in the indexes shown in Table 7 are a symptom of a real national economic loss, even if these price movements do not reveal the net effect on income. However, they do indicate the magnitude of the harvest failures, i.e., the fall in agricultural output, which, together with the share that grain production has in aggregate national income, determines the effect on real national income. A severe harvest deficiency in an economy ruled by agriculture necessarily results in a fall in aggregate income; an economy that fails to produce as much grain as formerly becomes poorer. It is not just a question of consumers paying more for a measure of grain; more hours must be worked and more resources must be surrendered for the same quantity of cereals. In effect, the net loss to the economy in 1816 was the grain that failed to mature.

In general outline, the postwar economic contraction conformed to the preindustrial depressions depicted by Camille-Ernest Labrousse in his explication of trade cycles in eighteenth-century France.[6] According to Labrousse, the economy contracts because the majority of grain producers suffer a decline in income as a consequence of the fall in the volume of output. Since the rural population makes up the great majority of the nation, the market for manufactured goods slumps, and this decline in demand is extended by the impact of high food prices on the expenditures of poor urban consumers. Businesses find it necessary to retrench; both the output and price of manufactured articles fall; the level of employment also declines. The depression ends and the economy returns to normal when good harvests and lower grain prices restore the incomes of the working population. As in the eighteenth century, the economy in 1816 was still ruled by agricultural maladjustments, by the alternation of good and bad harvests. Further, the large agricultural price increases of 1816–17 remained doubly significant because the Western economy still operated in a ''specie regime.'' In addition, low-cost means of transportation were still substantially lacking, and each area had to shift largely for itself in counterbalancing the grain shortages. Labrousse's propositions, even if they cannot resolve every issue, nevertheless contribute to the understanding of the postwar trade cycle.

The quantitative evidence, even though no more than approximate, discloses not only that the harvest deficiencies of 1816 were significantly large but also that the relative product of the agricultural sector still occupied a preponderant position in the Western economy. In Britain, then the world's most industrialized economy, it has been estimated that agriculture accounted for 37.5 percent of national product in 1811, and that it occupied 33.0 percent of the labor force. The industrial sector, made up of manufactures, mining, and building, accounted for 20.8 percent of national product.[7] The value of the French agricultural product in 1815 has been estimated at 5 billion francs, compared to an industrial product of 4.5 billion francs, which includes the building industry and the large food-processing industry. Cereals and fodder made up 47 percent of the agricultural product, while potatoes accounted for slightly more than 2 percent.[8] Moreover, some 62–68 percent of the French population made a living from agriculture in 1816.[9] With the exception of the Netherlands and possibly Switzerland, agriculture's share in the national product of the remaining European economies would of course have been greater.

Labrousse's assumption that only a relatively few grain producers had holdings large enough to profit from the higher prices also seems to be borne out by the sparse knowledge of European land distribution during this period. Reputedly, there were 3,805,000 landholding families in France, but 2,882,000 possessed less than five hectares.[10] One method of testing the income effect produced by variations in the volume and price of grain is to calculate the net income for farms of modal sizes. This method of course yields no indication of profits based on the size of the farm or to what extent profits varied with prices. For analytical purposes assume that A, B, and C represent small, middling, and large farms; that the yield is ten hectoliters per hectare during an average wheat year; and that the market price is 20 francs per hectoliter:[11]

	A	B	C
Wheat harvest (hectoliters)	25	50	100
Consumption	20	30	40
Market sale	5	20	60
Income (francs)	100	400	1,200

If the wheat yield falls by 20 percent and the market price rises by 80 percent to 36 francs, these changes will occur:

	A	B	C
Wheat harvest (hectoliters)	20	40	80
Consumption	20	30	40
Market sale	0	10	40
Income (francs)	0	360	1,400

Because of consumption needs, farms of five hectares and smaller, which represented by far the largest fraction, failed to gain income from the higher prices, while farms of ten hectares and larger clearly benefited. Since approximately 1.1 million families averaged holdings of one-half hectare in 1815, they were compelled to be purchasers of grain at all times. Depending on family size and harvest yields, some of the 850,000 families who averaged holdings of one and two-thirds hectares were also purchasers of grain for consumption needs. By contrast, each of the 168,000 families who possessed an average of 62 hectares secured 9,280 francs in additional income as a result of higher prices. If the top category of 21,000 holdings averaging 880 hectares is subjected to the same analysis, each family improved its annual income, according to this rough calculation, by 140,160 francs.[12]

Neither the distribution of land holdings nor the structure of the rural community in Europe is reliably known until several decades after the postwar period. With the exception of England and some regions of Germany, however, the evidence suggests that some 65–75 percent of the landholding families of western and central Europe suffered a loss of income based on the above method of calculation. The Netherlands, like all Continental states at this time, remained a rural and agricultural economy, in spite of early industrialization in the Belgian provinces and the growth of several large commercial cities in the Dutch half of the kingdom. The rural population of the Netherlands amounted to more than 73 percent of the total; agriculture, moreover, was the principal occupation of more than 75 percent of the rural population. Domestic industry was practiced on a large scale in both Belgium and Holland by a rural population that combined spinning and weaving with agriculture. The evidence also suggests that land ownership in the Netherlands was more restricted than in France, and that a larger percentage of the population depended on money wages for subsistence.[13] Rural overpopulation and the miniaturization of peasant subsistence farms in southwestern Germany during this period are well established facts. Landholding patterns were, of course, different in eastern Germany, where the legacy of manorialism polarized land ownership into either large capitalistic enterprises producing grain surpluses for export or into prosperous peasant holdings of eight hectares or more.[14]

The agricultural population of the Austrian empire not only made up an overwhelming majority of the total, percentagewise even fewer landholders than in France possessed sufficient land to gain income from the rise of grain prices. Moreover, a significant fraction of the rural population was virtually landless. The working population of the Habsburg Monarchy was made up of purchasers rather than sellers of grain, with the exception of landholding peasants who produced surplus grain beyond family needs. Though the earliest comprehensive record of land distribution only dates from the 1840s, no substantial change in landholding patterns had taken place since 1815–20. Holdings in the Austrian empire were generally designated as either full, half, quarter, or smaller than a quarter, varying in acreage with location; but it is sufficient to note that only full or half holdings were large enough to demand the full-time labor of their occupants. The average peasant also worked at agricultural labor, both the compulsory *Robot* and hired, wage day-labor. Although occupational data compiled during the first half of the nineteenth century do not disclose the precise structure of the agricultural labor force, the number of peasants and the extent of their land holdings are known for four provinces. In Lower Austria, some 64 percent of peasant holdings were quarter or smaller in size; in Moravia, this figure reached 82 percent; in Hungary, small holders accounted for 84 percent; and in Styria, 78 percent of peasant holdings were quarter or smaller in size. Moreover, in each of these locations and in every land of the Monarchy, there were also unenumerated peasants who had a house but no land, and still others who possessed neither house nor land. In fact, cottagers and landless peasants in the Czech lands outnumbered those with holdings of all sizes. The lower strata of the agricultural community in the Austrian empire had to depend on wages of some kind to meet basic subsistence needs.[15]

Landless day-laborers in Europe, as well as small owners and tenants, suffered a loss of real income as a result of the decline in agricultural output and the rise in cereal prices. While it is difficult to measure real wage levels, since day-laborers might receive additional payments in kind for special tasks, be entitled to meals, and also secure higher earnings during some seasons, it is nevertheless clear that payment in grain only partially insulated a day-laborer against a loss of real income at the time of a severe harvest failure. A study of French day-laborers in the nineteenth century who were paid both in cash and in grain shows that the crop deficiencies of 1816 caused a large reduction in their real wages. The day-laborer (together with his wife and two small children) in this study was compelled to buy bread grain during nine months of the year. The day-laborer purchased a total of 49 *quartiers* at a cost of 146 francs in 1815, when the price of wheat stood at 16 francs the hectoliter. But in 1817, when the price of the same measure of wheat averaged 43 francs, his purchases totaled only 35 *quartiers* and he was required to spend 185 francs. The family was forced to reduce its consumption 30 percent, at the same time laying out 39 additional francs.[16] Moreover, work opportunities for day-laborers diminished with the poor harvest, since the amount of labor required to reap, move, store, and thresh the grain declined with the volume of the crop.

Labrousse's proposition that the slump is aggravated by the impact of high food prices on the expenditures of the poorer classes in the cities can scarcely be questioned, since urban wage rates were already so close to subsistence levels. As mentioned, contemporary observers believed that the income elasticity of demand for consumption goods was very high. *The Times* explained the sinking prices and stagnating sales at the great European fairs in the spring of 1817 by pointing to this concept: "Hence it is that while bread becomes dearer, or holds its value, the whole mass of luxuries, and many of the articles thought essential to comfort in ordinary times, sink below that price at which the manufacturers can live by selling them. The raw material falls with the manufactured goods. That alone would account for the gloomy prospects in the whole market."[17] Similar explanations were repeated in the Habsburg dominions: "Because of poor harvests the price of provisions rose extraordinarily and . . . the purchasing power of the population had also been very much diminished, so that sales openings continued to exist only for absolutely necessary goods."[18] An "economics professor" in Germany believed that the cause and effect sequence was axiomatic: "especially then in such . . . times trade stagnates; because bread after all is the first and most indispensable purchase. A new coat, a new shawl, a new shirt can be done without. If grain is expensive, linen is cheap,—that is an old watchword."[19] Conversely, when trade and industry began to recover in late 1817, explanations credited the improved harvests and lower bread prices. "The reduction in provisions will enable the poor man to spend his wages upon an article of dress as well as food; and an increase of wages as naturally follows upon an increase of trade, as that two and two makes four."[20] A standard proverb in nineteenth-century Bradford, England held that, "when the poor live cheaply, they clothe well.''[21] Similar expressions of optimism can be found in the French press on the eve of satisfactory harvests in 1817.[22]

It seemed evident to contemporaries that higher bread prices handicapped the sale of manufactured products. Ternaux, the greatest French industrialist and merchant of the period, accounted for the manufacturing slump in terms of a decline in real income, and buttressed his explanation with an early attempt at national income accounting:

Thirteen-twentieths of the nation live from income so limited that their expenditures totally absorb their daily earnings. *When they are obliged to use a much larger part of this income to purchase an indispensable commodity,* of necessity they employ a smaller share for the purchase of commodities of less urgent necessity.

Experience has taught that each inhabitant of a country like France consumes nearly a pound of bread daily . . .; but the totality of inhabitants does not consume the foodstuffs which make up their nourishment as a result of purchase. It is necessary to subtract from the 28 million inhabitants in France all those who do not buy their wheat or bread, or all those who buying it have enough sufficiency not to reduce their other expenditures to zero because of the dearness of provisions. It is difficult to estimate the number of these two classes of consumers: but one can hardly number them beyond a quarter of the inhabitants. The other three-quarters, that is to say 21 million, are obliged to buy their bread with wages or earnings, which in ordinary times are scarcely sufficient for all their expenditures. During the last dearth (1817), these 21 million persons instead of paying for bread on the basis of 3 *sous* per pound, the usual average price, paid 6 *sous* for it, its average price for 549 days in all of France. Now 21 million pounds of bread at 3 excess *sous* per pound, occasioned an added expenditure of 3,150,000 francs per day, and for 549 days, an extraordinary expenditure of 1,729,350,000 francs. *It was necessary that this entire sum enormous as it appears be subtracted from the consumption of the manufactured and commercial products of the country: our mills and factories by contrast finding themselves less employed, must furnish less employment to the working class and consequently increase its distress.*[23]

The higher price of bread, moreover, was not the only factor responsible for lower real wages and the decline in the demand for industrial goods. The supply of usable firewood for fuel, as an example, was reduced by the excessive precipitation of 1816, and the working population was forced to pay higher prices for another commodity which it could not do without. By November 1816, the price of firewood had doubled in the Rhineland region of Germany.[24] The weather proved detrimental to almost all plants and animals; and this fact caused commodity prices to rise, which inhibited their sale and likewise reduced employment levels. In addition to losses of grain, grapes, and livestock, such industrial crops as hemp and silk also suffered. The "failure of the silk-worms" in France resulted in a deficient supply for silk manufacturers, leading to a reduction in the duty on foreign raw silk in 1817.[25] Numerous smaller casualties also contributed to the net economic loss. The wetness of the summer created an "almost unprecedented" scarcity of honey, by interfering with the normal activity of bees.[26] The total failure of the European chestnut crop represented not only an economic loss but was a social tragedy in some districts of France and Italy.[27] Elsewhere in the Western world, the output of oils, tobacco, and cotton was also adversely affected by the weather.

At the same time, harvest failures of the magnitude of those experienced in 1816 also lead to a significant redistribution of income in favor of the agricultural sector as the result of higher price levels, and its effects call for examination. To begin with, unless the redistributed income escapes from the circular flow of money, the effective demand of the rural sector for industrial goods and services should rise and offset to an extent the decline that ensued from the lower real income of wage-earners and small peasants. In fact, it would not be unreasonable to assume that transferring income from peasants and wage-earners to large and middling grain producers might result in higher demand for manufactured products, since subsistence peasants were poor customers for industrial goods, even in times of prosperity. David Landes has advanced a solution to this problem, which, when applied to the specific mechanisms and the observed patterns of social disruption that flowed from the famine of 1816–17, helps to explain why aggregate demand was so adversely affected and why the economic crisis proved so severe.

Landes has shown that the steep rise in grain prices during a famine finally reaches a level where profits fall into few hands, and that the beneficiaries tend to conceal wealth rather than to increase expenditures. At some point the gains in demand resulting from shifts in income are outweighed by the fall-off in demand that follows from social unrest, commercial disruption, and general insecurity. This threshold is passed before hunger and famine cripple the total economy.[28] The argument is convincing; the economic effect is produced as much by the social upheaval created by the famine as by changes in the flow of income. The end result is that aggregate demand fails to rise in proportion to the increase in agricultural revenue. The most apparent loss results from the tendency to conceal wealth; in preindustrial economies, farmers who profit from income redistribution tend to save, hoard, or to direct spending into different channels and thus to distort the normal flow of purchasing power, or to sterilize money temporarily outside the economic system.[29] The social unrest of 1816–17, however, also occasioned losses of income and brought about the destruction of wealth, and the weather responsible for the crop deficiencies produced similar consequences. These factors represented leakages from the potential windfall profits accruing from famine prices and help to account for the severity of the economic crisis.

One important leakage from the windfall profits and change in the flow of purchasing power in 1816–17 ensued from the fact that almost all individuals who were fortunate enough to possess discretionary income were faced with demands to assist the destitute. In the process of explaining the stagnation of commerce and industry in Germany, the economic writer Wilhelm Joseph Behr observed that: "The middling person in the towns and in the country, the largest class, is drained of all his funds for the scanty satisfaction of present necessities and with them the sources of future earnings. Even the well-to-do person, pressed by demands on his generosity, gives up the satisfaction of many wants, and by his curtailment contracts the sale of industrial goods."[30] The extraordinary private and public relief and welfare measures, which have been documented above, caused significant distortions in the flow of income. Moreover, it is easy to believe that the forbidding level of social distress inhibited expenditures for conspicious consumption, and therefore further reduced aggregate demand. Economic activity was also constrained by the prevailing typhus and plague epidemics, particularly in the Mediterranean ports.[31] Commercial channels were likewise disturbed by national embargoes placed on the export of foodstuffs, by large-scale emigration, and by the multiplication of rioting, vagrancy, and begging.

But it is also possible to identify specific leakages from the income redistributed to the agricultural sector, which often involved losses of real wealth as well. As a consequence of the incendiary violence committed against large farms situated near market towns, some gains were offset by destructive losses almost before they were realized. Arson became a European phenomenon during the dearth period, destroying grain, buildings, animals, and on occasion humans. Other farmers lost potential gains because of the extensive and widespread looting in the countryside by vagrant bands, while the institution of popular price controls and the endless food riots in the market towns spelled lost profits for sellers.[32] In these instances, however, the losses sustained were of minor significance for the economy, irrespective of individual tragedies.

Of more economic importance, the destructive weather exacted a high mortality among Europe's animal population. The excessive moisture was especially injurious to sheep and cattle. Reportedly, numerous landowners and peasants in Germany saw half or more of their flocks perish. Huge mortality among the livestock was also reported in the United Kingdom, France, the Netherlands, Switzerland, and the Habsburg Monarchy, particularly in Hungary.[33] According to Gustav von Gülich, losses from cattle deaths were frequently extensive enough to offset the income gains from high grain prices: "The producer on the other had gained from the enormously high grain prices which resulted from the poor harvests; yet in the majority of cases they were less than adequate to compensate him for the volume deficiencies, since husbandry expenses rose sharply owing to the unaccommodating weather and higher wages, and the loss which he suffered from cattle deaths frequently was so very great."[34] Since animal husbandry was mainly the business of substantial farmers, the replacement of cattle and sheep consumed some grain profits; in other cases, large grain producers doubtless used profits to add to flocks and herds. Smaller farmers found it necessary to replace cattle and sheep by purchasing from dealers on credit.[35] Also, the universal shortage of fodder had led to the slaughtering of animals who could not be fed through the winter months. Apart from the ruin of individuals, the death of millions of animals added a loss of real capital to the loss of aggregate income that befell the European economy as a consequence of the deficient grain output.

The high cereal prices prompted speculative as well as public grain purchases in eastern Europe and the Ottoman empire. Though such distinctions are difficult to make, a share of these cereal imports probably represented bad investment. Grain prices began to collapse in the ports of northern Europe as early as autumn 1817, and the press began to report commercial bankruptcies attributable to the steep decline in cereal prices. The quantity of grain imported into Amsterdam was so great that merchants had to store the surplus in Haarlem and other Dutch towns.[36] The bulk of the foreign grain purchases made by the French government did not arrive until the summer months of 1817; and, as grain prices were already declining, these supplies contributed to the speculative losses of merchants who had also placed orders abroad.[37] Moreover, because of the protracted time consumed in transporting grain from distant locations, the supplies often arrived in western Europe in poor or damaged condition. Speculation in grain was still widespread in the late summer of 1817, and complaints were voiced that landowners as well as merchants purchased grains of every description.[38] The extraordinary grain trade that developed at Trieste in 1816–18 as a consequence of high prices also led to speculative imports from Odessa, Smyrna, and Alexandria.[39] Merchant groups in Germany devoted large sums to grain purchases; the rising grain prices tended to attract large sums of commercial capital because of the quick profit involved, and also because the stagnation of industry had dried up investment opportunities.[40] The speculative importation of grain probably reached its highest point in Britain and the Netherlands.[41]

While dealers and merchants often risked their gains in commodity and security speculation, grain producers were more likely to invest windfall profits in land purchases and agricultural expansion or improvement. This circumstance was abundantly clear and has been well documented in the United States, where rising agricultural commodity and export prices inspired a movement into lands suitable for cotton and grain production.[42] Although the land boom was not so pronounced in Europe, investment in land and the expansion of grain production occurred on a major scale after 1816. Founded on the unprecedented European demand for grain, southern Russia experienced an expansion of agricultural production not unlike the American hinterland, resulting in the debut of Odessa as a leading wheat outport for European markets. Then, paralleling the overexpansion and subsequent contraction in the American west, the cereal and land boom collapsed in New Russia. The high prices and profits derived from the sale of grain to Europe in

1816–17 had occasioned the planting of large tracts of land previously neglected. The integration of these new lands into the Russian economy necessitated the commitment of large resources; but when the increased grain supplies arrived, European demand had contracted and prices had fallen sharply. Wheat supplies became a burden on the markets of southern Russia in the autumn of 1818 and prompted the view "that if Europe does not come to our assistance, we shall never be able to find vent for it."[43] By 1818, however, it was too late for European demand to drain off the surplus production of cereals either in Russia or America, for the new investment in grain production in western and central Europe in combination with improved weather resulted in excessive supply and falling prices everywhere in the Western world.

The extension of grain cultivation in 1817–18 was not confined to large producers in the Russian empire and North America. A new wave of land speculation developed in East Prussia, where the Edict of October 1807 had permitted even burghers to share in the ownership and free use of noble lands for commercial profit. The peasantry of Europe also participated in the movement to put more land into cereal production, once again prompted by the high prices of 1816–17. But in France, Germany, the Netherlands, and Switzerland, all too often farmers' income in 1819 proved insufficient to meet the higher rents and the mortgage debts contracted when grain prices were elevated. The abrupt fall of cereal prices bankrupted numerous producers. As many as one-half of the small peasant landowners and some 10 percent of the largest peasant proprietors in the Habsburg lands met with ruin in 1819. Forced auction sales of mortgaged peasant farms became commonplace in all provinces. Numerous producers of agricultural staples everywhere in the Western world were bound to commitments that could be fulfilled only if abnormally high prices continued to prevail in 1818–19. Many peasants in southwestern Germany had undertaken the liquidation of manorial dues and services by borrowing from moneylenders when famine grain prices were the rule; a considerable number of these emancipated peasants were hopelessly in debt to cattle dealers and money-lenders in 1819. In England and the grain lands of northeastern Europe, where the agricultural depression of 1815 had led to large tracts of land becoming untenanted, the high price of grain drove up land values and resulted in increased cereal production in 1817–18. The investment in expanded grain output produced, temporarily at least, overextended cultivators and surplus production.[44]

Even if the critical time series were available, in a complex total system like the Western economy it would still be difficult to demonstrate that economic activity declined primarily as a consequence of the harvest deficiencies. Yet the evidence points inescapably to that conclusion. The sharp drop in agricultural output and productivity resulted in a decline of aggregate income and real wages and, in addition, meant a multiple decline in redistributable agricultural incomes, since in a subsistence economy the saleable margin tended to evaporate. The redistribution of income to the large agricultural sector failed to produce a proportionate increase in the aggregate rural demand for goods and services, because of the social upheaval that inhibited expenditures and because of the loss of wealth and capital. Though high prices and windfall gains prompted investment in grain inventories and expanded capacity for grain production, the increased supplies proved too substantial for demand when they arrived.

THE FINANCIAL PANIC AND DEPRESSION OF 1818–1819

The influence of the crop deficiencies on economic activity did not end in 1817 and, together with the expanded capacity for the production of agricultural staples, continued to play a significant part in the postwar trade cycle. Although this is not the occasion to reexamine the commercial crisis, bank panic, and depression of 1818–19, it is appropriate to connect the weather patterns and agricultural commodity prices to these later economic events. The agricultural calamity of 1816 was probably the single most important factor in the trade cycle, yet its cyclical significance has been largely overlooked. While the boom in agricultural products represented in part the normal swing of a commodity inventory cycle, the production of world staples was expanded in 1817–18 chiefly in response to rising agricultural prices. The volume as well as the value of commodities in international trade rose, not only grain but all primary products that had been affected by the weather. The disappointing level of exports in 1818, which failed to match imports, and the collapse of prices were the inevitable out-come of the increased supply.

The postwar fluctuations of international trade reflected this sequence of events. To begin with the United States, the indifferent European harvests of 1815 and the harvest failures of 1816 brought prosperity to the American agrarian economy. The favorable European market for agricultural exports during the years 1816–18 was translated into higher income for American producers and for merchants engaged in commercial activities devoted to the import-export trade with the rural community. As in the years before the embargo, American agricultural products could again be sold abroad in large quantities and at high prices.

The rise of American grain prices in 1816–17 was influenced both by deficient domestic yields and by the enlarged European demand. The price levels of cotton and tobacco, though also influenced by the losses occasioned by the weather, particularly in the case of tobacco,[45] were determined chiefly by the export market. The importance of cotton exports in the American postwar economic expansion is well known. Table 17 shows that cotton

Table 17. Value of Exports and Imports—United States, 1815–20 (in millions of dollars)

Year[a]	Exports total	Exports U.S. products	Grain[b] exports	Cotton exports	Re-exports	General imports	Balance of trade
1815	53	46	11	18	7	113	−60
1816	82	65	13	24	17	147	−65
1817	88	68	23	23	19	99	−12
1818	93	74	19	31	19	122	−28
1819	70	51	10	21	19	87	−17
1820	70	52	8	22	18	74	− 5

[a]Fiscal years ending September 30.
[b]Includes wheat, corn, rice, and flour.
Sources: Charles H. Evans, "Exports, Domestic and Foreign, from the American Colonies to Great Britain, from 1697 to 1789, Inclusive. Exports, Domestic and Foreign, from the United States to all Countries from 1789 to 1883, Inclusive," House Miscellaneous Documents, 48 Cong., 1 Sess., No. 49, Part 2 (1884), Serial 2236, Table 2, pp. 46–47; United States, Bureau of the Census, Historical Statistics of the United States, Colonial Times to 1957 (Washington, D.C.: Government Printing Office, 1960), p. 538.

exports rose from $18 million in 1815 to $24 million in 1816, then declined slightly to $23 million in 1817, before reaching a peak of $31 million in 1818. At the same time the level of food exports promoted by the European subsistence crisis has gone relatively unnoticed. The figures in Table 17 indicate not only the boom in grain exports but also the fact that the value of American food products in international trade fluctuated with greater amplitude than cotton. Grain exports more than doubled, from $11 million in 1815 to $23 million in 1817, in which year their export value matched that of cotton. Unlike the case with cotton, grain exports declined with the easing of the European famine in 1818, and then fell off steeply to $10 million following the harvests of 1818. The sharp decline in grain exports also put an end to the land boom in the Northwest.

The rise of domestic export values from $46 million in 1815 to $65 million in 1816, and the continuing advance to $74 million in 1818, had inspired a westward movement into lands suitable for producing grain, cotton, and tobacco. Table 18 displays the United States Treasury's receipts from the sale of public lands and shows a strong correlation between the income from land sales and the value of grain and cotton exports, with the exception of 1819, in which the large figure is explained by the continuing interest in the newer lands of Alabama and Mississippi. The decline of land sales in the older public-land states of Ohio and Indiana mirrored the collapse of grain prices, whereas the activity in the Southwest matched the elevated cotton prices of 1818. Even though cotton export prices declined from $.330 cents per pound in 1818 to $.239 in 1819, cotton continued to return $.240 in New York and other markets throughout 1819, and new settlers continued to rush into the cotton lands of Alabama and Mississippi.[46] Prices remained at high levels

Table 18. U. S. Treasury's Receipts from the Sale of Public Lands, 1815–20 (in $000's)

Year	Ohio	Illinois	Indiana	Mississippi	Alabama	Total[a]
1815	$1,656	$ 53	$ 369	—	$ 157	$2,410
1816	1,332	207	1,202	—	398	3,640
1817	1,416	572	1,080	—	1,718	5,083
1818	881	1,491	1,272	793	8,676	13,619
1819	958	611	458	2,461	4,148	8,980
1820	142	87	272	128	1,067	1,736

[a]Nominal land purchases in Michigan and Missouri have been omitted.
Source: Arthur H. Cole "Cyclical and Seasonal Variations in the Sale of Public Lands, 1816–1860," *Review of Economic Statistics* 9 (January 1927): 52.

after the initial stimulus had substantially disappeared, largely because of the excessive speculation in land sales and the overtrading of commodities. The western land expansion was ultimately cut off by the decline in the demand for American staples and the collapse of prices at the end of 1818.[47]

Monetary factors also played a part in the boom and contraction, for monetary and real factors are invariably related. The monetary effects were in fact the proximate forces involved in the downturn. The Second Bank, for several reasons beyond its initiative, such as the rapid repayment of the federal debt and the balance-of-trade deficit, found it necessary to check the drain of specie in 1818, and this measure resulted in a severe contraction of the money supply. But the economic consequences that followed from the expansion of production and productive capacity were also critical variables. A decline of commodity prices was the inevitable result when the increased supplies of grain and tobacco became too substantial relative to world demand. The agricultural expansion resulted in a substantial shift in supply that depressed prices. At the same time, American merchants imported foreign products in amounts beyond the resources of the economy.[48] The net result was a continuing deficit in the balance of trade during the postwar years, which climbed from $12 million in 1817 to $28 million in 1818, and then was painfully corrected in the early 1820s.[49]

The movement of France's postwar international trade values also reflects the inordinate influence of the crop deficiencies on the trade cycle. The Restoration government, because of the threat of famine, was forced to import large quantities of grain in spite of its precarious fiscal situation. The trade statistics, which are apparently only approximate values, but nevertheless indicate trends, are shown in Table 19. The figures indicate that the trade in provisions was the key factor in the shift from a positive balance of trade in 1816 to negative positions in 1817–19, which in turn had a deflationary effect on domestic demand and led to a contraction of credit. While it is true that

Table 19. Value of Exports and Imports—France, 1815–20 (in millions of francs)

Year	Exports total	Exports provisions	Imports total	Imports provisions	Imports British	Balance of trade	Balance of provisions trade
1815	433	147	296	85	51	+137	+62
1816	444	124	334	108	46	+110	+16
1817	380	89	427	164	47	− 47	−75
1818	428	115	444	145	43	− 16	−30
1819	383	134	387	141	36	− 4	− 7
1820	373	137	360	153	38	+ 13	−16

Source: Alexandre Chabert, *Essai sur les movements des revenus et de l'activité économique en France de 1789 à 1820* (Paris: Médicis, 1949), pp. 321–24.

these funds would eventually flow back to France in the form of orders for French products, in the meantime the period of transition could be painful. Grain imports, moreover, normally had to be paid for in gold and silver, and consequently did not stimulate exports to any great degree. Speculation in the French public securities that were issued to pay off the war indemnity aggravated the credit stringency; at the least, normal credit flows to manufacturers and merchants were disrupted, which added to the liquidity crisis.[50] But the rapid rise of import values from 296 million francs in 1815 to 444 million francs in 1818 is the most notable feature of the trade figures. Imports from Britain declined during the same period; and it is apparent that agricultural commodities were mainly responsible for the rise in import values. According to the official statistics, the value of wheat imports rose from less than one million francs in 1815 to 71 million francs in 1817,[51] an increase almost as large as the deficit in the balance-of-provisions trade in 1817. French ships continued to carry large quantities of grain from Odessa well into 1818, despite the steep decline in prices.[52] By 1820, however, the value of French wheat imports had declined to 12 million francs and the balance of trade had returned to a positive position.

Great Britain was, of course, the leading commercial and industrial economy of the period, and any significant activity in world commodities would be mirrored in the movement of its foreign trade. Table 20 shows a rise in British imports during 1817, and then a further rise to a value of £80.7 million in 1818, an increase of nearly £20 million over the previous year. Exports and reexports rose only £6.9 million in 1818, however. This short-lived boom, which ended in the commercial crisis of 1818, was a further reverberation of the influence of the crop deficiencies on the Western economy. But three different forces were involved in the rise of imports in 1817–18. Part of the explanation is to be found in the low figures of 1816; the increase conformed to the swing of an inventory investment cycle. Commodity imports also increased as the agricultural sector improved its economic position at the beginning of 1817, and as the real income of wage-earners rose with the decline of bread prices in the last months of the year. Third, the prices of grain, wine, oils, wool, silk, hemp, beet-sugar, tobacco, cotton, all rose as the result of reduced yields in 1816 and promoted commercial optimism. Though most commodities did not exhibit the price increases observed for cereals, all advanced to some degree.[53]

Grain imports proved the most speculative commodity of 1818. Britain imported more than seven million quarters of grain during the years 1817–18.[54] While it remains difficult to determine the total expenditure for these imports, which customarily had to be paid for in gold, they were responsible for a considerable share of the balance of trade deficits during these years. The official values of £2.2 million for 1817, and £3.9 for 1818, understate the amounts expended. More accurate estimates of £7.8 million for 1817, and £13.3 for 1818, appeared in a contemporary publication.[55] If the 4.5 million quarters of grain imported during 1818 are multiplied by the average prices prevailing at Danzig and Königsberg, a value of £9.2 million results, with no allowance for freight, insurance, and other expenses.[56] In 1819, the Reports from the Committees on the Resumption of Cash Payments assigned values of £6.4 million for 1817 and £10.9 for 1818.[57] In any event, the sums help to explain the turn of the exchanges against Britain and the drain of gold in 1817–18.

The causal role of harvest fluctuations in the business cycle is nevertheless difficult to assess. The sums expended on grain imports in years like 1817 and 1818 were large enough to be counted as an important if not indeed a critical variable. At the same time, a theory of preindustrial trade cycles based solely on the periodicity of harvests will probably fail to do justice to the complexity of the economic system, notwithstanding the seemingly consistent relationship between grain imports and cycle movements.[58] However, from the movement of prices and international trade values during the postwar years, it appears almost certain that the deflationary pressures in 1818 originated in the collapse of commodity prices and that domestic monetary

Table 20. Value of Exports and Imports—United Kingdom, 1815–20 (in millions of pounds sterling)

Year	Exports	Reexports	Imports	Balance of trade	Balance of payments
1815	51.6	16.8	71.3	− 2.9	—
1816	41.7	12.6	50.2	+ 4.1	+14.6
1817	41.8	10.1	61.0	− 9.1	+ 6.3
1818	46.5	12.3	80.7	−21.9	+ 4.7
1819	35.2	10.2	56.0	−10.6	+ 7.3
1820	36.4	10.4	54.2	− 7.4	+ 3.2

Souce: Albert H. Imlah, *Economic Elements in the Pax Britannica* (Cambridge: Harvard University Press, 1958), pp. 37, 70.

restraint was a secondary factor. If famine food prices were the principal concern in 1816–17, from 1819 to the mid-1820s the main economic problem had shifted to depressed agricultural prices. This contrasting situation was due in part to the increased investment in agriculture during the war years and the further expansion of output and productive capacity during 1817–18. But the higher production also resulted from the improved weather patterns in 1818, and both factors combined to produce large grain yields in 1819, 1820, and 1821. Farms in northern Germany were depicted as being surrounded by grain heaped "almost as high as Egyptian pyramids."[59] Weather patterns still played a major role in the preindustrial economy of Europe; only this time the elements produced drastically lower grain prices everywhere in the Western world.

chapter
six

Political
Epilogue

European governments in the aftermath of the Napoleonic wars were confronted with an unending sequence of political dislocations, popular disturbances, and social unrest, which began in 1815 and persisted until 1819. Political boundaries were changed at the Congress of Vienna, and before governments could assimilate new subjects and new territories they were forced to deal with administrative problems that ensued from commercial depression, unemployment, hunger, rioting and looting, widespread begging and vagrancy, and large-scale emigration. Real and potential threats to public health also increased political anxiety. It seems plausible that these events affected the direction of European politics in the postwar years. While it may not be possible to establish a direct causal chain connecting the famine and crisis to political decisions, the political troubles both in Britain and on the Continent were linked with economic upsets. Governmental policies derive from conclusions arrived at by individuals and groups whose motivations are overdetermined, and in which ideological considerations play a significant role. As a result, intervening factors may break the causal connection between events or introduce a new set of causes. Moreover, there has been no guarantee that political policies will be relevant to social realities, whether adopted by leaders, ministries, or assemblies. Nonetheless, rather than ignore the events that followed the postwar crisis, it seems appropriate to remind the reader that the political decisions did not take place in a socioeconomic void. There are occasions when the social world departs so drastically from everyday expectations that political modifications become almost unavoidable. What is suggested here is that the series of economic and social reversals which marked the years 1816–19 tended to shift political views in a conservative direction. At the same time, the liberal forces spawned by the Revolutionary and Napoleonic wars continued to cause apprehension among established governments, no matter how remote the fears of conspiratorial revolution seem to present-day historians.[1] The few weak liberal compromises that made a timid appearance in 1815–16 vanished in a climate of distrust and fear in 1819–20. This pattern of liberal compromise followed by repression arose in several European states; the socioeconomic factors were less noticeable in France but strikingly evident in Germany.

FRANCE

The year 1820 in France marked a return to the repressive political program that had been replaced in 1816 by a policy of reconciliation aimed at those elements most likely to support a constitutional monarchy. A period which has been characterized as one of "restoration and reaction" had in fact experienced a four-year interval that was relatively free of political repression. This interval began in the early stages of a severe economic crisis and ended when neither dearth nor social unrest were any longer a threat and economic recovery was on the horizon. From the dismissal of the ultraroyalist *Chambre introuvable* in September 1816, to the assassination of the duc de Berry in February 1820, the successive Paris ministries pursued a course calculated to conciliate moderate views. While the government's orientation remained firmly royalist, more tolerance toward individual views appeared, along with an attempt to win over the opposition with concessions. The government proposed, to repeat the well-known watchword, to *royaliser la nation et de nationaliser la royaute.*[2]

There were several reasons for the change of political course in 1816. First of all, the Allies, who feared that excessive repression, such as the White Terror, could lead to revolution, urged a shift in policy. Bonapartists, republicans, and revolutionaries made up the potential opposition to the Bourbon monarchy, and no doubt these fears were not completely unfounded. The necessity to win over the commercial and financial interests and the peasantry was more compelling, however; otherwise the restored monarchy could not hope to comply with the financial terms imposed by the Treaty of Paris. Since the *Chambre introuvable* had treated state creditors almost as traitors, the dissolution of the assembly served more ends than preserving France from political rebellion. An optional clause in the treaty limited occupation to three years instead of five, if the indemnity called for was paid in advance of the schedule; and it was a goal to strive for in order to end the foreign occupation as early as possible. Indefinite occupation also loomed as a possibility, a pessimistic alternative which would have been fatal to the prestige of the Bourbon dynasty in France.

The period from 1816 to 1820 was the calmest political episode of the entire Restoration. The new elections in 1816 returned a Chamber of Deputies of a more moderate stripe, and the ministry headed by the duc de Richelieu pursued a moderately liberal program. The king and his ministry were supported in both chambers by majorities made up of constitutional royalists and liberals, the latter elected under the political label of *indépendants*. Electoral reform represented one conspicuous example of the policy of conciliating the potential opposition. A new law on February 5, 1817, abolished the system of indirect elections established by the Charter and in its place conferred a direct vote on all male citizens who were thirty years or older and paid a minimum of 300 francs in direct taxes. The intention was to enlarge the influence of the liberal bourgeoisie in future elections at the relative expense of the ultraroyalists.[3]

The subsistence crisis of 1817 intervened, however, and to some degree reshaped the course and destiny of the Richelieu ministry. For example, when the law of October 1815 that had established emergency police powers and had restricted personal liberty came up for reconsideration in 1817, the illiberal provisions were substantially reenacted, owing in large part to concern over the popular disturbances engendered by the dearth.[4] The liberal faction tended to dissociate itself from ministerial policies of this kind and, in opposition, to represent itself as the champion of popular demands. The Bonapartists and the ultraroyalists also exploited the economic crisis for political ends. Public opinion, as so often happens in times of economic adversity, held the government responsible for much of the distress and hardship. The ministry was harrassed, moreover, by friends attempting to be helpful as well as by enemies fishing in the troubled waters.[5] The usual rumors appeared, some malicious others simply founded in credulousness. The outstanding example of the latter was the familiar charge that the royal family sold grain to England during the dearth; in this case the issue was raised by the duc de FitzJames in the Chamber of Peers, and the rumor was given wide circulation by the free distribution of thousands of copies of the speech.[6] But no organized opposition to the Bourbon monarchy existed. Even though the vagrant bands that ravaged the countryside often were led by former imperial soldiers, the concern with basic subsistence, not politics, remained paramount.[7] Belief in the existence of an opposition mattered more. The government's surprisingly mild response to the social disorders, as noticed above, was inspired in part by a strategy that tried to avoid forcing the disaffected into the camp of political opponents.

In the September 1817 elections, contested under the new law, the independents on the left won 25 seats, while the moderate ministerial royalists captured 150 seats and the ultraroyalists 80. The elections of 1818, in which again one-fifth of the deputies were to be replaced, produced additional gains for the independent candidates, who now held 45 of the 250 seats in the chamber.[8] Despite the great triumph of the duc de Richelieu at Aix-la-Chapelle in October 1818, the meeting at which the final financial details of the war indemnity were worked out and where the Allies agreed to withdraw their army of occupation under the optional clause of the treaty, and despite a policy of moderation and conciliation, the Richelieu ministry was unable to stay in office. Richelieu's ministry, moreover, had pursued a sincere constitutional policy; whatever legal restrictions existed that affected personal freedom or the press were not seriously enforced by Élie Decazes, the prefect of police. The newspapers suspended were, almost without exception, those suspected of Bonapartism.[9] The liberation of French territory and the admission of France into the European alliance system were major political victories for the Bourbon monarchy and the moderate Richelieu ministry. When Richelieu returned in triumph to Paris in November, his minister of interior, Joachim Lainé, persuaded him that the last elections had demonstrated that the danger to a constitutional monarchy now emanated from the left rather than from the right. Lainé advocated a coalition with the ultraroyalists, in order to oppose a growing Jacobinism; the Allies, who had noticed the reappearance of revolutionary symptoms in Germany and Italy, also supported this view. Decazes, however, opposed this policy, and when the king insisted that Decazes remain in the ministry, Richelieu resigned.[10]

The fall of the Richelieu ministry at the end of 1818 has been explained by the king's unwillingness to be separated from his favorite minister, and no doubt this view has some validity; but personal preference was not the only reason for the change of ministries. To begin with, when Decazes was named a peer early in 1818, a private correspondent of *The Times* interpreted this move to represent a commitment by the king to a policy of conciliation and constitutionalism, as well as a reward for his favorite.[11] The Chamber of Deputies also must have shared this preference for Decazes, unless it is maintained that the assembly was indifferent to the membership of the royal council, or, on the other hand, that the king was indifferent to the opinion of the chamber. In fact, Richelieu's ministry, from an economic viewpoint, was burdened with a series of liabilities that were awkward to explain away. The ministry had been formed when France was caught in the postwar economic doldrums. It was inseparably linked with the subsistence crisis, and now it was weighed in the balance on the morrow of the financial panic of 1818. Moderates as well as liberals were becoming convinced that aristocratic direction of the state was tantamount to economic failure. The results of the 1818 elections also suggest disenchantment with aristocratic candidates and a rejection of ultraroyalist positions; for not one of the twenty-five ultraroyalist members up for reelection was returned to the chamber.[12] No doubt the episode of the Secret Note proved a serious liability for the ultraroyalists in the elections.[13] Moreover, its appearance was scarcely calculated to promote ultraroyalist views among moderate royalists or to impress the king. In any event, the new Dessolles–Decazes government (General Dessolles was the nominal head, but Decazes as minister of interior and police was in control) had the support of the king, the support of two-thirds of the Chamber of Deputies, and the overwhelming approval of Paris, and the new ministry was pledged to a more liberal program.[14]

The financial crisis that materialized in France at the same time as the political crisis probably hastened the replacement of the Richelieu ministry. The Bank of France was forced to curtail the discounting of bills owing to an alarming outflow of specie, and finally the Bank had to limit the period of the bills to forty-five days instead of the usual ninety days. This measure was followed by a liquidity crisis in the French money market. The most serious consequence was a sharp drop in the price of the government's *rentes* from 74 to 68. Much of the new debt was held by individuals who lacked the means to make their installment payments in the absence of bank accommodation. A majority of the holders were in effect speculators now forced to sell their shares.[15] The continuing depressed price of the funds in December led to the replacement of Richelieu's minister of finance, a step that had been anticipated by the business community. The expected rise in the *rentes* occurred, but within several days the quoted price of the French funds declined to 63, and the real price was probably as low as 60.[16] At the end of December, after news of Richelieu's retirement reached London, *The Times* reported that the new political arrangement appeared to have had a beneficial influence on the French funds, and added that under the conditions of many large holders abroad and attempts to liquidate the last war indemnity payments, the funds "must be looked to with great anxiety throughout Europe."[17] According to the private correspondent of *The Times* in Paris, who might have been in the pay of Decazes, the king, struck with the difficulties that Richelieu encountered in trying to form a ministry representing all parties and with the expression of public opinion, asked Decazes to form a ministry.[18] According to an "occasional correspondent" of *The Times* in Paris, the fear of an ultraroyalist ministry increased the number of Decazes's supporters both in the Chamber of Deputies and among the public.[19] *The Times* speculated that the new ministry, together with the prospect of a speedy sale of the royal forests (long opposed by the ultraroyalists), would have the effect of raising the price of the French stocks.[20] The depressed economy of the first half of 1819, however, inhibited any significant rise in the French funds.

The depression, moreover, was instrumental in bringing down the Decazes ministry. But viewed from the standpoint of European political history, the liberal government fell because of a succession of domestic and international events that created a widespread fear of impending revolution. One of the first measures of the Decazes ministry was to lift the remaining limitations on freedom of the press.[21] The most progressive press law of the Restoration period made it possible, however, for the ultraroyalist journals, i.e.,

Quotidienne, Conservateur, and *Debats,* to continue their war to the death against Decazes. The conservative press attributed every popular disturbance in France and Europe to the liberal ministerial forces, even the murder of Kotzebue in Germany.[22] Nonetheless, the elections of 1819 to replace one-fifth of the Chamber of Deputies again favored the left independents and the left-center royalists.[23] According to Chancelier Pasquier, the election results not only exasperated the ultraroyalists but also had a distressing effect abroad, where changes in France were still believed to be a threat to domestic governments.[24] Britain was experiencing another wave of unemployment and popular agitation; although the British depression of 1819 was less severe than the subsistence crisis of 1816–17, the political crisis was more acute. Radical protest climaxed in the "Peterloo Massacre" of August 1819, and in November Parliament enacted the well-known repressive Six Acts.[25] The duke of Wellington, referring to this legislation, commented to the Russian minister (in a letter dated November 25): "Our example will render some good in France as well as in Germany, and we must hope that the whole world will escape the universal revolution which seems to menace us all."[26] Ultraroyalists in France and conservative statesmen in Germany used similar language in 1819; moreover, in Germany revolutionary agitation had already occasioned the repressive decrees adopted at the conference in Carlsbad.

Liberal ideas appeared all the more revolutionary in France because of the repressive European political climate in 1819. When the regicide Abbé Gregoire was elected to the Chamber of Deputies in 1819, even moderates began to wonder whether the time had come for the king to rely on a more royalist ministry.[27] The assassination of the king's nephew, the duc de Berry, on February 13, 1820, doomed the liberal Decazes ministry.[28] The king summoned Richelieu to form a new ministry; and the year 1820 saw a series of illiberal legislative measures which strengthened the electoral influence of the largest taxpayers and reintroduced press censorship. The attempt to bridge the chasm between the Old Regime and the Revolution with a constitutional monarchy had in effect failed.

A genuine fear of revolution from the left was no doubt the motivation behind the retreat from moderate liberalism by the king. At the same time modifications in economic and social conditions during the Decazes ministry predisposed the constitutional royalists to the right. The most apparent economic change was the return of low grain prices and cheap bread, which in turn was paralleled by the return of the countryside to its traditional repose. Fear of peasant rebellion had vanished and with it faded the possibility of a Jacobin-peasant revolutionary coalition. Manufacturing towns were still occasionally disturbed by machine-breaking artisans, but as long as subsistence was plentiful and cheap the disaffection could be kept within limits.

On the other hand, the succession of crises had gradually fostered a community of interest among the various sectors of the French economy—an alliance that focused on monopolistic control of the domestic economy. French policy between 1814 and 1819 evolved from a relatively laissez-faire position to extreme protectionism. The postwar economic crises were responsible, moreover, for the trend toward tariff walls everywhere in the Western world.[29] Whatever political differences existed among the French parties and wings did not extend to the economic sphere. Because of the restricted franchise and high property qualifications for election to the Chamber of Deputies, landed proprietors, merchants, financiers, and manufacturers dominated the legislature. Successive Restoration legislatures, whether controlled by ultraroyalists or constitutional royalists, erected a customs fortress around France. The protective legislation was the common work of all political parties. Textile manufacturers and iron producers demanded import prohibitions and tariffs from the beginning and won notable victories in 1814, 1816, and 1820. Tariff protection for agriculture, however, was not a familiar phenomenon in France. Moreover, with the harvest failures of 1816 and the ensuing dearth, all grain legislation was directed toward the encouragement of imports. But excellent harvests in 1818 and abundant wheat imports from Russia combined to force grain prices down, and as a result numerous wheat producers were driven into bankruptcy during the commercial crisis. Proprietors blamed Russian wheat for their predicament, claiming that it could be delivered in France for as little as 12 or 13 francs per hectoliter while French wheat could hardly be produced for less than 23 francs. In 1819 the legislature decided to subordinate the interests of the consumers to those of grain producers and adopted a duty system patterned after the British Corn Law of 1815.[30] By 1820 all political parties in the chamber were in agreement in economic matters; forces which might have been hostile to one another politically found a mutually beneficial device in protectionism. Propertied interests were to be protected by eliminating foreign competition, while at home the first line of defense would be the suppression of radical liberal innovations. The moderately liberal elements of the bourgeoisie were required to accept aristocratic direction of the state and to curtail their enthusiasm for a freer press and more representative political institutions as the price of this protection.

GERMANY

The trend toward political conservatism was even more marked in postwar Germany, but, as in France, economic events influenced the timing and the direction of the movement. While the settlement of 1815 has been viewed as embodying the principles of "restoration and reaction," despite the relevancy of the phrase, the Vienna settlement also incorporated a series of compromises. The political arrangements were no doubt based on the principle of legitimacy, but the institutions of the Old Regime were not revived and restored in their pristine forms. The two outstanding modernizing tendencies in the postwar German states were the continuing emancipation of the peasantry, a practice initiated during the period of French domination, and the introduction of representative assemblies in accordance with Article XIII of the Federal Constitution (*Bundesakte*). The delayed and limited implementation of these two measures can be explained by doubting the original sincerity of the German princes, who came to regret the rash promises made during the effervescent period of national liberation. This case has been made many times over, with Metternich viewed as the grey eminence behind a calculated policy of reaction. By contrast, a supplementary explanation is advanced here which sees the growing conservatism as a response to the seemingly endless sequence of dislocations and disturbances.

A tendency to confuse economic discontent with political disaffection became unavoidable as social disorder mounted, and, at the same time, economic and social complaints became inextricably tied up with political demands.[31] Moreover, the degree of postwar political dislocation alone rendered constitutional innovations an unrealistic expectation for the first year or so. Prussia was, of course, confronted with the maximum administrative demands due to extensive territorial additions; however, Austria, Bavaria, Württemberg, Hanover, and Saxony also had experienced significant territorial adjustments either in 1803 or 1815. By the time these political rearrangements were assimilated, the subsistence crisis and its attendant social upheaval claimed the attention of the political machinery.

Nonetheless, peasant emancipation, with the notable exception of Prussia, continued unabated during the early postwar years. Though the agrarian legislation of the French era was repealed in Hanover and Hesse-Cassel, this reactionary peasant policy proved to be only temporary. Elsewhere in Germany, particularly in the southwestern states, manorial dues and labor services were converted into rents, which in turn were being extinguished by redemption payments. The pace and the details of reform varied from state to state, but the trend away from a manorial agricultural system was unmistakable.[32] However, this same trend was suddenly reversed in Prussia, and the possible causes require some discussion.

Peasant emancipation in Prussia dated back to the law of September 14, 1811. Though many peasants had been excluded from the terms of the decree, and though those emancipated had to forfeit half of the land occupied in order to obtain a freehold in the remaining half, a definite start had been made in the direction of peasant ownership. Few peasants were able to realize freedom from manorial tenure and services during the war years, however, largely because of the unsettled conditions. In the meantime, *Junker* opposition to the terms of emancipation persisted, and with the return of peace the landowners pressed the government for revisions. Finally, the Declaration of May 29, 1816 revised the terms of emancipation to the advantage of the landowners and the more prosperous peasants. In effect, the right to end manorial dues by ceding land was restricted to peasants who held eight hectares or more, and as a consequence reduced by two-thirds the number of peasants eligible for freehold possession.[33] The Declaration of May 29, 1816 reflected the decision of the Prussian state to rely on the landowning aristocracy as its principal support. The landowners had also strengthened their position in the army and the bureaucracy during the preceding years, and for these reasons the *Junker* class was made the chief beneficiary of the Declaration.

If, on the other hand, the Declaration was also motived by the concern of the Hardenberg ministry for the well-being of the Prussian economy, then the decision can be understood against the background of the northern European economic conjuncture. The effect of the Declaration, apart from the political and social features, was to transform Prussian agriculture from manorial or subsistence tenure to capitalistic enterprise. To begin with, Britain had been Prussia's largest market for agricultural exports before the wars, and it was assumed, or at least hoped, that with the lifting of the blockades the Prussian economy would recover to its former level on the strength of grain exports. The immediate postwar years proved these expectations to be illusory, for Prussian hopes were dashed by the passage of the new Corn Law in 1815, which raised the protection accorded to British wheat. If grain exports from Prussia to Britain were disappointingly low at 186,200 quarters in 1814, in 1815 the total dropped calamitously to 19,400 quarters.[34] In order to compete in the protected British grain market Prussian landowners had to realize the same economies of scale and in addition had to adopt the scientific methods which the enclosure movement had facilitated in Britain. The Declaration of 1816 clearly promoted capitalistic agriculture, albeit at the expense of the majority of the Prussian peasantry.

The subsistence crisis and the concomitant brisk demand for Prussian grain in 1817 and 1818 were of course fortuitous. Nevertheless, the dearth occasioned huge grain imports by western European states, particularly Britain, which purchased 1,243,000 quarters in Prussian ports during this two-year period. Grain exports to Britain fell off progressively from the end of 1818, however, declining to 39,300 quarters by 1821.[35] Prussian hopes were again disappointed, despite the temporary reprieve, and grain prices fell steadily until the mid-1820s.[36] This agricultural depression, which was matched by the stagnation of trade and industry, was accompanied by a deepening political conservatism. While it would be unwarranted to conclude that economic distress, disappointment, and frustration were primarily responsible for the conservative trend in postwar Prussia, neither can these circumstances be ignored. The agricultural crisis can only have added to the tension that was engendered by social upheaval and political discontent.

Even though resurgent German conservatism blocked the implementation of the constitutional provisions of Article XIII in Prussia, nevertheless representative institutions embodying varying degrees of liberalism were installed in the southwestern states of Württemberg, Bavaria, Baden, and Hesse-Darmstadt between 1818 and 1820.[37] While some period of time was necessary before conflicting views could be accommodated within an acceptable constitutional system, it is interesting to note that these arrangements were not instituted until the subsistence crisis had passed. Hesse-Darmstadt, moreover, which was still occupied with an incipient peasant revolt in the Odenwald district in 1819, failed to institute a constitution until the end of 1820.[38] Princes in part granted constitutions in order to win support in the new districts that were added to their realms. At the same time, the postwar economic chaos must have convinced the propertied classes, who were the sole beneficiaries of the constitutional liberties, that princely governments were incompatible with economic progress.[39]

Political rearrangement, economic distress, and social upheaval combined not only to delay the implementation of constitutional promises but also to support and enlarge conservative public opinion. For example, Hans von Gagern warned the Diet that the migrations of 1817 gave rise to social and political dangers which posed a threat to the internal security of Germany. The uprooted and destitute status of the emigrants not only encouraged criminality and spread epidemic disease but also produced a bitterness that could be translated into hostile political behavior.[40] Metternich, in the same vein, proved sensitive to the inherent political dangers in the chiliastic activities of Madame de Krüdener. When the baroness distributed newspapers to the poor, who were in turn to sell them to the well-to-do in order to buy food, Metternich complained that her teachings were a challenge to the established social order. He even suggested to the Austrian minister at St. Petersburg that the Great Powers should "stifle" this evil "in its beginning."[41] Neither Metternich nor other German policy-making officials feared a working-class revolution as such; rather they feared that revolutionaries might capitalize on popular discontent to advance their conspiracies. However, numerous contemporary publications cited the subsistence crisis as a revolutionary danger,[42] and accordingly every effort was made by the state and by the propertied to alleviate distress.

If almost all popular disturbances ended with the subsistence crisis, the worsening economic stagnation nevertheless continued to breed or to aggravate social and political disaffection. Despite the lack of revolutionary content in the student movement, and despite the absence of meaningful support for revolutionary circles, German governments considered these bourgeois movements a graver threat to the established order than working-class protest. The presence of nationalistic ideas and liberal opinions, along with middle-class economic discontent, accounted for this political differentiation. German officials also understood that in the absence of appalling distress neither peasants nor artisans constituted a genuine revolutionary danger at this time. The peasantry remained devoted to the Prussian administration throughout the crisis; whereas the educated classes in the Rhenish provinces villified the government. When the conjunction of famine and economic stagnation raised anxiety to a peak, the *Oberpräsident* of Lower Rhine advised Berlin to redeem the pledge for a constitution in order to prevent disorder and to put an end to the Rhinelanders' grievances; the administration in Cleves advised the same course of action. The Berlin ministry, however, saw no necessity to appease the Rhenish bourgeoisie.[43] While the student movement created the impression of political activism in the minds of many state officials, the famous Wartburg festival of October 1817 possessed little political content. But the interpretation given the proceedings mattered more, and the liberal press hailed the festival as a great political event.[44] A few students utilized their literary education to draft petitions and constitutions, while the most famous student revolutionary, Carl Follen, composed a political song that became popular among the rural rebels in Hesse-Darmstadt.[45]

The official attack on the German academic community was directed against the university professors not the students. Moreover, professors were not feared as potential revolutionaries; rather the concern was to prevent a revolutionary generation from being spawned at the universities. Metternich expressed this view to Friedrich von Gentz just prior to the Carlsbad meeting. "I have never feared that the revolution would be engendered by the universities; but that a whole generation of revolutionaries must be formed at them, seems certain to me, unless the evil is restrained."[46] This viewpoint was shared in Berlin, where in fact it seems to have originated with the Prussian professor Theodor Schmalz. According to Schmalz's thesis, his university colleagues were the propagators of the new radical nationalism. Schmalz concluded that it was necessary to win over public opinion to counteract the efforts to incite student organizations to political activity. A campaign of counterpropaganda initiated by Schmalz resulted in action by the Prussian government against radical professors; these persecutions, known as the *Demagogenverfolgungen,* were actively pursued after the murder of Kotzebue in March 1819.[47]

The economic crisis, the student movement, and the radical professors notwithstanding, the threat of revolution in postwar Germany appears, in retrospect, to have been slight. Carl Follen among the students stood nearly alone as a revolutionary. The resistance of the Odenwald peasantry in Hesse-Darmstadt during 1818–19 presented an ideal opportunity for student political activism. The Odenwald uprising had its origin in the famine, excessive taxation, and economic distress. Entire communities in this forest district resisted the authorities. But few students participated; though some among the radical *Schwarzen* groups at the nearby University of Giessen acted as messengers for the rebels. While Follen remained an active participant in the Odenwald resistance, he was no longer a student. The leadership of the rebellion was made up mostly of village elders and lawyers.[48] A more distinct revolutionary stirring occurred among the liberal elements in the Rhenish towns. The political discontent was based mainly on the failure of Prussian constitutionalism, but it also reflected the prevailing economic distress and Rhenish particularism. The disaffection inspired pamphlets and newspaper articles which suggested the possibility of a German revolution. In June 1819 a pamphlet entitled "Is a Revolution To Be Feared in Germany?" circulated in Wiesbaden (Nassau). The public excitement that the writing provoked affords some indication of the political climate of the Rhineland. Its author was the respected liberal publicist Johannes Weitzel, editor of the *Rheinischen Blätter* of Wiesbaden. The echoes created by this pamphlet continued to resound until submerged in the sensation produced by Joseph Görres's booklet with the pithy title "Germany and the Revolution," which was published in Koblenz in September 1819.[49] But this heady intellectual activity ceased abruptly in the repressive atmosphere created by the Carlsbad Decrees and the demagogue persecutions, and critics like Görres were forced to take refuge abroad.

German urban popular discontent was more forcefully expressed in a series of anti-Semitic outrages which broke out in the summer of 1819. Even though most writers of Jewish history have viewed these riots as the product of ignorance and fanaticism stimulated by anti-Jewish literature,[50] the disturbances suggest a case of displaced protest in the psychodynamic sense. While it is true that religious and zenophobic elements were at work, and also that the outbreaks cannot be explained as merely crude economic competition aimed at spoliation, neither can the disorders be viewed apart from the accumulated economic frustrations and disappointments.[51] It is possible that the thwarting of German political aspirations increased the fury of the riots; however, since the outrages occurred chiefly in the southwestern states, which had instituted constitutional governments, the political ingredient can be exaggerated.

The basic question of Jewish emancipation had been raised in the drafting of the Federal Constitution. The Hanseatic towns of Hamburg, Bremen, and Lübeck in particular favored the reestablishment of Jewish disabilities, but the opposition of Metternich and Hardenberg at the Congress of Vienna resulted in the constitutional protection of the rights acquired by Jews during the French domination. The constitutional safeguard was not unequivocal, however, and reflected a compromise to placate the hostile German states; for the wording adopted made it possible for some states to withhold full civic equality.[52] Moreover, the position of Jews within the German body politic continued to be a topic of intellectual debate during 1816. Ignoring the more virulent anti-Semitic views, two proposed solutions to the Jewish question secured wide attention. Friedrich Rühs advanced the thesis that Jews in Germany could only be subjects, excluded from civic life; that while it might prove necessary to control the increase of Jews and to supervise their economic life, they were to be protected from persecution and violence and that it might be necessary to reinstitute compulsory badges of identity. However, Jews converted to Christianity were to be accepted as full citizens. By contrast, Jakob Friedrich Fries, a physician and professor of natural science at Heidelberg, insisted that Judaism must disappear. While Jews were to be protected by equal rights, Jewry was not to be tolerated.[53] Reputedly, Fries work was widely read in taverns and public-houses. His writing, moreover, found a receptive chord and was followed by an avalanche of literature hostile to Jews and Judaism.[54] But despite such incendiary provocations no anti-Semitic outbreaks occurred at this time.

The initial outrage in fact took place three years later, on August 2, 1819, in the Bavarian university town of Würzburg. The riot was preceded by an incident at the university; a group of students evicted a professor who had defended Jews in his writings. The students chanted the expression Hep-Hep!, followed by *Jude verreck!* or Jew, drop dead. The origin of Hep-Hep is obscure, but the expression was universally used to ridicule Jews during these outbursts, which consequently became known as the Hep-Hep riots.[55] The student disorder in Würzburg was followed by physical assaults on Jews and by attacks on shops and property; several Jews were killed and many were injured attempting to defend their property. A military detachment had to be called on to put down the violence and to prevent further bloodshed. The townspeople, nevertheless, forced the municipal officials to banish all Jews from Würzburg, and the next day some 400 persons had to abandon their homes and wait until the state authorities intervened several days later. The persecution of Jews was repeated in almost every northern Bavarian town, particularly in Bamberg and Bayreuth.[56]

From northern Bavaria the Hep-Hep riots spread to the free city of Frankfurt on August 9. Windows were smashed, and Jews were driven from the public walks with insulting brutality. A large number of clerks and artisans invaded houses and shops belonging to Jews; gunfire was exchanged, and several persons were wounded. Several wealthy Jewish families, including Amschel Rothschild, prepared to leave Frankfurt. At this point Metternich intervened and threatened to restore order with the federal military garrison stationed at Mainz. Order was quickly restored by the Frankfurt officials, although the local police and town-watch had made no previous attempt to prevent the violence. The disorders radiated to the towns of northern Baden, however; Karlsruhe, Heidelberg, and Mannheim witnessed anti-Semitic outbursts. Students and professors at Heidelberg were forced to intervene in behalf of victimized Jews when the town-watch abdicated its responsibilities. Attacks against Jews in rural communities necessitated the institution of military patrols in order to guarantee protection. The attacks finally subsided in Baden when the state made each town and village financially responsible for damages and losses suffered by Jews.[57]

Although the most outrageous assaults on Jews took place in Bavaria, Frankfurt, and Baden, similar Hep-Hep disturbances occurred in Hamburg, Leipzig, Dresden, Meiningen (Thuringia), and in the Hessen towns of Fulda, Cassel, and Darmstadt, during the months of August and September. The anti-Semitic violence peaked at Darmstadt, where the population attacked persons and property, and troops were required to patrol the streets for several days. Prussia, by contrast, escaped anti-Semitic outrages with only a few minor incidents in Danzig and Düsseldorf. Not only was there a relative absence of the Hep-Hep mentality in Prussia but the state also publicly disapproved of anti-Semitism.[58] At the same time the anti-Semitic outbursts were more than a German phenomenon. Disturbances occurred in Amsterdam, and in Copenhagen Jews were stoned to the taunting cry of Hep-Hep! Martial law ended the violence in Copenhagen, but the abuse and ridicule of Jews continued long afterward.[59]

These attacks were carried out mainly by members of the urban working classes. Even if merchants and landowners shrank before the prospect of smashing doors and windows, they did not hesitate to incite and even to pay the rioters. The propertied classes also controlled the police and townwatch, who were indifferent to the fate of Jewish victims. Though a measure of religious anti-Semitism was displayed by the rioters, economic frustration clearly furnished the principal motivation. The educated urban population proved to be the most dangerous enemies of the Jews. Jews had become the competitors of the urban merchants by entering trade and finance after emancipation. Jews, unhindered by German commercial traditions, traded in English goods and adopted the English practices of credit sales, stock speculation, and large quantity transactions in manufactured products. The commercial success of these Jews became painfully apparent to the distressed urban merchants and also to the German manufacturers who were confronted with British competition and declining domestic consumption. These social groups were victimized by the economic transformation, which had the effect of fomenting hostility toward Jewish competitors. The majority of the attacks on Jews took place in southwestern Germany, where, unlike the situation in more developed Prussia, Jewish merchants and financiers remained conspicuous in the smaller and less developed states.[60]

Rural economic discontent in the southwestern states also gave rise to anti-Semitic outbursts. To begin with, many cattle-dealers, shopkeepers, and moneylenders in rural Baden and Bavaria were Jews, beyond their proportion of the population. Peasants in these locations had borrowed from Jews to buy cattle and seed, and also to fulfill financial commitments arising from emancipation and the liquidation of manorial dues and services. As indicated, the majority of these obligations were undertaken when grain prices stood at dearth levels. In addition, the weather of 1816 had inflicted a heavy toll on the cattle herds, and the year also had been a business disaster for small grain producers. By contrast, grain prices declined to record lows in 1819. Numerous emancipated peasants in Baden and Bavaria found themselves in debt to cattle-dealers and moneylenders, most of whom were Jews.[61] The loans must have appeared not only onerous in 1819 but even unscrupulous to peasants who no doubt departed from objectivity under economic pressures and frustration. Moreover, some families had perished during the famine, and Jews were believed to have been disproportionately represented among those who had withheld cereals in order to obtain higher prices. This popular view also persisted in some urban locations; the grain riot that had occurred at Mainz in 1817, for example, displayed a noticeable anti-Semitic tone.[62] Even when popular disturbances were absent the famine had promoted anti-Semitism. The government of Hamburg entertained a demand that Jews be confined to their quarter; it was claimed that Jews had earned a great deal of money during the calamitous times and unless restricted would end up monopolizing everything.[63]

In the minds of German officials, however, the Hep-Hep riots were another source of social commotion—one more disturbance in a series of unsettling events. Because of the uneasiness created by the student movement and the liberal agitation, some authorities tended to view the riots as a disguised revolutionary uprising, which in part explains the willingness to use military force to suppress them. The authorities in Prussia and Austria believed that the outbreaks were nothing less than the rehearsals of secret revolutionary societies. The constitutional states cited the disorders as proof that the majority of the population was not ready to participate in government.[64] If nothing else, the Hep-Hep riots furnished the political authorities with additional justification for repression, arrests, and police examinations.

It has been suggested that the riots appeared in 1819 and not earlier because the repression of Germanizing movements engendered the need for a scapegoat. The helpless Jews were selected as sacrificial victims, for the students and the nationalists did not dare to attack German statesmen.[65] But it is not always clear whether those who have advanced this view were aware that the Carlsbad Decrees were announced after the anti-Semitic outbreak and not before. It is true that the negotitations between Austria and Prussia, aimed at suppressing revolutionary activity, had already begun at Teplitz when the Hep-Hep riots occurred. Most likely, these popular excesses served the purpose of timely evidence to support conservative opinions. As Metternich explained to the president of the Bundestag and to the Austrian ambassador at Frankfurt, ''when outbreaks of the vulgar masses . . . have once appeared in a state . . . no security exists, for the same thing could arise again at any moment and over any other matter.''[66]

The Carlsbad Decrees were the culmination of the drift toward repression in postwar German politics. The Decrees were aimed at liberalism and nationalism, which were perceived as threats to the established order. The jittery response of government officials to the psychopathic murder of Kotzebue indicates that some authorities believed in a conspiratorial student movement. The outcry which the assassination elicited was also a reflection of the supercharged atmosphere in Germany. This excitement was in part engendered by political issues, by the threat of revolution, real or imagined, but also by the more elusive economic and social factors. Postwar German history was marked by an endless succession of disturbances. The more spectacular events included the economic dislocation and stagnation following the lifting of the blockades, the territorial and population transfers, the agricultural calamity and famine, the mass vagrancy and emigration, the student movement, the commercial depression, the anti-Semitic riots, and political assassination. These experiences produced a climate of unrest, distrust, and fear; moreover, the social disequilibrium in turn fostered political disequilibrium. The postwar economic and social upheaval reinforced conservative opinion everywhere in western Europe, not merely in Germany, and all states shared in the trend toward political reaction.

CONCLUSION

The reaction of the European governments to the wave of social and political unrest can be seen as the last link in a connected sequence of events that began with the meteorological effects of the volcanic dust clouds of 1815. The anomalous weather patterns produced a sharp fall off in agricultural productivity and output, particularly in the case of bread grains; the resulting scarcity and high price of basic foodstuffs led to a subsistence crisis reminiscent of the economic and social distress that marked famines before 1750. Agricultural shortfalls disrupted Western commodity markets, which were already disturbed by the postwar commercial dislocations and the general economic downturn. The decline of real income that ensued from the drop in agricultural productivity in turn amplified the cyclical downswing. Agricultural output and prices fluctuated widely in the succeeding years as a consequence both of the ecological upset and the economic decisions based on real or illusory opportunities which materialized, and this variable continued to exert a key influence on successive economic turns.

As the prices of essential foodstuffs doubled and tripled and real national income declined, consumer demand shifted away from industrial goods and services and unemployment levels rose still higher. Moreover, the inordinate increase in the price of grains and other agricultural commodities produced a drastic redistribution of income, which aggravated the economic disequilibrium by altering patterns of investment and by interfering with the normal flow of credit. The elevated price of foodstuffs not only promoted hoarding and speculation; windfall profits induced a wave of inventory investment in basic commodities and also investment in land suitable for the production of agricultural staples. Then, when the increased productive capacity was joined by the return of favorable weather in 1818, the two factors produced overabundant harvests and put an end to the economic boom. The succeeding years saw surplus agricultural commodities, sharply lower prices for both farm and industrial products, and lingering economic stagnation.

The economic distress and the subsistence crisis also provoked a wide range of social responses. When the cost of living climbed beyond the reach of the majority of the working population, hundreds of thousands found themselves dependent on public charity or reduced to begging. A minority, but still a large number, of the distressed opted for a temporary life of vagrancy or attempted to emigrate to America or to the Russian empire; fewer but nevertheless many thousands turned to rioting and crime. Yet the majority of the population beset by hunger and distress suffered in resignation. Whatever were the individual responses, the severity of the crisis was clearly reflected in the movement of demographic variables: the number of births declined in step with the number of marriages, and mortality levels rose from the inroads of malnutrition, starvation, and infectious disease. The threat of famine and epidemic disease, particularly typhus and bubonic plague, impelled European governments to institute an array of administrative measures to provide relief for the distressed. They also were compelled to curb the mounting agitation.

The specific political policies that were followed derived from a series of motivations determined in part by the nature and gravity of the crisis and in part by state and regional precedents. Traditional paternalistic guidelines governed the course of action in the majority of states, while others applied at least in part the tenets of economic liberalism. In either case, however, public opinion, whether official or private, moved toward the acceptance of public welfare and relief of distress as a responsibility of governments or community organizations. In some countries, a half century of accelerated economic development now also supplied the resources to transform desirable goals into attainable ends. While the pressure of unrelieved social and political unrest frightened European governments into a retreat to conservative and even repressive policies, these same pressures also resulted in the series of positive administrative programs that signified a commitment to social welfare and security in times of economic crisis. Most of these social programs outlasted not only the brief crisis but also the political repression prompted by the calamity.

Notes

Introduction

1. For full discussion see H. H. Lamb, *The Changing Climate* (London, 1966); idem, *Climate: Present, Past and Future*, vol. I, *Fundamentals and Climate Now* (London, 1972); Hans von Rudloff, *Die Schwankungen und Pendelungen des Klimas in Europa seit dem Beginn der regelmässigen Instrumenten-Beobachtungen (1670)* (Braunschweig, 1967); E. Le Roy Ladurie, *Times of Feast, Times of Famine: A History of Climate since the Year 1000* (Garden City, N.Y., 1971); C. E. P. Brooks, *Climate through the Ages* (rev. ed.; New York, 1949); and *Inadvertent Climate Modification: Report of the Study of Man's Impact on Climate* (Cambridge, Mass., 1971).

2. See H. H. Lamb, "Volcanic Dust in the Atmosphere: with a Chronology and an Assessment of its Meteorological Significance," *Philosophical Transactions of the Royal Society*, Ser. A, 266 (1970): 425–533; and *Inadvertant Climate Modification*, pp. 280–83.

3. Pierre Goubert, *The Ancien Regime*, trans. by Steve Cox (London, 1973), p. 41.

Chapter I

1. C. E. P. Brooks, *Climate through the ages* (rev. ed.; New York, 1949).

2. See Gustaf Utterström, "Climatic Fluctuations and Population Problems in Early Modern History," *Scandinavian Economic History Review* 3 (1955): 1–47; idem, "Population and Agriculture in Sweden, *circa* 1700–1830," ibid. 9 (1961): 176–94.

3. For a progressively less skeptical view, see E. Le Roy Ladurie, "Histoire et Climat," *Annales: E. S. C.* 14 (1959): 3–34; idem, *Histoire du climat depuis l'an mil* (Paris, 1967); idem, *Times of Feast, Times of Famine: A History of Climate since the Year 1000* (Garden City, N.Y., 1971); E. Le Roy Ladurie and J. -P. Desaive, "Le climat et la France (1776–1792): séries thermiques," in J. -P. Desaive et al., *Médecins, climat et épidemies à la fin du XVIIIe siècle* (Paris, 1972), pp. 23–89. For a discussion of these works and the issues, see John D. Post, "Meteorological Historiography," *Journal of Interdisciplinary History* 3 (Spring 1973): 721–32.

4. H. H. Lamb, *The Changing Climate* (London, 1966).

5. Hans von Rudloff, *Die Schwankungen und Pendelungen des Klimas in Europa seit dem Beginn der regelmässigen Instrumenten-Beobachtungen (1670)* (Braunschweig, 1967).

6. H. H. Lamb, *Climate: Present, Past and Future*, vol. 1, *Fundamentals and Climate Now*

(London, 1972), p. 254. For an extended discussion of the causes of climatic fluctuation, see pp. 254–306, 385–464.

7. This explanation has been reduced to essentials. A long literature on the subject exists. The following citations represent a chronological listing of significant works valuable for historians. C. G. Abbot and F. E. Fowle, "Volcanoes and Climate," *Smithsonian Miscellaneous Collections* 60, no. 2176 (March 28, 1913): 3–22; William J. Humphreys, "Volcanic Dust and Other Factors in the Production of Climatic Changes and Their Possible Relation to Ice Ages," *Bulletin of the Mount Weather Observatory* 6 (1913): 1–34; Harry Wexler, "Volcanoes and World Climate," *Scientific American* 186 (April 1952): 74–76; H. H. Lamb, "Volcanic Dust in the Atmosphere: with a Chronology and an Assessment of its Meteorological Significance," *Philosophical Transactions of the Royal Society,* Ser. A, 166 (1970): 425–533; idem, *Climate,* pp. 47–49, 410–35.

8. *Inadvertent Climate Modification: Report of the Study of Man's Impact on Climate* (Cambridge, Mass., 1971), pp. 280–83; Lamb, "Volcanic Dust," pp. 461–69; idem, *Climate,* p. 47.

9. The discussion in these two paragraphs has also been reduced to minimum essentials. For diagrams showing the pressure variations of the atmospheric circulation since 1750, and for the location of the average latitude of lowest (Iceland low) and highest (Azores high) atmospheric pressure in the North Atlantic, see H. H. Lamb and A. I. Johnson, "Secular Variations of the Atmospheric Circulation since 1750," *Geophysical Memoirs,* no. 110, Meteorological Office (London, 1966), pp. 117–21; for a more comprehensive explanation of the fundamentals of climatic variations with diagrams indicating the average barometric pressure recorded in the twentieth century, see Lamb, *Changing Climate,* pp. 48–55; for discussion of the anomalous patterns of the atmosphere, see idem, *Climate,* pp. 254–63, 336–38; for a study of the economic and ecological effects of climate change in the twentieth century, see A. B. Pittock, "How Important Are Climatic Changes," *Weather* 27 (July 1972): 262–71.

10. Lamb, "Volcanic Dust," pp. 500–25.

11. F. von Wolff, *Der Vulkanismus* (2 vols.; Stuttgart, 1914), 2: 236–37; Karl Sapper, *Vulkankunde* (Stuttgart, 1927), pp. 268–69.

12. Lamb, "Volcanic Dust," pp. 485–96, 528–31; idem, *Climate,* pp. 423–24.

13. For comprehensive and detailed collections of first-hand reports of the uninterrupted cold weather of this winter, see C. Easton, *Les hivers dans l'Europe occidentale* (Leiden, 1928), pp. 119–24; Curt Weikinn, *Quellentexte zur Witterungsgeschichte Europas von der Zeitenwende bis zum 1850* (4 vols.; Berlin, 1958–67), 4: 34–63.

14. Wilhelm Abel, *Massenarmut und Hungerkrisen im vorindustriellen Europa* (Hamburg and Berlin, 1974), pp. 169–77.

15. See Adolf Erman, *Reise um die Erde durch Nord-Asien und die beiden Oceane in den Jahren 1828, 1829 und 1830,* vol. 3, *Historischer Bericht* (Berlin, 1848), pp. 261–62, 353–56; Alexander von Humboldt, *Cosmos,* trans. by E. C. Otte and W. S. Dallas (5 vols.; New York, 1862–63), 5: 340–44; Sapper, *Vulkankunde,* pp. 312–13; Lamb, "Volcanic Dust," p. 506.

16. For an extended discussion of these issues with historical examples, see Lamb, "Volcanic Dust," pp. 442–59; for a recent summary of the theory, see A. J. Dyer, "The Effect of Volcanic Eruptions on Global Turbidity, and an Attempt to Detect Longterm Trends Due to Man," *Quarterly Journal of the Royal Meteorological Society* 100 (October 1974): 563–71.

17. For detailed evidence of the weather patterns of 1740 and the social crises of 1740–42 see, Easton, *Hivers,* pp. 127–30; Weikinn, *Witterungsgeschichte,* 4: 242–69; Rudloff, *Schwankungen,* pp. 102–25; Abel, *Hungerkrisen,* pp. 179–87; Thomas Short, *New Observations on City, Town and Country Bills of Mortality* (London, 1750), pp. 217, 230–33, 344–46; T. Southwell, "An Account of the Severe Winter of 1739–40 and of Its Effects in the County of Norfolk in the Year following," *Norfolk and Norwich Naturalists Society, Transactions* 2 (1875): 125–30; J. D. Marshall, ed., *Autobiography of William Stout of Lancaster 1665–1752* (Manchester, 1967), pp. 227–36; H. Gille, "The Demographic History of the Northern European Countries in the Eighteenth Century," *Population Studies* 3 (1949–50): 3–65; Francois Lebrun, *Les hommes et la mort en Anjou aux 17e et 18e siècles* (Paris, 1971), pp. 138–39, 367–73; Michael Drake, "The Irish Demographic Crisis of 1740–41," *Historical Studies* 6 (1968): 101–26.

18. Lamb, *Climate,* p. 425.

19. Temperature readings during the early nineteenth century were collected according to the Centigrade, Réaumur, and Fahrenheit scales. Since English language readers are accustomed to Fahrenheit values, all readings and deviations have been converted to this scale whenever necessary. In dealing with deviations from mean temperature, tenths of degrees have been retained when available. Average temperatures, however, have usually been rounded to whole numbers, since decimal point precision is neither regularly available nor essential.

20. For meteorological investigations of the weather in 1816, see Joseph B. Hoyt, "The Cold Summer of 1816," *Annals of the Association of American Geographers* 48 (June 1958): 118–31; Alfred J. Henry, "Abnormal Summers in the United States," U.S. Weather Bureau, *Monthly Weather Review* 55 (August 1927): 349–53; Willis I. Milham, "The Year 1816, the Causes of Abnormalities," ibid. 52 (December 1924): 563–70.

21. A summary of the weather log is found in Chester Dewey, "Results of Meteorological Observations Made at Williamstown, Massachusetts," *Memoirs of the American Academy of Arts and Sciences* 4 (1818–21): 387–92. Dewey was Professor of Mathematics and Natural Philosophy, Williams College. An excellent meteorological analysis of the weather log is found in Milham, "The Year 1816."

22. Dewey, "Observations," pp. 388–89.

23. Michael Treshow, *Environment and Plant Response* (New York, 1970), pp. 78–91.

24. Lorin Blodget, *Climatology of the United States* (Philadelphia, 1857), pp. 68–69; Edward A. Holyoke, "Observations Made with Fahrenheit's Thermometer, at Salem, Mass. from the Year 1793 to the Year 1818," *Memoirs of the American Academy of Arts and Sciences* 4 (1818–21): 373–80; Parker Cleaveland, "Communications in Consequence of the Request of the Society, on the Circumstances Attending the Season of 1816," *Memoirs of the Philadelphia Society for Promoting Agriculture* 4 (1818): 192–94; Milham, "The Year 1816," p. 565; Hoyt, "Summer of 1816," p. 126.

25. *Daily National Intelligencer* (District of Columbia), May 13, 1816, p. 2.

26. Isaiah Thomas, "Diary, 1805–1828," ed. by Benjamin Thomas Hill, in *Transactions and Collections of the American Antiquarian Society* 9 (1909): 311–14; Thomas Robbins, *Diary of Thomas Robbins*, ed. by Increase N. Tarbox (2 vols.; Boston, 1886), 1: 665–70.

27. *Albany Advertiser*, June 22, 1816; Zadock Thompson, *History of Vermont* (2d ed.; 3 vols.; Burlington, 1842), 1: 20; Arthur W. Peach, ed., "As the Years Pass—The Diaries of Seth Shaler Arnold (1788–1871), A Vermonter," *Vermont Historical Society, Proceedings* 8 New Ser. (June 1940): 109; Hosea Beckley, *The History of Vermont* (Brattleboro, 1846), pp. 171–72; George Barstow, *History of New Hampshire* (Concord, 1842), p. 392; John Milton Whiton, *Sketches of the History of New Hampshire* (Concord, 1834), p. 188; William D. Williamson, *The History of the State of Maine* (2 vols.; Hallowell, 1832), 2: 664; *National Intelligencer*, June 19, 1816, p. 3; Hoyt, "Summer of 1816," pp. 120–21; Thomas, "Diary," p. 316; Robbins, *Diary*, 1: 671; Chauncy Jerome, *History of the American Clock Business of the Past Sixty Years and Life of Chauncy Jerome* (New Haven, 1860), pp. 31–32.

28. Milham, "The Year 1816," p. 564; Hoyt, "Summer of 1816," pp. 119, 122; Robbins, *Diary*, 1: 673–75; Peach, "Diaries," p. 109; Williamson, *Maine*, 2: 664; Nathan Hoskins, *A History of the State of Vermont* (Vergennes, 1831), pp. 232–33; *Albany Argus*, July 19, 1816; *National Intelligencer*, July 24, 1816, p. 2.

29. Thomas, "Diary," p. 323; Robbins, *Diary*, 1: 678, 681; Cleaveland, "Communications," p. 194; Beckley, *Vermont*, p. 171; Williamson, *Maine*, 2: 665; Samuel Griswold Goodrich, *Recollections of a Lifetime* (2 vols.; New York, 1856), 1: 78; Barstow, *New Hampshire*, p. 392; Peach, "Diaries," p. 109; *National Intelligencer*, August 13, 1816, p. 2; Hoyt, "Summer of 1816," p. 122.

30. *Niles' Weekly Register*, August 10, 1816, pp. 385–86.

31. *Memoirs of the Philadelphia Society for Promoting Agriculture* 4 (1818).

32. *National Intelligencer*, September 6, 1816, p. 2; *Western Intelligencer* (Columbus, Ohio), December 5, 1816, p. 2; *Nashville Whig*, February 5, 1817, p. 3.

33. Mr. Jackson's Weather Log, January 1814—December 1848. Farmers College, College Hill, Ohio. National Archives, Washington, D.C.; David Thomas, *Travels through the Western Country in the Summer of 1816* (Auburn, N.Y., 1819), pp. 55, 72–73, 105–06; *Western Intelligencer*, May 16, 1816, p. 2; *Missouri Gazette* (St. Louis), June 15, 1816, p. 2; Clarence E. Carter, ed., *The Territorial Papers of the United States*, vol. 10, *The Territory of Michigan*

1805–1820 (Washington, D.C., 1942), p. 644; *National Intelligencer,* September 9, 1816, p. 2; Solon J. Buck, ed., "Pioneer Letters of Gershom Flagg," *Transactions of the Illinois State Historical Society* 15 (1910): 147–49; William Henry Alexander, *A Climatological History of Ohio* (Columbus, 1924), p. 709.

34. Copied by *National Intelligencer,* August 27, 1816, p. 3; see also Letter to David B. Warden, dated Monticello, May 17, 1816, in *Thomas Jefferson's Farm Book,* ed. by Edwin Morris Betts, vol. 35, Memoirs of the American Philosophical Society (Princeton, 1953), p. 303; *Raleigh Register,* June 14, 1816, p. 3; *National Intelligencer,* September 3, 1816, p. 3; September 13, 1816, p. 2.

35. *Records of the Moravians in North Carolina 1752–1879,* ed. by Adelaide L. Fries (11 vols.; Raleigh, 1947), 7: 3,294–3,313.

36. Ibid., p. 3,318.

37. *Raleigh Register,* September 13, 1816, p. 3; *National Intelligencer,* August 16, 1816, p. 2; *The Papers of Thomas Ruffin,* ed. by J. G. de Rolhac Hamilton (4 vols.; Raleigh, 1918–20), 1: 172.

38. *Niles' Weekly Register,* September 21, 1816, p. 64; *Raleigh Register,* September 20, 1816, p. 3; James Haynsworth, M.D., "Account of the Winter Epidemic of 1815, 16, and 17, As It Appeared in Salem and Claremont Counties," *New York Medical Repository,* New ser., 4 (1818): 8.

39. *Raleigh Register,* September 20, 1816, p. 3; *Niles' Weekly Register,* September 21, 1816, p. 64; February 8, 1817, p. 400; *Missouri Gazette,* October 12, 1816, p. 3; Richard Breckenridge, "Diary 1816," in *Transactions of the Alabama Historical Society* 3 (1898–99): 149; Carter, *Territorial Papers,* vol. 18, *The Territory of Alabama, 1817–1819,* pp. 24, 35, 88; *Nashville Whig,* February 5, 1817, p. 3; *National Intelligencer,* May 6, 1817, p. 2; *Western Spy,* November 22, 1816, p. 3.

40. E. F. F. Chladni, "Ueber die Ursachen des nasskalten Sommer von 1816, und zum Theil auch 1817," *Annalen der Physik* 62 (1819): 133–34; *Raleigh Register,* January 10, 1817, p. 3; *North American Review* 3 (July 1816): 285.

41. *The Times* (London), July 18, 1817, p. 2.

42. *The Times,* June 23, 1817, p. 3.

43. *Montreal Gazette,* June 8, 1816; *Western Spy,* May 24, 1816, p. 3; *The Times,* July 20, 1816, p. 3.

44. *The Times,* September 9, 1816, p. 1.

45. *Western Spy,* August 9, 1816, p. 3; November 1, 1816, p. 1; *Raleigh Register,* October 25, 1816, p. 3; *The Times,* November 18, 1816, p. 2.

46. Milham, "The Year 1816," p. 565; Henry, "Abnormal Summers," p. 351.

47. Gordon Manley, "The Mean Temperature of Central England 1698–1952," *Quarterly Journal of the Royal Meteorological Society* 79 (1953): 242–60.

48. Idem, "Temperature Trend in Lancashire, 1753–1945," ibid., 72 (1946): 15–17, 19.

49. Idem, "Central England Temperatures: Monthly Means 1659 to 1973," ibid., 100 (1974): 393–98.

50. I. D. Margary, "The Marsham Phenological Record in Norfolk, 1735–1925, and Some Others," ibid., 52 (1926): 42–43. Phenology may be summarized as the study of the influence of climate on the recurrence of such phenomena as the budding or ripening of plant life; the major premise is that the warmer and sunnier the weather the earlier fruit will ripen and cultivated plants be ready for harvest. Unfortunately, the longer English series observed near Norfolk from 1736 to 1925 has a break in the record from 1811 to 1835. It is interesting to note, however, that the latest hawthorn flowering date during the entire period occurred on June 8, 1740, compared to an average date of May 12.

51. Robert C. Mossman, "The Meteorology of Edinburgh," *Transactions of the Royal Society of Edinburgh* 39 (1896–99): 91.

52. William Harty, M.D., *An Historic Sketch of the Causes, Progress, Extent, and Mortality of the Contagious Fever Epidemic in Ireland during the Years 1817, 1818 and 1819* (Dublin, 1820), pp. 113–15.

53. Drake, "Crisis," pp. 101–13.

54. Stout, *Autobiography,* pp. 227–29.

55. *The Times,* July 20, 1816, p. 3.

56. Ibid., September 2, 1816, p. 3; September 3, 1816, p. 2.

57. D. J. V. Jones, "The Amlwich Riots of 1817," *Anglesey Antiquarian Society and Field Club Transactions* (1966): 39; David J. Wood, "The Complicity of Climate in the 1816 Depression in Dumsfriesshire," *Scottish Geographical Magazine* 81 (1965): 7–10; *The Times,* September 7, 1816, p. 2; September 9, 1816, p. 2; September 11, 1816, p. 3; September 4, 1816, p. 3; November 26, 1816, p. 3; October 1, 1816, p. 3.

58. Mossman, "Edinburgh," pp. 143, 145.

59. *Annual Register,* 1816, "Chronicle," p. 355.

60. Dewey, "Observations," pp. 387–88.

61. The manuscript containing the observations made at Ghent by Guillaume Schamp is reproduced in Emile Vanderlinden, "Chronique des événements météorologiques en Belgique jusq'en 1834," *Mémoirs de l'Académie royale de Belgique,* Classe des sciences, 2d Ser., 6 (1924): 1–329.

62. Aart Labrijn, *Het klimaat van Nederland, gedurende de laatste twee en een halve eeuw* (Schiedam, 1945), pp. 86–93.

63. *Annual Register,* 1816, "Chronicle," p. 95; *The Times,* August 2, 1816, p. 3; October 26, 1816, p. 2.

64. D. Brunt, "Periodicities in European Weather," *Philosophical Transactions of the Royal Society,* Ser. A, 215 (1925): 299; M. H. Duchaussoy, "Le bans de vendanges de la région parisienne," *La météorologie* (March–April 1934), p. 130.

65. France, Ministère de l'Intérieur, *Circulaires, instructions et autre actes émanés du ministère de l'intérieur de 1797 à 1821 inclusivement* (2d ed; 6 vols.; Paris, 1821–30), 3: 136–40; Roger Marlin, *La crise des subsistances de 1816–1817 dans le Doubs* (Becançon, 1960), pp. 15–16; Marquise de Montcalm, *Mon journal, 1815–1818: pendant le premier ministère de mon frère,* ed. by Sébastien Charléty (Paris, 1936), p. 167; Paul Leuilliot, *L'Alsace au début du XIXᵉ siècle (1815–1830)*(3 vols.: Paris, 1959–60), 2: 158; Maurice Vergnaud, "Agitation politique et crise de subsistance à Lyon de septembre 1816 à juin 1817," *Cahiers d'histoire* 2 (1957): 173; Louis Guéneau, "La disette de 1816–1817 dans une région productrice de blé, la Brie," *Revue d'histoire moderne* 9 (January–February 1929): 21–22; Collette C. Girard, "La catastrophe agricole de 1816 dans le département de la Meurthe," *Annales de l'Est,* 5th ser., 5, no. 2 (1954): 135–37; Pierre-Paul Viard, "La disette de 1816–1817, particulièrement en Côte-d'Or," *Revue historique* 159 (September–October 1928): 96.

66. "Résumé des observations météorologiques faite à l'Observatoire royal de Paris," *Annales de chimie et de physique,* 2d ser., 6 (December 1817): 441; ibid. 9 (December 1818): 430; ibid. 12 (December 1819): 422.

67. Duchaussoy, "Vendanges," p. 115.

68. Le Roy Ladurie, *Times of Feast,* see Appendix 12, pp. 345–71. It is interesting to note that the latest grape-harvest date in France during the eighteenth century occurred in 1740.

69. Eduard Brückner. "Klimaschwankungen seit 1700," *Geographische Abhandlungen* 4, no. 2 (1890): 295.

70. Ministère de l'Intérieure, *Circulaires* 3: 103–04, 136–40.

71. Staatsrath Joseph von Hazzi, *Betrachtungen über Theurung und Noth der Vergangenheit und Gegenwart* (Munich, 1818), pp. 76–91.

72. *Württembergishes Jahrbuch für 1818,* pp. 3–9.

73. Johann Gottfried von Pahl, *Geschichte von Wirtemberg* (6 vols.; Stuttgart, 1827–31), 6: 201–12; *Württembergishes Jahrbuch für 1818,* pp. 8–9; Christian A. Schuerring, "Die Teuerungs- und Hungerjahre 1816 und 1817 in Württemberg," *Württembergische Jahrbücher für Statistik und Landeskunde,* 1916, p. 49.

74. A. J. V. Heunisch, *Das Grossherzogtum Baden* (Heidelberg, 1857), p. 127.

75. *The Times,* July 22, 1816, p. 2.

76. Ibid., December 6, 1816, p. 2.

77. Heinrich Bechtolsheimer, "Die Provinz Rheinhessen in den beiden ersten Jahrzehnten ihres Bestehens," *Quellen und Forschungen zur hessischen Geschichte* 4 (1916): 57–70; *The Times,* July 9, 1816, p. 2; July 24, 1816, p. 2.

78. For the weather in the Rhenish provinces during 1816, see Johann Friedrich Benzenberg, *Ueber Handel und Gewerbe, Steuren und Zölle* (Elberfeld, 1819), p. 170; Gustav von Gülich, *Geschichtliche Darstellung des Handels, der Gewerbe, und des Ackerbaus der bedeutendsten handeltreibenden Staaten unserer Zeit* (2 vols.; Jena, 1830), 2: 362–64; Friedrich Schnurrer,

Chronik der Seuchen (2 vols.; Tübingen, 1823–25), 2: 530–31; William Jacob, *A View of the Agriculture, Manufacture, Statistics and State of Society, of Germany, and Parts of Holland and France* (London, 1820), pp. 102–03.

79. Wilhelm Sandkaulen, *Das Notjahr 1816/17 mit besonderer Berücksichtigung der Verhältnisse am Niederrhein* (Münster, 1927), pp. 1–14.

80. Chladni, "Sommer von 1816," p. 133; *The Times*, May 27, 1816, p. 3; *Landwirthschaftliche Zeitung oder Der Land- und Hauswirth* 15, no. 16 (1817): 137–39.

81. Günther Meinhardt, "Die Auswirkungen der Hungerjahre in der ersten Hälfte des 19. Jahrhunderts auf Göttingen," *Göttinger Jahrbuch* 14 (1966): 213–15.

82. *Landwirthschaftliche Zeitung* 15, no. 10 (1817): 86–87.

83. *The Times*, November 18, 1816, p. 2.

84. Chladni, "Sommer of 1816," p. 133; Ludwig Wilhelm Gilbert, ed., "Aus einem Schreiben des Professor Brandes zu Breslau, meteorologischen Inhalts," *Annalen der Physik* 55 (1817): 112; *Gentleman's Magazine* 86 (December 1816): 551; *The Times*, August 15, 1816, p. 2; September 4, 1816, p. 2; November 7, 1816, p. 2; January 13, 1817, p. 2; March 21, 1817, p. 3.

85. Arcadius Kahan, "Natural Calamities and Their Effect upon the Food Supply in Russia (An Introduction to a Catalog)," *Jahrbücher für Geschichte Osteuropas*, N. F., 16 (September 1968): 373–76; Chladni, "Sommer of 1816," p. 133.

86. Easton, *Hivers*, pp. 119–24, 127–30; Weikinn, *Witterungsgeschichte* 4: 243–66; Abel, *Hungerkrisen*, pp. 180–81; Stout, *Autobiography*, p. 228.

87. Gille, "Northern Countries," pp. 50–52.

88. Ruprecht Zollikofer, *Der Osten meinen Vaterlandes, oder die Kantone St. Gallen und Appenzell im Hungerjahre 1817* (2 vols.; St. Gall, 1818–19), 1: 4; Wilhelm Oechsli, *Geschichte der Schweiz im neunzehnten Jahrhundert* (2 vols.; Leipzig, 1913), 2: 475–76.

89. Hans Brugger, *Die schweizerische Landwirtschaft in der ersten Hälfte des 19. Jahrhunderts* (Frauenfeld, 1956), p. 36. This system was developed and maintained by C. K. Muller, Director of the Statistical Office at Zürich.

90. *Schweizerische Monathschronik*, 1816, pp. 202–03; Zollikofer, *Meinen Vaterlandes* 1: 191; Oechsli, *Schweiz* 2: 476.

91. Freiherr Anton Baldacci, "Über die inneren Zustände Österreichs. Eine Denkschrift aus dem Jahr 1816," ed. by F. von Krones, in *Archiv für österreichische Geschichte* 74 (1889): 30, 78–88. Baldacci was *Präsident* of the General-Rechnungs-Directorium in 1816; in 1829 the emperor placed him at the head of the new Austrian statistical bureau.

92. *Oekonomische Neuigkeiten und Verhandlungen. Zeitschrift für alle Zweige der Land- und Hauswirthschaft, des Forst- und Jagdwesens im oesterreichischen Kaiserthum und dem ganzen Deutschland*, January, 1817, no. 1, pp. 6–7; *The Times*, January 27, 1816, p. 3.

93. Johann von Csaplovics, *Gemälde von Ungern* (2 vols.; Budapest, 1829), 1: 139–42; *Gentleman's Magazine* 86, part I (January–June 1816): 267; *Quotidienne* (Paris), March 4, 1816, p. 2.

94. *Oekonomische Neuigkeiten*, January 1817, no. 1, p. 2; Baldacci, "Zustände," pp. 83–84; *Landwirthschaftliche Zeitung* 15, no. 10 (1817): 89–90; C. A. Macartney, *The Habsburg Empire, 1790–1918* (London, 1968), p. 200.

95. *Oekonomische Neuigkeiten*, May 1818, no. 7, p. 49; January 1817, no. 1, p. 4; Baldacci, "Zustände," pp. 80–82.

96. *Oekonomische Neuigkeiten*, January 1817, no. 1, pp. 2–7.

97. Ibid., April 1817, no. 5, p. 35.

98. Baldacci, "Zustände," pp. 77–78; *The Times*, July 27, 1816, p. 3.

99. *Oekonomische Neuigkeiten*, January 1817, no. 1, pp. 6–7; April 1817, no. 6, p. 47; Baldacci, "Zustände," pp. 58–69, 77–78.

100. Baldacci, "Zustände," pp. 70, 87–88; Hermann Meynert, *Kaiser Franz I* (Vienna, 1872), pp. 397–98.

101. *The Times*, July 24, 1816, p. 2.

102. *Quotidienne*, February 14, 1816, pp. 1–2; August 22, 1817, p. 1; *Moniteur* (Paris), April 27, 1817, p. 463.

103. Baldacci, "Zustände," p. 76; H. W. Dove, "Über die nicht periodischen Änderungen der Temperaturvertheilung auf der Oberflasche der Erde," *Abhandlungen der Königlichen*

Akademie der Wissenschaften zu Berlin (1838), part 1, p. 362; ibid., part 3, p. 125; Jos. Alex. von Helfert, *Zur Geschichte des Lombardo-Venezianischen Königreichs* (Vienna, 1908), p. 31; R. John Rath, "The Habsburgs and the Great Depression in Lombardo-Venetia, 1814–1818," *Journal of Modern History* 13 (September 1941): 309.

104. Rath, "Depression," pp. 308–09; Helfert, *Geschichte,* p. 31.

105. Helfert, *Geschichte,* p. 32.

106. *Quotidienne,* May 5, 1816, p. 2; January 27, 1817, p. 3; February 14, 1817, p. 2; February 17, 1817, p. 1; February 20, 1817, p. 1; March 10, 1817, p. 1; *Gentleman's Magazine* 86 (March 1816): 266; Henry Matthews, *The Diary of an Invalid. Being the Journal of a Tour in Poursuit of Health in Portugal, Italy, Switzerland and France in the Years 1817, 1818, and 1819* (3d ed.; Paris, 1825), p. 209; G. Monteleone, "Le carestie de 1816–1817 nelle Province Venete," *Archivio Veneto* 86–87 (1969): 23–86; Mario Romani, *Storia economica d'Italia nel secolo XIX* (2d ed.; Milan, 1970), pp. 33–37.

107. *The Times,* September 5, 1816, p. 3; March 3, 1817, pp. 2–3; May 12, 1817, p. 2; May 26, 1817, p. 2; Nicolás Sanchez-Albornoz, *Las crisis de subsistencias de España en el siglo XIX* (Rosario, Argentina, 1963), pp. 8–9; Jaime Vicens Vives, *An Economic History of Spain,* trans. by Frances López-Morillas (3d. ed.; Princeton, 1969), pp. 733–35.

108. Vitorino Magalhães Godinho, *Prix et monnaies au Portugal, 1750–1850* (Paris, 1955), pp. 70–74; *The Times,* November 5, 1816, p. 2.

109. *Niles' Weekly Register,* February 1, 1817, p. 379.

110. Magalhães Godinho, *Prix au Portugal,* pp. 77–78.

111. M. H. Cherif, "Expansion européene et difficultés tunisiennes de 1815 à 1830," *Annales: E. S. C.* 15 (May–June 1970): 721–22; *The Times,* October 6, 1817, p. 2; *Gentleman's Magazine* 86 (December 1816): 551.

112. H. Arakawa, "Meteorological Conditions of the Great Famines in the Last Half of the Tokugawa Period, Japan," *Papers in Meteorology and Geophysics* 6, no. 2 (September 1955): 105–06.

113. Koji Aoki, *Hyakushō Ikki no Nenjiteki Kenkyā [A Study by Years of Peasant Uprisings]* (Tokyo, 1966), pp. 15–18.

114. James Jameson, *Report on the Epidemick Cholera Morbus as It Visited the Territories Subject to the Presidency of Bengal in the Years 1817, 1818, and 1819* (Calcutta, 1820), pp. xxvix–li, 92–94.

115. *Lexington* (Kentucky) *Gazette,* September 23, 1816, p. 2.

116. For contemporary discussion of the association between sunspots and meteorological phenomena, see W. M. Mosely, "Bemerkungen über die Sonnenflecken des Jahres 1816," *Annalen der Physik* 58 (1818): 406–13; *Gentleman's Magazine* 87 (February 1817): 109–10; *Western Spy,* May 13, 1816, p. 2; June 27, 1816, p. 2; *Württembergishes Jahrbuch für 1818,* p. 509.

117. Lamb, *Climate,* pp. 440–58; Milham, "The Year 1816," pp. 566–67; Hoyt, "Summer of 1816," p. 128; David Shaw, "Sunspot Changes and Temperature," *Journal of Geophysical Research* 70 (October 15, 1965): 4,997–98; H. H. Clayton, "Sunspot Changes and Weather Changes," *Smithsonian Miscellaneous Collections* 104, no. 19 (March 6, 1946): 1–29.

118. Dr. Thomas D. Mitchell, "Atmospheric Constitution of New York, from March to July 1816," *New York Medical Repository,* New ser., 3 (1817): 304; Chladni, "Sommer von 1816," p. 132; Gilbert, "Schreiben," pp. 112–14; *Gentleman's Magazine* 88 (February 1818): 136.

119. Lamb, *Climate,* pp. 301–03, 330–33, 337–41, 385–88.

120. Mitchell, "Atmospheric Constitution," pp. 301–02.

121. *The Works of Benjamin Franklin,* ed. by Jared Sparks (10 vols.; Boston, 1836–40), 6: 456–57.

122. Humphreys, "Volcanic Dust," pp. 25–26; Lamb, "Volcanic Dust," pp. 430–35.

123. *National Intelligencer,* May 17, 1816, p. 2.

124. Charles M. Wilson, "The Year without a summer," *American History Illustrated* 5 (June 1970): 24–29.

125. Quoted in *The Old Farmers Almanac* 174 (1966): 47.

126. Abbot and Fowle, "Volcanoes and Climate," p. 4.

127. *Annual Register,* 1815, "Chronicle," pp. 36–37.

128. Sir Thomas Raffles, *The History of Java* (2d ed.; 2 vols.; (London, 1830), 1: 29–30. A more detailed account with documents is found in *Memoir of the Life and Public Service of Sir Thomas Raffles,* ed. by Lady Sophia Raffles (London, 1830), pp. 241–50.
129. Franz Wilhelm Junghuhn, *Java: seine Gestalt, Pflanzendecke und innere Bauart,* trans. by J. K. Hasskarl from the Dutch (3 vols.; Leipzig, 1857), 2: 822–23.

Chapter II

1. *Annual Register,* 1816, pp. 91–92.
2. François Crouzet, "Wars, Blockade, and Economic Change in Europe 1792–1815," *Journal of Economic History* 24 (December 1964): 570–73.
3. Gustav von Gülich, *Geschichtliche Darstellung des Handels, der Gewerbe und des Ackerbaus der bedeutendsten handeltreibenden Staaten unserer Zeit* (2 vols.; Jena, 1830), 2: 368–70, 387–88; William Jacob, *A View of the Agriculture, Manufacture, Statistics and State of Society, of Germany, and Parts of Holland and France* (London, 1820), pp. 91, 245; Julius Andreas Demian, *Der deutsche Bund in seiner Gesammtkraft* (Leipzig, 1818), pp. 58–60, 245; Wilhelm Treue, *Wirtschaftszustände und Wirtschaftspolitik in Preussen 1815–1825* (Stuttgart, 1937), pp. 36–37; Wolfram Fischer, *Der Staat und die Anfänge der Industrialisierung in Baden 1800–1850* (Berlin, 1962), pp. 277–79; W. O. Henderson, The Zollverein (2d ed.; London, 1959), passim; Johann Slokar, *Geschichte der österreichischen Industrie und ihrer Förderung unter Kaiser Franz I* (Vienna, 1914), pp. 358–68.
4. Victor Fris, *Histoire de Gand* (Brussels, 1913), pp. 337–38; Henri Pirenne, *Histoire de Belgique* (7 vols.; Brussels, 1909–26), 6: 273; Slokar, *Industrie,* pp. 358–68; Demian, *Deutsche Bund,* pp. 58–60; Jacob, *View,* p. 91; Gülich, *Geschichtliche Darstellung,* 2: 387–88; Treue, *Wirtschaftszustände,* pp. 36–37.
5. Jacob, *View,* pp. 91, 245; Gülich, *Geschichtliche Darstellung,* 2: 387–88; Demian, *Deutsche Bund,* pp. 58–60, 245; Treue, *Wirtschaftszustände,* pp. 36–37; Fischer, *Industrialisierung,* pp. 277–79.
6. Wilhelm Treue, *Wirtschaftsgeschichte der Neuzeit im Zeitalter der Industriellen Revolution 1700 bis 1960* (Stuttgart, 1962), pp. 355–56.
7. Slokar, *Industrie,* pp. 64–65; Jerome Blum, *Noble Landowners and Agriculture in Austria 1815–1848* (Baltimore, 1948), pp. 102–03; Hans G. A. V. Schenk, *The Aftermath of the Napoleonic Wars* (London, 1947), p. 66.
8. Alexandre Chabert, *Essai sur les mouvements des revenues et de l'activitié économique en France de 1798 à 1820* (Paris, 1949), p. 126, David S. Landes, *The Unbound Prometheus* (Cambridge, 1970), pp. 143–45. 162: G. de Bertier de Sauvigny. *La Restauration* (2d ed.; Paris, 1963), p. 11.
9. Jan Craeybeckx, "The Beginnings of the Industrial Revolution in Belgium," trans. from the French, in *Essays in French Economic History,* ed. by Rondo E. Cameron (Homewood, Ill., 1970), pp. 191–200; Robert Demoulin. *Guillaume Ier, et la transformation èconomique des provinces belges, 1815–1830* (Liège, 1938), pp. 17–18; J. Dhondt, "The Cotton Industry at Ghent during the French Regime," trans. by Michael B. Palmer, in *Essays in European Economic History,* ed. by F. Crouzet, W. H. Chaloner, and W. M. Stern (London, 1969), p. 45; Laurent Dechesne, *Histoire économique et sociale de la Belgique* (Liège, 1932), p. 357.
10. Gülich, *Geschichtliche Darstellung,* 2: 368–70; Demian, *Deutsche Bund,* p. 63.
11. B. M. Biucchi, "The Industrial Revolution in Switzerland 1700–1914," trans. by Muriel Grindrod, in vol. 4, *The Fontana Economic History of Europe,* ed. by Carlo M. Cipolla (London, 1969), pp. 631–32; *Schweizerische Monathschronik,* 1816, pp. 203–04; Ruprecht Zollikofer, *Der Osten meinen Vaterlandes oder die Kantone St. Gallen und Appenzell im Hungerjahre 1817* (2 vols.; St. Gall, 1818–19), 1: 66–67; Wilhelm Oechsli, *Geschichte der Schweiz im neunzehnten Jahrhundert* (2 vols.; Leipzig, 1913), 2: 447; Kurt B. Mayer, *The Population of Switzerland* (New York, 1952), pp. 9, 22, 140, 248; Biucchi, "Industrial Revolution," pp. 648–52.

12. Slokar, *Industrie*, pp. 268–72; Treue, *Wirtschaftsgeschichte*, p. 343; Schenk, *Aftermath*, p. 66.

13. Arthur D. Gayer, W. W. Rostow, and Anna Jacobson Schwartz, *The Growth and Fluctuation of the British Economy 1790–1850* (2 vols.; London, 1953), 1: 117, 122; Harold R. C. Wright, *Free Trade and Protection in the Netherlands 1816–1830* (Cambridge, 1955), pp. 97–98; Demoulin, *Guillaume Ier*, pp. 41, 119–22.

14. B. R. Mitchell and Phyllis Deane, *Abstract of British Historical Statistics* (Cambridge, 1962), pp. 282–83.

15. Peter Mathias, *The First Industrial Nation* (London, 1969), p. 65.

16. Wright, *Free Trade*, p. 98; Demoulin, *Guillaume Ier*, p. 324; Pirenne, *Belgique*, 4: 273; Frederick B. Artz, *Reaction and Revolution 1814–1832* (New York, 1963), p. 27; Dechesne, *Histoire économique*, p. 357; Fris, *Gand*, p. 337; Crouzet, "Economic Change," p. 572.

17. Demoulin, *Guillaume Ier*, p. 325; Wright, *Free Trade*, pp. 100–01.

18. Dhont, "Cotton Industry," pp. 41–42.

19. For a definitive discussion of these issues see Albert H. Imlah, *Economic Elements in the Pax Britannica* (Cambridge, Mass., 1958), esp. pp. 21–40.

20. Wright, *Free Trade*, p. 31, has constructed an index of British exports to the Netherlands which includes the year 1815 and indicates the same high percentage of nonmanufactured products:

Year	Products of Great Britain	Colonial, Irish and Foreign Products	Total
1815	235	398	325
1816	207	304	261
1817	160	187	175
1818	155	158	157
1819	164	158	161
1820	169	121	142

21. Demoulin, *Guillaume Ier*, pp. 105–06.

22. For discussion of the unavailability and unreliability of French statistical data during the early Restoration period, see Rondo E. Cameron, *France and the Economic Development of Europe, 1800–1914* (Princeton, 1961), pp. 14, 67–74; David S. Landes, "The Statistical Study of French Crises," *Journal of Economic History* 10 (1950), 201–04; Sebastien Charléty, *La Restauration* (Paris, 1921), pp. 288–89.

23. R. John Rath, "The Habsburgs and the Great Depression in Lombardo-Venetia, 1814–1818," *Journal of Modern History* 13 (September 1941): 307–08; idem, "Economic Conditions in Lombardy and Venetia, 1813–1815, and Their Effects on Public Opinion," *Journal of Central European Affairs* 23 (October 1963): 276–77; G. Monteleone, "Le Carestie de 1816–1817 nelle Province Venete," *Archivio Veneto* 86–87 (1969): 23–35.

24. Charles Dupin, *Forces productives et commerciales de la France* (2 vols.; Paris, 1827), 1: iii.

25. Bertier, *Restauration*, p. 128; Charléty, *Restauration*, p. 74.

26. E. Levasseur, *Histoire des classes ouvrières et de l'industrie en France de 1789 à 1820* (2d ed.; 2 vols.; Paris, 1903–04), 1: 561; Charléty, *Restauration*, p. 115. This figure is the sum of the 700 million franc war indemnity, the 633 million francs expended to maintain the occupation troops, and the foreign debt claims that were ultimately scaled down from 1,600 million to 500 million francs.

27. Étienne Denis Pasquier, *Histoire de mon temps: Mémoires du Chancelier Pasquier*, ed. by M. le duc D'Audiffret-Pasquier (3d ed.; 6 vols.; Paris, 1894–95), 4: 99; Charléty, *Restauration*, pp. 100–01.

28. Marcel Marion, *Histoire financière de la France depuis 1715* (5 vols.; Paris, 1914–28), 4: 402–10. Without examining budgetary details, which are difficult to present briefly and comprehensively and which would add little to this study, some factors nevertheless should be mentioned. There still remained an unpaid arrears of 696 million francs extending back to the

unpaid arrears of 462 million francs in 1814 and including the accumulated deficit of the first nine months of the Restoration. It was impossible to pay such a sum with the tax receipts expected in 1816. However, the ordinary and extraordinary expenses of 1816 had to be budgeted and met. These expenses were estimated at a total of about 838 million francs, of which 140 million francs were for the first one-fifth of the war indemnity, 130 million francs for the maintenance of the armies of occupation, and 5.3 million frances for payments arising out of the peace treaty. For discussion of the 1816 budget, see Charléty. *Restauration*, pp. 99–100. For official figures of receipts and expenditures, see Statistique générale, *Documents statistiques sur la France* (Paris, 1835), pp. 117–43.

29. Marion, *Histoire financière*, 4: 410. In the six-month period beginning May 1, 1816 about one-third of all outstanding *rentes* were transferred to different owners; it became clear that the credit of the royal government was in jeopardy. The *rentes* returned a 5 percent income on the face value of the security. When a source speaks of 5 million *rentes*, it refers to a par value of 100 million francs. If these securities were sold below par, as they were in the postwar years, the actual proceeds received by the government were reduced proportionately. A loan contract was signed February 10, 1817, with Baring Brothers & Company, Hope & Company, and smaller foreign banking contractors. The significance of these loans for this study will be dealt with below.

30. Thomas Tooke, *Thoughts and Details on the High and Low Prices of the Last Thirty Years* (London, 1823), part 3, p. 177; Thomas Tooke and William Newmarch, *A History of Prices and of the State of Circulation from 1792 to 1856* (6 vols.; New York, 1857), 2: 2–4; *Annual Register*, 1815, p. 144; J. D. Chambers and G. E. Mingay, *The Agricultural Revolution 1750–1880* (London, 1966), pp. 112–24; David J. Wood, "The Complicity of Climate in the 1816 Depression in Dumsfriesshire," *Scottish Geographical Magazine* 81 (1965): 5–7; William Smart, *Economic Annals of the Nineteenth Century 1801–1820* (New York, 1964), pp. 372–89, 407–17, 445–60.

31. Lord Ernle, *English Farming Past and Present* (6th ed.; Chicago, 1961), pp. 322–23.

32. Treue, *Wirtschaftszustände*, p. 21.

33. For discussion of German industry at this time, see Hans Mottek, *Wirtschaftsgeschichte Deutschlands* (2d ed.; 2 vols.; Berlin, 1974), 2: 105–18; Jürgen Kuczynski, *Germany, 1800 to the Present Day*, vol. 3, part 1, *A Short History of Labour Conditions under Industrial Capitalism* (4 vols.; London, 1942–46), p. 25; Reinhart Koselleck, *Preussen zwischen Reform und Revolution* (Stuttgart, 1967), p. 608; Staatsrath Joseph von Hazzi, *Betrachtungen über Theurung und Noth der Vergangenheit und Gegenwart* (Munich, 1818), p. 98; Treue, *Wirtschaftszustände*, pp. 94–95, 100, 104–08.

34. William Jacob, *Report of the Trade in Foreign Corn, and on the Agriculture of the North of Europe* (3d ed.; London, 1826), p. 50; for discussion of the landholding structure of Prussia, see Walter M. Simon, *The Failure of the Prussian Reform Movement, 1807–1819* (Ithaca, N.Y., 1955), pp. 91–104.

35. Max Peters, *Die Entwicklung der deutschen Rhederei* (2 vols.; Jena, 1899–1905), 1: 51–56.

36. France, Statistique gènèrale, *Archives statistiques du ministère des trauvaux publics, de l'agriculture et du commerce* (Paris, 1837), pp. 20–21; Paul Leuilliot, *L'Alsace au début de XIXe siècle 1815–1830* (3 vols.; Paris, 1959–60), 2: 63.

37. Mathias, *Industrial Nation*, p. 65.

38. Sir William H. Beveridge, "Weather and Harvest Cycles," *Economic Journal* 31 (1921): 429–30, 450–51. Crop or agricultural years begin on September 1; for example, the year 1816 began on September 1, 1816, and ended August 31, 1817; thus the index for any given year represents the average price at which the crop of that year was sold. The 48 market locations are found in England (4), Scotland (4), Holland (2), Flanders (5), France (11), North Germany (14), South Germany (4), Alsace (2), Bohemia (1), and Austria (1).

39. M. J. R. Healy and E. L. Jones, "Wheat Yields in England, 1815–57," *Journal of the Royal Statistical Society*, Ser. A (1962): 578.

40. U.K., Parliamentary Papers, *Report from Committee on the Agriculture of the United Kingdom*, Session 23 January to 11 July, 1821, 9: 264–65.

41. Tooke and Newmarch, *Prices*, 2: 14–15.

42. France, Ministère de l'Intérieur, *Circulaires, instructions et autre actes émanés du ministère de l'intérieur de 1797 à 1821 inclusivement* (2d ed.; 6 vols.; Paris, 1821–30), 3: 136–40.

43. Quoted in Louis Guéneau, "La disette de 1816–1817 dans une région productrice de blé, la Brie," *Revue d'histoire moderne* 9 (January–February 1929): 21–22.

44. *Württembergishes Jahrbuch für 1818,* pp. 9–10.

45. Wilhelm, Abel, *Massenarmut und Hungerkrisen im vorindustriellen Europa* (Hamburg and Berlin, 1974), p. 318; Hazzi, *Theurung,* p. 79.

46. *Oekonomische Neuigkeiten,* January 1817, no. 1, pp. 2–7.

47. Ibid., April 1817, no. 5, p. 35.

48. Rath, "Great Depression," pp. 308–09; Jos. Alex. von Helfert, *Zur Geschichte des Lombardo-Venezianischen Königreichs* (Vienna, 1908), p. 31.

49. For the relevant price data in France, see Alexandre Chabert, *Essai sur les movements des prix en France de 1798 à 1820* (Paris, 1945), pp. 59, 65, 76; for Austria, see Alfred Francis Pribram, *Materialien zur Geschichte der Preise und Löhne in Österreich* (Vienna, 1938), pp. 388, 393, 398, 400, 415–19, 432, 436, 439, 443, 445; for Germany, see Moritz J. Elsas, *Umriss einer Geschichte der Preise und Löhne in Deutschland vom ausgehenden Mittelalter bis zum Beginn des 19. Jahrhunderts* (2 vols.; Leiden, 1936–49), 1: 649, 677; 2, B: 107, 124, 127, 131; for Britain see Tooke, *Prices,* part 3, p. 177.

50. Arthur H. Cole, *Wholesale Commodity Prices in the United States, 1700–1861* (Cambridge, Mass., 1938), supplement, pp. 171–91.

51. See Abel, *Hungerkrisen,* pp. 319–20, in support of this conclusion and also for a demonstration that in Hanover prices per calorie remained considerably lower for rye, wheat, and bread, despite the fact that grain prices rose twice as steeply as meat prices between January 1816 and November 1817.

52. Chabert, *Prix,* p. 50.

53. Louis François Benoiston de Chateauneuf, *Recherches sur les consommations de tout genre de la ville de Paris en 1817, comparées à ce qu'elles étaient en 1789* (2d ed.; Paris, 1821), p. 151.

54. Collette Girard, "La disette de 1816–1817 dans la Meurthe," *Annales de l'Est,* 5th ser., 6, no. 4 (1955): 338–39; P. Truchon, "La vie ouvrière à Lyon sous la Restauration," *Revue d'histoire de Lyon* 11 (May–June 1912): 198.

55. Statistique générale, *Archives statistiques,* pp. 8–13, 20–21.

56. Demoulin, *Guillaume Ier,* p. 408.

57. Nicholaas W. Posthumus, *Inquiry into the History of Prices in Holland* (2 vols.; Leiden, 1946–64), 1: 14, 22, 36, 98–99; I. J. Brugmans, "Economic Fluctuations in the Netherlands in the Nineteenth Century," in Crouzet, ed., *Essays,* p. 48.

58. Sir William Henry Beveridge and Others, *Prices and Wages in England from the Twelfth to the Nineteenth Century* (London, 1939), p. 210. Prices are given in shillings and decimal pence per 15 lbs. Troy.

59. *The Times,* May 2, 1816, p. 3; May 18, 1817, p. 3; June 25, 1817, p. 3; *Blackwoods Edinburgh Magazine* 1 (June 1817): 336.

60. Carl von Clausewitz, *Politische Schriften und Briefe,* ed. by Hans Rothfels (Munich, 1922), pp. 189–91.

61. *Oekonomische Neuigkeiten,* February 1818, no. 11, p. 88; *Württembergishes Jahrbuch für 1818,* pp. 13–14; ibid., 1819, pp. 9–10.

62. A. J. V. Heunisch, *Das Grossherzogtum Baden* (Heidelberg, 1857), pp. 127, 454; Fischer, *Baden,* p. 381.

63. Elsas, *Preise,* I, pp. 674, 677.

64. Heinrich Bechtolsheimer, "Die Provinz Rheinhessen in den beiden ersten Jahrzehnten ihres Bestehens," *Quellen und Forschungen zur hessischen Geschichte* 4 (1916): 70–74.

65. Johann Friedrich Benzenberg, *Ueber Handel und Gewerbe, Steuren und Zölle* (Elberfeld, 1819), pp. 335–36; Wilhelm Sandkaulen, *Das Notjahr 1816/17 mit besonderer Berücksichtigung der Verhältnisse am Niederrhein* (Münster, 1927), pp. 10–13, 29–30; Wilhelm Abel, *Agrarkrisen und Agrarkonjunktur* (2d ed.; Hamburg and Berlin, 1966), p. 290; Jacob, *Foreign Corn,* pp. 167–68; Anna Neumann, *Die Bewegung der Löhne der ländlichen "freien" Arbeiter im Königreich Preussen gegenwärtigen Umfangs vom Ausgang des 18. Jahrhundert bis 1850* (Ber-

lin, 1911), p. 117; Wolfgang Köllmann, *Sozialgeschichte der Stadt Barmen im 19. Jahrhundert* (Tübingen, 1960), pp. 39, 138–39.

66. Abel, *Agrarkrisen*, p. 290; Gunther Meinhardt, "Die Auswirkungen der Hungerjahre in der ersten Hälfte des 19. Jahrhundert auf Göttingen," *Göttinger Jahrbuch* 14 (1966): 214–15.

67. Jacob, *Foreign Corn*, pp. 50, 211, 242–43.

68 Elsas, *Preise*, 2, B, p. 127; Abel, *Agrarkrisen*, p. 290.

69. Pribram, *Preise*, pp. 270, 338.

70. See A. Tebeldi, *Die Geldangelegenheiten Oestreichs* (Leipzig, 1847), pp. 51, 60, 80, for the exchange rate of paper currency during the second decade of the nineteenth century.

71. Adolf Beer, *Die Finanzen Oesterreichs im XIX. Jahrhundert* (Prague, 1877), pp. 92–101, 111. In essence the state repudiated 60 percent of its floating debt in 1816; but the government's offer proved tempting, for the current quotation of the paper money (Wiener Währung as it was called) stood at 346. Those surrendering *Papiergeld* received not merely 40 florins in *Banknoten* but also bonds worth perhaps an additional 20 florins. (Austrian public indebtedness at the end of 1815 still amounted to more than 800 million florins, excluding the issued and unredeemed paper money.) But because the paper currency was being redeemed at a figure much more attractive than the quoted discount, a rush ensued to exchange *Papiergeld* for *Banknoten* and state obligations, and there was a corresponding rush to exchange the bank notes for specie, especially by business and industry. In the first few weeks 13 million florins in bank notes were issued and 11 million florins were exchanged for silver. Since the government's sinking fund was to be financed principally from the French indemnity (initially the sum of 47 million florins was planned for the sinking fund; the French indemnity of 150 million francs approximated 43 million florins), which became available only in small quarterly payments, various expedients had to be adopted to tempt state creditors to postpone redemption into specie. By the end of 1817, only 46.5 million florins had been redeemed. The redemption figure reached 226 million florins at the end of 1819, with approximately 450 million florins remaining in circulation.

72. Pribram, *Preise*, pp. 415–45.

73. *Oekonomische Neuigkeiten*, June 1817, no. 8, p. 64: July 1817, no. 9, p. 72; December 1818, no. 72, p. 576.

74. Pribram, *Preise*, pp. 400, 432, 436, 439.

75. C. A. Macartney, *The Habsburg Empire 1790–1918* (London, 1968), p. 200.

76. *Oekonomische Neuigkeiten*, January 1817, no. 1, pp. 6–7; April 1817, no. 6, p. 47; Freiherr Anton von Baldacci, "Über die inneren Zustände Österreichs. Eine Denkschrift aus dem Jahr 1816," ed. and introduced by F. von Krones in *Archiv für österreichische Geschichte* 74 (1889): 58, 70–77, 87–88; Hermann Meynert, *Kaiser Franz I* (Vienna, 1872), pp. 397–98; *The Times*, July 24, 1816, p. 2; *Quotidienne* (Paris), February 14, 1816, pp. 1–2; August 22, 1817, p. 1.

77. Abel, *Agrarkrisen*, p. 290. Measured in the silver equivalent of lire, wheat prices in Lombardy–Venetia rose from an average of 24.82 per 100 kilograms in 1814 to 41.03 in 1816; by 1819, however, prices had declined to 13.58 lire.

78. Meynert, *Franz I*, pp. 394–95; Baldacci, "Zustände," p. 76; *Quotidienne*, May 5, 1816, p. 2; January 2, 1817, p. 3; January 27, 1817, p. 2; February 14, 1817, p. 2; February 17, 1817, p. 1; February 20, 1817, p. 1; March 10, 1817, p. 1; Rath, "Great Depression," pp. 308–09; Helfert, *Geschichte*, pp. 32–33.

79. Hans Brugger, *Die schweizerische Landwirtschaft in der ersten Hälfte des 19. Jahrhunderts* (Frauenfeld, 1956), p. 110.

80. Zollikofer, *Meinen Vaterlandes*, 1: 136, 282.

81. Christoph Bernoulli, *Schweizerische Archiv für Statistik und Nationalökonomie* (5 vols.; Basel, 1827–31), 4: 117–18; *Schweizerische Monathschronik*, 1817, pp. 65–67; Oechsli, *Schweiz*, 2: 476–77.

82. William Harty, M.D., *An Historic Sketch of the Causes, Progress, Extent, and Mortality of the Contagious Fever Epidemic in Ireland during the Years 1817, 1818, and 1819* (Dublin, 1820), p. 183.

83. Cole, *Prices*, supplement, pp. 171, 174–75, 178–89, 182, 186–87, 191.

84. Arthur G. Peterson, "Wheat and Corn Prices Received by Producers in Virginia, 1801–1928," *Journal of Economic and Business History* 2 (February 1930): 389.

85. William Durkee Williamson, *The History of the State of Maine* (2 vols.; Hallowell, 1832), 2: 665.

86. Samuel Griswold Goodrich, *Recollections of a Lifetime* (2 vols.; New York, 1850), 2: 78–79; also see John Milton Whiton, *Sketches of the History of New Hampshire* (Concord, 1834), p. 189; George Barstow, *History of New Hampshire* (Concord, 1842), p. 392.

87. Pliney H. White, "Coventry," in *Vermont Historical Gazetteer* (Claremont, N.H., 1877), pp. 146–47.

88. Nathan A. Hoskins, *A History of the State of Vermont* (Vergennes, 1831), p. 232; Lewis Dayton Stilwell, *Migration from Vermont* (Montpelier, 1948), pp. 129–30.

89. *National Intelligencer*, November 26, 1816, p. 3; January 3, 1817, p. 2; *Western Intelligencer* (Worthington, Ohio), December 5, 1816, p. 2; *Nashville Whig*, February 5, 1817, p. 3.

90. *National Intelligencer*, April 10, 1817, p. 3; *Raleigh Register*, April 12, 1816, p. 3.

91. Clarence E. Carter, ed., *The Territorial Papers of the United States*, vol. 18, *The Territory of Alabama, 1817–1819* (Washington, D.C., 1952), pp. 35, 88; Thomas P. Abernethy, *The South in the New Nation* (Baton Rouge, 1961), p. 466; *Nashville Whig*, June 16, 1817, p. 3.

92. Thomas P. Abernethy, *The Formative Period in Alabama, 1815–1828* (University, Alabama, 1965), p. 37.

93. Williamson, *Maine*, 2: 669.

94. *American Monthly Magazine and Critical Review* 1 (July 1817): 228.

95. For discussion of these issues, see Arthur L. Bowley, *Wages in the United Kingdom in the Nineteenth Century* (Cambridge, 1900), pp. 26, 41; for an investigation of the availability of cottage-gardens, garden-allotments, and "potato-grounds" to alleviate poverty in Britain, see D. C. Barnett, "Allotments and the Problem of Rural Poverty, 1780–1840," in E. L. Jones and G. E. Mingay, *Land, Labour and Population in the Industrial Revolution* (London, 1967), pp. 162–83.

96. Bowley, *Wages*, pp. 33–34, 60, 82–89; Mitchell and Deane, *Statistics*, pp. 348–49.

97. J. D. Chambers and G. E. Mingay, *The Agricultural Revolution 1750–1880* (London, 1966), p. 129; Bowley, *Wages*, p. 34.

98. A. J. Peacock, *Bread or Blood: A Study of the Agrarian Riots in East Anglia in 1816* (London, 1965), pp. 39–42, 174–76.

99. Sir Edward Baines, *History of the Cotton Manufacture in Great Britain* (London, 1835), p. 438; Bowley, *Wages*, p. 60.

100. Smart, *Economic Annals*, p. 595.

101. Paul Paillat, "Les salaires et la condition ouvrière en France à l'aube du machinisme (1815–1830)," *Revue économique* 2 (November 1951): 768–70.

102. Leuilliot, *L'Alsace*, 2: 163; Girard, "Disette," pp. 338–39.

103. Köllmann, *Barmen*, pp. 39, 138–39.

104. Gülich, *Geschichtliche Darstellung*, 2: 370, 388; Treue, *Wirtschaftszustände*, pp. 75–107.

105. Adolf Lewin, *Geschichte der badischen Juden 1738–1909* (Karlsruhe, 1909), p. 190; Fischer, *Baden*, p. 364; Mack Walker, *Germany and the Emigration 1816–1885* (Cambridge, Mass., 1964), p. 2.

106. Slokar, *Industrie*, pp. 273, 319, 373.

107. *Schweizerische Monathschronik*, 1817, p. 67; Oechsli, *Schweiz*, 2: 477; Louis Simond, *Switzerland; or a Journal of a Tour and Residence in that Country, in the Years 1817, 1818, and 1819* (2 vols.; Boston, 1822), 1: 76–77.

108. Zollikofer, *Meinen Vaterlandes*, 1: 8, 43.

109. Chabert, *Revenus*, pp. 81–88, 201; Charléty, *Restauration*, p. 315; Henri Sée, *La vie économique de la France sous la monarchie censitaire (1815–1848)* (Paris, 1951), pp. 14–15; Richard Cobb, *The Police and the People: French Popular Protest 1789–1820* (Oxford, 1970), pp. 278–81.

110. Connell, *Ireland*, p. 228; Charles Creighton, *A History of Epidemics in Britain* (2 vols.; Cambridge, 1891–94), 2: 256–57.

111. Brugger, *Landwirtschaft*, p. 227.

112. Sandkaulen, *Notjahr*, pp. 10–11.

113. Newmann, *Löhne*, p. 117.

114. *Oekonomische Neuigkeiten,* October 1816, no. 8, p. 59; Blum, *Noble Landowners,* pp. 187–90.

115. Blum, *Noble Landowners,* p. 50.

116. *Oekonomische Neuigkeiten,* October 1816, no. 8, p. 59.

117. For descriptions of the subsistence crisis in Italy see *Quotidienne,* February 14, 1817, p. 2; February 20, 1817, p. 2; January 2, 1817, p. 3; *The Times,* October 2, 1817, p. 2; October 31, 1817, p. 2.

118. France, *Collection complète des lois, décrets, ordonnances, réglements, et avis du Conseil-d'État,* ed. by Jean Baptiste Devergier de Hauranne (24 vols.; Paris, 1824–32), 21: 2, 64–66, 73.

119. Jean Vidalenc, *Le département de l'Eure sous la monarchie constitutionnelle 1814–1848* (Paris, 1952), pp. 167, 177; Louis Guéneau, "La disette de 1816–1817 dans une région productrice de blé, la Brie," *Revue d'histoire moderne* 9 (January–February 1929): 27–28; Leuilliot, *L'Alsace,* 2: 163–66; Henry Contamine, *Metz et la Moselle de 1814 à 1870* (2 vols.; Nancy, 1932), 1: 308–11; Pierre-Paul Viard, "La disette de 1816–1817, particulièrement en Côte-d'Or," *Revue historique* 159 (September–October 1928): 100; Cobb, *People,* pp. 115–17; Chabert, *Revenus,* p. 414.

120. *The Times,* December 21, 1816, p. 2; June 28, 1817, p. 3; Demoulin, Guillaume Ier, pp. 122, 182; *Annual Register,* 1816, p. 128; Dechesne, *Histoire économique,* p. 358.

121. Meynert, *Franz I,* pp. 360–61.

122. Wilfred von Eisenhart Rothe and A. Ritthaler, *Vorgeschichte und Begründung des deutschen Zollvereins, 1815–1834* (3 vols.; Berlin, 1934), 1: 299, 314–15; Heinrich Ritter von Srbik, *Metternich* (3 vols.; Munich, 1925), 1: 533.

123. Maximilian Grafen von Montgelas, *Denkwürdigkeiten 1799–1817,* ed. by Ludwig Grafen von Montgelas (Stuttgart, 1887), p. 542; Wilhelm Joseph Behr, *Das Recht und die Pflicht der Regierungen in Beziehung auf die gegenwärtige Theurungsangelegenheit* (Würzburg, 1817), pp. 24–25.

124. Abel, *Hungerkrisen,* pp. 326–30; Wolf-Heino Struck, *Die Auswanderung aus dem Herzogtum Nassau, 1806–1866* (Wiesbaden, 1966), pp. 8–9.

125. Zollikofer, *Meinen Vaterlandes,* 1: 19; *Schweizerische Monathschronik,* 1817, p. 62; Oechsli, *Schweiz,* 2: 481.

126. *The Times,* October 2, 1817, p. 2; Helfert, *Geschichte,* pp. 33–34; Meynert, *Franz I,* pp. 360–61.

127. Wilhelm Roscher, *Ueber Kornhandel und Theuerungspolitik* (3d ed.; Stuttgart and Tübingen, 1852), pp. 5–14.

128. *The Times,* January 22, 1817, p. 2.

129. Vernon J. Puryear, "Odessa: Its Rise and International Importance 1815–1850," *Pacific Historical Review* 3 (1934): 195–97; Ludwik Tengoborskii, *Commentaries on the Productive Forces of Russia,* English translation (2 vols.; London, 1855–56), 2: 294; S. A. Pokrovskii, *Vneshniaia torgovlia i vneshniaia torgovaia politika Rossii* (Moscow, 1947), p. 246; *The Times,* November 2, 1816, p. 2; *Gentleman's Magazine* 88 (May 1818): 459. The grain measure *chetvert* or *tchetwert* is equivalent to 0.72 of a British imperial quarter.

130. Hedwig Pavelka, *English-österreichische Wirtschaftsbeziehungen in der ersten Hälfte des 19. Jahrhunderts* (Graz, 1968), pp. 143–44.

131. Charles H. Evans, "Exports, Domestic and Foreign, from the United States to all Countries from 1789 to 1883, Inclusive," House Miscellaneous Documents, 48th Cong., 1st sess., no. 49, part 2, 1884, Serial 2236, Table 2; U.S., Bureau of the Census, *Historical Statistics of the United States, Colonial Times to 1957* (Washington, D.C., 1960), p. 538.

132. *Quotidienne,* June 6, 1817, p. 2.

133. Claude Étienne Chaillou-Des Barres, *Essai historique et critique sur la legislation des grains jusqu'à ce jour* (Paris, 1820), p. 84.

134. Bertier, *Restauration,* p. 217; Levasseur, *Classes ouvrières,* 1: 643; Chabert, *Revenus,* pp. 414–15.

135. Henri Sée, *Histoire économique de la France: Les temps modernes (1789–1914)* (Paris, 1951), p. 123; Chaillou-Des Barres, *Grains,* pp. 85–86; Chabert, *Revenus,* pp. 321–24, 415; Bertier, *Restauration,* p. 217.

136. Charles Le Sur, *La France et les Français en 1817* (Paris, 1817), p. 279.

137. Ralph W. Hidy, *The House of Baring in American Trade and Finance* (Cambridge, Mass., 1949), pp. 58–60, 498. The foreign banking contractors imposed Draconian conditions, offering to buy at a price of 55 francs enough 5 percent *rentes* to produce 100 million francs for the French government. The price of *rentes* rose as anticipated, and a second loan was effected on July 30, 1817, which provided 115,200,000 francs in exchange for 5 percent *rentes* purchased at 64 francs. The expenses of the foreign occupation were covered by the proceeds of the first loan, while the indemnity installment was paid by the second. The French government created 30 million francs in *rentes*, or annual interest, during 1817. In May 1818 the government borrowed by means of a domestic loan, realizing about 200 million francs through the sale of securities at 66½; this last loan was oversubscribed more than ten times.

138. P. J. Blok, *Geschiedenis van het Nederlandsche Volk* (8 vols.; Leiden, 1892–1908), 7: 372; Pirenne, *Belgique*, 6: 273–74; *Quotidienne*, February 7, 1817, p. 2. The minister of interior had assured the states-general that some 11,400,000 hectoliters of grain were on hand in the kingdom on January 1, 1817, and that since consumption during the eight months prior to the next harvest would amount only to 9,100,000 hectoliters, in fact the Netherlands had a surplus of some 2,300,000 hectoliters beyond its consumption needs. Despite these calculations, grains were being cut in the fields and potatoes unearthed for food as early as May.

139. Demoulin, *Guillaume Ier*, p. 422.

140. *Annual Register*, 1817, p. 139.

141. Richard Tilly, "The Political Economy of Public Finance and the Industrialization of Prussia, 1815–1866," *Journal of Economic History* 26 (December 1966): 495.

142. Koselleck, *Preussen*, pp. 299, 570–71; W. O. Henderson, *The State and the Industrial Revolution in Prussia 1740–1870* (Liverpool, 1958), pp. 82–83; Jacob, *Foreign Corn*, p. 51.

143. Sandkaulen, *Notjahr*, pp. 7, 11, 49.

144. Clausewitz, *Politische Schriften*, pp. 189–91; Sandkaulen, *Notjahr*, pp. 37–38, 53–54, 58–61. The Prussian taler was valued at about three marks and thus also equal to three British shillings.

145. Clausewitz, *Politische Schriften*, pp. 190–91; *Moniteur*, July 22, 1817, p. 801.

146. Sandkaulen, *Notjahr*, p. 64.

147. *The Times*, August 22, 1817, p. 2.

148. Clausewitz, *Politische Schriften*, p. 190.

149. Sandkaulen, *Notjahr*, pp. 47–48.

150. *The Times*, August 22, 1817, p. 2.

151. Hazzi, *Theurung*, pp. 83–85, 94–95; Benzenberg, *Handel*, p. 172; Abel, *Hungerkrisen*, pp. 330–31; Wolfgang Zorn, *Handels- und Industriegeschichte Bayerisch-Schwabens 1648–1870* (Augsburg, 1961), p. 128. For example, the Augsburg merchants advanced 300,000 florins in private funds for foreign grain purchases in 1816–17.

152. *Württembergishes Jahrbuch für 1819*, p. 101.

153. Eugen von Philippovich, "Auswanderung und Auswanderungspolitik in Grossherzogtum Baden," in idem, ed., *Auswanderung und Auswanderungspolitik in Deutschland* (Leipzig, 1892), pp. 111–12; Bechtolsheimer, "Rheinhessen," pp. 70–74; Struck, *Nassau*, pp. 8–9.

154. Meinhardt, "Göttingen," pp. 214–15.

155. For a complete account of the activities and operating details of the Elberfeld *Kornverein* by its director, see Benzenberg, *Handel*, pp. 170–242; for an account of several municipal *Kornvereine*, see Abel, *Hungerkrisen*, pp. 338–40.

156. *Schweizerische Monathschronik*, 1817, p. 62; Zollikofer, *Meinen Vaterlandes*, 1: 19; 2: 44–45.

157. *Schweizerische Monathschronik*, 1817, p. 62; Oechsli, *Schweiz*, 2: 481–82.

158. Zollikofer, *Meinen Vaterlandes*, 2: 232; Bernoulli, *Schweizerische Archiv*, 4: 130; Oechsli, *Schweiz*, 2: 481–82.

159. *Quotidienne*, January 28, 1817, p. 1.

160. Ibid., March 16, 1817, p. 2; April 22, 1817, p. 2; May 4, 1817, p. 4; Helfert, *Geschichte*, p. 35; Pavelka, *Wirtschaftsbeziehungen*, pp. 143–44.

161. Tooke, *Prices*, part III, p. 181; Mitchell and Deane, *Statistics*, pp. 95–96; *The Times*, May 2, 1816, p. 3; June 25, 1817, p. 3.

162. For a detailed discussion of the regulations adopted in Germany, see Abel, *Hungerkrisen*, pp. 326–42.

163. Chaillou-Des Barres, *Grains*, pp. 85–86; Chabert, *Revenus*, p. 415; Sée, *Histoire*

économique, p. 123; Bertier, *Restauration*, p. 217; Demoulin, *Guillaume Ier*, p. 182; Zollikofer, *Meinen Vaterlandes*, 2: 232; *Württembergishes Jahrbuch für 1818*, pp. 16–27; Meinhardt, "Göttingen," pp. 214–15; Sandkaulen, *Notjahr*, pp. 37–38, 53–54, 58–61.

164. *Württembergishes Jahrbuch für 1818*, pp. 16–27.

165. *Quotidienne*, January 31, 1817, pp. 1–2; February 26, 1818, pp. 1–2; Cobb, *People*, pp. 278–81.

166. Abel, *Hungerkrisen*, p. 334.

167. Fris, *Gand*, p. 338; Demoulin, *Guillaume Ier*, pp. 157–59; Benzenberg, *Handel*, pp. 170–242.

168. Ministère de l'Intérieur, *Circulaires*, 3: 123, 187.

169. Demoulin, *Guillaume Ier*, pp. 105–06.

170. Oechsli, *Schweiz*, 2: 481–82.

171. Sandkaulen, *Notjahr*, pp. 34–85; Henderson, *Prussia*, pp. 82–83.

172. Helfert, *Geschichte*, pp. 39–40; Meynert, *Franz I*, pp. 393–98; Rath, "Great Depression," pp. 315–20.

173. M. W. Flinn, "The Poor Employment Act of 1817," *Economic History Review*, 2d ser., 14 (August 1961): 82–92; Smart, *Economic Annals*, p. 543.

174. Fris, *Gand*, p. 338; Demoulin, *Guillaume Ier*, pp. 157–59.

175. Herbert Matis, "Über die sozialen und wirtschaftlichen Verhältnisse österreichischer Fabrik- und Manufakturarbeiter um die Wende vom 18. zum 19. Jahrhundert," *Vierteljahrschrift für Sozial- und Wirtschaftsgeschichte* 80 (1966): 464; Slokar, *Industrie*, pp. 68–69, 272, 368–69.

176. Quoted in *The Times*, December 21, 1816, p. 2.

177. Demoulin, *Guillaume Ier*, pp. 157–59; Fris, *Gand*, p. 338; *Moniteur*, May 27, 1817, p. 578.

178. Demoulin, *Guillaume Ier*, pp. 224, 325, 400, 420. The actual figure cited in this work is 413,986 paupers for Belgium, but the larger number is required as the sum of the individual Belgian provinces. For the entire kingdom, the number reached 745,023, or 12 percent of the total population.

179. Vidalenc, *l'Eure*, pp. 159–62; Robert Marjolin, "Troubles provoqués en France par la disette de 1816–1817," *Revue d'histoire moderne*, New ser., 10 (November–December 1933): 425–48; for press accounts of these activities see *Quotidienne*, January 24, 1817, p. 3; January 25, 1817, p. 3; January 31, 1817, pp. 1–2; February 2, 1817, p. 2; May 2, 1817, p. 2; June 11, 1817, p. 3; February 26, 1818, pp. 1–2.

180. Ministère de l'Intérieur, *Circulaires*, 3: 125.

181. Sandkaulen, *Notjahr*, pp. 35–40; Henderson, *Prussia*, pp. 82–83.

182. Meinhardt, "Göttingen," pp. 214–15.

183. Hazzi, *Theurung*, pp. 83–85, 94–95; Hansjörg Gruber, *Die Entwicklung der pfälzischen Wirtschaft 1816–1834* (Saarbrücken, 1962), p. 98; Abel, *Hungerkrisen*, pp. 330–33.

184. For a detailed account of the relief measures in Nuremberg during the subsistence crisis, see Abel, *Hungerkrisen*, pp. 333–37.

185. *Württembergishes Jahrbuch für 1818*, pp. 16–27; Abel, *Hungerkrisen*, p. 341.

186. Philippovich, "Baden," pp. 111–12; Bechtolsheimer, "Rheinhessen," pp. 70–74; Struck, *Nassau*, pp. 8–9.

187. Zollikofer, *Meinen Vaterlandes*, 1: 38–47; Oechsli, *Schweiz*, pp. 481–82; *Schweizerische Monathschronik*, 1816, p. 204.

188. Helfert, *Geschichte*, pp. 34–40; Meynert, *Franz I*, pp. 393–98; Monteleone, "Carestie," pp. 73–74; Rath, "Great Depression," pp. 315–20.

189. *Quotidienne*, January 2, 1817, p. 3; February 14, 1817, p. 2; February 20, 1817, p. 2; *The Times*, October 31, 1817, p. 2.

190. *Oekonomische Neuigkeiten*, January, 1817, no. 1, p. 6.

191. *Moniteur*, April 27, 1817, p. 463.

192. Meynert, *Franz I*, p. 397.

193. Smart, *Economic Annals*, pp. 543, 706.

194. Arthur H. Dodd, *The Industrial Revolution in North Wales* (2d ed., Cardiff, 1951), p. 384.

195. Thomas Baines, *History of the Commerce and Town of Liverpool* (London, 1852), pp. 574–75.

196. *Gentleman's Magazine* 87 (April 1817): 368.

197. *Report of the Committee, Appointed at a General Meeting of the Inhabitants of Edinburgh, for Affording Relief to the Labouring Classes in the City and Suburbs* (Edinburgh, 1817), pp. 3–23.

198. E. L. Jones, "The Agricultural Labour Market in England, 1793–1872," *Economic History Review*, 2d ser., 17 (December 1964): 325; Ernle, *English Farming*, pp. 316–17, 323–24; *Annual Register*, 1816, p. 93; Smart, *Economic Annals*, pp. 489–90, 543.

199. *Quotidienne*, May 24, 1817, p. 3; for other press accounts of the methods of financing relief measures, see *Quotidienne*, March 8, 1817, p. 2; April 22, 1817, p. 2; April 30, 1817, p. 2; January 10, 1818, p. 2.

200. Truchon, "Lyon," p. 198.

201. For discussion of the financing of welfare and relief in Germany, see Abel, *Hungerkrisen*, pp. 337–42.

202. *Schweizerische Monathschronik*, 1816, p. 204; ibid., 1817, pp. 69–70; Zollikofer, *Meinen Vaterlandes*, 1: 38–47.

203. Ernest J. Knapton, *The Lady of the Holy Alliance: The Life of Julie de Krüdener* (New York, 1939), pp. 170–78; Charles Eynard, *Vie de Madame de Krüdener* (2 vols.; Paris, 1849), 2: 153–73, 222–80; *Schweizerische Monathschronik*, 1817, pp. 72, 115–16; Zollikofer, *Meinen Vaterlandes*, 1: 38–50.

204. Meynert, *Franz I*, pp. 393–98; *Quotidienne*, March 14, 1817, p. 1; April 17, 1817, p. 1; April 26, 1817, p. 1; May 1, 1817, p. 1; Helfert, *Geschichte*, pp. 34–40.

205. Ministère de l'Intérieur, *Circulaires*, 3: 125.

206. *Quotidienne*, January 24, 1817, p. 3; January 25, 1817, p. 3; January 31, 1817, pp. 1–2; February 2, 1817, p. 2; May 2, 1817, p. 2; June 11, 1817, p. 3; Chaillou-Des Barres, *Grains*, p. 86; Comte de Rambuteau, *Mémoirs* (Paris, 1905), pp. 199–200; Marquise de Montcalm, *Mon journal, 1815–1818: pendant le premier ministère de mon frère*, ed. by Sébastien Charléty (Paris, 1936), p. 261; Vidalenc, *l'Eure*, pp. 160–64; Guéneau, "Brie," p. 28; Leuilliot, *L'Alsace*, 2: 166–68; Contamine, *Metz*, 1: 308–11; Collette C. Girard, "La catastrophe agricole de 1816 dans le département de la Meurthe," *Annales de l'Est*, 5th ser., 5, no. 2 (1954): 134; Maurice Vergnaud, "Agitation politique et crise de subsistance à Lyon de septembre 1816 à juin 1817," *Cahiers d'histoire* 2 (1957): 176–77.

207. *Blackwoods Edinburgh Magazine* 1 (April 1817): 113.

208. Eric Richards, "The Industrial Face of a Great Estate: Trentham and Lilleshall, 1780–1860," *Economic History Review*, 2d ser., 27 (August 1974): 420–23.

209. *Gentleman's Magazine* 87 (March 1817): 270.

210 *The Times*, January 1, 1818, p. 2; *Gentleman's Magazine* 87 (March 1817): 270; ibid. (1817), supplement, 620.

211. *The Times*, December 17, 1816, p. 3.

212. *Blackwoods Edinburgh Magazine* 1 (August 1817): 545; W. A. Maguire, *The Downshire Estates in Ireland 1801–1845* (Oxford, 1972), pp. 224–27.

213. *Annual Register*, 1817, p. 139.

214. Abel, *Hungerkrisen*, pp. 339–41.

215. In fact, the crop failures of 1740 prompted the wider introduction of potatoes, and despite the slow growth of adoption by 1750 it had become a field crop in some European regions; see Aldo de Maddalena, "Rural Europe 1500–1750," in vol. 3, *The Fontana Economic History of Europe*, ed. by Carlo M. Cipolla (London, 1974), p. 315; and Walter Minchinton, "Patterns and Structure of Demand 1500–1750," ibid., p. 125. But as Fernand Braudel has pointed out that the "miracle" crops—maize and potatoes—were only established late in Europe, and apart from its early success in Ireland and Germany the potato is a phenomenon of the nineteenth century; see Fernand Braudel, *Capitalism and Material Life*, trans. by Miriam Kochan (New York, 1973), p. 39. In France, to be specific, the potato harvest in 1816 amounted to 25.8 million hectoliters and then increased to 47.5 million in 1817; see Statistique générale, *Archives*, p. 79. In Switzerland potatoes had remained primarily garden plants until the famine of 1770–72, which eliminated the prejudice against the use of potatoes for human consumption, and at which time extensive field cultivation began. Then the further multiplication of potato culture and production ensued from the famine of 1817; see Stefano Francini, *Statistique de la Suisse* (Bern, 1855), p. 206, and Brugger, *Landwirtschaft*, pp. 39, 127–28. Expanded potato cultivation in Hungary was also seen as the one consolation deriving from the harvest deficiencies of 1816; see *Oekonomische Neuigkeiten*, January 1817, no. 1, p. 2, and *Landwirtschaftliche Zeitung* 15, no. 10 (1817):

89–90; however, for evidence of greatly expanded potato culture in Europe between 1750 and 1816, see William L. Langer, "American Foods and Europe's Population Growth," *Journal of Social History* (Winter 1975): 51–66.
216. For details, see Abel *Hungerkrisen*, pp. 242–51. For a similar conclusion as to the effectiveness of administrative measures in reducing mortality from harvest failures, see M. W. Flinn, "The Stabilisation of Mortality in Pre-industrial Western Europe," *Journal of European Economic History* 3 (Fall 1974): 285–318.
217. Reinhold A. Dorwart, *The Prussian Welfare State before 1740* (Cambridge, Mass., 1971), pp. 101–05, 111.
218. Olwen H. Hufton, *The Poor of Eighteenth-Century France 1750–1789* (Oxford, 1974), pp. 132–201; Pierre Goubert, *The Ancien Regime,* trans. by Steve Cox (London, 1973), p. 40; Françoise Lebrun, *Les hommes et la mort an Anjou aux 17ᵉ et 18ᵉ siècles* (Paris, 1971), pp. 140, 367–73, 491–93.
219. For discussion of the government's program and policies in 1811–12, see Cobb, *People,* pp. 104–05, 115–17.

CHAPTER III

1. Richard Cobb, *The Police and the People: French Popular Protest 1789–1820* (Oxford, 1970), pp. 92–93, 104–05, 257–59; George Rudé, *The Crowd in History: A Study of Popular Disturbances in France and England 1730–1848* (New York, 1964), pp. 5, 21–22.
2. Rudé, *Crowd,* pp. 19–22; R. W. Wearmouth, *Methodism and the Common People in the Eighteenth Century* (London, 1945), pp. 19–91.
3. Rudé, *Crowd,* pp. 22–31, 38–45; R. B. Rose, "Eighteenth-Century Price Riots and Public Policy in England," *International Review of Social History* 6 (1961), part 2, 277–92.
4. Thomas Tooke and William Newmarch, *A History of Prices and of the State of Circulation from 1792 to 1856* (6 vols.; New York, 1857), 2: 14–15, 20, 390; A. J. Peacock, *Bread or Blood: A Study of the Agrarian Riots in East Anglia in 1816* (London, 1965), p. 63.
5. *The Times* (London), May 21, 1816, p. 3.
6. Ibid., May 14, 1816, p. 3.
7. Ibid., May 23, 1816, p. 3.
8. Ibid., October 14, 1816, p. 2.
9. For an account of the riots at Sunderland near Newcastle, and at Heckington near Boston, see *The Times,* October 25, 1816, p. 3.
10. Ibid., December 11, 1816, p. 3.
11. Ibid., January 24, 1817, p. 3.
12. Ibid., November 16, 1816, p. 3.
13. See Élie Halévy, *The Liberal Awakening 1815–1830,* trans. by E. I. Watkin (New York, 1961), pp. 3–69; Frank O. Darvall, *Popular Disturbances and Public Disorder in Regency England* (London, 1934), pp. 152–55, 160–65; R. J. White, *Waterloo to Peterloo* (London, 1957); E. P. Thompson, *The Making of the English Working Class* (London, 1965), pp. 603–710.
14. Robert Marjolin, "Troubles provoqués en France par la disette de 1816–1817," *Revue d'histoire moderne,* new ser., 10 (November–December 1933); 425–26.
15. Marjolin, "Troubles," pp. 426–27.
16. France, Ministère de l'Intérieur, *Circulaires, instructions et autre actes émanés du ministère de l'intérieur de 1797 à 1821 inclusivement* (2d ed.; 6 vols.; Paris, 1821–30), 3: 130–31.
17. Marjolin, "Troubles," pp. 427–29; Jean Vidalenc, *Le département de l'Eure sous la monarchie constituionelle 1814–1848* (Paris, 1952), pp. 158–62; *The Times,* December 4, 1816, p. 3. With a few exceptions, the riots and popular disturbances were not reported in the French press until spring 1817.
18. *Schweizerische Monathschronik,* 1816, p. 204.
19. R. John Rath, "The Habsburgs and the Great Depression in Lombardo-Venetia, 1814–1818," *Journal of Modern History* 13 (September 1941): 312–13.
20. *The Times,* June 10, 1816, p. 3.
21. Ibid., June 3, 1816, p. 3.
22. Gunther Meinhardt, "Die Auswirkungen der Hungerjahre in der ersten Hälfte des 19.

194   NOTES TO PAGES 72–77

Jahrhunderts auf Göttingen,'' *Göttinger Jahrbuch* 14 (1966): 213; Wilhelm Abel, *Massenarmut und Hungerkrisen im vorindustriellen Europa* (Hamburg and Berlin, 1974), p. 324.

23. For an account of grain riots near Leicester and Carlisle, see *The Times,* January 27, 1817, p. 3; March 11, 1817, p. 2; March 18, 1817, p. 3.

24. Samuel Bamford, *Passages in the Life of a Radical* (2 vols.; London, 1844), 1: 6–7.

25. *Annual Register,* 1816, "Chronicle," p. 165.

26. D. J. V. Jones, "The Amlwich Riots of 1817," *Anglesey Antiquarian Society and Field Club Transactions* (1966): 93–101.

27. For accounts of famine, distress, vagrancy, begging, and violence in North Wales 1816–17, see D. J. Jones, "Distress and Discontent in Cardiganshire, 1814–1819," *Ceredigion* 5 no. 3 (1966): 281–85; W. J. Lewis, "The Condition of Labour in Mid-Cardiganshire in the Early Nineteenth Century," ibid. 4 no. 4 (1963): 326–29; Arthur H. Dodd, *The Industrial Revolution in North Wales* (2d ed.; Cardiff, 1951), pp. 383–84.

28. Galen Broeker, *Rural Disorder and Police Reform in Ireland, 1812–36* (London, 1970), pp. 95–96.

29. *The Times,* March 4, 1817, p. 3; March 10, 1817, p. 3.

30. *Blackwoods Edinburgh Magazine* 1 (August 1817): 545.

31. *Gentleman's Magazine* 87 (1817), supplement, 619–20.

32. W. A. Maguire, *The Downshire Estates in Ireland 1801–1845* (Oxford, 1972), pp. 224–26.

33. Vidalenc, *Eure,* pp. 158–59; Marjolin, "Troubles," pp. 429–30.

34. Vidalenc, *Eure,* pp. 159–62.

35. Ibid., pp. 162–69; Jean Vidalenc, *La societé française de 1815 à 1848: Le peuple des campagnes* (Paris, 1970), pp. 71–72; Marjolin, "Troubles," pp. 431–33.

36. *Gentleman's Magazine* 88 (January 1818): 72; Franz Schnabel, *Deutsche Geschichte im neunzehnten Jahrhundert* (2d ed.; 4 vols.; Freiburg im Breisgau, 1949–50), 2: 217; *Landwirthschaftliche Zeitung* 16, no. 9 (1818): 86.

37. *The Times,* January 1, 1817, p. 2.

38. *Quotidienne* (Paris), October 24, 1817, p. 1.

39. *The Times,* July 26, 1817, p. 2.

40. *Quotidienne,* October 3, 1817, p. 2; *The Times,* October 7, 1817, p. 2; October 25, 1817, p. 2; Abel, *Hungerkrisen,* p. 324.

41. *The Times.* August 27, 1817, p. 2; August 29, 1817, p. 2.

42. Abel, *Hungerkrisen,* p. 324.

43. George Rudé, *Paris and London in the Eighteenth Century* (New York, 1971), p. 24.

44. *Quotidienne,* October 23, 1817, p. 2; Ruprecht Zollikofer, *Der Osten meinen Vaterlandes, oder die Kantone St. Gallen und Appenzell im Hungerjahre 1817* (2 vols.; St. Gall, 1818–19), 1: 66–67.

45. *Oekonomische Neuigkeiten und Verhandlungen,* October 1817, no. 13, p. 97; *Quotidienne,* June 5, 1817, p. 2; *The Times,* July 26, 1817, p. 2.

46. Rath, "Great Depression," pp. 312–13.

47. For discussion of the postwar social commotion in Norway, see the reports of private correspondents in Stockholm and Hamburg in *The Times,* January 13, 1817, p. 2; March 21, 1817, p. 2.

48. For notice and discussion of these events in Spain, see *The Times,* March 3, 1817, pp. 2–3; May 26, 1817, p. 2.

49. M. H. Cherif, "Expansion européene et difficultés tunisiennes de 1815 à 1830," *Annales, E. S. C.* 25 (May–June 1970): 721–22.

50. Robert Demoulin, *Guillaume Ier et la transformation économique des provinces belges 1815–1830* (Liège, 1938), pp. 224, 325, 400, 420; *The Times,* October 1, 1816, p. 2.

51. *Moniteur* (Paris), June 30, 1817, p. 713. Curiously, the official French newspaper, which virtually ignored popular disturbances at home (no doubt for political and security reasons), printed numerous detailed reports of the social protest in the Netherlands. Some accounts were copied from Belgian newspapers, while others were direct communications from correspondents.

52. Ibid., pp. 713–14.

53. Ibid., July 2, 1817, p. 722.

54. Ibid., June 26, 1817, p. 697.

55. Ibid., July 2, 1817, p. 722.

56. Ibid., July 5, 1817, p. 733; July 16, 1817, p. 777; July 20, 1817, p. 793; July 22, 1817, p. 801.

57. Harold R. C. Wright, *Free Trade and Protection in the Netherlands 1816–1830* (Cambridge, 1955), p. 103; Henri Pirenne, *Histoire de Belgique* (7 vols.; Brussels, 1909–26), 6: 274.

58. Félix Ponteil, *La monarchie parlementaire, 1815–1848* (Paris, 1949), p. 52.

59. Marjolin, "Troubles," p. 437. For discussion of the geographical variables involved in French popular disturbances arising from the dearth years between 1789 and 1812, see Cobb, *People,* pp. 257–61.

60. Jacques Antoine Dulaure, *Histoire civile, physique et morale de Paris* (3d ed.; 10 vols.; Paris, 1825), 9: 467.

61. Alexandre Chabert, *Essai sur les mouvements des revenus et de l'activité économique en France de 1789 à 1820* (Paris, 1949), p. 169.

62. *Quotidienne,* June 6, 1817, p. 2; June 8, 1817, p. 2; Marjolin, "Troubles," pp. 437–41.

63. *Moniteur,* June 4, 1817, pp. 611–12; *Quotidienne,* June 4, 1817, p. 3; Marjolin, "Troubles," pp. 442–45.

64. Louis Guéneau, "La disette de 1816–1817 dans une région productrice de blé, la Brie," *Revue d'histoire moderne* 159 (September–October 1928): 18–29. Since the beginning of the empire, a special organization called l'Approvisionnement de Reserve de Paris had been responsible for supplying the capital with provisions; one of its storehouses was located at Meaux, the largest town in the department.

65. *Quotidienne,* June 4, 1817, p. 2; June 6, 1817, p. 2; Guéneau, "Disette," pp. 30–34.

66. Guéneau, "Disette," p. 36.

67. For these popular beliefs in Brie during 1816–17, see Guéneau, "Disette," pp. 31–32; for discussion of these public policies and popular beliefs during the revolutionary and imperial years, see Cobb, *People,* pp. 278–89.

68. Cobb, *People,* p. 279.

69. For examples, see Roger Marlin, *La crise des subsistances de 1816–1817 dans le Doubs* (Besançon, 1960), p. 48; Vidalenc, *Eure,* pp. 158, 174; Guéneau, "Disette," pp. 31–32; Marjolin, "Troubles," passim.

70. Marjolin, "Troubles," p. 448; Guéneau, "Disette," pp. 31–33, 36–38, 40–41.

71. Maurice Vergnaud, "Agitation politique et crise de subsistances à Lyon de septembre 1816 à juin 1817," *Cahiers d'histoire* 2 (1957): 163–66, 169–72, 177. The term "liberal" is used by Vergnaud and many other French historians of this period. It has been adopted for the sake of uniformity and for simplification, but perhaps signifies little beyond middle-class dissatisfaction with an old regime monarchy.

72. P. Truchon, "La vie ouvrière à Lyon sous la Restauration," *Revue d'histoire de Lyon* 11 (May–June 1912): 198; Vergnaud, "Lyon," p. 173.

73. Georges and Hubert Bourgin, eds., *Les patrons, les ourvrièrs et l'état: Le régime de l'industrie en France de 1814 à 1830,* vol. 1: May 1814–May 1821 (Paris, 1912), pp. 54–55; Vergnaud, "Lyon," pp. 174–75.

74. Quoted in Vergnaud, "Lyon," pp. 173–77.

75. For the account of the disturbances printed in the *Journal des Maires,* see *Quotidienne,* June 13, 1817, p. 3; June 15, 1817, p. 3.

76. M. le chevalier Desuttes, *Réponse de M. le chevalier Desuttes, Prevôt du Département du Rhône, à un Écrit intitule Lyon en 1817 Par M. le Colonel Fabvier* (Lyon, 1818), pp. 3–28. In this work the departmental provost summed up and refuted the charges of Colonel Fabvier, chef de l'État Major du Lieutenant du Roi. Almost all of the principals in the "Events" published a version as they perceived it.

77. M. le comte Chabrol de Crousol, *Sur les événements de Lyon, au mois de juin 1817* (Paris, 1818), pp. 2–8, 32, 43–44, 56.

78. *Quotidienne,* June 15, 1817, p. 3.

79. Marquise de Montcalm, *Mon journal, 1815–1818: pendant le premier ministère de mon frère,* ed. by Sébastien Charléty (Paris, 1936), pp. 269–70, 292.

80. Étienne Denis duc Pasquier, *Histoire de mon Temps: Mémoirs du Chancelier Pasquier,* ed. by M. le duc D'Audiffret-Pasquier (3d ed.; 6 vols.; Paris, 1894–95), 4: 169, 181.

81. One of the outstanding examples of this view is found in Thompson, *English Working Class,* see esp. pp. 62–63, 389–90, 573–74, 618–20, 633–98.

82. *The Times,* June 25, 1817, p. 3.

83. *Annual Register,* 1816, "Chronicle," pp. 68–127; Thompson, *English Working Class,* pp. 633–69; William Smart, *Economic Annals of the Nineteenth Century 1801–1820* (New York, 1964), pp. 550–54; White, *Waterloo to Peterloo,* pp. 155, 162–75.

84. Reinhart Koselleck, *Preussen zwischen Reform and Revolution* (Stuttgart, 1967), pp. 462–63, 542, 570–71.

85. Philip Resnick, *The White Terror and the Political Reaction after Waterloo* (Cambridge, Mass., 1966), pp. 96–97.

86. Ibid., p. 115. Since Resnick's principal concern was with the years 1815–16, no attempt was made to assess the courts' activities against the background of a provisions crisis.

87. For press accounts of these cases see *Quotidienne*, June 8, 1817, p. 3; June 9, 1817, p. 2; June 11, 1817, p. 4; June 13, 1817, p. 3; July 1, 1817, p. 3; July 8, 1817, p. 4; July 23, 1817, p. 3; August 14, 1817, p. 2; August 22, 1817, p. 2.

88. Marlin, *Doubs,* pp. 45–48, 56, 60.

89. Cobb, *People,* pp. 104–05.

90. Ministère de l'Intérieur, *Circulaires* 3: 280; *Quotidienne*, October 17, 1817, p. 2; Cobb, *People,* p. 105.

91. Thomas Baines, *History of the Commerce and Town of Liverpool* (London, 1852), pp. 574–75.

92. M. C. Buer, "The Trade Depression following the Napoleonic Wars," *Economica* 1 (May 1921): 162.

93. *The Speech of Thomas Fowell Buxton Esq. at the Egyptian Hall, on the 26th November, 1816 on the Subject of the Distress in Spitalfields* (London, 1816), p. 19.

94. *The Times,* December 2, 1816, p. 3.

95. Jones, "Amlwich Riots," p. 93, quoting the *North Wales Gazette,* February 5, 1818.

96. Jones, "Cardiganshire," p. 282; Lewis, "Mid-Cardiganshire," p. 327; Dodd, *North Wales,* p. 384; Smart, *Economic Annals,* pp. 542–43.

97. James E. Handley, *The Irish in Scotland, 1798–1845* (2d ed.; Cork, 1945), pp. 173–76.

98. William Harty, M.D., *An Historic Sketch of the Causes, Progress, Extent, and Mortality of the Contagious Fever Epidemic in Ireland During the Years 1817, 1818, and 1819* (Dublin, 1820), Appendix, p. 114.

99. Montcalm, *Mon journal,* p. 261; *Quotidienne,* July 17, 1817, p. 3; October 17, 1817, p. 3.

100. Louis Simond, *Switzerland; or a Journal of a Tour and Residence in that Country, in the Years 1817, 1818, and 1819* (2 vols.; Boston, 1822), 1: 9–10.

101. Thomas Raffles, *Letters, during a Tour through Some Parts of France, Savoy, Switzerland, Germany, and the Netherlands in the Summer of 1817* (Liverpool, 1818), pp. 149, 151, 158–60.

102. *Quotidienne,* January 10, 1818, p. 2.

103. Charles Creighton, *A History of Epidemics in Britain* (2 vols.; Cambridge, 1891–94), 2: 256–57; K. H. Connell, *The Population of Ireland 1750–1845* (London, 1950), p. 228; George O'Brien, *The Economic History of Ireland from the Union to the Famine* (London, 1921), pp. 17–19, 227–28.

104. Harty, *Ireland,* p. 83.

105. *Landwirthschaftliche Zeitung* 16, no. 9 (1818): 85–86.

106. Staatsrath Joseph Ritter von Hazzi, *Betrachtungen über Theurung und Noth der Vergangenheit und Gegenwart* (Munich, 1818), pp. 76–77.

107. Hazzi, *Theurung,* pp. 81–82.

108. Abel, *Hungerkrisen,* pp. 322–23.

109. Johann Gottfried von Pahl, *Geschichte von Wirtemberg* (6 vols.; Stuttgart, 1827–31), 6: 212–13.

110. Simond, *Switzerland,* 1: 70.

111. Charles Eynard, *Vie de Madame de Krüdener* (2 vols.; Paris, 1849), 2: 163.

112. Hans Richter, "Hessen und die Auswanderung 1815–55," *Mitteilungen des Oberhessischen Geschichtsvereins,* H. F. 32 (1934): 52. For press accounts of indigent migrants on the road to Holland, see *Quotidienne,* May 1, 1817, p. 1; May 5, 1817, p. 2; May 19, 1817, p. 1; June 4, 1817, p. 2; July 9, 1817, p. 2.

113. Wilhelm Sandkaulen, *Das Notjahr 1816/17 mit besonderer Berücksichtigung der Verhältnisse am Niederrhein* (Münster, 1927), pp. 65–66.

114. Meinhardt, "Göttingen," pp. 213–15; Heinrich Bechtolsheimer, "Die Provinz Rheinhessen in den beiden ersten Jahrzehten ihres Bestehens," *Quellen und Forschungen zur hessischen Geschichte* 4 (1916): 76–77; Antje Kraus, *Die Unterschichten Hamburgs in den ersten*

Hälfte des 19. Jahrhunderts (Stuttgart, 1965), pp. 97–98; Koselleck, *Preussen,* passim; Sandkaulen, *Notjahr,* p. 7; Wolfgang Köllmann, *Sozialgeschichte der Stadt Barmen im 19. Jahrhundert* (Tübingen, 1960), pp. 109–10; Johann Friedrich Benzenberg, *Ueber Handel und Gewerbe, Steuren und Zölle* (Elberfeld, 1819), pp. 230–31.

115. Johann Slokar, *Geschichte der österreichischen Industrie und ihrer Förderung unter Kaiser Franz I* (Vienna, 1914), p. 69.

116. *Quotidienne,* June 5, 1817, p. 2.

117. *Oekonomische Neuigkeiten und Verhandlungen,* October 1817, no. 13, p. 97.

118. *The Times,* July 26, 1817, p. 2.

119. Ibid., April 23, 1817, p. 2; R. John Rath, "Economic Conditions in Lombardy and Venetia, 1813–1815, and Their Effects on Public Opinion," *Journal of Central European Affairs* 23 (October 1963): 276.

120. *Quotidienne,* March 10, 1817, p. 1.

121. *Schweizerische Monathschronik,* 1816, p. 204; Simond, *Switzerland,* 1: 91–92.

122. *The Times,* May 9, 1817, p. 3.

123. Simond, *Switzerland,* 1: 91–92.

124. Ibid., p. 77.

125. Ibid., p. 195.

126. Zollikofer, *Osten,* 1: 8–9.

127. Ibid., pp. 11, 34.

128. Ibid., p. 38.

129. *The Times,* May 9, 1817, p. 3.

130. *Schweizerische Monathschronik,* 1816, p. 204.

131. Simond, *Switzerland,* 1: 77, 91–92.

132. Zollikofer, *Osten,* 1: 8–38.

133. *Gentleman's Magazine* 87 (September 1817): 267; Rath, "Great Depression," pp. 312–13; *Quotidienne,* January 2, 1817, p. 3.

134. Freiherr Jos. Alex. von Helfert, *Zur Geschichte des Lombardo-Venezianischen Königreichs* (Vienna, 1908), p. 44.

135. Schnabel, *Deutsche Geschichte,* 2: 217.

136. *Landwirthschaftliche Zeitung* 16, no. 9 (1818): 86.

137. *The Times,* June 3, 1816, p. 3.

138. *Gentleman's Magazine* 88 (January 1818): 72.

139. *Moniteur,* June 17, 1817, p. 661; June 30, 1817, p. 713.

140. *The Times,* May 10, 1816, p. 3.

141. E. J. Hobsbawm, "Les soulèvements de la campagne anglaise 1780–1850," *Annales,* E. S. C. 12 (January–February 1968): 15, note.

142. For accounts of arson and cases of suspected arson, see *Gentleman's Magazine* 87 (April 1817): 367–68; *The Times,* August 30, 1816, p. 2; November 28, 1816, p. 3; December 23, 1816, p. 3; January 27, 1817, p. 3; February 17, 1817, p. 3; April 19, 1817, p. 3.

143. E. J. Hobsbawm and George Rudé, *Captain Swing* (New York, 1968), p. 79.

144. A. J. V. Heunisch, *Das Grossherzogtum Baden* (Heidelberg, 1857), p. 454.

145. *The Times,* April 15, 1817, p. 2.

146. Joseph Fletcher, "Moral and Educational Statistics of England and Wales," *Journal of the Statistical Society* 12 (1849): 167–68. Commitments for larceny traced the following course during a ten-year period:

1813	4,623	1818	9,303
1814	4,259	1819	9,653
1815	5,409	1820	9,160
1816	6,123	1821	8,725
1817	9,396	1822	8,445

England's population was of course increasing at its highest rate during this period, and thus the rate of crime did not advance quite so sharply and conversely decreased somewhat more rapidly after 1817.

147. Guéneau, "Disette," pp. 43–45.

148. Vidalenc, *Eure,* p. 171.

149. Marlin, *Doubs,* pp. 44–46, 60.

150. Collette Girard, "Famine et criminalité dans la Meurthe en 1816–1817," *Annales de l'Est*, 5th ser., 12, no. 3 (1961): 213–20, 225–28.

151. Dulaure, *Paris*, 9: 477. This report appeared in the Paris press in 1821. The number of trials were not given for the years beyond 1817, but the number of prison sentences involving hard labor are known, and they indicate a decline from 3,329 in 1817 to 2,569 in 1818 to 2,015 in 1819, and then by 1825 they show the much lower figure of 1,622; allowing for a population increase of 1.2 million between the two extreme dates, the rate of criminality declined from 1 per 9,192 persons in 1817 to 1 per 19,359 in 1825; see Charles Dupin, *Forces productives et commerciales de la France* (2 vols.; Paris, 1827), 1: xxxviii–xxxix.

152. France, *Collection complète de lois, décrets, ordonnances, réglements, et avis du Conseil-d'État*, ed. by Jean Baptiste Duvergier de Hauranne (24 vols.; Paris, 1824–32), 21: 259–60.

153. For example, see *Quotidienne*, August 16, 1817, p. 4; August 28, 1817, p. 2; September 10, 1817, p. 3; October 6, 1817, p. 2.

154. John Milton Whiton, *Sketches of the History of New Hampshire* (Concord, 1834), p. 189.

155. Joshua Bradley, *Accounts of Religious Revivals in Many Parts of the United States from 1815 to 1818* (Albany, 1819), pp. 41–42, 95–96, 130, 138.

156. *The Times*, May 2, 1817, p. 2.

157. Ibid., May 3, 1817, p. 2, quoting the *Bavarian National Gazette*.

158. Ibid.

159. For a detailed account, see A..Fr. von Ludwig, *Die chiliastische Bewegung in Franken und Hessen im ersten Drittel des 19. Jahrhundert* (Regensburg and Rome, 1913), pp. 8–31.

160. Quoted in Ernest J. Knapton, *The Lady of the Holy Alliance: The Life of Julie de Krüdener* (New York, 1939), p. 178.

161. Ibid., p. 170; Eynard, *Krüdener*, 2: 274–80; *The Times*, July 22, 1817, p. 2.

162. *Schweizerische Monathschronik*, 1817, p. 72.

163. Ibid., pp. 115–16; Zollikofer, *Osten* 1: 49–50; Eynard, *Krüdener*, 2: 222–25.

164. *The Times*, July 22, 1817, p. 2.

165. *Quotidienne*, September 30, 1817, p. 2.

166. Imre Ferenczi, *International Migrations*, ed. by Walter F. Willcox (2 vols.; New York, 1929), 1: 81.

167. Kurt B. Mayer, *The Population of Switzerland* (New York, 1952), p. 116.

168. Ernest Steineman, "Die schaffhauserische Auswanderung und ihre Ursachen. Ein Beitrag zur Wirtschaftsgeschichte," *Revue suisse d'histoire* 14, no. 4 (1934): 405–06; Wilhelm Oechsli, *Geschichte der Schweiz im neunzehnten Jahrhundert* (2 vols.; Leipzig, 1913), 2: 483–84; *Schweizerische Monathschronik*, 1817, pp. 187–88.

169. *Schweizerische Monathschronik*, 1817, pp. 187–88.

170. Mayer, *Switzerland*, p. 200; *Quotidienne*, May 5, 1817, p. 2; Oechsli, *Schweiz*, 2: 484.

171. Walther Kirchner, "Emigration to Russia," *American Historical Review* 55 (April 1950): 560–61; Knapton, *Lady*, pp. 181, 190.

172. Zollikofer, *Osten*. 1: 52.

173. Wolf-Heino Struck, *Die Auswanderung aus dem Herzogtum Nassau, 1806–1866* (Wiesbaden, 1966), p. 16.

174. Mayer, *Switzerland*, pp. 200–01.

175. Louis Chevalier, "L'émigration française au XIXe siècle," *Étude d'histoire moderne et contemporaine* 1 (1947): 127, 131.

176. Ferenczi, *International Migrations*, 1: 105–06.

177. *Gentleman's Magazine* 87 (July 1817): 75: *Blackwood's Edinburgh Magazine* 1 (July 1817): 428.

178. Ferenczi, *International Migrations*, 1: 105–06; Paul Leuilliot, *L'Alsace au début de XIXe siècle (1815–1830)* (3 vols.; Paris, 1959–60), 2: 33–35.

179. M. S. Flanningham, "The Rural Economy of Northwestern France and the Bavarian Palatinate 1815–1830," *Agricultural History* 24 (July 1950): 167. The Bavarian Palatinate had in fact been under French rule after 1792, but was separated from France by the treaties of 1814 and 1815.

180. Leuilliot, *Alsace*, 2: 37; Ferenczi, *International Migrations*, 1: 106.

181. Leuilliot, *Alsace*, 2: 36–37; Ferenczi, *International Migrations*, 1: 105.

182. B. R. Mitchell and Phyllis Deane, *Abstract of British Historical Statistics* (Cambridge, 1962), p. 47.

183. William Savage, *Observations on Emigration to the United States of America* (London, 1819), p. 5.

184. Hans G. A. V. Schenk, *The Aftermath of the Napoleonic Wars* (London, 1947), p. 179.

185. Smart, *Economic Annals*, p. 545.

186. William F. Adams, *Ireland and Irish Emigration to the New World from 1815 to the Famine* (New Haven, 1932), pp. 120–23 ,426.

187. Hans C. von Gagern, *Mein Antheil an der Politik* (5 vols.; Stuttgart and Tübingen, 1823–45), 3: 145–46. Von Gagern represented Luxembourg in the *Bundestag* in the service of William of Orange.

188. Mack Walker, *Germany and the Emigration 1816–1885* (Cambridge, Mass., 1964), pp. 17–19, 34.

189. Ibid., pp. 3–4.

190. In addition to Walker's study, drawn upon here, for German emigration in the postwar period, see Gagern, *Mein Antheil,* 3: pp. 145–51; Schnabel, *Deutsche Geschichte,* 3: 359–61; Joseph Scheben, "Die Frage nach der Geschichte der deutschen Auswanderung," *Rheinische Vierteljahrsblätter* 5 (1935): 180; A. Sartorius von Waltershausen, *Deutsche Wirtschaftsgeschichte, 1815–1914* (2d ed.; Jena, 1923), pp. 34–36.

191. Schnabel, *Deutsche Geschichte,* 3: 359.

192. Walker, *Emigration,* pp. 30–33.

193. Karl Stumpp, ed., *Akten über die Auswanderung der Württemberger nach Russland 1816–1822* (Leipzig, 1914), p. xiii.

194. Eugen von Philippovich, "Auswanderung und Auswanderungspolitik im Grossherzogtum Baden," in Eugen von Philippovich, ed., *Auswanderung und Auswanderungspolitik in Deutschland* (Leipzig, 1892), p. 117.

195. Struck, *Nassau,* p. 121.

196. Walker, *Emigration,* pp. 30–31.

197. Bechtolsheimer, "Rheinhessen," pp. 77, 89.

198. *Quotidienne,* May 5, 1817, p. 2. For similar press accounts relating the large number of destitute elderly and children see ibid., April 17, 1817, p. 1; June 4, 1817, p. 2.

199. Struck, *Nassau,* pp. 16–17; Gagern, *Mein Antheil,* 3: 149–50; Walker, *Emigration,* pp. 8–9, 29; Bechtolsheimer, "Rheinhessen," p. 89; *Gentleman's Magazine* 87 (July 1817): 75.

200. Walker, *Emigration,* pp. 6, 28; *Quotidienne,* June 4, 1817, p. 2; July 9, 1817, p. 2; *The Times,* September 5, 1817, p. 2; September 27, 1817, p. 2; Schnabel, *Deutsche Geschichte,* 3: 360.

201. Philippovich, "Baden," pp. 115–16.

202. Struck, *Nassau,* p. 17.

203. *The Times,* September 5, 1817, p. 2; this account also reports additional emigrant deaths from epidemic disease aboard the ship *Avril.*

204. Ibid., September 27, 1817, p. 2, quoting a letter from Boston dated July 1, 1817.

205. Stumpp, *Württemberger,* p. xiii.

206. Joseph Hässler, *Die Auswanderung aus Baden nach Russland und Polen im 18. und 19. Jahrhundert, Beiträge zur Familien- und Heimatkunde in Baden,* no. 1 (1961), p. 39; Georg Leibbrandt, *Die Auswanderung aus Schwaben nach Russland, 1816–1823* (Stuttgart, 1928), p. 165.

207. Walker, *Emigration,* pp. 9–16; Leibbrandt, *Schwaben,* pp. 91–125; Stumpp, *Württemberger,* pp. ix–x.

208. Ludwig, *Chiliastische Bewegung,* pp. 8–31.

209. Walker, *Emigration,* p. 12.

210. Stumpp, *Württemberger,* pp. xix, 21.

211. Friedrich List, who was commissioned by the Württemberg Interior Ministry in April 1817 to investigate the reasons for emigration, concluded that the principal cause was political oppression and that economic difficulties were secondary. However, it seems probable that List's findings reflected his own concerns rather than the responses of the 600–700 emigrants whom he interviewed. For an account of this episode in List's career see Paul Gehring, *Friedrich List: Jugend- und Reifejahre 1789–1825* (Tübingen, 1964), pp. 150–53. Leibbrandt, *Schwaben,* pp.

93–94, on the other hand, concluded that the emigration could be best explained as a chiliastic movement, although he suggested that the movement received its immediate impulse from the subsistence crisis.

212. Walker, *Emigration*, pp. 16–19; Struck, *Nassau*, p. 14; Leibbrandt, *Schwaben*, p. 126.

213. Gagern, *Mein Antheil*, 3: 147–48; Walker, *Emigration*, pp. 29–30; Philippovich, "Baden," p. 115; Struck, *Nassau*, p. 17.

214. Walker, *Emigration*, pp. 19–20, 36–37.

215. Joseph B Hoyt, "The Cold Summer of 1816," *Annals of the Association of American Geographers* 48 (June 1958): esp. 126–27.

216. Arthur C. Boggess, *Settlement of Illinois, 1778–1830* (Chicago, 1908), pp. 120–21.

217. William Durkee Williamson, *The History of the State of Maine* (2 vols.; Hallowell, 1832), 2: 664–68.

218. George Barstow, *History of New Hampshire* (Concord, 1842), p. 392; for a similar account, see Whiton, *New Hampshire*, p. 189.

219. Lewis Dayton Stilwell, *Migration from Vermont* (Montpelier, 1948), pp. 125–29.

220. Zadock Thompson, *History of Vermont* (2d ed.; 3 vols.; Burlington, 1842), 3: 76; Rev. J. H. Woodward, "Westford," in *Vermont Historical Gazetteer* (Burlington, 1867), p. 893; Stilwell, *Vermont*, pp. 129–30.

221. Hoyt, "Summer of 1816," pp. 126–27.

222. Samuel Griswold Goodrich, *Recollections of a Lifetime* (2 vols.; New York, 1850), pp. 79–80.

223. *Raleigh Register*, September 20, 1816, p. 3; Boggess, *Illinois*, pp. 120–21.

224. Clarence E. Carter, ed., *The Territorial Papers of the United States*, vol. 18, *The Territory of Alabama, 1817–1819* (Washington, D.C., 1952), p. 23.

CHAPTER IV

1. This expression is borrowed from Fernand Braudel, *Capitalism and Material Life 1400–1800*, trans. by Miriam Kochan (New York and London, 1973), p. 37.

2. For one of the earliest descriptions of the nature of an Old Regime demographic crisis, see Jean Meuvret, "Les crises de subsistances et de la démographie de la France d'Ancien Régime," *Population* 1 (October–December 1946): 643–50; also see idem, "Demographic Crisis in France from the Sixteenth to the Eighteenth Century," in D. V. Glass and D. E. C. Eversley, eds., *Population in History* (London, 1965), pp. 507–22. Jean Meuvret was one of the first historians to become interested in demography and together with a number of statisticians and demographers contributed to the new journal *Population,* which began publication in 1946. The two groups eventually merged into the Société de Démographie Historique. Meuvret was the pioneer in the investigation of the nature of Old Regime demographic crises; for a collection of his work see Jean Meuvret, *Études d'histoire économique* (Paris, 1971). For discussion of the validity of Meuvret's findings see Pierre Goubert, "Historical Demography and the Reinterpretation of Early Modern French History: A Research Review," in T. K. Rabb and R. I. Rotberg, eds., *The Family in History* (New York and London, 1973), pp. 17–20.

3. Goubert, "Historical Demography," p. 19.

4. These demographic relationships are well known and universally accepted; for a discussion of the interaction of the economic and population movements, see D. E. C. Eversley, "Population, Economy, and Society," in Glass and Eversley, *Population,* pp. 23–69; for discussion of famine and the incidence of amenorrhoea in the twentieth century, see E. Le Roy Ladurie, "Famine Amenorrhoea (Seventeenth-Twentieth Centuries)," in Robert Forster and Orest Ranum, eds., *Biology of Man in History,* trans. from the French by Elborg Forster and Patricia M. Ranum (Baltimore and London, 1975), pp. 163–78.

5. Charles H. Pouthas, *La population française pendant la première moitié du XIXe siècle* (Paris, 1956), p. 17.

6. Wesley D. Camp, *Marriage and the Family in France since the Revolution* (New York, 1961), p. 22; Pouthas, *Population francaise,* p. 23.

7. Erwin H. Ackerknecht, *Geschichte und Geographie der wichtigsten Krankheiten* (Stuttgart,

1963), pp. 32–33; idem, *Medicine at the Paris Hospital 1794–1848* (Baltimore, 1967), p. 111; J. A. F. Ozanam, *Histoire médicale générale et particulière des maladies épidémiques, contagieuses et épizootiques* (2d ed.; 4 vols.; Paris, 1835), 4: 22. Typhus reached European epidemic proportions during the Napoleonic wars, with a high mortality rate.

8. For evidence of this fertility trend in Germany especially, see Franz Schnabel, *Deutsche Geschichte im neunzehnten Jahrhundert* (2d ed.; 4 vols.; Freiburg im Breisgau, 1949–50), 3: 359; Gustav von Gülich, *Geschichtliche Darstellung des Handels, der Gewerbe und des Ackerbaus der bedeutendsten handeltreibenden Staaten unserer Zeit* (2 vols.; Jena, 1830), 2: 367; Mack Walker, *Germany and the Emigration 1816–1885* (Cambridge, Mass., 1964), p. 3.

9. Wilhelm Roscher, *Ueber Kornhandel und Theuerungspolitik* (3d. ed.; Stuttgart and Tübingen, 1852), p. 55; Karlheinz Blaschke, *Bevölkerungsgeschichte von Sachsen bis zur industriellen Revolution* (Weimar, 1967), p. 30.

10. These data lack precision, to be sure, but unlike the English parochial records they appear to be accurate enough to follow short-term demographic trends. English vital statistics have not been included because of the general agreement that the omission of burials and baptisms reached an extremely high percentage during the period from 1800 to 1820; possibly more than 30 percent of the deaths escaped registration during the years 1816–19; see P. E. Razzell, "The Evaluation of Baptisms as a Form of Birth Registration through Cross-Matching Census and Parish Register Data," *Population Studies* 26 (March 1972): 139–45; J. T. Krause, "Changes in English Fertility and Mortality, 1781–1850," *Economic History Review*, 2d ser., 10 (August 1958): 52–70.

11. See Carl von Clausewitz, *Politische Schriften und Briefe,* ed. by Hans Rothfels (Munich, 1922), pp. 189–91; Wilhelm Sandkaulen, *Das Notjahr 1816/17 mit besonderer Berücksichtigung der Verhältinsse am Niederrhein* (Münster, 1927); Alexander Stollenwerk, "Der Regierungsbezirk Koblenz während der grossen Hungersnot in Jahre 1816/1817," *Jahrbuch für Geschichte und Kunst des Mittelrheins und seiner Nachbargebiete* 22–23 (1970–71): 109–49.

12. Athos Belletini, *La popolazione di Bologna dal secolo XV all' unificazione italiana* (Bologna, 1961), pp. 95, 96, 147, 149, 428, 429.

13. G. Monteleone, "Le Carestie de 1816–1817 nelle Province Venete," *Archivio Veneto* 86–87 (1969): 75.

14. Statistisches Bureau, *Schweizerische Statistik / Statistique de la Suisse* (Bern, 1862–1919), Lieferung no. 128 (1901), pp. 191, 195.

15. Siegfried Becker, *Die Bevölkerungs-Verhältinsse der österreichischen Monarchie* (Vienna, 1846), pp. 293, 341, 347; L. Maschek, "Zur Geschichte und Praxis der Volkzählung in Dalmatien," *Statistische Monatschrift* 6 (1880): 353–54; Joseph Hain, *Handbuch der Statistik des österreichischen Kaiserstaates* (2 vols.; Vienna, 1852–53), 1: 490; Johann Springer, *Statistik der österreichischen Kaiserstaates* (2 vols.; Vienna, 1840), 1: 93. The 1818 census in Dalmatia returned a smaller population by 1,146 than the census of 1817; and the census in the Military Frontier returned 14,188 fewer persons in 1817 than had been counted in 1815.

16. André Armengaud, "Population in Europe 1700–1914," in *The Fontana Economic History of Europe,* vol. 3, *The Industrial Revolution* (London, 1973), p. 44; C. A. Macartney, *The Habsburg Empire 1790–1918* (London, 1968), p. 200; *Oekonomische Neuigkeiten,* January 1817, no. 1, p. 2; Anton von Baldacci, "Über die inneren Zustände Österreichs. Eine Denkschrift aus dem Jahr 1816," ed. and introduced by F. von Krones in *Archiv für österreichische Geschichte* 84 (1889): 83–84; *Landwirthschaftliche Zeitung* 15, no. 10 (1817): 89–90; *The Times* (London), July 26, 1817, p. 2.

17. Staatsrath Joseph Ritter von Hazzi, *Betrachtungen über Theurung und Noth der Vergangenheit und Gegenwart* (Munich, 1818), pp. 84–85; A. J. V. Heunisch, *Das Grossherzogtum Baden* (Heidelberg, 1857), pp. 231, 248, 252.

18. Pavla Horska, "L'État actuel des recherches sur l'évolution de la population dans les pays tchèques aux XVIIIe et XIX e siècles," *Annales de démographie historique,* 1967, p. 183.

19. Sweden, Statistiska Centralbyrån, *Historisk Statistik för Sverige,* 1, *Befolkning 1720–1967* (Stockholm, 1969), p. 93.

20. Wilhelm Abel, *Agrarkrisen und Agrarkonjunktur* (2d ed.; Hamburg and Berlin, 1966), p. 290. Prices are given in the equivalent of silver *Reichsmark.*

21. Michael Drake, *Population and Society in Norway 1735–1865* (Cambridge, 1969), p. 73.

22. The figures given for the number of plague deaths represent the traditionally accepted

account found in the standard work by Georg Sticker, *Die Pest: Die Geschichte der Pest* (Giessen, 1908), pp. 213–22. The figures appear incredibly large, measured against the estimated populations of these cities around 1700. For example, the population of Danzig is generally believed to have been about 50,000 in 1710. A total of 32,000 deaths from plague would imply a morbidity and a case-fatality rate difficult to accept. Perhaps the population counted as dying in Danzig covered a geographical area wider than the term suburbs suggests. According to the calculations made by T. H. Hollingsworth, even the smaller number of 24,353 deaths which is sometimes given, if a morbidity rate of 50 percent is assumed, would still imply a population of 193,000; see T. H. Hollingsworth, *Historical Demography* (Ithaca, N.Y., 1969), pp. 372–73.

23. Charles Creighton, *A History of Epidemics in Britain* (2 vols.; 2d ed.; London, 1965), 2: 53–58.

24. Thomas Short, *New Observations on City, Town and Country Bills of Mortality* (London, 1750), pp. 85–88.

25. J. D. Chambers, *The Vale of Trent*, supplement no. 3, *Economic History Review* (London, 1957), pp. 25–28, 34–35.

26. Meuvret, "Demographic Crisis," p. 518.

27. François Lebrun, *Les hommes et la mort en Anjou aux 17ᵉ et 18ᵉ siècles* (Paris, 1971), pp. 362–66, 509.

28. Pierre Goubert, *Beauvais et le Beauvaisis de 1600 à 1730* (2 vols.; Paris, 1961), 1: 51–59; 2: 56–61; idem. "Les fondements démographiques," in Fernand Braudel and Ernest Labrousse, eds., *Histoire économique et sociale de la France*, vol. 2, 1660–1789 (Paris, 1970), pp. 38–49, 60, 67.

29. Marcel Reinhard, André Armengaud, and Jacques Dupaquier, *Histoire générale de la population mondiale* (3d ed.; Paris, 1968), pp. 185, 268.

30. Maurice-A. Arnould, "Mortalité et épidemies sous l'Ancien Régime dans le Hainaut et quelques régions limitrophes," in *Problèmes de mortalité*, Actes du Colloque International de demographie historique, ed. by Paul Harsin and Étienne Hélin, Liège, 1963 (Liège, 1965), pp. 478–79; Joseph Ruvet, "Les inégalités devant la mort. Les Pays-Bas et la principauté de Liège du XVIᵉ au XVIIIᵉ siècle," in ibid., p. 454; Étienne Hélin, "Le déroulement de trois crises à Liège au XVIIIᵉ siècle," in ibid., pp. 487–90.

31. B. H. Slicher van Bath, "Report on the Study of Historical Demography in the Netherlands," in Harsin and Hélin, eds., *Problèmes de mortalité*, pp. 192–93.

32. Wilhelm Abel, *Massenarmut und Hungerkrisen im vorindustriellen Europa* (Hamburg and Berlin, 1974), pp. 170–74; Erich Keyser, *Bevölkerungsgeschichte Deutschlands* (2d ed.; Leipzig, 1941), pp. 355–65.

33. Wilhelm Bickel, *Bevölkerungsgeschichte und Bevölkerungspolitik der Schweiz* (Zürich, 1947), pp. 78–87.

34. H. Gille, "The Demographic History of the Northern European Countries in the Eighteenth Century," *Population Studies* 3 (1949–50): 65; Drake, *Norway*, p. 192; *Historisk Statistik*, p. 86.

35. Drake, *Norway*, pp. 169, 173; *Historisk Statistik*, p. 86; Gille, "Demographic History," pp. 60–61.

36. Gustaf Utterström, "Some Population Problems in Preindustrial Sweden," *Scandinavian Economic History Review* 2, no. 1 (1954): 121–36; Gille, "Demographic History," pp. 50–51; Eino Jutikkala, "Finland's Population Movement in the Eighteenth Century," in Glass and Eversley, *Population*, pp. 558–60.

37. Sticker, *Pest*, pp. 240–44.

38. Sølvi Sogner, "Aspects of the Demographic Situation in Seventeen Parishes in Shropshire, 1711–60," *Population Studies* 17 (November 1963): 136, 146.

39. Creighton, *Epidemics*, 2: 78–83.

40. Short, *New Observations*, p. 33.

41. Chambers, *Trent*, pp. 29–30, 34–35.

42. D. E. C. Eversley, "Mortality in Britain in the Eighteenth Century: Problems and Prospects," in *Problèmes de mortalité*, p. 358.

43. Jean-Pierre Goubert, *Malades et médecins en Bretagne 1770–1790* (Rennes, 1974), pp. 328–32; Yves Blayo and Louis Henry, "Données démographiques sur la Bretagne et l'Anjou de

1740 à 1829," in *Annales de démographie historique* (1967): 100–04; Reinhard, Armengaud, and Dupaquier, *Population mondiale*, pp. 260–61.
44. Lebrun, *Anjou*, pp. 368–71.
45. Pierre Goubert, *Beauvais*, 2: 56–61.
46. Reinhard, Armengaud, and Dupaquier, *Population mondiale*, p. 268.
47. Pierre Goubert, "Fondements," pp. 61–62, 67.
48. Arnould, "Hainaut," pp. 479–80; Hélin, "Liège," pp. 490–93.
49. Slicher van Bath, "Netherlands," pp. 192–93; P. Deprez, "The Demographic Development of Flanders in the Eighteenth Century," in Glass and Eversley, *Population*, pp. 611–13.
50. Karl L. Helleiner, "The Population of Europe from the Black Death to the Eve of the Vital Revolution," in *The Cambridge Economic History of Europe*, vol. 4 (Cambridge, 1967), pp. 92–93; Keyser, *Bevölkerungsgeschichte*, pp. 355–65; Abel, *Massenarmut*, pp. 179–87; Bickel, *Schweiz*, pp. 78–87; Carlo M. Cipolla, "Four Centuries of Italian Demographic Development," in Glass and Eversley, *Population*, pp. 573–75.
The fragmentary statistics for Germany found in Johann Peter Süssmilch, *Die göttliche Ordnung in den Veränderungen des menschlichen Geschlechts*, ed. by Christian Jacob Baumann (3d ed.; Berlin, 1798) yield an impression of the quantitative order of the increase in mortality in 1740–41. The number of deaths in Berlin rose fom 3,502 in 1739 to 4,749 (or 36 percent) in 1740, and then declined to 3,921 in 1741, to 3,492 in 1742, and to 2,967 in 1743. The annual number of deaths in Berlin for the decade 1737–46 averaged 3,672, and thus the number of deaths in 1740 stood at 29 percent above this figure; see ibid., 1, Tables, p. 24. The number of deaths in Vienna rose from 6,158 in 1739 to 6,913 (or 11 percent) in 1740, and then declined to 6,585 in 1741, to 6,513 in 1742, and to 5,372 in 1743. The annual number of deaths in Vienna for the decade 1735–44 averaged 6,256, and thus the number of deaths in 1740 stood at 11 percent above this figure; see ibid., 1, Tables, p. 26. The number of deaths in the duchy of Magdeburg rose from 8,235 in 1739 to 9,496 (or 15 percent) in 1740, rose further to 9,615 in 1741, and then declined to 7,845 in 1742, and to 6,652 in 1743. The annual number of deaths for the decade 1733–42 averaged 7,795, and thus the number of deaths in 1741 stood at 23 percent above this figure; see ibid., 1, Tables, pp. 104–05. The number of deaths in the west German territory of Minden and Ravensberg rose from 4,057 in 1739 to 4,962 (or 22 percent) in 1740, and then declined to 4,762 in 1741, to 4,195 in 1742, to 3,467 in 1743; see ibid., 1, Tables, p. 118. By contrast, the number of deaths in the province of East Prussia and Lithuania declined from 15,896 in 1739 to 15,390 in 1740, to 15,288 in 1741, to 14,015 in 1742; see ibid., 1, Tables, p. 85. These examples can be multiplied, but the general trends would not change; see ibid., 1, Tables, pp. 101–02, 110, 121.
51. Michael Drake, "The Irish Demographic Crisis of 1740–41," *Historical Studies* 6 (1968): 101, 116–117; Creighton, *Epidemics*, 2: 242–43.
52. Creighton, *Epidemics*, 2: 244; Drake, "Irish Crisis," pp. 120–21.
53. Drake, "Irish Crisis," p. 121.
54. K. H. Connell, *The Population of Ireland, 1750–1845* (Oxford, 1950), p. 25.
55. Louis Henry, "The Population of France in the Eighteenth Century," in Glass and Eversley, *Population*, p. 448.
56. Meuvret, "Demographic Crisis," p. 511; however, Jean Pierre Goubert's recent study of Brittany in the eighteenth century concludes that it is rare to find a "pure epidemic crisis" where the death rate has not been influenced by a food crisis, although this influence diminishes as the century progresses; also that subsistence crises exact a higher toll in the countryside than in urban districts, which may help to explain the slight correlation between high bread prices and epidemic disease found in Andrew B. Appleby, "Nutrition and Disease: The Case of London, 1550–1750," *Journal of Interdisciplinary History* 6 (Summer 1975): 1–22; see Goubert, *Malades*, pp. 31–33, 277–79, 290–92, 308–15, 343–48, 379–80.
57. J. D. Chambers, *Population, Economy, and Society in Pre-Industrial England* (London, 1972), pp. 82–88.
58. Meuvret, "Demographic Crisis," p. 511.
59. Braudel, *Material Life*, p. 51.
60. E. A. Wrigley, *Population and History* (New York and Toronto, 1969), p. 76.
61. N. L. Tranter, *Population Since the Industrial Revolution* (London, 1973), pp. 64, 89, for these views.

62. For discussion and for clinical evidence supporting this view, see Vernon R. Young and Nevin S. Scrimshaw, "The Physiology of Starvation," *Scientific American* 224 (October 1971), reprinted in *Readings from Scientific American* (San Francisco, 1973), pp. 44–51; George F. Cahill, Jr. M.D., "Starvation in Man," *New England Journal of Medicine* 282 (March 1970): 668–75.

63. N.S. Scrimshaw, C. E. Taylor, and J. E. Gordon, *Interaction of Nutrition and Infection* (Geneva, 1968), pp. 11–14.

64. Per Helweg-Larsen et al., *Famine Disease in German Concentration Camps, Complications and Sequels*, supplement 274, *Acta Medica Scandinavica* (Copenhagen, 1952), pp. 74, 77, 124–33.

65. Helweg-Larsen, *Famine Disease*, p. 73.

66. Ozanam, *Histoire médicale*, 1: 67; Friedrich Schnurrer, *Chronik der Seuchen* (2 vols.; Tübingen, 1823–25), 2: 543–44; Heinrich Haeser, *Lehrbuch der Geschichte der Medicin und der epidemischen Krankheiten* (3d ed.; 3 vols.; Jena, 1875–82), 3: 618–21.

67. Hans-Ludwig Schaefer, *Bremens Bevölkerung in der ersten Hälfte des neunzehnten Jahrhunderts* (Bremen, 1957), p. 36; Günther Meinhardt, "Die Auswirkungen der Hungerjahre in der ersten Hälfte des 19. Jahrhunderts auf Göttingen," *Göttinger Jahrbuch* 14 (1966): 215.

68. Schnurrer, *Seuchen*, 2: 532–35.

69. Jacques Antoine Dulaure, *Histoire civile, physique et morale de Paris* (3d ed.; 10 vols.; Paris, 1825), 9: 453–55.

70. *Moniteur* (Paris), May 27, 1817, p. 578; Haeser, *Epidemischen Krankheiten*, 3: 661.

71. Creighton, *Epidemics*, 2: 571–80.

72. Hain, *Statistik*, 1: 71, 73.

73. Haeser, *Epidemischen Krankheiten*, 3: 659.

74. Scrimshaw, Taylor, and Gordon, *Nutrition and Infection*, pp. 60–64, 68–70. For evidence of an increase in tuberculosis mortality in Bavaria during 1816–17, see W. Robert Lee, "Zur Bevölkerungsgeschichte Bayerns 1750–1850: Britische Forschungsergebnisse," *Vierteljahrschrift für Sozial- und Wirtschaftsgeschichte* 62, Heft 3 (1975): 335.

75. Sir Macfarlane Burnet and David O. White, *Natural History of Infectious Disease* (4th ed.; Cambridge, 1972), pp. 215–17.

76. Helweg-Larsen, *Famine Disease*, pp. 279, 330–31.

77. Schnurrer, *Seuchen*, 2: 539–41; Haeser, *Epidemischen Krankheiten*, 3: 663.

78. *The Times*, May 5, 1817, p. 3; Paul Leuilliot, *L'Alsace au début de XIXᵉ siècle (1815– 1830)* (3 vols.; Paris, 1959–60), p. 170.

79. Thomas Raffles, *Letters, during a Tour through Some Parts of France, Savoy, Switzerland, Germany, and the Netherlands in the Summer of 1817* (Liverpool, 1818), pp. 149–51.

80. Louis Simond, *Switzerland; or a Journal of a Tour and Residence in that Country, in the Years 1817, 1818, and 1819* (2 vols.; Boston, 1822), 1: 9.

81. Hazzi, *Theurung*, p. 85.

82. Johann Gottfried von Pahl, *Geschichte von Wirtemberg* (6 vols.; Stuttgart, 1827–31), 6: 212.

83. Stollenwerk, "Hungersnot," pp. 143–44.

84. Wolf-Heino Struck, *Die Auswanderung aus dem Herzogtum Nassau, 1806–1866* (Wiesbaden, 1966), p. 121; Hansjörg Gruber, *Die Entwickelung der pfälzischen Wirtschaft 1816–1834* (Saarbrücken, 1962), p. 20.

85. Schnurrer, *Seuchen*, 2: 540–41; Macartney, *Habsburg Empire*, p. 200.

86. Scrimshaw, Taylor, and Gordon, *Nutrition and Infection*, pp. 216–29.

87. Schnurrer, *Seuchen*, 2: 540–43.

88. *The Times*, May 5, 1817, p. 3.

89. *Württembergishes Jahrbuch für 1818*, pp. 27–28.

90. Stollenwerk, "Hungersnot," p. 143; Sandkaulen, *Notjahr*, pp. 7–8.

91. *Württembergishes Jahrbuch für 1818*, p. 28.

92. Hazzi, *Theurung*, p. 85.

93. George Barger, *Ergot and Ergotism* (London, 1931), pp. 56–60, 98; this study is the standard work.

94. Ozanam, *Histoire médicale*, 4: 22; Barger, *Ergotism*, p. 61.

95. *Landwirthschaftliche Zeitung* 16, no. 21 (1818): 212; Schnurrer, *Seuchen,* 2: 541; Stollenwerk, "Hungersnot," p. 114.

96. Barger, *Ergotism,* pp. 75–77.

97. Stollenwerk, "Hungersnot," p. 114; Sandkaulen, *Notjahr,* p. 44; Barger, *Ergotism,* p. 77.

98. Schnurrer, *Seuchen,* 2: 543–44.

99. Haeser, *Epidemischen Krankheiten,* 3: 621; Schnurrer, *Seuchen,* p. 543; *Schweizerische Monathschronik,* 1817, pp. 71–72.

100. Ozanam, *Histoire médicale,* 1: 67.

101. Quoted in Hermann Meynert, *Kaiser Franz I* (Vienna, 1872), p. 394.

102. Meynert, *Franz I,* pp. 394–95.

103. Dr. Henry Holland, "On the Pellagra, a Disease Prevailing in Lombardy," *Medico-Chirurgical Transactions* 8 (1817): 326.

104. Holland, "Pellagra," p. 336. Pellagra results of course from undue reliance on maize for subsistance; the disease appeared in northern Italy during the eighteenth century; by 1817 it was estimated that 15–20 percent of the population in the worst affected districts were pellagrous; Goethe described the pathetic condition of the hill people when he was traveling in northern Italy in 1786; for this discussion and pellagra in history, see Daphne A. Roe, *A Plague of Corn* (Ithaca and London, 1973), esp. p. 39.

105. Schnurrer, *Seuchen,* 2: 543–44; *The Times,* April 23, 1817, p. 2; April 25, 1817, p. 3; May 1, 1817, p. 2; August 6, 1817, p. 2; October 2, 1817, p. 2; October 31, 1817, p. 2; *Quotidienne* (Paris), April 26, 1817, p. 1; January 5, 1818, p. 2; February 11, 1818, p. 2.

106. *The Times,* August 6, 1817, p. 2.

107. Ibid., October 31, 1817, p. 2.

108. *Schweizerische Monathschronik,* 1817, p. 71.

109. Quoted in Ernest J. Knapton, *The Lady of the Holy Alliance: The Life of Julie de Krüdener* (New York, 1939), p. 170.

110. Ruprecht Zollikofer, *Der Osten meinen Vaterlandes, oder die Kantone St. Gallen und Appenzell im Hungerjahre 1817* (2 vols.; St. Gall, 1818–19), 1: 36.

111. Simond, *Switzerland,* 1: 93.

112. Helweg-Larsen, *Famine Disease,* pp. 76–77, 95, 124, 157–58. The contemporary observation in Switzerland that starving persons died when normal diets returned because "their organs became impaired" is significant. In fact, the findings of *Famine Disease* indicate that hunger not only produced atrophic changes in the small intestine and impaired intestinal function but also that the greatest relative weight loss occurred in the intestines, spleen, and liver, ranging from 50 to 60 percent; see pp. 91, 152.

113. Zollikofer, *Osten,* see table inserted at end of vol. 1.

114. Christoph Bernoulli, *Schweizerische Archiv für Statistik und Nationalökonomie* (5 vols.; Basel, 1827–31), 2: 87.

115. Zollikofer, *Osten,* 1: 47, 51, 128; *Schweizerische Monathschronik,* 1817, pp. 71–72; Schnurrer, *Seuchen,* 2: 143; Haeser, *Epidemischen Krankheiten,* 3: 621; the case-fatality rate averaged 16 percent of those infected but reached 37 percent in the worst instances.

116. William Harty, M.D., *An Historic Sketch of the Causes, Progress, Extent, and Mortality of the Contagious Fever Epidemic in Ireland during the Years 1817, 1818, and 1819* (Dublin, 1820), appendix, pp. 158–59, quoting a letter from Samuel Smith Thomson, M.D., Belfast Fever Hospital, dated April 2, 1818, in which he sums up the medical consensus.

117. Sir William Macarthur, "Famines and Fevers in England and Ireland," *Journal of the British Archaeological Association,* 3d ser., 9 (1944): 66–67; idem, "Medical History of the Famine," in R. Dudley Edwards and T. Desmond Williams, eds., *The Great Famine* (New York, 1959), p. 271; Stanhope Bayne-Jones, "Epidemic Typhus in the Mediterranean Area during World War II," in F. R. Moulton, ed., *Rickettsial Diseases of Man* (Washington, D.C., 1948), pp. 8–9; Creighton, *Epidemics,* 2: 257.

118. Creighton, *Epidemics,* 2: 259–60.

119. Harty, *Contagious Fever,* pp. 21, 119, 127.

120. Andrew Yeomans, "The Symptomatology, Clinical Course and Management of Louse-borne Typhus Fever," in Moulton, *Rickettsial Diseases,* pp. 129–30; Bayne-Jones, "Epidemic Typhus," p. 9.

121. Creighton, *Epidemics,* 2: 264–65, citing F. Baker and J. Cheyne, *Account of the Fever Lately Epidemical in Ireland* (London, 1821).

122. Creighton, *Epidemics,* 2: 266.

123. Ibid., pp. 258, 265–66; Macarthur, "Medical History," pp. 268–69, 284–87, 289.

124. Connell, *Ireland,* pp. 226–31.

125. Robert Cowan, M.D., "Vital Statistics of Glasgow, Illustrating the Sanatory Condition of the Population," *Journal of the Statistical Society* 2 (1840–41): 270–71, 288–89.

126. James E. Handley, *The Irish in Scotland, 1789–1845* (2d ed.; Cork, 1945), pp. 173–76.

127. *The Times,* April 23, 1817, p. 3; September 30, 1818, p. 3; Creighton, *Epidemics,* 2: 174–78; Harty, *Contagious Fever,* appendix, pp. 111–14.

128. "Tracts on the Causes, Cure, and Prevention of Contagious Fever," *The Edinburgh Review,* 21, no. 62 (March 1819): 414–16.

129. Creighton, *Epidemics,* 2: 170–73; *The Times,* April 12, 1817, p. 3; April 23, 1817, p. 2; *Gentleman's Magazine* 88 (July 1818): supplement, part II: 597.

130. Thomas Bateman, M.D., *A Succinct Account of the Typhus or Contagious Fever of This Country, Exemplified in the Epidemic Which Prevailed in the Metropolis in 1817 and 1818* (2d ed.; London, 1820), pp. 16–18.

131. Bateman, *Typhus,* pp. 1–5.

132. *The Times,* July 24, 1818, p. 2.

133. Bateman, *Typhus,* pp. 75–83.

134. Creighton, *Epidemics,* 2: 173; *The Times,* July 24, 1818, p. 2.

135. Macarthur, "Medical History," pp. 280–81.

136. Helweg-Larsen, *Famine Disease,* pp. 263–71.

137. Burnet and White, *Infectious Disease,* p. 147.

138. Scrimshaw, Taylor, and Gordon, *Nutrition and Infection,* pp. 70, 177–82.

139. Sticker, *Pest,* pp. 285–89; Schnurrer, *Seuchen,* 2: 511–12, 518–20, 524, 526–27; Haeser, *Epidemischen Krankheiten,* 3: 627; *Quotidienne,* February 14, 1816, pp. 1–2; *The Times,* January 27, 1816, p. 3; April 12, 1816, p. 2.

140. *The Times,* February 22, 1816, p. 3; *Quotidienne,* March 19, 1816, p. 2; *Maryland Gazette,* April 11, 1816, p. 3.

141. René-Clovis Prus, *Rapport à l'Academié Royal de Médecine sur la peste et les quarantines* (2 vols.; Paris, 1846), 1: 493. This work is an invaluable source for any investigation of Europe's "conquest of plague." Volume one is divided into two parts: the report of the medical commission on the question of the necessity of quarantine; and, two, a collection of documents containing testimony and evidence from physicians and public health officials who were active in controlling plague in the Ottoman empire, from Morocco in the west to Armenia in the east, during the first half of the nineteenth century. Volume two contains the medical opinions heard by the commission concerning the etiology of plague, now mainly out of date.

142. Sticker, *Pest,* pp. 289–94; Prus, *Rapport,* 1: 277–82; *The Times,* October 6, 1817, p. 2; October 25, 1817, p. 2; September 10, 1818, p. 2; M. H. Cherif, "Expansion européene et difficultés tunisiennes de 1815 à 1830," *Annales, E. S. C.* 25 (May–June 1970): 721–22; C. Bacaloglu, "La peste dans les Pays Roumains au XVIIIe et XIXe siècle," in *Neuvième congrès international d'histoire de la medécine* (Bucharest, 1932), p. 520.

143. *Quotidienne,* May 1, 1817, p. 3.

144. Prus, *Rapport,* 1: 42, 497–98; L. Fabian Hirst, *The Conquest of Plague* (Oxford, 1953), pp. 378–81; S. Fairlee, "Shipping in the Anglo-Russian Grain Trade, to 1870, Part I," *Maritime History* 1 (1971): 166; Charles F. Mullett, *The Bubonic Plague and England* (Lexington, Kentucky, 1956), pp. 331–32, 351; Helleiner, "Population," p. 84. For an extended discussion of the history of quarantines in Britain in the seventeenth and eighteenth centuries, see M. C. Buer, *Health, Welfare, and Population in the Early Days of the Industrial Revolution* (London, 1926), pp. 171–80.

145. Sticker, *Pest,* pp. 288–89; *The Times,* January 27, 1816, p. 3; April 12, 1816, p. 2; *Quotidienne,* February 14, 1816, pp. 1–2.

146. Helleiner, "Population," p. 84.

147. Gunther E. Rothenberg, "The Austrian Sanitary Cordon and the Control of the Bubonic Plague: 1710–1871," *Journal of the History of Medicine and Allied Sciences* 28 (January 1973): 15–21; Sticker, *Pest,* pp. 240–41; 252–69; Bacaloglu, "Peste," p. 520.

148. Prus, *Rapport*, 1: 42, 497–98, 620–21.

149. Hirst, *Plague*, p. 388; Helleiner, "Population," p. 85. For agreement with these statements and for the standard work on the epidemiology and ecology of plague, see R. Pollitzer, *Plague* (Geneva, 1954), esp. pp. 315–408, 483–521. For more recent findings, see *Bulletin of the World Health Organization* 23, nos. 2–3 (1960): 135–418, which is devoted to the epidemiology and ecology of plague.

150. Jacques Revel, "Autour d'une épidémie ancienne: la peste de 1666–1670," *Revue d'histoire moderne et contemporaine* 17 (October–December 1970): 957, 974; J. Charlier, *La peste à Bruxelles de 1667 à 1669 et ses conséquences démographiques* (Brussels, 1969), p. 37; Sticker, *Pest*, p. 175.

151. Prus, *Rapport*, 1: 592–94.

152. For discussion of the role of flea transport in the spread of plague, see Pollitzer, *Plague*, pp. 385–88; also see J. F. D. Shewsbury, *A History of Bubonic Plague in the British Isles* (Cambridge, 1970), p. 29.

153. P. Samarian, "Histoire de la peste en Roumanie," in *Neuvième congrès*, p. 536; Sticker, *Pest*, pp. 287–88; Prus, *Rapport*, 1: 255.

154. A. Lenghel, "Histoire de la peste à Cluj, en 1738–39," in *Neuvième congrès*, pp. 522–23; for an account of the plague epidemic in the Balkans, Turkey, the Levant, North Africa, and Sicily 1738–43, see Sticker, *Pest*, pp. 239–43.

155. Burnet and White, *Infectious Disease*, pp. 142–43; Aidan Cockburn, M.D., *The Evolution and Eradication of Infectious Diseases* (Baltimore and London, 1963), pp. 80–85, 99; Thomas McKeown and R. G. Record, "Reasons for the Decline of Mortality in England and Wales during the Nineteenth Century," *Population Studies* 16 (November 1962): 110–11.

156. Shrewsbury, *Plague*, p. 6.

157. Pollitzer, *Plague*, pp. 14–15; Helleiner, "Population," p. 84; Shrewsbury, *Plague*, p. 6; Sticker, *Pest*, pp. 285–94.

158. For morbidity and mortality rates during the seventeenth century, see Pierre Deyon, *Amiens, capitale provinciale* (Paris, 1967), p. 32; Carlo M. Cipolla, *Christofano and the Plague* (Berkeley, 1973), pp. 103–05; Shrewsbury, *Plague*, p. 487; Charlier, *Peste*, pp. 173–99; Helleiner, "Population," p. 84.

159. Hirst, *Plague*, pp. 338–45.

160. M. Baltazard, "Déclin et destin d'une maladie infectieuse: la peste," *Bulletin of the World Health Organization* 23, nos. 2–3 (1960): 250–52; Hirst, *Plague*, pp. 335–36; Helleiner, "Population," pp. 84–85, 95; Buer, *Health*, pp. 172–73.

161. R. Pollitzer, M.D., "A Review of Recent Literature on Plague," *Bulletin of the World Health Organization* 23, nos. 2–3 (1960): 355–57; Baltazard, "Peste," ibid., p. 251; Dr. Ernest Schwarz, "Classification, Origin, and Distribution of Commensal Rats," ibid., pp. 414–15; Hirst, *Plague*, pp. 345–46.

162. Ricardo Jorge, "Les anciennes épidémies de peste en Europe comparées aux épidémies modernes," in *Neuvième congrès*, p. 372; Sticker, *Pest*, pp. 252–57; John T. Alexander, "Catherin II, Bubonic Plague, and Industry in Moscow," *American Historical Review* 79 (June 1974): 661.

163. Pollitzer, *Plague*, pp. 340–73, 483–86.

164. Ibid., pp. 378–81.

165. Ernst Rodenwaldt, "Pest in Venedig 1575–1577. Ein Beitrage zur Frage der Infektkette bei den Pestepidemien West-Europas," *Sitzungsbericht der Heidelberger Akademie der Wissenschaften*, Mathematisch-naturwissenschaftliche Klasse, Jahrgang 1952, 2 (1953): 218–63; see also Erich Keyser, "Die Pest in Deutschland und ihre Erforschung," in *Problemes de mortalite*, pp. 376–77.

166. Baltazard, "Peste," pp. 253–56.

167. Buer, *Health*, pp. 77–92; Alan Armstrong, *Stability and Change in an English County Town: A Social Study of York 1801–51* (London, 1974), pp. 111–12.

168. Buer, *Health*, pp. 78–79.

169. Reinhold A. Dorwart, *The Prussian Welfare State before 1740* (Cambridge, Mass., 1971), pp. 293–96.

170. Braudel, *Material Life*, pp. 47, 192–99; Helleiner, "Population," pp. 84–85.

171. Alexander, "Catherine II," pp. 642–43, 660–61.

172. Pollitzer, "Review," p. 355.
173. J.-N. Biraben and Jacques Le Goff, "The Plague in the Early Middle Ages," in Forster and Ranum, *Biology,* pp. 52–55; E. T. Renbourn, *Materials and Clothing in Health and Disease* (London, 1972), pp. 419–20; Shrewsbury, *Plague,* pp. 4, 7, 34–36; Helleiner, "Population," pp. 7, 85; Buer, *Health,* 172–73; Pollitzer, "Review," p. 360.
174. Prus, *Rapport,* 1: 29–30.
175. Ibid., p. 42.
176. Ibid., p. 32.
177. Pollitzer, *Plague,* p. 502.
178. R. B. Mackenzie, "Public Health Importance of Rodents in South America," *Bulletin of the World Health Organization* 47 (1972): 161–64.
179. For the genesis of this conclusion, see Edwin D. Kilbourne, M.D., and Wilson G. Smillie, M.D., eds., *Human Ecology and Public Health* (4th ed.; London, 1969), esp. Walsh McDermott, "Demography, Culture, and Economics and the Evolutionary Stages of Medicine," pp. 72–77; and Edwin D. Kilbourne, "Approaches to the Control of Human Infections," pp. 209–54.
180. Prus, *Rapport,* p. 200.

CHAPTER V

1. B. H. Slicher van Bath, *The Agrarian History of Western Europe, A.D. 500–1850,* trans. by Olive Ordish (London. 1963), pp. 3–4; J. D. Chambers and G. E. Mingay, The *Agricultural Revolution 1750–1880* (London, 1964), pp. 108–09; Peter Mathias, *The First Industrial Nation* (London, 1969), p. 65.
2. E. L. Jones, *Seasons and Prices* (London, 1964), pp. 21–22; T. S. Ashton, *Economic Fluctuations in England 1700–1800* (London, 1959), pp. 37–38, 42–43.
3. R. C. O. Matthews, *A Study in Trade Cycle History: Economic Fluctuations in Great Britain 1833–1842* (Cambridge, 1954), p. 224.
4. Mathias, *Industrial Nation,* p. 65; George Rudé, *The Crowd in History: A Study of Popular Disturbances in France and England* (New York, 1964), p. 21.
5. For this view, see *The Times* (London), September 4, 1817, p. 2.
6. For the development of this model, see C. E. Labrousse, *Esquisse du mouvement des prix et des revenus en France au XVIIIe siècle* (Paris, 1932); it was refined in idem, *La crise de l'économie française à la fin de l'ancien régime et au début de la Revolution* (Paris, 1944), esp. pp. 172–80; idem, *Le mouvement ouvrier et les idées sociales en France de 1815 à la fin du XIXe siècle* (Paris, 1948), pp. 30–31. For the most illuminating summary of the Labrousse thesis in English, see David S. Landes, "The Statistical Study of French Crises," *Journal of Economic History,* 10 (November 1950): 196–201, which is relied upon here. This is the point to acknowledge my indebtedness to Professor Landes for his kindness in furthering my understanding by personal communication.

The theoretical validity of the Labrousse thesis has long been debated. His critical proposition that a severe harvest deficiency does not lead to a net gain in revenue for the agricultural sector despite a twofold or threefold increase in grain prices is difficult to confirm. Landes has examined the question by computing the annual supply of wheat available in 1817, 1818, and 1819 and then multiplying these figures by the annual average prices to determine the net market value of the crops; see David S. Landes, "Reply to Mr. Daniere and Some Reflections on the Significance of the Debate," *Journal of Economic History* 18 (September 1958): 337. While Landes's conclusion that the smaller production of 1816 resulted in a much larger value than the higher production of 1817 and 1818 is convincing, it should be noted that the grain production figures for France at this period are too imprecise for refined statistical analysis.
7. Phyllis Deane and W. A. Cole, *British Economic Growth 1688–1959* (2d. ed., Cambridge, 1967), pp. 142–43, 161, 166–67.
8. M. Lévy-Leboyer, "La croissance économique en France au XIXe siècle. Resultats préliminaires," *Annales, E. S. C.* 23 (1968): 803; Alexandre Chabert, *Essai sur les mouvements des revenus et de l'activité économique en France de 1789 à 1820* (Paris, 1949), p. 427; Tihomir J. Markovitch, *L'industrie française de 1789 à 1964.—Sources et méthods* (Paris, 1965), p. 143.

9. J. C. Toutain, *La population de la France de 1700 à 1959* (Paris, 1963), pp. 54, 57.

10. Sébastien Charléty, *La Restauration* (Paris, 1921), p. 315.

11. This hypothetical mechanism is borrowed from Wilhelm Abel, *Agrarkrisen und Agrarkonjunktur* (2d ed.; Hamburg and Berlin, 1966), pp. 23–25. According to official statistics, the wheat yield fell just below 10 hectoliters per hectare in 1816, which postulates a small farm at 2 ½ hectares, a middling farm at 5 hectares, and a large farm at 10 hectares. See Statistique générale, *Archives statistiques,* pp. 78–79. In approximate terms, French national grain production amounted to 4–5 hectoliters per capita, so the consumption figures are not too arbitrary, assuming an average family size of four or five persons.

12. Charléty, *Restauration,* p. 315. The land distribution as reported probably needs a large margin for error, but would have to be fictional to change these results significantly.

13. Robert Demoulin, *Guillaume Ier et la transformation économique des provinces belges 1815–1830* (Liège, 1938), pp. 182, 199, 213, 400; J. Dhont, ''The Cotton Industry at Ghent during the French Regime,'' trans. from the French by Michael B. Palmer, in *Essays in European Economic History 1789–1914,* ed. by F. Crouzet, W. H. Chaloner, and W. M. Stern (London, 1969), p. 27; Ernest Baasch, *Holländische Wirtschaftsgeschichte* (Jena, 1927), p. 454; Rondo E. Cameron, *France and the Economic Development of Europe, 1800–1914* (Princeton, 1961), pp. 14, 334.

14. Reinhart Koselleck, *Preussen zwischen Reform und Revolution: Allgemeines Landrecht, Verwaltung und Soziale Bewegung von 1791 bis 1848* (Stuttgart, 1967), pp. 491–92; Walter M. Simon, *The Failure of the Prussian Reform Movement 1807–1819* (Ithaca, 1955), pp. 91–99; Franz Schnabel, *Deutsche Geschichte im neunzehnten Jahrhundert* (2d ed.; 4 vols.; Freiburg im Breisgau, 1949–50), 2: 291–97.

15. Jerome Blum, *Noble Landowners and Agriculture in Austria 1815–1848* (Baltimore, 1948), pp. 153, 171–72; Joseph Marx von Liechtenstern, *Vollständiger Umriss der Statistik des österreichischen Kaiserstaats, mit Rücksicht auf dessen neueste Zustände* (Brünn, 1820), p. 293.

16. Ronald-Henri Hubscher, ''Une contribution à la connaissance des milieux populaires ruraux au XIXe siècle. Le livre de compte de la famille Flahaut (1811–1877),'' *Revue d'histoire économique et sociale* 47, no. 3 (1969): 367–70.

17. *The Times,* June 3, 1817, p. 2.

18. Johann Slokar, *Geschichte der österreichischen Industrie und ihrer Förderung unter Kaiser Franz I* (Vienna, 1914), p. 68.

19. Johann Friedrich Benzenberg, *Ueber Handel und Gewerbe, Steuren und Zölle* (Elberfeld, 1819), p. 172.

20. *The Times,* September 4, 1817, p. 2.

21. Mathias, *Industrial Nation,* p. 229.

22. See, for example, *Quotidienne* (Paris), August 12, 1817, p. 1; August 18, 1817, p. 1; September 9, 1817, p. 1.

23. Quoted in Chabert, *Revenus,* p. 213.

24. *The Times,* October 25, 1816, p. 2; December 6, 1816, p. 2.

25. Ibid., September 23, 1817, p. 2; September 30, 1817, p. 2.

26. Ibid., October 12, 1816, p. 3.

27. Ibid., December 4, 1816, p. 3; Henry Matthews, *The Diary of an Invalid. Being the Journal of a Tour in Poursuit of Health in Portugal, Italy, Switzerland and France in the Years 1817, 1818, and 1819* (3d ed.; Paris, 1825), p. 209.

28. Landes, Personal communication, dated November 25, 1974; also see idem, ''French Crises,'' pp. 197, 200–01.

29. Mathias, *Industrial Nation,* pp. 229–30.

30. Wilhelm Joseph Behr, *Das Recht und die Pflicht der Regierungen in Beziehung auf die gegenwärtige Theuerungsangelegenheit* (Würzburg, 1817), p. 25.

31. See *The Times,* September 25, 1817, p. 2; and for a detailed discussion of Marseilles and the Mediterranean typhus and plague epidemics, see the article reprinted from the *Journal de Marseille* in *Quotidienne,* May 1, 1817, p. 3.

32. For France, see *Quotidienne,* June 4, 1817, pp. 2–3; June 6, 1817, p. 2; June 15, 1817, p. 3; Robert Marjolin, ''Troubles provoqués en France par la disette de 1816–1817,'' *Revue d'histoire moderne,* new ser., 10 (November–December 1933): 425–48; for the Netherlands, *Moniteur* (Paris), June 17, 1817, p. 661; June 30, 1817, p. 713; *Quotidienne,* August 11, 1817,

p. 3; for Germany, see *The Times*, May 10, 1816, p. 3; January 1, 1817, p. 2; July 26, 1817, p. 2; *Gentleman's Magazine* 88 (January 1818): 72; for the United Kingdom, see *The Times*, May 10, 1816, p. 3; August 30, 1816, p. 2; November 28, 1816, p. 3; December 23, 1816, p. 3; January 27, 1817, p. 3; February 17, 1817, p. 3; April 19, 1817, p. 3.

33. Gustav von Gülich, *Geschichtliche Darstellung des Handels, der Gewerbe, und des Ackerbaus der bedeutendsten handeltreibenden Staaten unserer Zeit* (2 vols.; Jena, 1830), 2: 362–64; *Landwirthschaftliche Zeitung oder Der Land- und Hauswirth*, 15, no. 10 (1817): 92; Jones, *Seasons and Prices*, pp. 84–85, 160; Louis Guéneau, "La disette de 1816–1817 dans une région productrice de blé, la Brie," *Revue d'histoire moderne* 9 (January–February 1929): 21; *The Times*, August 22, 1818, p. 2; Johann von Csaplovics, *Gemälde von Ungern* (2 vols.; Budapest, 1829), 1: 142.

34. Gülich, *Geschichtliche Darstellung*, 2: 263.

35. Eleonore O. Sterling, "Anti-Jewish Riots in Germany in 1819: A Displacement of Social Protest," *Historia Judaica* 12 (April 1950): 112.

36. *The Times*, September 23, 1817, p. 3; October 18, 1817, p. 3.

37. Claude Étienne Chaillou-Desbarres, *Essai historique et critique sur la législation des grains jusqu'à ce jour* (Paris, 1820), p. 84.

38. *The Times*, September 2, 1817, p. 2.

39. Hedwig Pavelka, *Englisch-österreichische Wirtschaftsbeziehungen in der ersten Hälfte des 19. Jahrhunderts* (Graz, 1968), pp. 143–44.

40. Benzenberg, *Ueber Handel*, p. 172; Wolfgang Zorn, *Handels-und Industriegeschichte Bayerisch-Schwabens 1648–1870* (Augsburg, 1961), p. 128.

41. Thomas Tooke, *Thoughts and Details on the High and Low Prices of the Last Thirty Years* (London, 1823), part I, pp. 157–58; *The Times*, December 11, 1818, p. 2; William Jacob, *A View of the Agriculture, Manufacture, Statistics and State of Society, of Germany, and Parts of Holland and France* (London, 1820), p. 43.

42. Arthur H. Cole, "Cyclical and Seasonal Variations in the Sale of Public Lands 1816–1860," *Review of Economic Statistics* 9 (January 1927): 52; Malcolm J. Rohrbough, *The Land Office Business: The Settlement and Administration of American Public Lands, 1789–1837* (New York, 1968), pp. 91–92.

43. *The Times*, October 15, 1818, p. 2; Vernon J. Puryear, "Odessa: Its Rise and International Importance, 1815–1850," *Pacific Historical Review* 3 (1934): 195–97; Ludwik Tengoborskii, *Commentaries on the Productive Forces of Russia*, English translation (2 vols.; London, 1855–56), 2: 294.

44. Ignez Beidtel, *Geschichte der österreichischen Staatsverwaltung 1740–1848* (2 vols.; Innsbruck, 1896–98), 2: 303–04; Jean Vidalenc, *Le peuple des campagnes: la société française de 1815 à 1848* (Paris, 1969), p. 337; Abel, *Agrarkrisen*, pp. 209–23; Demoulin, *Guillaume Ier*, pp. 213–14; Hans Brugger, *Die schweizerische Landwirtschaft in der ersten Hälfte des 19. Jahrhundert* (Frauenfeld, 1956), pp. 127–28; William Jacob, *Report of the Trade in Foreign Corn, and on the Agriculture of the North of Europe* (3d ed.; London, 1826), p. 110, passim; United Kingdom, Parliamentary Papers, *Report from Committee on the Agriculture of the United Kingdom*, Session 23 January to 11 July, 1821, 9, p. 267; *The Times*, April 5, 1817, p. 3; Eleonore Sterling, *Er ist wie Du. Aus der Frühgeschichte des Antisemitismus in Deutschland (1815–1850)* (Munich, 1956), pp. 36–37; Gustav Otruba, "Wirtschaft und soziale Lage Österreichs im Vormärz," *Österreich in Geschichte und Literatur* 10 (1966): 161–76; Mario Romani, *Storia economica d'Italia nel secolo XIX* (2d ed.; Milan, 1970), pp. 37–45.

45. The wholesale price of leaf tobacco averaged $0.145 per pound in New Orleans in 1816 (in contrast to $0.085 in 1815 and $0.078 in 1817), and climbed to a monthly peak of $0.22 at Philadelphia from February through June 1816. Americans in London expressed amazement at the continuing high tobacco prices in the United States, in light of the depressed European demand and prices. Nonetheless, tobacco prices remained high through the winter of 1816–17. The unseasonable frosts and untimely precipitation of 1816 reduced the output of tobacco considerably. The early estimates of the 1816 crop in Virginia and North Carolina (the Virginia District) varied from 40,000 to 50,000 hogsheads, but only 29,222 were inspected by July 1, 1817, and the final volume of the crop amounted to 32,217 hogsheads (41,000 were inspected in 1816). See Joseph C. Robert, *The Tobacco Kingdom: Plantation, Market and Factory in Virginia*

aṅd North Carolina, 1800–1860 (Durham, N.C., 1938), pp. 17, 129, 137–38, 240; *Daily National Intelligencer* (District of Columbia), June 13, 1817, p. 2; *Thomas Jefferson's Farm Book,* ed. by Edwin Morris Betts (Princeton, 1953), pp. 215–16, 237, 256, 303–04; Lewis C. Gray, *History of Agriculture in the Southern United States to 1860* (2 vols.; Washington, D.C., 1931), 2: 1,038.

46. Rohrbough, *Land Office,* pp. 91–92; Matthew B. Hammond, *The Cotton Industry* (New York, 1897), p. 358.

47. As is well known, a tendency developed to impute both the rise of price levels and the subsequent deflation to the mismanagement of the money supply. The policies of the Second Bank of the United States were deemed to be dysfunctional. But it seems that overexpansion in the West would have taken place in the absence of the Second Bank. That high agricultural prices should have occasioned a boom in western lands is not surprising. Land speculation had long been a common phenomenon in America; and it would recur again under similar agricultural conditions. Deflation, moreover, would have ensued inevitably from the fall in world prices. For this view, see Douglass C. North, *The Economic Growth of the United States 1790–1860* (Englewood Cliffs, N.J., 1961), pp. 182–84; and Walter B. Smith, *Economic Aspects of the Second Bank of the United States* (Cambridge, Mass., 1953), pp. 113–14; for a view more critical of the Second Bank's role in facilitating the overexpansion, see Leon M. Schur, "The Second Bank of the United States and the Inflation after the War of 1812," *Journal of Political Economy* 68 (April 1960): 126–27, 132–33.

48. North, *Economic Growth,* pp. 13–14, 181–84; Murray N. Rothbard, *The Panic of 1819: Reactions and Policies* (New York and London, 1962), pp. 6–7; for an explanation of the similar economic events of 1836–37, see Matthews, *Trade-Cycle History,* pp. 59–60.

49. U.S., Bureau of the Census, *Historical Statistics of the United States: Colonial Times to 1957* (Washington, D.C., 1960), p. 538.

50. Bertrand Gille, *La banque et le crédit en France de 1815 à 1848* (Paris, 1959), pp. 294–97; for a similar view, see Clément Juglar, *Des crises commerciales et leur retour périodique en France, en Angleterre, et aux États-Unis* (2d ed.; Paris, 1889), pp. 14–15.

51. France, Statistique générale, *Statistique de la France: Commerce extérieur* (Paris, 1838), p. 263.

52. *The Times,* December 7, 1818, p. 2; see also *Quotidienne,* May 8, 1818, p. 3.

53. *The Times,* September 23, 1817, p. 2; Thomas Tooke and William Newmarch, *A History of Prices and of the State of Circulation from 1792 to 1856* (6 vols.; New York, 1857), 2: 24–25; *Quotidienne,* May 8, 1818, p. 3.

54. B. R. Mitchell and Phyllis Deane, *Abstract of British Historical Statistics* (Cambridge, 1962), p. 95; Tooke, *Prices,* part III, p. 181.

55. *Gentleman's Magazine* 89 (June 1819): 573.

56. The following unit prices were used in this computation: wheat 70s. per quarter, rye 35s.; barley 30s., oats 20s. These prices are based on the average grain prices at the Danzig market found in Jacob, *Foreign Corn,* p. 211; and the prices for wheat in Danzig and Königsberg, in Tooke, *Prices,* part 4, p. 65.

57. A. W. Acworth, *Financial Reconstruction in England 1815–1822* (London, 1925), p. 80.

58. For the same conclusion, see Arthur D. Gayer, W. W. Rostow, and Anna Jacobson Schwartz, *The Growth and Fluctuation of the British Economy 1790–1850* (2 vols.; London, 1953), 2: 563–64.

59. Abel, *Agrarkrisen,* p. 210.

CHAPTER VI

1. For example, Hans von Gagern began his account of the postwar years with the statement that Europe, particularly Germany, lived in constant apprehension of a conspiratorial revolution; see Hans C. von Gagern, *Mein Antheil an der Politik* (5 vols.; Stuttgart and Tübingen, 1823–45), 3: 1.

2. E. Levasseur, *Histoire des classes ouvrières et de l'industrie en France de 1789 à 1870* (2d ed.; 2 vols.; Paris, 1903–04), 1: 539.

3. Frederick B. Artz, *France under the Bourbon Restoration 1814–1830* (New York, 1963),

pp. 19, 70; G. de Bertier de Sauvigny, *La Restauration* (New ed.; Paris, 1955), p. 144; Sébastien Charléty, *La Restauration* (Paris, 1921), p. 144.

4. France, *Archives Parlementaries de 1787 à 1860*. *Recueil complet des débats législatifs & politiqes des chambres françaises*, 2d ser., vols. 15–26 (Paris, 1862–1913), 18: 128–29, 189, 640.

5. Félix Ponteil, *La monarchie parlementaire, 1815–1848* (Paris, 1949), pp. 58–59; Marquise de Montcalm, *Mon journal, 1815–1818: pendant le premier ministère de mon frère*, ed. by Sébastien Charléty (Paris, 1936), pp. 269, 278.

6. For a copy of the speech, see *The Times* (London), January 19, 1818, p. 2.

7. For similar conclusions, see Louis Guéneau, "La disette de 1816–1817 dans une région productrice de blé, la Brie," *Revue d'histoire moderne* 9 (January–February 1929): 31; Robert Marjolin, "Troubles provoqués en France par la disette de 1816–1817," ibid., New ser., 10 (November–December 1933): 459–60; Maurice Vergnaud, "Agitation politique et crise de subsistances à Lyon de Septembre 1816 à juin 1817," *Cahiers d'histoire* 2 (1957): 177; Jean Vidalenc, *Le département de l'Eure sous la monarchie constitutionnelle 1814–1848* (Paris, 1952), p. 153.

8. Ponteil, *Monarchie,* pp. 59–60; Bertier de Sauvigny, *Restauration,* pp. 142, 145.

9. Irene Collins, *The Government and the Newspaper Press in France 1814–1881* (London, 1959), p. 11; Charléty, *Restauration,* p. 110.

10. Bertier de Sauvigny, *Restauration,* p. 154.

11. *The Times,* February 6, 1818, p. 3.

12. Ibid., November 7, 1818, p. 3.

13. The ultraroyalists had failed to persuade the Allies to refuse to accept the accelerated indemnity payments and to continue the occupation. This attempted measure was promoted more by an unreconciled attitude toward the constitutional monarchy than by fear of revolution from the left. Apparently the explanation behind this *Note Secrète* was that it originated as a note requested by the Comte d'Artois, but fell into the hands of Decazes, who had a truncated version published; see Bertier de Sauvigny, *Restauration,* pp. 149–50.

14. *The Times,* January 1, 1819, p. 2; Bertier de Sauvigny, *Restauration,* pp. 154–57.

15. Marcel Marion, *Histoire financière de la France depuis 1815* (5 vols.; Paris, 1914–28), 4: 422–26; for discussion of the liquidity crisis, see the editorial essays in *The Times,* November 3, 1818, p. 2; November 4, 1818, p. 2; November 5, 1818, p. 2.

16. *The Times,* December 11, 1818, p. 2; December 16, 1818, p. 2.

17. Ibid., December 31, 1818, p. 2. The French government in 1818 still owed the Allies 280 million francs as the balance of the war indemnity, and also had agreed on April 25, 1818, to pay an additional 265 million francs in settlement of the claims of foreign individual creditors against the imperial and revolutionary governments. Once again, foreign banking contractors (Baring, Rothschild, Parish, among others) were called upon to collect and export the payments, particularly since the Allies insisted on this additional security. The foreign banking houses agreed to purchase 24 million in *rentes* (par value of 480 million francs). By December 12, 1818, the price of *rentes* on the Bourse had dropped to 60, after having been artificially sustained by the French government and the Bank of France in order to make a better bargain at Aix-la-Chapelle. Because of the bank panic, the foreign banking houses were not able to deliver the monthly payments to the Allies called for from January to September 1819. As a solution the Allies agreed to exchange their *rentes* for 100 million francs in 5 percent bonds that were not due until 1820 and 1821; see Ralph W. Hidy, *The House of Baring in American Trade and Finance* (Cambridge, Mass., 1949), pp. 60–62; Charléty, *Restauration,* pp. 114–15; Bertier de Sauvigny, *Restauration,* pp. 151–52.

18. *The Times,* January 1, 1819, p. 2.

19. Ibid.

20. Ibid., January 2, 1819, p. 2.

21. For a detailed analysis of the new press laws, see Collins, *Newspaper Press,* pp. 15–27.

22. Charléty, *Restauration,* p. 121.

23. Ponteil, *Monarchie,* p. 61.

24. Étienne Denis duc Pasquier, *Histoire de mon temps. Mémoirs du Chancelier Pasquier,* ed. by M. le duc D'Audiffret-Pasquier (3d ed.; 6 vols.; Paris, 1894–95), 4: 309–10.

25. For a description of the protest and these events, see R. J. White, *Waterloo to Peterloo*

(London, 1957), pp. 176–92; William Smart, *Economic Annals of the Nineteenth Century, 1801–1820* (New York, 1964), pp. 720–26; E. P. Thompson, *The Making of the English Working Class* (London, 1965), pp. 669–710.

26. Quoted in Frederick B. Artz, *Reaction and Revolution 1814–1832* (New York, Evanston, and London, 1963), pp. 124–26.

27. Pasquier, *Mémoirs*, 4: 355.

28. Charléty, *Restauration*, pp. 142–43. For the discussion in the Chamber of Deputies, which almost accused Decazes of complicity in the assassination, see France, *Archives parlementaires*, 26, p. 195.

29. Rondo E. Cameron, *France and the Economic Development of Europe* (Princeton, 1961), p. 36; for an account of the trend to protectionism in Prussia, see Wilhelm Treue, *Wirtschaftszustände und Wirtschaftspolitik in Preussen 1815–1825* (Stuttgart, 1937), pp. 83–89, 94–95, 121, 149; W. O. Henderson, *The Zollverein* (2d ed.; London, 1959), pp. 34–39.

30. Levasseur, *Classes ouvrières*, 1: 562–74; Shepard B. Clough, *France: A History of National Economics, 1789–1939* (New York, 1939), pp. 92–99; Charléty, *Restauration*, pp. 272–79; Artz, *France*, pp. 216–17; C. E. Labrousse, *Le mouvement ouvrier et les idées sociales en France de 1815 à la fin du XIXe siècle* (Paris, 1948), p. 68; Claude Étienne Chaillou-Des Barres, *Essai historique et critique sur la législation des grains jusqu'à ce jour* (Paris, 1820), pp. 157–60.

31. Reinhart Koselleck, *Preussen zwischen Reform und Revolution. Allgemeines Landrecht, Verwaltung und soziale Bewegung von 1791 bis 1848* (Stuttgart, 1967), pp. 299, 462–63, 570–71; for accounts of these mixed complaints in Württemberg, see the reports from Stuttgart in *Quotidienne* (Paris), March 4, 1816, p. 2; May 15, 1817, p. 3.

32. Theodore S. Hamerow, *Restoration, Revolution, Reaction: Economics and Politics in Germany 1815–1871* (Princeton, 1958), p. 48.

33. Walter M. Simon, *The Failure of the Prussian Reform Movement, 1807–1819* (Ithaca, N.Y., 1955), pp. 91–99; Franz Schnabel, *Deutsche Geschichte im neunzehnten Jahrhundert* (2d ed.; 4 vols.; Freiburg im Breisgau, 1949–50), 2: 291–97; Hamerow, *Restoration*, p. 4; Koselleck, *Preussen*, pp. 491–92.

34. Max Peters, *Die Entwicklung der deutschen Rhederei* (2 vols.; Jena, 1899–1905), 1: 55–56.

35. Ibid., pp. 56–57.

36. Wilhelm Abel, *Agrarkrisen und Agrarkonjunktur* (2d ed.; Hamburg and Berlin, 1966), p. 211.

37. Schnabel, *Deutsche Geschichte*, 2: 77–86.

38. F. Gunther Eyck, "The Political Theories and Activities of the German Academic Youth between 1815 and 1819," *Journal of Modern History* 27 (March 1955): 33–34.

39. For similar conclusions, see Gunther Meinhardt, "Die Auswirkungen der Hungerjahre in der ersten Hälfte des 19. Jahrhunderts auf Göttingen," *Göttinger Jahrbuch* 14 (1966): 215; and *The Times*, October 7, 1817, p. 2 (for a long article based on the observations of a traveler through Germany).

40. Gagern, *Mein Antheil*, 3: 149–50.

41. Prince Clemens L. W. Metternich, *Aus Metternich's nachgelassen Papieren*, ed. by Fürsten Richard Metternich-Winneburg (8 vols.; Vienna, 1880–84), 3: 52; Charles Eynard, *Vie de Madame de Krüdener* (2 vols.; Paris, 1849), 2: 222–25.

42. Karl-Georg Faber, "Görres, Weitzel und die Revolution (1819)," *Historische Zeitschrift* 194, Heft 1 (1962): 38, note.

43. Koselleck, *Preussen*, p. 299.

44. Schnabel, *Deutsche Geschichte*, 2: 245–48; Eyck, "German Academic Youth," pp. 27–28; Simon, *Prussian Reform Movement*, p. 122.

45. Eyck, "German Academic Youth," pp. 28, 34.

46. Metternich, *Papiere*, 3: 250–51.

47. Simon, *Prussian Reform Movement*, pp. 118–22.

48. Eyck, "German Academic Youth," p. 34.

49. Faber, "Görres," p. 37.

50. For explanations of this nature, see Selma Stern-Taeubler, "Der literarische Kampf um die Emanzipation in den Jahren 1816–1820 und seine ideologischen und soziologischen

Voraussetzungen," *Hebrew Union College Annual* 22, part 2 (1950–51): 179–80; J. M. Jost, *Neuere Geschichte der Israeliten von 1815–1845* (3 vols.; Berlin, 1846–47), 1: 48–105; Simon Dubnow, *Weltgeschichte des jüdischen Volkes*, vol. 9 (Berlin, 1929), pp. 11–22; Heinrich Graetz, *History of the Jews*, trans. by Bella Löwy (6 vols.; Philadelphia, 1891–98), 5: 520–28; Ismar Elbogen, *Geschichte der Juden in Deutschland* (Berlin, 1935), pp. 208–09; Adolf Lewin, *Geschichte der badischen Juden 1738–1909* (Karlsruhe, 1909), pp. 193–94.

51. For this view, see Eleonore O. Sterling, "Anti-Jewish Riots in Germany in 1819: A Displacement of Social Protest," *Historia Judaica* 12 (April 1950): 106–12; idem, *Er ist wie Du. Aus der Frühgeschichte des Antisemitismus in Deutschland 1815–1850* (Munich, 1956), pp. 32–37, 179–80.

52. For discussion of the constitutional and legal struggle over Jewish emancipation in 1814–15, see Dubnow, *Weltgeschichte*, pp. 12–15; Graetz, *Jews*, 5: 520.

53. Jakob Friedrich Fries, *Über der Gefährdung des Wohlstandes und Charakters der Deutschen durch die Juden. . . .* (Heidelberg, 1816), p. 10. The work also appeared in the *Heidelberger Jahrbücher der Literatur in 1816*. For discussion of Rühs' thought and similar German views, see Jost, *Israeliten*, 1: 48–50; Dubnow, *Weltgeschichte*, pp. 17–18.

54. Waldemar Gurian, "Antisemitism in Modern Germany," in *Essays on Anti-Semitism*, ed. by Koppel S. Pinson (New York, 1946), p. 224; Elbogen, *Juden*, p. 208; Graetz, *Jews*, 5: 521; Jost, *Israeliten*, 1: 51–52.

55. The term Hep-Hep has been associated with the initials of the Latin expression *Hierosolyma est perdita* (i.e., Jerusalem is destroyed), but whether this expression was revived from the time of the Crusades or originated in student slang is unsettled; see Graetz, *Jews*, 5: 528; Lewin, *Juden*, p. 193.

56. Dubnow, *Weltgeschichte*, pp. 22–23; Graetz, *Jews*, 5: 528–29; Jost, *Israeliten*, 1: 205; Elbogen, *Juden*, p. 210.

57. Sterling, *Er ist wie Du*, p. 181; Dubnow, *Weltgeschichte*, pp. 23–24; Graetz, *Jews*, 5: 529–30; Lewin, *Juden*, pp. 193–94.

58. Sterling, "Anti-Jewish Riots," pp. 129, 132–33; Jost, *Israeliten*, 1: 105–06; M. M. Haarbleicher, *Aus der Geschichte Deutsch-Israelitischen Gemeinde in Hamburg* (2d ed.; Hamburg, 1886), pp. 140–41; Dubnow, *Weltgeschichte*, p. 24.

59. Graetz, *Jews*, 5: 531–32; Jost, *Israeliten*, 1: 205; Elbogen, *Juden*, pp. 210–11.

60. Sterling, *Er ist wie Du*, pp. 180–81; idem, "Anti-Jewish Riots," pp. 107–32; Graetz, *Jews*, 5: 529–30.

61. Sterling, *Er ist wie Du*, pp. 36–37; idem, "Anti-Jewish Riots," p. 112; Gustav von Gülich, *Geschichtliche Darstellung des Handels, der Gewerbe und des Ackerbaus der bedeutendsten handeltreiben Staaten unserer Zeit* (2 vols.; Jena, 1830), 2: 363.

62. *The Times*, August 26, 1817, p. 2; Sterling, "Anti-Jewish Riots," p. 108.

63. *Quotidienne*, September 4, 1817, p. 1.

64. Graetz, *Jews*, 5: 531–32; Sterling, "Anti-Jewish Riots," p. 140.

65. Graetz, *Jews*, 5: 528; Dubnow, *Weltgeschichte*, p. 22; Elbogen, *Juden*, p. 208.

66. Quoted in Sterling, *Er ist wie Du*, p. 182.

Bibliography

PRIMARY SOURCES

American Monthly Magazine and Critical Review, 1817–18.

Annales de chimie de physique, 1816–19.

Annual Register, 1815–19

"Aus einem Schreiben des Professor Brandes zu Breslau, meteorologischen Inhalts." *Annalen der Physik* 55 (1817): 112–14.

Baines, Sir Edward. *History of the Cotton Manufacture in Great Britain and a View of the Present State of the Manufacture and the Conditions of the Classes Engaged in Its Several Departments.* London, 1835.

Baines, Thomas. *History of the Commerce and Town of Liverpool.* London, 1852.

Baldacci, Freiherr Anton von. "Über die inneren Zustände Österreichs. Eine Denkschrift aus dem Jahr 1816." Edited by F. von Krones. *Archiv für österreichische Geschichte* 74 (1889): 1–160.

Bamford, Samuel. *Passages in the Life of a Radical.* 2 vols. London, 1844.

Barstow, George. *History of New Hampshire.* Concord, N.H., 1842.

Bateman, Thomas, M.D. *A Succinct Account of the Typhus or Contagious Fever of this Country, Exemplified in the Epidemic which Prevailed in the Metropolis in 1817 and 1818.* 2d ed. London, 1820.

Beckley, Hosea. *The History of Vermont.* Brattleboro, 1846.

Behr, Wilhelm Joseph. *Das Recht und die Pflicht der Regierungen in Beziehung auf die gegenwärtige Theurungsangelegenheit.* Würzburg, 1817.

Bell, John, M.D. "A History of a Contagious Fever which Prevailed throughout Italy during the Greater Part of the Year 1817." *Philadelphia Journal of the Medical and Physical Sciences* 1 (1820): 22–34.

Benoiston de Chateauneuf, Louis François. *Considérations sur les enfans trouvés dans les principaux états de l'Europe.* Paris, 1824.

———. *Recherches sur les consommations de tout genre de la Ville de Paris en 1817; comparées à ce qu'elles etaient en 1789.* 2d ed. Paris, 1821.

Benzenberg, Johann Friedrich. *Ueber Handel und Gewerbe, Steuren und Zölle.* Elberfeld, 1819.

Bernoulli, Christoph. *Schweizerisches Archiv für Statistik und Nationalökonomie.* 5 vols. Basel, 1827–31.

Blackwoods Edinburgh Magazine. 1817–19.

Bourgin, Georges, and Bourgin, Hubert, eds. *Les patrons, les ouvriers et l'état. Le régime de l'industrie en France de 1814 à 1830.* Vol. 1: May 1814–May 1821. Paris, 1912.

Bradley, Joshua. *Accounts of Religious Revivals in Many Parts of the United States from 1815 to 1818.* Albany, 1819.

Breckenridge, Richard. "Diary, 1816." Alabama Historical Society, *Transactions of the Alabama Historical Society* (1898–99): 142–53.

Buck, Solon J., ed. "Pioneer Letters of Gershom Flagg." *Transactions of the Illinois State Historical Society* 15 (1910): 139–83.

Buxton, Sir Thomas Fowell. *The Speech of Thomas Fowell Buxton Esq. at the Egyptian Hall, on the 26th November, 1816 on the Subject of the Distress in Spitalfields. To Which Is Added the Report of the Spitalfields Association Read at the Meeting.* London, 1816.

Carter, Clarence E., ed. *The Territorial Papers of the United States.* 25 vols. Washington, D.C., 1934–.

Chabrol de Crousol, M. le Comte. *Sur les événements de Lyon, au mois de juin 1817.* Paris, 1818.

Chaillou-Des Barres, Claude Étienne. *Essai historique et critique sur la législation des grains jusqu'à ce jour.* Paris, 1820.

Chaptal de Chanteloupe, Comte Antoine Claude. *De l'industrie française.* 2 vols. Paris, 1819.

Chladni, E. F. F. "Ueber die Ursachen des nasskalten Sommer von 1816, und zum Theil auch 1817." *Annalen der Physik* 62 (1819): 132–36.

Clausewitz, Carl von. *Politische Schriften und Briefe.* Edited by Hans Rothfels. Munich, 1922.

Cowan, Robert, M.D. "Vital Statistics of Glasgow, Illustrating the Sanatory Conditions of the Population." *Journal of the Statistical Society* 3 (1840–41): 257–92.

Csaplovics, Johann von. *Gemälde von Ungern.* 2 vols. Budapest, 1829.

Demian, Julius Andrea. *Der deutsche Bund in seiner Gesammtkraft.* Leipzig, 1818.

Desuttes, M. le Chevalier. *Réponse de M. le Chevalier Desuttes, Prevôt du Département du Rhône, à un Écrit intitulé Lyon en 1817, Par m. le Colonel Fabvier.* Lyons, 1818.

Dewey, Chester. "Results of Meteorological Observations Made at Williamstown, Massachusetts." *Memoirs of the American Academy of Arts and Sciences* 4 (1818–21): 387–92.

Dulaure, Jacques Antoine. *Histoire civile, physique et morale de Paris.* 3d ed. 10 vols. Paris, 1825.

Dupin, Charles Baron. *Forces productives et commerciales de la France.* 2 vols. Paris, 1827.

Foot, Malachi. "Atmospheric Constitution of New York, from October, 1816 to January 1, 1817." *New York Medical Repository,* N. S., 3 (1817): 408–11.

France. *Archives parlementaires de 1787 à 1860. Recueil complet des débats législatifs & politiques dans chambres françaises.* 2d Ser. Vols. 15–26. Paris, 1862–1913.

———. *Collection complète des lois, décrets, ordonnances, réglements, et avis du Conseil-d'État.* Edited by Jean Baptiste Duvergier de Hauranne. 24 vols. Paris, 1824–32.

———. Ministère de l'Intérieur. *Circulaires, instructions et autre actes émanés du ministère de l'intérieur de 1797 à 1821 inclusivement.* 2d ed. 6 vols. Paris, 1821–30.

———. Statistique générale. *Documents statistiques sur la France.* Paris, 1835.

———. Statistique générale. *Archives statistiques du ministère des travaux publics, de l'agriculture et du commerce.* Paris, 1837.

————. Statistique générale. *Statistique de la France: Territoire, population.* Paris, 1837.

————. Statistique générale. *Statistique de la France: Commerce extérieur.* Paris, 1838.

————. Statistique générale. *Statistique de la France: Administration publique.* 2 vols. Paris, 1843.

Franscini, Stefano. *Statistique de la Suisse: La Suisse, géographique, industrielle et agricole.* Bern, 1855.

Fries, Jakob Friedrich. *Über der Gefährdung des Wohlstandes und Charakters der Deutschen durch die Juden.* Heidelberg, 1816.

Gagern, Hans C. von. *Mein Antheil an der Politik.* 5 vols. Stuttgart and Tübingen, 1823–45.

Gentleman's Magazine, 1816–19.

Goodrich, Samuel Griswold. *Recollections of a Lifetime.* 2 vols. New York, 1850.

Gülich, Gustav von. *Geschichtliche Darstellung des Handels, der Gewerbe und des ackerbaus der bedeutendsten handeltreibenden Staaten unserer Zeit.* 2 vols. Jena, 1830.

Harty, William M.D. *An Historic Sketch of the Causes, Progress, Extent, and Mortality of the Contagious Fever Epidemic in Ireland during the Years 1817, 1818, and 1819.* Dublin, 1820.

Haynsworth, James, M.D. "Some Account of the Winter Epidemic of 1815, 16, and 17, as It Appeared in Salem and Claremont Counties." *New York Medical Repository,* N. S., 4 (1818): 1–14.

Hazzi, Staatsrath Joseph Ritter von. *Betrachtungen über Theurung und Noth der Vergangenheit und Gegenwart.* Munich, 1818.

Hoffmann, Johann Gottfried. "Uebersicht der im Preussischen Staate im Jahre 1841 vorgekommenen Geburten, Trauungen und Todesfälle . . . von 1816 bis mit 1840." *Sammlung kleiner Schriften.* Berlin, 1843.

Holyoke, Edward A. "Observations Made with Fahrenheit's Thermometer, at Salem, Mass. from the Year 1793 to the Year 1818." *Memoirs of the American Academy of Arts and Sciences* 4 (1818–21): 361–82.

Hoskins, Nathan. *A History of the State of Vermont.* Vergennes, Vermont, 1831.

Jacob, William. "An Inquiry into the Causes of Agricultural Distress." *Pamphleteer* 10 (1817): 395–418.

————. *Report of the Trade in Foreign Corn, and on the Agriculture of the North of Europe.* 3d ed. London, 1826.

————. *A View of the Agriculture, Manufacture, Statistics and State of Society, of Germany, and Parts of Holland and France.* London, 1820.

Jameson, James. *Report on the Epidemick Cholera Morbus, As It Visited the Territories Subject to the Presidency of Bengal in the Years 1817, 1818, and 1819.* Calcutta, 1820.

Thomas Jefferson's Farm Book. Edited by Edwin Morris Betts. Princeton, 1953.

Jerome, Chauncy. *History of the American Clock Business for the Past Sixty years and Life of Chauncy Jerome.* New Haven, 1860.

Jones, Pomroy. *Annals & Recollections of Oneida County.* Rome, New York, 1851.

Jost, J. M. *Neuere Geschichte der Israeliten von 1815–1845.* 3 vols. Berlin, 1846–47.

Junghuhn, Franz Wilhelm. *Java: seine Gestalt, Pflanzendecke und innere Bauart.* Trans. from the Dutch by J. K. Hasskarl. 3 vols. Leipzig, 1857.

Landwirthschaftliche Zeitung oder Der Land- und Hauswirth, XIV–XVI, 1816–18.

Leichtenstern, Joseph Marx von. *Statistisch-topographischer Landesschematismus des Herzogthums Steyermark.* Vienna, 1818.

————. *Vollständiger Umriss der Statistik des österreichischen Kaiserstaats, mit Rücksicht auf dessen neueste Zustände.* Brünn, 1820.

Le Sur, Charles Louis. *La France et les Français en 1817.* Paris, 1817.

Marshall, J. D., ed. *Autobiography of William Stout of Lancaster 1665–1752*. Manchester, 1967.

Matthews, Henry. *The Diary of an Invalid. Being the Journal of a Tour in Poursuit of Health in Portugal, Italy, Switzerland and France in the Years 1817, 1818, and 1819*. 3d ed. Paris, 1825.

Memoirs of the Philadelphia Society for Promoting Agriculture 4 (1818).

Metternich, Prince Clemens L. W. *Aus Metternich's nachgelassenen Papieren*. Edited by Fürsten Richard Metternich-Winneburg. 8 vols. Vienna, 1880–84.

Missouri Gazette. 1816.

Mr. Jackson's Weather Log, Jan. 1814–Dec. 1848. Farmer's College, College Hill, Ohio. National Archives, Washington, D.C.

Mitchell, Dr. Thomas D. "Atmospheric Constitution of New York, from March to July 1816." *New York Medical Repository*, N. S., 3 (1817): 301–07.

Moniteur (Paris). 1815–18.

Montcalm, Marquise de. *Mon journal, 1815–1818: pendant le premier ministère de mon frère*. Edited by Sébastien Charléty. Paris, 1936.

Montgelas, Maximilian Grafen von, *Denkwürdigkeiten (1799–1817)*. Edited by Ludwig Grafen von Montgelas. Trans. from the French by Max Freiherrn von Freyberg-Eisenberg. Stuttgart, 1887.

Moseley, W. M. "Bemerkungen über die Sonnenflecken des Jahres 1816." *Annalen der Physik* 58 (1818): 406–16.

Nashville (Tennessee) *Whig*. 1816–17.

National Intelligencer (District of Columbia). 1816–17.

Niles' Weekly Register. 1816–17.

North American Review 3 (1816).

Oekonomische Neuigkeiten und Verhandlungen. Zeitschrift für alle Zweige der Land- und Hauswirthschaft, des Forst- und Jagdwesens im oesterreichischen Kaiserthum und dem ganzen Deutschland. 1816–18.

Ozanam, J. A. F. *Histoire médicale générale et particulière des maladies épidémiques, contagieuses et épizootiques*. 2d ed. 4 vols. Paris, 1835.

Pahl, Johann Gottfried von. *Geschichte von Wirtemberg*. 6 vols. Stuttgart, 1827–31.

Pasquier, Étienne Denis duc. *Histoire de mon temps. Mémoires du Chancelier Pasquier*. Edited by M. le duc D'Audiffret-Pasquier. 3d ed. 6 vols. Paris, 1894–95.

Peach, Arthur W., ed. "As the Years Pass—The Diaries of Seth Shaler Arnold (1788–1871), A Vermonter." *Vermont Historical Society Proceedings*, N. S., 8 (June 1940): 107–93.

Porter, G. R. *The Progress of the Nation*. 2 vols. London, 1836–38.

Prus, René-Clovis. *Rapport à l'Académie Royale de Médecine sur la peste et les quarantines*. 2 vols. Paris, 1846.

Prussia. *Preussische Statistik* 48, A (1879).

Quetelet, Adolphe. *Sur l'homme et le développement de ses facultés*. 2 vols. Paris, 1835.

Quotidienne (Paris). 1816–18.

Raffles, Sophia, ed. *Memoir of the Life and Public Services of Sir Thomas Raffles*. London, 1830.

Raffles, Thomas. *Letters, during a Tour through Some Parts of France, Savoy, Switzerland, Germany, and the Netherlands in the Summer of 1817*. Liverpool, 1818.

Raffles, Sir Thomas Stamford. *The History of Java*. 2d ed. 2 vols. London, 1830.

Raleigh Register and North Carolina Gazette. 1816–17.

Rambuteau, Claude-Philibert Barthelot comte de. *Mémoires*. Paris, 1905.

Records of the Moravians in North Carolina 1752–1879. Edited by Adelaide L. Fries. 11 vols. Raleigh, N.C., 1947.

Report of the Committee, Appointed at a General Meeting of the Inhabitants of Edinburgh, for Affording Relief to the Labouring Classes in the City and Suburbs. Edinburgh, 1817.

Robbins, Thomas. *Diary of Thomas Robbins.* Edited by Increase N. Tarbox. 2 vols. Boston, 1886.

The Papers of Thomas Ruffin. Edited by J. G. Roulhac Hamilton. 4 vols. Raleigh, N.C., 1918–20.

Savage, William. *Observations on Emigration to the United States of America.* London, 1819.

Schnurrer, Friedrich. *Chronik der Seuchen. Die Krankheiten des Menschen-Geschlechts.* 2 vols. Tübingen, 1823–25.

Schweizerische Monathschronik. 1816–17.

Simond, Louis. *Switzerland; or, a Journal of a Tour and Residence in that Country, in the Years 1817, 1818, and 1819.* 2 vols. Boston, 1822.

Short, Thomas. *New Observations on City, Town and Country Bills of Mortality.* London, 1750.

Somerville, Alexander. *The Autobiography of a Working Man.* Edited by John Carswell. London, 1951.

Southwell, T. "An Account of the Severe Winter of 1739–40 and of Its Effects in the County of Norfolk in the Year Following." *Norfolk and Norwich Naturalists Society, Transactions* 2 (1875): 125–30.

Sparks, Jared, ed. *The Works of Benjamin Franklin.* 10 vols. Boston, 1836–40.

Springer, Johann. *Statistik der österreichischen Kaiserstaates.* 2 vols. Vienna, 1840.

Süssmilch, Johann Peter. *Die göttliche Ordnung in den Veränderungen des menschlichen Geschlechts.* Edited by Christian Jacob Baumann. 3d ed. 2 vols. Berlin, 1798.

Sweden. Statistiska Centralbyrån. *Historisk Statistik för Sverige.* Vol 1: *Befolkning 1720–1967.* Stockholm, 1969.

Switzerland. Statistisches Bureau. *Schweizerische Statistik/Statistique de la Suisse.* Lieferungen No. 103 (1895), No. 112 (1897), no. 128 (1901).

Thomas, David. *Travels through the Western Country in the Summer of 1816.* Auburn, New York, 1819.

Thomas, Isaiah. "Diary, 1805–1828." Edited by Benjamin Thomas Hill. *Transactions and Collections of the American Antiquarian Society* 9 (1909).

Thompson, Zadock. *History of Vermont, Natural, Civil, and Statistical.* 2d ed. 3 vols. Burlington, Vermont, 1842.

The Times (London). 1816–19.

Tooke, Thomas. *Thoughts and Details on the High and Low Prices of the Last Thirty Years.* London, 1823.

———, and Newmarch, William. *A History of Prices and of the State of Circulation from 1792 to 1856.* 6 vols. New York, 1857.

"Tracts on the Causes, Cure, and Prevention of Contagious Fever." *The Edinburgh Review* 21 no. 62 (March 1819): 413–40.

United Kingdom. Parliamentary Papers. *Report from Committee on the Agriculture of the United Kingdom.* Vol. 9. 1821.

United States. Bureau of the Census. *Historical Statistics of the United States. Colonial Times to 1957.* Washington, D.C., 1960.

———. Congress. House. Evans, Charles H. "Exports, Domestic and Foreign, from the American Colonies to Great Britain, from 1697 to 1789, Inclusive. Exports, Domestic and Foreign, from the United States to all Countries from 1789 to 1883, Inclusive." *House*

Miscellaneous Documents, 48th Cong., 1st sess., No. 49, Part 2, 1884, Serial 2236, Table 2.

———. Department of Agriculture, Bureau of Statistics—Circular 32. *Cotton Crop of the United States, 1790–1911.* Compiled by George K. Holmes. Washington, D.C., 1912.

———. Department of Agriculture, Bureau of Statistics—Circular 33. *Tobacco Crop of the United States, 1612–1911.* Compiled by George K. Holmes. Washington, D.C., 1912.

———. Department of Agriculture, Bureau of Statistics—Circular 34. *Rice Crop of the United States, 1712–1911.* Compiled by George K. Holmes. Washington, D.C., 1912.

Vanderlinden, Émile. "Chronique des événements météorologiques en Belgique jusqu'en 1834." *Mémoires de l'Académie Royale de Belgique, Classe des Sciences,* 2d Ser., 6 (1924): 1–329.

Vaterländisches Archiv des Königreichs Hannover. 1820–21.

Vermont Historical Gazetteer. Edited by Abby Maria Hemenway. 5 vols. Burlington, Vermont, 1867.

Western Intelligencer (Columbus, Ohio). 1816–17.

Western Spy (Cincinnati). 1816–17.

Whiton, John Milton. *Sketches of the History of New-Hampshire.* Concord, New Hampshire, 1834.

Williamson, William Durkee. *The History of the State of Maine.* 2 vols. Hallowell, Maine, 1832.

Württembergishes Jahrbuch. 1818–19.

Zollikofer, Ruprecht. *Der Osten meinen Vaterlandes, oder die Kantone St. Gallen und Appenzell im Hungerjahre 1817. Ein Denkmal jener Schreckens-Epoche. Von einem Mitglied der Hülfsgesellschaft in St. Gallen.* 2 vols. St. Gall, 1818–19.

SECONDARY WORKS

Abbot, C. G., and Fowle, F. E. "Volcanoes and Climate." *Smithsonian Miscellaneous Collections* 60, no. 29, Publication no. 2176, March 28, 1913.

Abel, Wilhelm. *Agrarkrisen und Agrarkonjunktur.* 2d ed. Hamburg and Berlin, 1966.

———. *Massenarmut und Hungerkrisen im vorindustriellen Europa.* Hamburg and Berlin, 1974.

Abernethy, Thomas Perkins. *The Formative Period in Alabama, 1815–1828.* University, Alabama, 1965.

———. *The South in the New Nation.* Baton Rouge, Louisiana, 1961.

Ackerknecht, Erwin H. *Geschichte und Geographie der wichtigsten Krankheiten.* Stuttgart, 1963.

———. *Medicine at the Paris Hospital 1794–1848.* Baltimore, 1967.

Adams, William F. *Ireland and Irish Emigration to the New World from 1815 to the Famine.* New Haven, 1932.

Alexander, John T. "Catherine II, Bubonic Plague, and Industry in Moscow." *American Historical Review* 79 (June 1974): 637–71.

Alexander, William Henry. *A Climatological History of Ohio.* Columbus, Ohio, 1924.

Aoki, Koji. *Hyakushō Ikki no Nenjiteki Kenkyā.* Tokyo, 1966.

Appleby, Andrew B. "Nutrition and Disease: The Case of London 1550–1750." *Journal of Interdisciplinary History* 6 (Summer 1975): 1–22.

Arakawa, H. "Meteorological Conditions of the Great Famines in the Last Half of the Tokugawa Period, Japan." *Papers in Meteorology and Geophysics* 6 (September 1955): 101–16.

Armengaud, André. "Population in Europe 1700–1914." *Fontana Economic History of Europe,* vol. 3, section 1. Edited by Carlo M. Cipolla. London and Glasgow, 1970.

Armstrong, Alan. *Stability and Change in an English County Town: A Social Study of York 1801–51.* London, 1974.

Artz, Frederick B. *France under the Bourbon Restoration 1814–1830.* New York, 1963.

————. *Reaction and Revolution 1814–1832.* New York, Evanston, and London, 1963.

Ashton, Thomas Southcliffe. *Economic Fluctuations in England 1700–1800.* London, 1959.

————. *Iron and Steel in the Industrial Revolution.* London, 1924.

Assante, Franca. La Puglia demografica nel secolo XIX°. Naples, 1967.

Baasch, Ernst. *Hollandische Wirtschaftgeschichte.* Jena, 1927.

Baker, T. H. *Records of the Seasons, Prices of Agricultural Produce, and Phenomena Observed in the British Isles.* London, 1884.

Baltazard, M. "Déclin et Destin d'une Maladie infectieuse: la peste." *Bulletin of the World Health Organization* 23, nos. 2–3 (1960): 247–62.

Bandettini, Pierfrancesco, ed. *La popolazione della Toscana dal 1810 al 1959.* Florence, 1961.

Barger, George. *Ergot and Ergotism.* London, 1931.

Barnett, D. C. "Allotments and the Problem of Rural Poverty, 1780–1840." *Land, Labour and Population in the Industrial Revolution.* Edited by E. L. Jones and G. E. Mingay. London, 1967.

Bechtolsheimer, Heinrich. "Die Provinz Rheinhessen in den beiden ersten Jahrzehnten ihres Bestehens." *Quellen und Forschungen zur hessischen Geschichte* 4 (1916): 1–143.

Becker, Siegfried. *Die Bevölkerungs-Verhältnisse der österreichischen Monarchie.* Vienna, 1846.

Beer, Adolf. *Die Finanzen Oesterreichs im XIX. Jahrhundert.* Prague, 1877.

Beidtel, Ignaz. *Geschichte der österreichischen Staatsverwaltung 1740–1848.* 2 vols. Innsbruck, 1896–98.

Belletini, Athos. *La popolazione di Bologna dal secolo XV all'unificazione italiana.* Bologna, 1961.

Berry, Thomas Senior. *Western Prices before 1861.* Cambridge, Massachusetts, 1943.

Bertier de Sauvigny, G. de. *La Restauration.* New ed. Paris, 1955.

Beveridge, Sir William H. "Weather and Harvest Cycles." *Economic Journal* 31 (December 1921): 429–52.

————, and Others. *Prices and Wages in England from the Twelfth to the Nineteenth Century.* Vol 1: *Price Tables: Mercantile Era.* London, 1939.

Bickel, Wilhelm. *Bevölkerungsgeschichte und Bevölkerungspolitik der Schweiz.* Zürich, 1947.

Biraben, J.-N., and Le Goff, Jacques. "The Plague in the Early Middle Ages." *Biology of Man in History.* Edited by Robert Forster and Orest Ranum. Trans. from the French by Elborg Forster and Patricia M. Ranum. Baltimore and London, 1975.

Biucchi, B. M. "The Industrial Revolution in Switzerland." Trans. by Muriel Grindrod. *Fontana Economic History of Europe,* Vol. 4, Section 10. Edited by Carlo M. Cipolla. London, 1969.

Blaschke, Karlheinz. *Bevölkerungsgeschichte von Sachsen bis zur industriellen Revolution.* Weimar, 1967.

Blayo, Yves, and Henry, Louis. "Données démographiques sur la Bretagne et l'Anjou de 1740 à 1829." *Annales de démographie historique,* 1967.

Blodgett, Lorin. *Climatology of the United States.* Philadelphia, 1857.

Blok, Pieter Jan. *Geschiedenis van het Nederlandsche Volk.* 8 vols. Leiden, 1892–1908.

Blum, Jerome. *Noble Landowners and Agriculture in Austria, 1815–1848.* Baltimore, 1948.

————. "Transportation and Industry in Austria 1815–1848." *Journal of Modern History* 15 (March 1943): 24–38.

Blumberg, Horst. *Die deutsche Textilindustrie in der industriellen Revolution.* Berlin, 1965.

Boggess, Arthur C. *Settlement of Illinois, 1778–1830.* Chicago, 1908.

Bondi, Gerhard. *Deutschlands Aussenhandel 1815–1870.* Berlin, 1958.

Bowley, Arthur O. *Wages in the United Kingdom in the Nineteenth Century.* Cambridge, 1900.

Braudel, Fernand. *Capitalism and Material Life 1400–1800.* Trans. by Miriam Kochan. New York, and London, 1973.

———, and Labrousse, Ernest, eds. *Histoire économique et sociale de la France.* Vol. 2: *1660–1789.* Paris, 1970.

Broeker, Galen. *Rural Disorder and Police Reform in Ireland, 1812–36.* London, 1970.

Brooks, C. E. P. *Climate through the Ages.* Rev. ed. New York, 1949.

Brückner, Eduard. "Klimaschwankungen seit 1700." *Geographische Abhandlungen* 4, no. 2 (1890): 155–325.

Brugger, Hans. *Die schweizerische Landwirtschaft in der ersten Hälfte des 19. Jahrhunderts.* Frauenfeld, 1956.

Brugmans, I. J. "Economic Fluctuations in the Netherlands in the Nineteenth Century." Trans. from the Dutch by Alice C. Carter and Sytha Hart. *Essays in European Economic History 1789–1914.* Edited by F. Crouzet, W. H. Chaloner, and W. M. Stern. London, 1969.

Brunt, D. "Periodicities in European Weather." *Philosophical Transactions of the Royal Society of London,* Series A, 215 (1925): 247–302.

Buck, Norman Sydney. *The Development of the Organization of Anglo-American Trade, 1800–1850.* New Haven, 1925.

Buer, M. C. *Health, Wealth, and Population in the Early Days of the Industrial Revolution.* London, 1926.

———. "The Trade Depression following the Napoleonic Wars." *Economica* 1 (May 1921): 159–79.

Bulletin of the World Health Organization 23, nos. 2–3 (1960).

Burnet, Sir Macfarlane, and White, David O. *Natural History of Infectious Disease.* 4th ed. Cambridge, 1972.

Cahill, George F., Jr., M.D. "Starvation in Man." *New England Journal of Medicine* 282 (March 1970): 668–75.

Cameron, Rondo E. *France and the Economic Development of Europe, 1800–1914.* Princeton, 1961.

Camp, Wesley D. *Marriage and the Family in France since the Revolution.* New York, 1961.

Castellan, Georges. "Fourrages et bovins dans l'économie rurale de la Restauration." *Revue d'histoire économique et sociale* 38, no. 1 (1960): 77–97.

Catterall, Ralph C. H. *The Second Bank of the United States.* Chicago, 1903.

Chabert, Alexandre. *Essai sur les mouvements des prix en France de 1798 à 1820.* Paris, 1945.

———. *Essai sur les mouvements des revenus et de l'activité économique en France de 1789 à 1820.* Paris, 1949.

Chambers, J. D. *Population, Economy, and Society in Pre-Industrial England.* London, 1972.

———. *The Vale of Trent.* Supplement No. 3, *Economic History Review.* London, 1957.

———, and Mingay, G. E. *The Agricultural Revolution 1750–1880.* London, 1966.

Charléty, Sébastien. *La Restauration.* Paris, 1921.

Charlier, J. *La peste à Bruxelles de 1667 à 1669 et ses conséquences démographiques.* Brussels, 1969.

Chatelain, Abel. "Recherches et enquêtes démogéographiques: les migrations française vers le Nouveau Monde aux XIXᵉ et XXᵉ siècles." *Annales: E. S. C.* 2 (January–March 1947): 53–70.

Cherif, M. H. "Expansion européenne et difficultés tunisiennes de 1815 à 1830." *Annales: E. S. C.* 25 (May–June, 1970): 714–45.

Chevalier, Louis. "L'émigration française au XIXe siècle." *Études d'histoire moderne et contemporaine* 1 (1947): 127–71.

Cipolla, Carlo A. *Christofano and the Plague.* Berkeley, 1973.

————. "Four Centuries of Italian Demographic Development." *Population in History.* Edited by D. V. Glass and D. E. C. Eversley. London, 1965.

Clark, John C. *The Grain Trade in the Old Northwest.* Urbana, Illinois, 1966.

Clayton, H. H. "Sunspot Changes and Weather Changes." *Smithsonian Miscellaneous Collections* 104, no. 19 (March 6, 1946): 1–29.

Clough, Shepard Bancroft. *France. A History of National Economics, 1789–1939.* New York, 1939.

Cobb, Richard. *The Police and the People: French Popular Protest 1789–1820.* Oxford, 1970.

Cockburn, Aidan, M.D. *The Evolution and Eradication of Infectious Diseases.* Baltimore and London, 1963.

Cole, Arthur H. "Cyclical and Seasonal Variations in the Sale of Public Lands, 1816–60." *Review of Economic Statistics* 9 (January 1927): 42–53.

————. *Wholesale Commodity Prices in the United States, 1700–1861.* Cambridge, Massachusetts, 1938.

Collins, Irene. *The Government and the Newspaper Press in France 1814–1881.* London, 1959.

Connell, K. H. *The Population of Ireland 1750–1845.* London, 1950.

Contamine, Henry. *Les conséquences financières des invasions de 1814 et de 1815 dans les départements de la Moselle et de la Meurthe.* Metz, 1932.

————. *Metz et la Moselle de 1814 à 1870.* 2 vols. Nancy, 1932.

Craeybeckx, Jan. "The Beginnings of the Industrial Revolution in Belgium." Trans. from the French by Rondo E. Cameron. *Essays in French Economic History.* Edited by Rondo E. Cameron. Homewood, Illinois, 1970.

Crawley, C. W., ed. *War and Peace in an Age of Upheaval 1793–1830.* Vol. IX of *The New Cambridge Modern History.* Cambridge, 1965.

Creighton, Charles. *A History of Epidemics in Britain.* 2 vols. Cambridge, 1891–94.

Crouzet, François. "Wars, Blockade, and Economic Change in Europe 1792–1815." *Journal of Economic History* 24 (December 1964): 567–90.

Danière, Andre. "Feudal Incomes and the Demand Elasticity for Bread in the Late Eighteenth Century." *Journal of Economic History* 18 (September 1958): 317–31, 339–41.

Darvall, Frank O. *Popular Disturbances and Public Order in Regency England.* London, 1934.

Dechesne, Laurent. *Histoire économique et sociale de la Belgique.* Liège, 1932.

Demoulin, Robert. *Guillaume Ier et la transformation économique des provinces belges, 1815–1830.* Liège, 1938.

Deprez, P. "The Demographic Development of Flanders in the Eighteenth Century." *Population in History.* Edited by D. V. Glass and D. E. C. Eversley. London, 1965.

Deyon, Pierre. *Amiens, capitale provinciale.* Paris, 1967.

Dhondt, J. "The Cotton Industry at Ghent during the French Regime." Trans. from the French by Michael B. Palmer. *Essays in European Economic History 1789–1914.* Edited by F. Crouzet, W. H. Chaloner, and W. M. Stern. London, 1969.

Ditz, Heinrich. *Die ungarische Landwirthschaft.* Leipzig, 1867.

Dodd, Arthur H. *The Industrial Revolution in North Wales.* 2d ed. Cardiff, 1951.

Dorwart, Reinhold A. *The Prussian Welfare State before 1740.* Cambridge, Massachusetts, 1971.

Dove, H. W. "Über die nicht periodischen Änderungen der Temperaturvertheilung auf der Oberfläsche der Erde." *Abhandlungen der Königlichen Akademie der Wissenschaften zu Berlin.* Erste Abhandlung (1838): 285–415. Zweite Abhandlung (1839): 305–440. Dritte Abhandlung (1842): 117–241.

Drake, Michael. "The Irish Demographic Crisis of 1740–41." *Historical Studies* 6 (1968): 101–24.

―――. *Population and Society in Norway 1735–1865.* Cambridge, 1969.

Dubnow, Simon. *Weltgeschichte des jüdischen Volkes.* Vol. 9. Berlin, 1929.

Duchaussoy, M. H. "Les bans de vendanges de la région parisienne." *La Météorologie* (March–April, 1934): 111–88.

Dunham Arthur L. "Economic History of France 1815–1870." *Journal of Modern History* 21 (June 1949): 121–39.

―――. *The Industrial Revolution in France 1815–48.* New York, 1955.

Dyer, A. J. "The Effect of Volcanic Eruptions on Global Turbidity, and an Attempt to Detect Long-term Trends Due to Man." *Journal of the Royal Meteorological Society* 100 (October 1974): 563–71.

Easton, C. *Les hivers dans l'Europe occidentale.* Leiden, 1928.

Eisenhart Rothe, Wilfried, and Ritthaler, A. *Vorgeschichte und Begründung des deutschen Zollvereins, 1815–1834.* 3 vols. Berlin, 1934.

Elbogen, Ismar. *Geschichte der Juden in Deutschland.* Berlin, 1935.

Ellison, Thomas. *The Cotton Trade of Great Britain.* New York, 1968.

Elsas, Moritz J. *Umriss einer Geschichte der Preise und Löhne in Deutschland vom ausgehenden Mittelalter bis zum Beginn des 19. Jahrhunderts.* 2 vols. Leiden, 1936–49.

Erman, Adolf. *Reise um die Erde durch Nord-Asien und die beiden Oceane in den Jahren 1828, 1829, and 1830.* Vol. 3: *Historischer Bericht.* Berlin, 1848.

Ernle, Lord. *English Farming Past and Present.* 6th ed. Chicago, 1961.

Eversley, D. E. C. "Population, Economy and Society." *Population in History.* Edited by D. V. Glass and D. E. C. Eversley. London, 1965.

Eyck, F. Gunther. "The Political Theories and Activities of the German Academic Youth between 1815 and 1819." *Journal of Modern History* 27 (March 1955): 27–38.

Eynard, Charles. *Vie de Madame de Krüdener.* 2 vols. Paris, 1849.

Faber, Karl-Georg. "Görres, Weitzel und die Revolution (1819)." *Historische Zeitschrift* 194, no. 1 (1962): 37–61.

Fairlee, S. "Shipping in the Anglo-Russian Grain Trade, to 1870, Part I." *Maritime History* 1 (1971).

Ferenczi, Imre. *International Migrations.* Edited by Walter F. Willcox. 2 vols. New York, 1929.

Fischer, Wolfram. *Der Staat und die Anfänge der Industrialisierung in Baden 1800–1850.* Berlin, 1962.

Flamingham, Miletus L. "The Rural Economy of Northeastern France and the Bavarian Palatinate 1815 to 1830." *Agricultural History* 24 (July 1950): 166–70.

Fletcher, Joseph. "Moral and Educational Statistics of England and Wales." *Journal of the Statistical Society* 12 (1849): 151–76.

Flinn, M. W. "The Poor Employment Act of 1817." *Economic History Review,* 2d ser., 14 (August 1961): 82–92.

―――. "The Stabilisation of Mortality in Pre-industrial Western Europe." *Journal of European Economic History,* 3 (Fall 1974): 285–318.

The Fontana Economic History of Europe. Vol. 2: *The Sixteenth and Seventeenth Centuries.* Edited by Carlo M. Cipolla. London and Glasgow, 1974.

The Fontana Economic History of Europe. Vol. 3: *The Industrial Revolution.* Edited by Carlo M. Cipolla. London and Glasgow, 1973.

Fris, Victor. *Histoire de Gand.* Brussels, 1913.

Garnier, Marcel. "Contribution de la phénologie à l'étude des variations climatiques." *La Météorologie* (October–December 1955): 291–300.

Gates, Paul Wallace. *The Farmer's Age: Agriculture, 1815–1860.* New York, 1960.

Gayer, Arthur D., Rostow, W. W., and Schwartz, Anna Jacobson. *The Growth and Fluctuation of the British Economy, 1790–1850.* 2 vols. London, 1953.

Gehring, Paul. *Friedrich List: Jugend- und Reifejahre 1789–1825.* Tübingen, 1964.

Gille, Bertrand. *La Banque et le Crédit en France de 1815 à 1848.* Paris, 1959.

————. "Les crises vues par la presse économique et financière, 1815–1848." *Revue d'histoire moderne* 11 (1964): 5–30.

Gille, H. "The Demographic History of the Northern European Countries in the Eighteenth Century." *Population Studies* 3 (1949–50): 3–65.

Girard, Colette C. "La catastrophe agricole de 1816 dans le département de la Meurthe." *Annales de l'Est,* 5th ser., 5, no. 2 (1954): 133–56.

————. "Les conséquences démographiques de la famine de 1816–1817 dans le département de la Meurthe." *Annales de l'Est,* 5th ser., 7, no. 1 (1956): 18–38.

————. "La disette de 1816–1817 dans la Meurthe." *Annales de l'Est,* 5th ser., 6, no. 4 (1955): 333–62.

————. "Famine et criminalité dans la Meurthe en 1816–17." *Annales de l'Est,* 5th ser., 12, no. 3 (1961): 213–33.

Glass, D. V. "Population and Population Movements in England and Wales, 1700–1850." *Population and History.* Edited by D. V. Glass and D. E. C. Eversley. London, 1965.

Goehlert, J. V. "Die Entwickelung der Bevölkerung der Steiermark vom Jahre 1754 bis auf die Gegenwart." *Statistische Monatschrift* 5 (1879): 59–64.

————. "Die Entwickelung der Bevölkerung von Tirol und Vorarlberg." *Statistische Monatschrift* 6 (1880): 52–64.

Goehlert, Vincenz. "Die Entwickelung der Bevölkerung Krains seit dem vorigen Jahrhundert." *Statistische Monatschrift* 8 (1882): 184–91.

Goubert, Jean-Pierre. *Malades et médecins en Bretagne 1770–1790.* Rennes, 1974.

Goubert, Pierre. *The Ancien Regime.* Trans. by Steve Cox. London, 1973.

————. *Beauvais et le Beauvaisis de 1600 à 1730.* 2 vols. Paris, 1961.

————. "Historical Demography and the Reinterpretation of Early Modern French History: A Research Review." *The Family in History.* Edited by T. K. Rabb and R. I. Rotberg. New York and London, 1973.

Graetz, Heinrich. *History of the Jews.* Trans. by Bella Löwy. 6 Vols. Philadelphia, 1891–98.

Gray, Lewis C. *History of Agriculture in the Southern United States to 1860.* 2 vols. Washington, D.C., 1933.

Greer, Thomas H. "Economic and Social Effects of the Depression of 1819 in the Old Northwest." *Indiana Magazine of History* 44 (September 1948): 227–43.

Gruber, Hansjörg. *Die Entwickelung der pfälzischen Wirtschaft 1816–1834.* Saarbrücken, 1962.

Guéneau, Louis, "La disette de 1816–1817 dans une région productrice de blé, la Brie." *Revue d'histoire moderne* 9 (January–February 1929): 18–46.

Gurian, Waldemar. "Antisemitism in Modern Germany." *Essays on Anti-Semitism.* Edited by Koppel S. Pinson. New York, 1946.

Haarbleicher, M. M. *Aus der Geschichte der Deutsche-Israelitischen Gemeinde in Hamburg.* 2d ed. Hamburg, 1886.

Haeser, Heinrich. *Lehrbuch der Geschichte der Medicin und der epidemischen Krankheiten.* 3d ed. 3 vols. Jena, 1875–82.

Hain, Joseph. *Handbuch der Statistik des österreichischen Kaiserstaates.* 2 vols. Vienna, 1852–53.

Halévy, Élie. *The Liberal Awakening 1815–1830.* Trans. by E. I. Watkin. New York, 1961.

Hammond, Barbara. "Urban Death-rates in the Early Nineteenth Century." *The Economic Journal* 3 (January 1928): supplement, 419–28.

Hammond, Matthew B. *The Cotton Industry, an Essay in American Economic History.* New York, 1897.

Handley, James E. *The Irish in Scotland, 1798–1845.* 2d ed. Cork, 1945.

Harsin, Paul, and Hélin, Étienne, eds. *Problèmes de mortalité.* Actes du Colloque International de démographie historique, Liège, 1963. Liège, 1965.

Hässler, Joseph. *Die Auswanderung aus Baden nach Russland und Polen im 18. und 19. Jahrhundert.* Heft 1 of *Beiträge zur Familien- und Heimatkunde in Baden,* 1961.

Healy, M. J. R., and Jones, E. L. "Wheat Yields in England, 1815–57." *Journal of the Royal Statistical Society,* Series A (1962): 574–79.

Helfert, Jos. Alex. Freiherr von. *Zur Geschichte des Lombardo-Venezianischen Königreichs.* Vienna, 1908.

Helleiner, Karl L. "The Population of Europe from the Black Death to the Eve of the Vital Revolution." *The Cambridge Economic History of Europe,* Vol. 4. Cambridge, 1967.

Helweg-Larsen, Per, et al. *Famine Disease in German Concentration Camps, Complications and Sequels.* Supplement 274, *Acta Medica Scandinavica.* Copenhagen, 1952.

Henderson, W. O. *Britain and Industrial Europe 1750–1870.* 2d ed. Leicester, 1965.

————. *The State and the Industrial Revolution in Prussia 1740–1870.* Liverpool, 1958.

————. *The Zollverein.* 2d ed. London, 1959.

Henry, Alfred J. "Abnormal Summers in the United States." *United States Weather Bureau, Monthly Weather Review* 55 (August 1927): 349–53.

Heunisch, A. J. V. *Das Grossherzogtum Baden.* Heidelberg, 1857.

————. *Grossherzogthums Baden.* Stuttgart, 1837.

Hidy, Ralph W. *The House of Baring in American Trade and Finance.* Cambridge, Massachusetts, 1949.

Hirst, L. Fabian. *The Conquest of Plague.* Oxford, 1953.

Hobsbawm, E. J. "Les soulèvements de la campagne anglaise 1780–1850." *Annales: E. S. C.* 23 (January–February 1968): 9–30.

Holland, Dr. Henry. "On the Pellagra, a Disease Prevailing in Lombardy." *Medico-chirurgical Transactions* 8 (1817): 317–48.

Hollingsworth, T. H. *Historical Demography.* Ithaca, 1969.

Horska, Pavla. "L'État actuel des recherches sur l'évolution de la population dans les pays tchèques aux XVIIIᵉ et XIXᵉ siècles." *Annales de démographie historique* (1967): 173–95.

Houtte, J. A. van. "The Low Countries." *War and Peace in an Age of Upheaval 1793–1830.* Edited by C. W. Crawley. Vol. 9 of *The New Cambridge Modern History.* Cambridge, 1965.

Hoyt, Joseph B. "The Cold Summer of 1816." *Annals of the Association of American Geographers* 48 (June 1958): 118–31.

Huber, F. C. "Auswanderung und Auswanderungspolitik im Königreich Württemberg." *Auswanderung und Auswanderungspolitik in Deutschland.* Edited by Eugen von Philippovich. Leipzig, 1892.

Hubscher, Ronald-Henri. "Une contribution à la connaissance des milieux populaires ruraux au XIXᵉ siècle. Le livre de compte de la famille Flahaut (1811–1877)." *Revue d'histoire économique et sociale* 47, no. 3 (1969): 361–403.

Hufton, Olwen H. *The Poor of Eighteenth-Century France 1750–1789*. Oxford, 1974.

Humboldt, Alexander von. *Cosmos*. Trans. by E. C. Otte and W. S. Dallas. 5 vols. New York, 1862–63.

Humphreys, William J. "Volcanic Dust and Other Factors in the Production of Climatic Changes and Their Possible Relation to Ice Ages." *Bulletin of the Mount Weather Observatory* 6 (1913): 1–34.

Imlah, Albert H. *Economic Elements in the Pax Britannica*. Cambridge, Massachusetts, 1958.

Inadvertant Climate Modification: Report of the Study of Man's Impact on Climate. Cambridge, Massachusetts, 1971.

Jones, D. J. V. "The Amlwich Riots of 1817." *Anglesey Antiquarian Society and Field Club Transactions* (1966): 93–102.

_____. "Distress and Discontent in Cardiganshire, 1814–1819." *Ceredigion* 5, no. 3 (1966): 280–89.

Jones, E. L. *Seasons and Prices*. London, 1964.

_____. "The Agricultural Labour Market in England, 1793–1872." *Economic History Review*, 2d ser., 17 (December 1964): 322–38.

Juglar, Clément. *Des crises commerciales et de leur retour périodique en France, en Angleterre, et aux États-Unis*. 2d ed. Paris, 1889.

Jutikkala, Eino. "Finland's Population Movement in the Eighteenth Century." *Population in History*. Edited by D. V. Glass and D. E. C. Eversley. London, 1965.

Kahan, Arcadius. "Natural Calamities and Their Effect upon the Food Supply in Russia (An Introduction to a Catalog)." *Jahrbücher für Geschichte Osteuropas*, N. F., 16 (September 1968): 353–77.

Kamer van Koophandel en Fabrieken Rotterdam 1803–1928. Rotterdam, 1928.

Kelsch, A. *Traité des maladies épidémiques*. Paris, 1894.

Keyser, Erich. *Bevölkerungsgeschichte Deutschlands*. 2d ed. Leipzig, 1941.

Kilbourne, Edwin D., M.D., and Smillie, Wilson G., M.D., eds. *Human Ecology and Public Health*. 4th ed. London, 1969.

Kirchner, Walther. "Emigration to Russia." *American Historical Review* 55 (April 1950): 552–66.

Knapton, Ernest J. *The Lady of the Holy Alliance: The Life of Julie de Krudener*. New York, 1939.

Köllmann, Wolfgang. *Sozialgeschichte der Stadt Barmen im 19. Jahrhundert*. Tübingen, 1960.

Köppen, W. "Ueber mehrjährige Perioden der Witterung." *Zeitschrift der österreichischen Gesellschaft für Meteorologie* 8 (September 1873): 257–67.

Koselleck, Reinhart. *Preussen zwischen Reform und Revolution. Allgemeines Landrecht, Verwaltung und soziale Bewegung von 1791 bis 1848*. Stuttgart, 1967.

Kraus, Antje. *Die Unterschichten Hamburgs in der ersten Hälfte des 19. Jahrhunderts*. Stuttgart, 1965.

Krause, J. T. "Changes in English Fertility and Mortality, 1781–1850." *Economic History Review*, 2d ser., 11 (August 1958): 52–70.

_____. "The Changing Adequacy of English Registration, 1690–1837." *Population in History*. Edited by D. V. Glass and D. E. C. Eversley. London, 1965.

_____. "English population Movements between 1700 and 1850." *Population in Industrialization*. Edited by Michael Drake. London, 1969.

Kuczynski, Jürgen. *Germany, 1800 to the Present Day*. Vol. 3, Part 1: *A Short History of Labour Conditions under Industrial Capitalism*. London, 1945.

Labrijn, Aart. *Het klimaat van Nederland gedurende de laatste twee en een halve eeuw*. Schiedam, 1945.

Labrousse, Camille Ernest. *La crise de l'économie française à la fin de l'ancien régime et au début de la Revolution*. Paris, 1944.

_____. *Esquisse du mouvement des prix et des revenus en France au XVIIIe siècle*. Paris, 1932.

_____. *Le mouvement ouvrier et les idées sociales en France de 1815 à la fin du XIXe siècle*. Paris, 1948.

Lamb, H. H. *Climate: Present, Past and Future*. Vol. 1, *Fundamentals and Climate Now*. London, 1972.

_____. *The Changing Climate*. London, 1966.

_____. "Volcanic Dust in the Atmosphere: with a Chronology and an Assessment of its Meteorological Significance." *Philosophical Transactions of the Royal Society*, Series A, 266 (1970): 425–533.

_____, and Johnson, A. I. "Secular Variations of the Atmospheric Circulation since 1750." *Geophysical Memoirs*, no. 110. Meteorological Office. London, 1966.

Landes, David S. "Recent Work in the Economic History of Modern France." *French Historical Studies* 1, no. 1 (1958): 73–94.

_____. "Reply to Mr. Danière and Some Reflections on the Significance of the Debate." *Journal of Economic History* 18 (September 1958): 331–38, 342–44.

_____. "The Statistical Study of French Crises." *Journal of Economic History* 10 (November 1950): 195–211.

_____. *The Unbound Prometheus*. Cambridge, 1970.

Langer, William L. "American Foods and Europe's Population Growth." *Journal of Social History* (Winter 1975): 51–66.

Lebrun, François. *Les hommes et la mort en Anjou aux 17e et 18e siècles*. Paris, 1971.

Lee, W. Robert. "Zur Bevölkerungsgeschichte Bayerns 1750–1850: Britische Forschungsergebnisse." *Vierteljahrschrift für Sozial- und Wirtschaftsgeschichte*, 62, Heft 3 (1975): 309–38.

Leibbrandt, Georg. *Die Auswanderung aus Schwaben nach Russland, 1816–1823*. Stuttgart, 1928.

Léon, Pierre. *La naissance de la grande industrie en Dauphiné*. 2 vols. Paris, 1954.

Le Roy Ladurie, Emmanuel. "Famine Amenorrhoea (Seventeenth–Twentieth Centuries)." *Biology of Man in History*. Edited by Robert Forster and Orest Ranum. Trans. from the French by Elborg Forster and Patricia M. Ranum. Baltimore and London, 1975.

_____. *Histoire du climat depuis l'an mil*. Paris, 1967.

_____. "Histoire et Climat." *Annales: E. S. C.* 14 (January–March 1959): 3–34.

_____. *Times of Feast, Times of Famine: A History of Climate since the Year 1000*. Trans. by Barbara Bray. Garden City, New York, 1971.

_____, and Desaive, J.-P. "Le climat et la France (1776–1792): séries thermiques." J.-P. Desaive et al. *Médecins, climat et épidémies à la fin du XVIIIe siècle*. Paris, 1972.

Leuilliot, Paul. *L'Alsace au début de XIXe siècle (1815–1830): Essais d'histoire politique, économique et religieuse*. 3 vols. Paris, 1959–60.

_____. "Les crises économiques du XIXe siècle en France: de la disette de 1816–1817 à la famine du coton (1867)." *Annales, E. S. C.* 12 (April–June 1957): 317–25.

_____. "L'émigration alsacienne sous l'Empire et au début de la Restauration." *Revue historique* 155 (1930): 254–79.

_____. "L'usure judäique en Alsace sous l'Empire et la Restauration." *Annales historique de la Revolution française* 7 (May–June 1930): 231–50.

Levasseur, E. *Histoire des classes ouvrières et de l'industrie en France de 1789 à 1870*. 2d ed. 2 vols. Paris, 1903–04.

_____. *Histoire du commerce de la France*. 2 vols. Paris, 1911–12.

Lévy-Leboyer, Maurice. *Les banques européennes et l'industrialisation internationale dans la première moitié du XIXᵉ siècle.* Paris, 1964.

————. "La croissance économique en France au XIXᵉ siècle. Résultats preliminaires." *Annales: E. S. C.* 23 (1968): 788–807.

Lewin, Adolf. *Geschichte der badischen Juden 1738–1909.* Karlsruhe, 1909.

Lewis, W. J. "The Condition of Labour in Mid-Cardiganshire in the Early Nineteenth Century." *Ceredigion* 4, no. 4 (1963): 321–35.

Losch, Hermann. "Die Bewegung der Bevölkerung Württembergs im 19. Jahrhundert und im Jahre 1899" *Württembergische Jahrbücher für Statistik und Landeskunde,* 1900, Part 2: 55–165.

Ludlum, David M. *Early American Winters 1604–1820.* Boston, 1966.

Ludwig, A. Fr. von. *Die chiliastische Bewegung in Franken und Hessen im ersten Drittel des 19. Jahrhunderts.* Regensburg and Rome, 1913.

Macarthur, Sir William. "Famines and Fevers in England and Ireland." *Journal of the British Archaeological Association,* 3d ser., 9 (1944): 66–67.

————. "Medical History of the Famine." *The Great Famine.* Edited by R. Dudley Edwards and T. Desmond Williams. New York, 1959.

Macartney, C. A. "The Austrian Monarchy 1792–1847." *War and Peace in an Age of Upheaval 1793–1830.* Edited by C. W. Crawley. Vol. 9 of *The New Cambridge Modern History.* Cambridge, 1965.

————. *The Habsburg Empire 1790–1918.* London, 1968.

MacKenzie, R. B. "Public Health Importance of Rodents in South America." *Bulletin of the World Health Organization* 47 (1972): 161–69.

McKeown, Thomas, and Record, R. G. "Reasons for the Decline of Mortality in England and Wales during the Nineteenth Century." *Population Studies* 16 (November 1962): 94–122.

Magalhães Godinho, Vitorino. *Prix et monnaies au Portugal, 1750–1850.* Paris, 1955.

Maguire, W. A. *The Downshire Estates in Ireland 1801–1845.* Oxford, 1972.

Manley, Gordon. "Central England Temperatures: Monthly Means 1659 to 1973." *Quarterly Journal of the Royal Meteorological Society* 100 (July 1974): 389–405.

————. "The Mean Temperature of Central England 1698–1952." *Quarterly Journal of the Royal Meteorological Society* 79 (1953): 242–61.

————. "Temperature Trend in Lancashire, 1753–1945." *Quarterly Journal of the Royal Meteorological Society* 72 (1946): 1–31.

Margary, I. D. "The Marsham Phenological Record in Norfolk, 1735–1925, and Some Others." *Quarterly Journal of the Royal Meteorological Society* 52 (June 1926): 27–52.

Marion, Marcel. *Histoire financière de la France depuis 1715.* 5 vols. Paris, 1914–28.

Marjolin, Robert. "Troubles provoqués en France par la disette de 1816–1817." *Revue d'histoire moderne,* New ser., 10 (November–December 1933): 423–60.

Markovitch, Tihomir J. "L'industrie française de 1789 à 1964.—Sources et méthodes." *Cahiers de l'I. S. E. A.,* Ser., A F, 4 (July 1965): 1–212.

Marlin, Roger. *La crise des subsistances de 1816–1817 dans le Doubs.* Besançon, 1960.

Marshall, J. *A Digest of All the Accounts.* London, 1833.

Maschek, L. "Zur Geschichte und Praxis der Volkszählung in Dalmatien." *Statistische Monatschrift* 6 (1880): 351–56.

Mathias, Peter. *The First Industrial Nation: An Economic History of Britain 1700–1914.* London, 1969.

Matis, Herbert. "Über die sozialen und wirtschaftlichen Verhältnisse österreichischer Fabrik- und Manufakturarbeiter um die Wende vom 18. zum 19. Jahrhundert." *Vierteljahrschrift für Sozial- und Wirtschaftsgeschichte* 80 (1966): 434–76.

Matthews, R. C. O. *A Study in Trade-Cycle History: Economic Fluctuations in Great Britain 1833–1842*. London, 1954.

Mayer, Kurt B. *The Population of Switzerland*. New York, 1952.

Meinhardt, Gunther. "Die Auswirkungen der Hungerjahre in der ersten Hälfte des 19. Jahrhunderts auf Göttingen." *Göttinger Jahrbuch* 14 (1966): 211–19.

Meuvret, Jean. "Les crises de subsistances et la démographie de la France d'Ancien Régime." *Population* 1 (October–December 1946); 643–50.

———. "Demographic Crisis in France from the Sixteenth to the Eighteenth Century." Trans. by Margaret Hilton. *Population in History*. Edited by D. V. Glass and D. E. C. Eversley. London, 1965.

———. *Études d'histoire économique*. Paris, 1971.

Meynert, Hermann. *Kaiser Franz I*. Vienna, 1872.

Milham, Willis I. "The Year 1816, the Causes of Abnormalities." *United States Weather Bureau, Monthly Weather Review* 52 (December 1924) 563–70.

Miller, Max. "Ursachen und Ziele der schwäbischen Auswanderung." *Württembergische Vierteljahrshefte für Landesgeschichte* 42 (1936): 184–218.

Milz, Herbert, *Das Kölner Grossgewerbe von 1750 bis 1835*. Cologne, 1962.

Mitchell, B. R., and Deane, Phyllis. *Abstract of British Historical Statistics*. Cambridge, 1962.

Mitchell, J. Murray, Jr. "Recent Secular Changes of Global Temperature." *Annals of the New York Academy of Sciences* 95 (1961): 235–50.

Monteleone, G. "Le carestie de 1816–1817 nelle Province Venete." *Archivio Veneto* 86–87 (1969): 23–86.

Mossman, Robert C. "The Meteorology of Edinburgh." *Transactions of the Royal Society of Edinburgh* 39 (1896–99): 63–207.

Mottek, Hans. *Wirtschaftsgeschichte Deutschlands*. 2d ed. 2 vols. Berlin, 1974.

Moulton, F. R., ed. *Rickettsial Diseases of Man*. Washington, D.C., 1948.

Mühlemann, C. "Einfluss der wichtigsten Nahrungsmittelpreise auf die Bewegung der Bevölkerung im Kanton Bern während dem 100 jährigen Zeitraum 1782–1881." *Zeitschrift für Schweizerische Statistik* 18 (1882): 59–70.

Mülinen, Comte de. *Les finances de l'Autriche*. Paris, 1875.

Mullett, Charles F. *The Bubonic Plague and England*. Lexington, Kentucky, 1956.

Mussey, Barrows, and Vigilante, Sylvester L. " 'Eighteen-Hundred-And-Froze-To-Death': The Cold Summer of 1816 and Westward Migration from New England." *Bulletin of the New York Public Library* 52 (September 1948): 454–57.

Neale, R. S. "The Standard of Living, 1780–1844: A Regional and Class Study." *Economic History Review*, 2d Ser., 19 (December 1966): 590–606.

Neumann, Anna. *Die Bewegung der Löhne der ländlichen "freien" Arbeiter im Königreich Preussen gegenwärtigen Umfangs vom Ausgang des 18. Jahrhunderts bis 1850*. Berlin, 1911.

Neuvième congrès international d'histoire de la médecine. Bucharest, 1932.

North, Douglass C. *The Economic Growth of the United States 1790–1860*. Englewood Cliffs, New Jersey, 1961.

O'Brien, George. *The Economic History of Ireland from the Union to the Famine*. London, 1921.

Oechsli, Wilhelm. *Geschichte der Schweiz im neunzehnten Jahrhundert*. 2 vols. Leipzig, 1913.

"The 150th Anniversary of the Cold Summer of 1816." *The (Old) Farmers Almanac* 174 (1966): 46–47.

Page, William, ed. *Commerce and Industry*. New York, 1968.

Paillat, Paul. "Les salaires et la condition ouvrière en France à l'aube du machinisme (1815–1830)." *Revue économique* 2 (November 1951): 767–77.

Pavelka, Hedwig. *Englisch-österreichische Wirtschaftsbeziehungen in der ersten Hälfte des 19. Jahrhunderts.* Graz, 1968.

Peacock, A. J. *Bread or Blood: A Study of the Agrarian Riots in East Anglia in 1816.* London, 1965.

Peters, Max. *Die Entwicklung der deutschen Rhederei.* 2 vols. Jena, 1899–1905.

Peterson, Arthur G. "Wheat and Corn Prices Received by Producers in Virginia, 1801–1928." *Journal of Economic and Business History* 2 (February 1930): 382–91.

Philippovich, Eugen von. "Auswanderung und Auswanderungspolitik im Grossherzogtum Baden." *Auswanderung und Auswanderungspolitik in Deutschland.* Edited by Eugen von Philippovich. Leipzig, 1892.

Pirchegger, Hans. *Geschichte und Kulturleben Deutschösterreichs von 1792 bis zum Weltkrieg.* Vienna and Leipzig, 1937.

Pirenne, Henri. *Histoire de Belgique.* 7 vols. Brussels, 1909–26.

Pittock, A. B. "How Important Are Climatic Changes." *Weather* 27 (July 1972): 262–71.

Plass, Gilbert. "Carbon Dioxide and Climate." *Scientific American* 201 (July 1959): 41–47.

Pokrovskii, S. A. *Vneshniaia torgovlia i vneshniaia torgovaia politika Rossii.* Moscow, 1947.

Pollitzer, R. *Plague.* Geneva, 1954.

Ponteil, Félix. *L'Éveil des nationalitiés et le mouvement liberal (1815–1848).* New ed. Paris, 1960.

―――. *La monarchie parlementaire, 1815–1848.* Paris, 1949.

Post, John D. "Famine, Mortality, and Epidemic Disease in the Process of Modernization." *Economic History Review,* 2d ser., 29 (February 1976): 14–37.

―――. "Meteorological Historiography." *Journal of Interdisciplinary History,* (Spring 1973): 721–32.

―――. "A Study in Meteorological and Trade Cycle History: The Economic Crisis Following the Napoleonic Wars." *Journal of Economic History* 24 (June 1974): 315–49.

Posthumus, Nicolaas W. *Inquiry into the History of Prices in Holland.* 2 vols. Leiden, 1946–64.

Pouthas, Charles H. *La population française pendant la première moitié du XIXe siècle.* Paris, 1956.

Powell, George. "A Description and History of Blount County." Alabama Historical Society, *Transactions at the Annual Meeting. . . .* July 9–10, 1855.

Pribram, Alfred Francis. *Materialien zur Geschichte der Preise und Löhne in Österreich.* Vienna, 1938.

Puryear, Vernon J. "Odessa: Its Rise and International Importance 1815–1850." *Pacific Historical Review* 3 (1934): 192–215.

Rath, R. John. "Economic Conditions in Lombardy and Venetia, 1813–1815, and Their Effects on Public Opinion." *Journal of Central European Affairs* 23 (October 1963): 267–81.

―――. "The Habsburgs and the Great Depression in Lombardo-Venetia, 1814–1818." *Journal of Modern History* 13 (September 1941): 305–20.

―――. *The Provincial Austrian Regime in Lombardy-Venetia 1814–1815.* Austin, Texas, 1969.

Razzell, P. E. "The Evaluation of Baptisms as a Form of Birth Registration through Cross-Matching Census and Parish Register Data." *Population Studies* 26 (March 1972): 121–46.

Reinhard, Marcel, Armengaud, André, and Dupaquier, Jacques. *Histoire générale de la population mondiale.* 3d ed. Paris, 1968.

Renbourn, E. T. *Materials and Clothing in Health and Disease.* London, 1972.

Resnick, Daniel Philip. *The White Terror and the Political Reaction after Waterloo.* Cambridge, Massachusetts, 1966.

Revel, Jacques. "Autour d'une épidémie ancienne: la peste de 1666–1670." *Revue d'histoire moderne et contemporaine* 17 (October–December 1970): 953–83.

Rezneck, Samuel. "The Depression of 1819–1822, a Social History." *American Historical Review* 39 (1933–34): 28–47.

Richards, Eric. "The Industrial Face of a Great Estate: Trentham and Lilleshall, 1780–1860." *Economic History Review,* 2d ser., 27 (August 1974): 414–30.

Richter, Hans. "Hessen und die Auswanderung 1815–55." *Mitteilungen des Oberhessischen Geschichtsvereins,* N. F., 32 (1934): 49–139.

Robert, Joseph Clark, *The Tobacco Kingdom: Plantation, Market and Factory in Virginia and North Carolina, 1800–1860.* Durham, North Carolina, 1938.

Roe, Daphne A. *A Plague of Corn.* Ithaca and London, 1973.

Rohrbough, Malcolm J. *The Land Office Business: The Settlement and Administration of American Public Lands, 1789–1837.* New York, 1968.

Romani, Mario. "Il movimento demografico in Lombardia dal 1750 al 1850." *Economica e Storia* 2, no. 4 (1955): 412–52.

_____. *Storia economica d'Italia nel secolo XIX.* 2d ed. Milan, 1970.

Roscher, Wilhelm. *Ueber Kornhandel und Theuerungspolitik.* 3d ed. Stuttgart and Tübingen, 1852.

Rose, R. B. "Eighteenth-Century Price Riots and Public Policy in England." *International Review of Social History* 6 (1961), part 2: 277–92.

Rostow, W. W. *British Economy of the Nineteenth Century.* Oxford, 1948.

Rothbard, Murray Newton. *The Panic of 1819: Reactions and Policies.* New York and London, 1962.

Rothenberg, Gunther E. "The Austrian Sanitary Cordon and the Control of the Bubonic Plague: 1710–1871." *Journal of the History of Medicine and Allied Sciences* 28 (January 1973): 15–23.

Rudé, George. *The Crowd in History: A Study of Popular Disturbances in France and England 1730–1848.* New York, 1964.

_____. *Paris and London in the Eighteenth Century.* New York, 1971.

Rudloff, Hans von. *Die Schwankungen und Pendelungen des Klimas in Europa seit dem Beginn der regelmässigen Instrumenten-Beobachtungen.* Braunschweig, 1967.

Sanchez-Albornoz, Nicolás. *Las crisis de subsistencias de España en el siglo XIX.* Rosario, Argentina, 1963.

Sandkaulen, Wilhelm. *Das Notjahr 1816/17 mit besonderer Berücksichtigung der Verhältnisse am Niederrhein.* Münster, 1927.

Sapper, Karl. *Vulkankunde.* Stuttgart, 1927.

Sartorius von Waltershausen, A. *Deutsche Wirtschaftsgeschichte, 1815–1914.* 2d ed. Jena, 1923.

Schaefer, Hans-Ludwig. *Bremens Bevölkerung in der ersten Hälfte des neunzehnten Jahrhunderts.* Bremen, 1957.

Scheben, Joseph. "Eifeler Amerika-Auswanderung im neunzehnten Jahrhundert." *Rheinische Vierteljahrsblätter* 2 (1932): 257–77.

_____. "Die Frage nach der Geschichte der deutschen Auswanderung." *Rheinische Vierteljahrsblätter* 5(1935): 175–82.

Schenk, Hans G. A. V. *The Aftermath of the Napoleonic Wars.* London, 1947.

Schimmer, G. A. "Die Bewegung der Bevölkerung in Wien seit dem Jahre 1770." *Statistische Monatschrift* 1 (1875): 119–33.

Schnabel, Franz. *Deutsche Geschichte im neunzehnten Jahrhundert.* 2d ed. 4 vols. Freiburg im Breisgau, 1949–50.

Schneider, Stephen H., and Mass, Clifford. "Volcanic Dust, Sunspots, and Temperature Trends." *Science* 190 (November 21, 1975): 741–46.

Schnerring, Christian A. "Die Teuerungs- und Hungerjahre 1816 and 1817 in Württemberg." *Württembergische Jahrbücher für Statistik und Landeskunde* (1916): 45–78.

Schott, Charles A. *Tables, Distribution, and Variations of the Atmospheric Temperature of the United States. Smithsonian Contributions to Knowledge*, 277. Washington, D.C., 1876.

Schumpeter, Joseph Alois. *Business Cycles*. 2 vols. New York, 1939.

Schur, Leon M. "The Second Bank of the United States and the Inflation after the War of 1812." *Journal of Political Economy* 68 (April 1960): 118–34.

Scrimshaw, N. S., Taylor, C. E., and Gordon, J. E. *Interaction of Nutrition and Infection.* Geneva, 1968.

Sée, Henri. *Histoire économique de la France: Les temps modernes (1789–1914)*. Paris, 1951.

———. *La vie économique de la France sous la monarchie censitaire (1815–1848)*. Paris, 1927.

Shannon, H. A. "Bricks—A Trade Index, 1785–1849." *Economica*, N. S., 3 (August 1934): 300–18.

Shaw, David. "Sunspots and Temperature." *Journal of Geophysical Research* 70 (October 15, 1965): 4,997–4,999.

Shewsbury, J. F. D. *A History of Bubonic Plague in the British Isles*. Cambridge, 1970.

Simon, Walter M. *The Failure of the Prussian Reform Movement, 1897–1819*. Ithaca, 1955.

Slicher van Bath, B. H. *The Agrarian History of Western Europe A.D. 500–1850*. Trans. from the Dutch by Olive Ordish. London, 1963.

Slokar, Johann. *Geschichte der österreichischen Industrie und ihrer Förderung unter Kaiser Franz I.* Vienna, 1914.

Smart, William. *Economic Annals of the Nineteenth Century 1801–1820*. New York, 1964.

Smith, Alfred G., Jr. *Economic Readjustment of an Old Cotton State, South Carolina 1820–1860*. Columbia, 1958.

Smith, Walter B. *Economic Aspects of the Second Bank of the United States*. Cambridge, Massachusetts, 1953.

———, and Cole, Arthur H. *Fluctuations in American Business 1790–1860*. Cambridge, Massachusetts, 1935.

Sogner, Sølvi. "Aspects of the Demographic Situation in Seventeen Parishes in Shropshire, 1711–60." *Population Studies* 17 (November 1963): 126–46.

Srbik, Heinrich Ritter von. *Metternich: der Staatsmann und Mensch*. 3 vols. Munich, 1925.

Steineman, Ernest. "Die schaffhauserische Auswanderung und ihre Ursachen. Ein Beitrag zur Wirtschaftesgeschichte." *Revue suisse d'histoire / Zeitschrift für schweizerische Geschichte* 14, no. 4 (1934): 401–50.

Sterling, Eleonore O. "Anti-Jewish Riots in Germany in 1819: A Displacement of Social Protest." *Historia Judaica* 12 (April 1950): 105–42.

———. *Er ist wie Du. Aus der Frühgeschichte des Antisemitismus in Deutschland (1815–1850)*. Munich, 1956.

Stern-Taeubler, Selma. "Der literarische Kampf um die Emanzipation in den Jahren 1816–1820 und seine ideologischen und soziologischen Voraussetzungen." *Hebrew Union College Annual* 23, part 2 (1950–51): 171–96.

Sticker, Georg. *Die Pest: Die Geschichte der Pest*. Giessen, 1908.

Stilwell, Lewis Dayton. *Migration from Vermont*. Montpelier, 1948.

Stollenwerk, Alexander. "Der Regierungsbezirk Koblenz während der grossen Hungersnot im Jahre 1816/17." *Jahrbuch für Geschichte und Kunst der Mittelrheins und seine Nachbargebiete* 22–23 (1970–71): 109–49.

Stratton, J. M. *Agricultural Records A.D. 220–1968*. Edited by Ralph Whitlock. London, 1969.

Struck, Wolf-Heino. *Die Auswanderung aus dem Herzogtum Nassau, 1806–1866.* Wiesbaden, 1966.

Stumpp, Karl, ed. *Ostwanderung. Akten über die Auswanderung der Württemberger nach Russland 1816–1822.* Leipzig, 1941.

Tapiès, le Chevalier F. de. *La France et l'Angleterre ou statistique morale et physique de la France comparée a celle de l'Angleterre.* Paris, 1845.

Taylor, George Rogers. "Wholesale Commodity Prices at Charleston, S.C., 1796–1861." *Journal of Economic and Business History* 4 (August 1932), supplement: 848–68.

Tebeldi, A. *Die Geldangelegenheiten Oestreichs.* Leipzig, 1847.

Teṅgoborskii, Ludwik. *Commentaries on the Productive Forces of Russia.* Trans. from the Russian. 2 vols. London, 1855–56.

Terlinden, Charles. "La politique économique de Guillaume Ier, roi des Pays-Bas en Belgique (1814–30)." *Revue historique* 139 (January–April 1922): 1–40.

Thompson, E. P. *The Making of the English Working Class.* London, 1965.

Thorp, Willard Long, and Mitchell, Wesley C. *Business Annals.* New York, 1926.

Tilly, Richard. "The Political Economy of Public Finance and the Industrialization of Prussia, 1815–1866." *Journal of Economic History* 26 (December 1966): 484–97.

Tranter, N. L. *Population Since the Industrial Revolution.* London, 1973.

Treshow, Michael. *Environment and Plant Response.* New York, 1970.

Treue, Wilhelm. *Wirtschaftsgeschichte der Neuzeit im Zeitalter der Industriellen Revolution 1700 bis 1960.* Stuttgart, 1962.

―――. *Wirtschaftszustände und Wirtschaftspolitik in Preussen 1815–1825.* Stuttgart, 1937.

Truchon, P. "La vie ouvrière à Lyon sous la Restauration." *Revue d'histoire de Lyon* 11 (May–June 1912): 195–222.

Utterström, Gustaf. "Climatic Fluctuations and Population Problems in Early Modern History." *Scandinavian Economic History Review* 3 (1955): 1–47.

―――. "Population and Agriculture in Sweden, *circa* 1700–1830." *Scandinavian Economic History Review* 9 (1961): 176–94.

Vergnaud, Maurice. "Agitation politique et crise de subsistances à Lyon de septembre 1816 à juin 1817." *Cahiers d'histoire* 2 (1957): 163–78.

Vial, Jean. *L'industrialisation de la sidérurgie française, 1814–1864.* 2 vols. Paris, 1967.

Viard, Pierre-Paul. "La disette de 1816–1817, particulièrement en Côte-d'Or." *Revue historique* 159 (September–October 1928): 95–117.

Vicens Vives, Jaime. *An Economic History of Spain.* Trans. by Frances M. López-Morillas. Princeton, 1969.

Vidalenc, Jean. *Le département de l'Eure sous la monarchie constitutionnelle 1814–1848.* Paris, 1952.

―――. *La société française de 1815 à 1848: le peuple des campagnes.* Paris, 1970.

Vopelius, Marie-Elisabeth. *Die altliberalen Ökonomen und die Reformzeit.* Stuttgart, 1968.

Wade, Richard C. *The Urban Frontier.* Chicago and London, 1964.

Walker, Mack. *Germany and the Emigration 1816–1885.* Cambridge, Massachusetts, 1964.

Wearmouth, R. W. *Methodism and the Common People in the Eighteenth Century.* London, 1945.

Weikinn, Curt. *Quellentexte zur Witterungsgeschichte Europas von der Zeitenwende bis zum 1850.* 4 vols. Berlin, 1958–67.

Wexler, Harry. "Volcanoes and World Climate." *Scientific American* 186 (April 1952): 74–80.

White, R. J. *Waterloo to Peterloo.* London, 1957.

Wilson, Charles M. "The Year without a Summer." *American History Illustrated* 5 (June 1970): 24–29.

Wolfer, A. "Revision of Wolf's Sun Spot Relative-Numbers." *Monthly Weather Review* 30 (April 1902): 171–76.

Wolff, F. von. *Der Vulkanismus.* 2 vols. Stuttgart, 1914.

Wood, J. David. "The Complicity of Climate in the 1816 Depression in Dumfriesshire." *Scottish Geographical Magazine* 81, no. 1 (1965): 5–17.

Wright, Harold R. C. *Free Trade and Protection in the Netherlands (1816–1830).* Cambridge, 1955.

Wrigley, E. A. *Population and History.* New York and Toronto, 1969.

Yeomans, Andrew. "The Symptomatology, Clinical Course and Management of Louse-borne Typhus Fever." *Rickettsial Diseases of Man.* Edited by F. R. Moulton. Washington, D.C., 1948.

Young, Vernon R., and Scrimshaw, Nevin S. "The Physiology of Starvation." *Scientific American* 224 (October 1971). Reprinted in *Readings from Scientific American.* San Francisco, 1973.

Zinsser, Hans. *Rats, Lice and History.* Boston, 1935.

Zorn, Wolfgang. *Handels- und Industriegeschichte Bayerisch-Schwabens 1648–1870.* Augsburg, 1961.

Index

The Johns Hopkins University Press

This book was composed in Times Roman text and display type by The Composing Room,
from a design by Marlene Bressler. It was printed on 50-lb. Publishers Eggshell Wove paper
and bound by The Maple Press Company.